narr **BACHELOR-WISSEN.DE**

Teaching English

narr BACHELOR-WISSEN.DE

Nancy Grimm, Michael Meyer,
Laurenz Volkmann

Teaching English

Nancy Grimm ist Wissenschaftliche Mitarbeiterin in englischer Fachdidaktik an der Friedrich-Schiller-Universität Jena.

Michael Meyer ist Professor für englische Literaturwissenschaft und Fachdidaktik an der Universität Koblenz-Landau, Campus Koblenz.

Laurenz Volkmann ist Professor für Englische Fachdidaktik an der Friedrich-Schiller-Universität Jena.

Idee und Konzept der Reihe: **Johannes Kabatek,** Professor für Romanische Philologie mit besonderer Berücksichtigung der iberoromanischen Sprachen an der Universität Zürich.

Bibliografische Information der Deutschen Nationalbibliothek

Die Deutsche Bibliothek verzeichnet diese Publikation in der Deutschen Nationalbibliografie; detaillierte bibliografische Daten sind im Internet über http://dnb.dnb.de abrufbar.

Internet: www.bachelor-wissen.de
E-Mail: info@narr.de
Satz: pagina GmbH, Tübingen
Printed in the EU

ISSN 1864-4082
ISBN 978-3-8233-6831-1

Contents

Contents

VIII

Preface

This volume bridges the gap between theoretical approaches to foreign language teaching and the needs of lecturers, students, teacher trainees, and those teaching at the grassroots level. This book should help readers to profit from their own learning and teaching of English through reflected practice. Using English as a target language and language of communication, we apply Content and Language Integrated Learning to Teaching English as a Foreign Language (TEFL). Technical terms will also be presented in German (unless the translation is evident) in order to facilitate the transfer to *Studienseminare*.

Teaching English covers – and reflects on – major issues and current trends in language learning and teaching, such as the turns towards constructivism, differentiation, empiricism, output-orientation, inter-/transcultural learning, and multimedia. The balance of practice and reflection in each chapter enables a flexible use of this volume in various teaching approaches. The sequence of the topics is structured for systematic introductions over the course of a semester. The first four chapters provide the historical background, the political framework, and the conceptual basis of TEFL in Educational Studies, Psychology, and Linguistics. All of the major topics of TEFL presented in the subsequent parts rely on this groundwork. In addition, individual readers can study the chapters in any order because core concepts are clearly defined at their first occurrence in the book and referenced in later chapters. The highlighting of *key terms* and *important phrases*, frequent cross-references, as well as the recapitulation and differentiation of core principles are designed to facilitate learning in the shape of a spiral curriculum.

Each chapter comes with a thought-provoking cartoon, an overview of the learning objectives, key concepts, study questions, rewarding examples of classroom activities, and recommended reading. Additional material in the form of PowerPoint-presentations for teaching TEFL and pdf-files for learners is provided online. Additional examples of classroom activities are also available online at www.bachelor-wissen.de/9783823368311.

Nancy Grimm deserves special recognition: in addition to writing 'her parts' of the book and competently commenting on the others, she masterminded the organization of the project with enormous zeal and great efficiency. Ultimately, each chapter gradually developed in a long and truly collaborative process. Many thanks are due to everyone who gave us plenty of helpful feedback on various chapters: the colleagues Melanie Green, Constanze Juchem-Grundmann, Andrew Liston, Christian Ludwig, Carol Ann Martin, Nicole Maruo-Schröder, Peter Starling, Fred Thompson, John Thomson, and Kim Willis, the teachers Peter Hohwiller and Sieglinde Spath, the students Jason D. Smith, Kirsten Weise, Benedikt Mediger, who prepared the groundwork for the PowerPoint-presentations. We would also like to thank Kathrin Heyng from Narr Verlag for her patience and her careful reading of the whole script. Last but not least, special thanks to Teresa Mönnich (aka Frollein Motte, www.frolleinmotte.com), whose cheeky as well as thought-provoking cartoons add extra spice to each of the chapters.

Jena and Koblenz, Spring 2015   N. Grimm – M. Meyer – L. Volkmann

The framework: history and politics

Contents

This chapter provides the historical background and current framework of Teaching English as a Foreign Language (TEFL). The overview of the historical development of basic issues in teaching and learning foreign languages helps to understand and evaluate contemporary discussions of language education and the development of TEFL in Germany within the *Common European Framework of Reference for Languages* (CEF, *Gemeinsamer Europäischer Referenzrahmen für Sprachen*). This chapter ends with a glance at the education and practical training of English teachers in Germany.

Abstract

Have a look at the cartoon on the next page: on the basis of your own experience, think about central aims, problems, and methods of teaching and learning English. Which of these do you consider to be fundamental at any time, and for which reasons?

1.1 | Teaching English as a Foreign Language

1.1.1 | The historical perspective

Fig. 1.1 |
William Hogarth:
Scholars at a Lecture
(1736)

Latin and Greek

The significance of (foreign) language teaching and learning is dependent upon a framework of social, economic, political, cultural, and academic interests, which have varied across history. It would be tempting – but wrong – to tell a linear story of progress in language teaching and learning. Many of the issues debated today have been part and parcel of teaching and learning languages since time immemorial. Pertinent topics include (1) principles of language acquisition and teaching a foreign language (FL), and (2) the political decision whether to train practical language skills only or pursue further educational objectives.

English is not the first and only global language. In the Roman Empire, Latin served as a *lingua franca*, a common language used among speakers not sharing a native language (cf. James 2008: 134, Musumeci 2011: 43). In the Middle Ages, the alliance of the church and the state in Europe was firmly based on Christianity. Many political and legal documents employed Latin, as did formal education and the central medium of religious service, the Bible. Renaissance Humanists of the 15th and 16th centuries favored Greek over Latin in order to be able to read fundamental literary, political, and philosophical texts to provide a rounded education (*Allgemeinbildung*) for a rather small elite.

The early modern period from the 15th to the 17th century was dominated by two models of teaching and learning a FL: (1) the instruction in *FL as a system* and (2) learning a modern *FL for communicative purposes* – often in the form of pattern drills to habitualize formulaic expressions: (1) using the *Grammar-Translation Method*, the Jesuits gave students Latin sample sentences and explained the words and the rules of grammar in detail and in the students' native language (cf. Musumeci 2011: 51–53). (2) However, international tradesmen acquired oral skills in the modern languages of their customers in order to negotiate business deals. The Czech scholar Comenius (see fig. 1.2), who was frustrated with the slow progress of language learners, found fault with the Grammar-Translation Method and the instructional material used. He considered efficient learning as a motivating process that should move from simple to complex issues and from content to form. He argued for a *holistic style of learning* (*ganzheitliches Lernen*), for which he developed multilingual textbooks with pictures and stories (e. g., Latin/English; see ch. 9.3). His objectives for foreign language learning were both practical communication and knowledge of the language system. In addition to learning their own language and Latin in vernacular schools at home, students should study modern languages abroad – an approach to FL learning which today is called '*immersion*' (cf. Musumeci 2011: 54–58; see ch. 4.4).

The English philosopher and teacher John Locke (1693) considered the Grammar-Translation Method as an apt way of teaching the reading of classical Latin texts, but recommended early beginning in modern foreign languages according to what is now called the *Direct or Natural Method*. Based on mechanisms of learning the mother tongue, and on the observation that learning grammar rules at school is far less efficient than practicing communication with a native speaker, he advocated extensive monolingual input and practice in the foreign language. The teacher should form the model to be emulated, using playful exercises rather than painful drills. Practice should take the form of playful habit formation through imitating good examples, being more effective than rules children forget, and mistakes should be avoided and immediately corrected. Locke's ideas apprehended those of the German reform movement and also Behaviorism (see ch. 3.2.1).

From the 17th to the late 19th century, the German upper class admired the French aristocracy both for their lifestyle and the philosophy of Enlightenment. French was considered the language of diplomacy and refined culture. It is often argued that French followed Latin as a lingua franca of international relations in Europe, but one must not forget that many members of the lower classes did not have the opportunity to attend schools regularly and were barely able to read – let alone speak – any foreign language before the end of the 18th century.

With the rise of the British Empire in the 18th and 19th centuries, followed by the global dominance of the USA in the 20th century, English became a

Early methods

| Fig. 1.2
Johan-Amos
Comenius

French

The spread
of English

world language. Some consider this a blessing, others a curse: in British colonies such as India or South Africa, educating the elite in English existed parallel to educating the rest of the population in their native tongues. However, British imperialists only trained the local elites to enlist their collaboration in running – and exploiting – their countries. In other British colonies, such as in Ireland, Canada, and New Zealand, the native cultures were repressed. Indigenous children were compelled to attend colonial schools, were forbidden to speak their native tongues, and were alienated from their own cultures with the aim to control them and form them into British subjects (cf. Phillipson 1992, 2010). The decline of the British Empire after World War II did not diminish the role of English in the world. Many former colonies did not completely turn their backs on Great Britain but rather joined the Commonwealth and formed their political and educational institutions along British lines, many of them pragmatically choosing English as one of their national languages. One can regard English as the *key to empowerment* or reject it as a *killer language* (cf. Schneider 2011: 213–15). Brutt-Griffler (2008: 30–31) argues that the major problem of the underprivileged is less the loss of their indigenous languages and cultures than the limited access to English as a skill required for economic participation and social rise. She regards this restriction as a colonial legacy of maintaining a manual labor force that served the imperial economy and now sustains class differences. In South Africa and in India, where English is one of several national languages, many middle-class families send their children to secondary schools in which English is the medium of instruction (see fig. 1.3). Since many of these schools charge fees the poor cannot afford, they are effectively excluded from advanced English deemed essential for white-collar jobs in, for example, the fields of IT, finance, or administration (cf. Brutt-Griffler 2008: 32–33; Verma 2008: 42–44, 47–49).

Language as threat Some consider the global US-American influence a great progressive force as politicians and the film industry have disseminated values and vistas of a democratic and capitalist culture as a potentially liberating alternative to authoritarian and repressive traditions. Others have criticized the rise of 'American cultural imperialism' as the 'McDonaldization' of the world (cf. Bryman 2004, Ritzer 2011). Linguists advocating language rights, such as Phillipson and Skutnabb-Kangas (cf. 2011: 28–30), consider the domination and teaching of English in close connection to US-American neoliberal ideology and economy as *linguistic imperialism* that continues colonial practices even today. Education in the medium of English deprives indigenous and minority children of their languages and the "intergenerational transfer" of culture and identity: English 'kills' other languages and cultures if it is not added as an L2 to education in the mother tongue (ibid.: 33–34). Whichever perspective is taken, Great Britain and the USA have been major forces in driving globalization and making English a global language.

Fig. 1.3 |
Rural English school
in Zimbabwe (1992)

> What are the most important historical models of language teaching and learning, and what are their major features? Can you identify tasks you used to learn or teach a FL that fit these models? How effective were these?

The international perspective | 1.1.2

Today, English has become the lingua franca of the world and dominates popular culture, the Internet, trade, finance, politics, and academia. However, which Englishes are used around the world and which are taught and learned? In the 'non-native-English peripheries' across the world, English has been appropriated and adapted to serve local purposes, establishing *hybrid and heterogeneous world Englishes*. According to Kachru (cf. 1996: n. p.), the Inner Circle of English consists of countries in which English is a native language (e. g., USA, UK, Australia), the Outer Circle of countries in which English serves as an official second language (L2; e. g., India, Nigeria, Singapore), and the Expanding Circle of countries in which English is studied as a FL (e. g., South America, Japan, China). Kachru's model raises the question of who is the more competent speaker in which situation. In some cases, the non-native, plurilingual (*mehrsprachig*) speaker of English may have an advantage over the native monolingual one (cf. Harmer 2007: 18).

Standard British English (BE, RP) and standard American English (SAE or GA) enjoy a great deal of prestige, which pays off for many learners and institutions alike. Mastering standard English forms cultural capital (knowledge and education), social capital (esteem and status), and economic capital (job opportunities): thus, English has become a valuable commodity (cf. Verma 2008: 44). Schools and universities in Great Britain, Canada, Australia, and the USA attract students from around the world and charge considerable fees. Native speaker teachers from these countries are in great demand in the language programs at many schools and universities in non-Anglophone countries.

Without a doubt, the local appropriation of English by non-native speakers has resulted in the development of numerous varieties of English with differences in vocabulary, grammar, and syntax (cf. Mair 2003: xviii-xix; Schneider 2011: 54–59, 189–205). As an alternative to the Anglo-American standards and to diverse global varieties of the language, linguists are discussing the development of *Global English* or *World Standard English*. However the problem is how to define its structural, sociolinguistic, and historical-political characteristics (cf. Gnutzmann 2008: 109, 113–14; James 2008). The most important purpose of English as a lingua franca is intelligibility, and features of standard English not relevant to understanding are often disregarded, such as the pronunciation of the phoneme / th/ (*/dis/), the inflection of the verb in the third

World English

person (*he talk), or 'would' in if-clauses (*If she would come, I would be there; cf. James 2008: 135–40; Jenkins 2008: 146–49).

> Imagine you are participating in a meeting of the Standing Commission of Ministers of Education and Cultural Affairs of the *Länder* (*Kultusministerkonferenz* or KMK) and are involved in a discussion on FL teaching. Find pros and cons of why English as a first FL should be complemented or even replaced with Spanish, Russian, or Chinese. In a group of four, one group member defends English against others who advocate one other language each. What are the most important reasons for/against English as the first FL in schools?

> Discuss reasons for/against learning standard British or American English according to the native-speaker norm.

1.1.3 | The national perspective

Beginnings How has the German educational system responded to the global rise of English? In the 18th century, English gained some ground in schools that focused on the education of the urban middle class, which included reading English literature and works of philosophy or practicing oral communication (cf. Hüllen 2005: 66). In the three-tiered and class-based 19th century system of the *Volksschule* for the common people (grades 1–8), the *Realschule* (grades 5–10) and the *Gymnasium* for the middle and upper classes (grades 5–13), the majority of the population was not taught any FL at all. Gradually, English became the second modern FL next to French in the *Realschule*, and a third or fourth option next to Latin and Greek in the *Gymnasium*. In the *Gymnasium*, teaching English in the classroom was often modeled on the Grammar-Translation Method used for Latin. The explicit teaching of vocabulary and grammar should enable students to ultimately read literary and philosophical 'classics' in order to support their general education.

Reform movement In the late 19th century, Viëtor (see fig. 1.4) called for a reform of language education with a pamphlet entitled *Der Sprachunterricht muss umkehren* (1882/1905). Instead of focusing on an elitist form of higher education, FL instruction should concentrate on functional skills of oral communication and knowledge about the target country ('*Realienkunde*,' today known as *Landeskunde*; see ch. 7.1.2). Viëtor advocated the so-called **Direct or Natural Method**, employing the FL as the medium of instruction in order to promote oral skills besides studying authentic texts. At the same time, the Berlitz schools were among the first institutions which implemented the monolingual, direct method of immersion in order to offer a fast track form of FL education (cf. Christ 2010: 18). It took about forty years to adopt the reformers'

Fig. 1.4 |
Wilhelm Viëtor

demands for something like *Landeskunde* as a classroom topic, and about one hundred years to implement communicative and intercultural competences on a broad scale.

In the 1920s, the target culture was taught in comparison to one's own culture, enhancing the awareness of national culture, which in fact supported the construction of stereotypes. In the 1930s, the fascists elected English as the first FL and fostered learning about culture in order to prove the superiority of German national culture (cf. Hüllen 2005: 126). Despite all their rhetoric about the *Volk*, the fascists maintained traditional class discrimination in education: the majority of learners – in the *Volksschule* – had no FL classes at all.

Volks- und Rassenkunde

Due to the separation of spheres of political influence among the USA, France, Great Britain, and Russia after 1945, the Federal Republic of Germany introduced English as a first FL in all secondary schools, and the German Democratic Republic Russian as the first FL. In the 1970s, *Communicative Language Teaching* (CLT) shifted the priority from teaching knowledge about language (grammar and syntax) to performance in language (e. g., listening comprehension and speaking; see chs. 4.3.1, 6).

After World War II

Today, teachers of English face multiple challenges:

21st century

▶ The pragmatic communicative approach to teaching and learning foreign languages put forward in the CEF has changed educational standards from a focus on content to *testable output* (see ch. 12.1).

▶ The learning objective of the native-speaker standard has been replaced by the norm of the *plurilingual speaker*, who connects his or her competences in diverse languages and cultures in order to communicate effectively with different interlocutors (cf. Council of Europe 2001: 4–5, Byram 1997, Schneider 2011: 226; see ch. 7).

▶ *Early foreign language teaching and learning* (*Fremdsprachenfrühbeginn*) has been widely proclaimed as the best solution for promoting excellent language competences (see ch. 4.5).

▶ *Bilingual or Content and Language Integrated Learning* has gained ground in Germany and is increasingly implemented in primary and secondary schools (*bilingualer Unterricht*; see ch. 4.4).

▶ The *digital revolution* and the transformation of the Internet into a mass medium has increased the media repertoire for schools in general and for the FL classroom in particular (see chs. 2.1.4, 9.4).

▶ The policy of *inclusion* increases heterogeneity among learners and demands more differentiation (see ch. 6.3).

1.2 | Current educational standards and curricula

If the introduction of CLT in the 1970s led to the biggest change in 20th-century language education, then the 'PISA-shock' of the year 2000 and the publication of the CEF in 2001 initiated a revision of language teaching and learning for the 21st century. The Organization for Economic Co-operation and Development (OECD) started *PISA* (Program for International Student Assessment) in order to test the learning outcomes of 15-year-old learners in reading, mathematical, and scientific literacy across Europe. Germany, which had always taken pride in its educational system, was shocked to learn that the overall performance of its learners was below the OECD average of more than 50 countries.

1.2.1 | *The Common European Framework of Reference for Languages*

A common framework
The CEF has served to redefine language learning policy in Germany. The objectives of the CEF are quite comprehensive, straddling the general divide between pragmatic and educational aims of language learning:

► Communicative skills in foreign languages
► Intercultural communicative competence
► Individual education and emancipation
► Social skills and values
► Economic empowerment and mobility
► Political participation in a democratic and multicultural Europe
► Learner-centered methods of teaching

In spite of the claim that the CEF only aims at making policy makers, teachers, and learners reflect on language education without "tak[ing] position on theories of language acquisition and learning or approaches to teaching" (Council of Europe 2001: 18), the CEF does, however, advance certain arguments in greater detail, such as the demise of the native-speaker model, the concept of the *learner as a social agent*, and *language as (inter-)action. The CEF favors an action-oriented approach to language and a task-based one to learning.* Individual members of society are understood as social agents, who use all of their competences to solve tasks together with other people in particular circumstances:

> Language use, embracing language learning, comprises the actions performed by persons who as individuals and as social agents develop a range of *competences*, both *general* and in particular *communicative language competences*. They draw on the competences at their disposal in various contexts under various *conditions* and under various *constraints* to engage in *language activities* involving *language processes* to produce and/or receive texts in relation to *themes* in specific *domains*, activating those *strategies* which seem most appropriate for carrying

out the *tasks* to be accomplished. The monitoring of these actions by the participants leads to the reinforcement or modification of their competences. (Council of Europe 2001: 9, emphasis added)

Competence is a comprehensive and fuzzy term. The CEF merges and goes beyond the conventional linguistic concepts of competence as knowledge of the language system and performance as its usage. However, the CEF is aware of the problems of merging competence and performance: certain conditions and constraints – for example, noise, the number of interlocutors, psychological stress (time pressure, exams) – may interfere with the display of competences in performances (cf. ibid.: 48–49). The CEF subsumes knowledge, know-how, ability, and skills under the heading of competences, as the following list reveals (cf. ibid.: 11–14, 101–09; see chs. 6.1, 7.2.2).

1. General competences:
   ▶ Declarative knowledge (*savoir*; knowing what, including sociocultural and intercultural knowledge)
   ▶ Know-how and skills (*savoir-faire*, including sociocultural and intercultural know-how)
   ▶ Existential competences (*savoir-être*; personality traits, points of view, attitudes)
   ▶ The ability to learn (*savoir apprendre*; e. g., learner strategies, metacognitive awareness, media literacy)
2. Communicative language competences:
   ▶ Linguistic competence about language structures and how to use these (vocabulary, grammar, pronunciation and intonation, spelling)
   ▶ Reception (listening and reading)
   ▶ Production (speaking and writing)
   ▶ Interaction
   ▶ Mediation

CEF competences

In order to avoid confusion, *'competence' will be used henceforth as a superordinate category including knowledge and performance*, such as communicative or intercultural competence, and *'skill' as a subordinate category that refers to listening, speaking, reading, writing, and mediating.*

Apart from the competences summarized above, the CEF established six reference levels, which are specified in 'can do'-descriptors (ibid: 24; see fig. 1.5):

Reference levels

Fig. 1.5 CEF common reference levels – global scale	Proficient User	C2	Can understand with ease virtually everything heard or read. Can summarise information from different spoken and written sources, reconstructing arguments and accounts in a coherent presentation. Can express him/herself spontaneously, very fluently and precisely, differentiating finer shades of meaning even in more complex situations.
		C1	Can understand a wide range of demanding, longer texts, and recognize implicit meaning. Can express him/herself fluently and spontaneously without much obvious searching for expressions. Can use language flexibly and effectively for social, academic and professional purposes. Can produce clear, well-structured, detailed text on complex subjects, showing controlled use of organisational patterns, connectors and cohesive devices.
	Independent User	B2	Can understand the main ideas of complex text [sic.!] on both concrete and abstract topics, including technical discussions in his/her field of specialisation. Can interact with a degree of fluency and spontaneity that makes regular interaction with native speakers quite possible without strain for either party. Can produce clear, detailed text on a wide range of subjects and explain a viewpoint on a topical issue giving the advantages and disadvantages of various options.
		B1	Can understand the main points of clear standard input on familiar matters regularly encountered in work, school, leisure, etc. Can deal with most situations likely to arise whilst travelling in an area where the language is spoken. Can produce simple connected text on topics which are familiar or of personal interest. Can describe experiences and events, dreams, hopes and ambitions and briefly give reasons and explanations for opinions and plans.
	Basic User	A2	Can understand sentences and frequently used expressions related to areas of most immediate relevance (e. g. very basic personal and family information, shopping, local geography, employment). Can communicate in simple and routine tasks requiring a simple and direct exchange of information on familiar and routine matters. Can describe in simple terms aspects of his/her background, immediate environment and matters in areas of immediate need.
		A1	Can understand and use familiar everyday expressions and very basic phrases aimed at the satisfaction of needs of a concrete type. Can introduce him/herself and others and can ask and answer questions about personal details such as where he/she lives, people he/she knows and things he/she has. Can interact in a simple way provided the other person talks slowly and clearly and is prepared to help.

Read through the descriptors for the different levels and rate your own language competence. In your opinion, which levels of language proficiency are expected of FL learners in, for example, grades four, ten, and twelve? Check your predictions against the reference levels postulated in the curriculum for the level and type of school you are teaching at or want to teach at.

Germany: new educational standards and more testing

| 1.2.2

The CEF has shifted attention from the input of teaching (next to communicative skills) to the *output* of learning and the *testing of functional competences*. This document has had an enormous impact on educational policy making and test design, on teaching, and on academic debates: the KMK used the CEF as the framework of the *national educational standards* in *Bildungsstandards für die erste Fremdsprache (Englisch/Französisch) für den Hauptschulabschluss* (2004), *für den Mittleren Abschluss* (2003), and *für die fortgeführte Fremdsprache (Englisch/Französisch) für die Allgemeine Hochschulreife* (2012a). The KMK has also created its own comprehensive list of competences for the *Sekundarstufe I* (see fig. 1.6).

KMK competences

Funktionale kommunikative Kompetenzen	
Kommunikative Fertigkeiten	**Verfügung über die sprachlichen Mittel**

▸ Hör- und Hör-/Sehverstehen
 ▸ Leseverstehen
 ▸ Sprechen
    – an Gesprächen teilnehmen
    – zusammenhängendes Sprechen
 ▸ Schreiben
 ▸ Sprachmittlung
	▸ Wortschatz
	 ▸ Grammatik
	 ▸ Aussprache und Intonation
	 ▸ Orthographie

Interkulturelle Kompetenzen	
▸ soziokulturelles Orientierungswissen ▸ verständnisvoller Umgang mit kultureller Differenz ▸ praktische Bewältigung interkultureller Begegnungssituationen	
Methodische Kompetenzen	
▸ Textrezeption (Leseverstehen und Hörverstehen) ▸ Interaktion ▸ Textproduktion (Sprechen und Schreiben) ▸ Lernstrategien ▸ Präsentation und Mediennutzung ▸ Lernbewusstheit und Lernorganisation	

| Fig. 1.6

KMK competence framework (Kultusministerkonferenz 2003: 8)

All over Europe, the CEF has influenced and validates the design of *language tests* (see the Association of Language Testers in Europe, www.alte.org; The European Language Certificates, www.sprachenzertifikate.de; the European Association for Quality Language Services, www.eaquals.org). Following the guidelines of the CEF, the KMK monitors the outcome of language education through the development and implementation of comparative tests.

Testing

The DESI test (*Deutsch-Englisch Schülerleistungen International*, 2003–2004) comprehensively examined the skills of listening comprehension, speaking, reading, and writing, language awareness, and intercultural awareness. DESI has revealed considerable heterogeneity in competence levels in all school types, fairly poor skills in listening and reading comprehension across the

DESI

board, but better results in oral and written skills. In general, female and pluri-lingual learners scored better than male learners with a monolingual back-ground. In addition, video recordings show that teachers talk most of the time in spite of the fact that communicative approaches to teaching and learning English as a Foreign Language (EFL) should provide plenty of opportunities for learners to interact (cf. Zydatiß 2005: 320, Nold et al. 2006).

VERA | VERA (*VERgleichs Arbeiten*) is a test taken a year before students finish pri-mary school (VERA 3) or secondary school (VERA 8) in order to give both teachers and learners *feedback* on what to improve to meet the required com-petence levels at the end of their level of schooling. However, VERA 2009 only examined listening and reading comprehension, a fact that might be related to both easy empirical assessment and to the problems the DESI test of 2003–2004 revealed in these particular skills (see above).

Portfolio | The European language portfolio complements the institutional monitor-ing of competences (Council of Europe 2011). A portfolio is the collection of a learner's output such as written exercises, drafts of essays, or results from pro-ject work, which documents the learner's progress and proficiency (see ch. 12.5.2). It aims at motivating learners to become aware of (plurilingual) lan-guage acquisition within and outside of school, to assess their own skills, to identify their strengths, and to assume responsibility for their own learning with regard to their aims, fostering both self-esteem and life-long learning. Apart from the functions for the learner, the portfolio may be used as addi-tional information for school or job applications.

Impact of the CEF | Many teachers are vaguely familiar with the CEF and do not see how it makes a difference in the classroom (cf. Beer 2007, Vogt 2012: 87–88). One might say that they have a point because communicative competence, a core element of the CEF, has formed the central goal of teaching for decades. How-ever, since the German federal states used the more comprehensive CEF as a framework for educational standards and subsequent curricula, pre- and in-service teachers must have noticed the many adjustments to the curricula they work with. After all, *curricula* provide the framework of teaching with regard to:

► Educational and functional *aims*
► *Orientation* for planning, implementing, and reflecting on teaching and learning
► The definition of *progression* toward certain levels of competences
► The *framework* for the design of materials and tests
► The *basis of comparable performances* of classes and schools within a state (cf. Hallet & Königs 2010: 54–58)

Criticism of the CEF | Academics have hotly debated the aims and standards of the CEF for some time (cf. Bausch et al. 2003, Zydatiß 2005, Bredella 2006, Harsch 2006, Timm 2006, Klieme 2007, Quetz & Vogt 2009, Decke-Cornill & Küster 2010, Bach &

Breidbach 2013). In general, they appreciate the basic function of the CEF as a guideline for developing comparable curricula and exams across Europe, and the focus on the positive 'can do'-statements of achievement rather than on learners' deficits. However, they also find fault with particular standards, competences, and descriptors for the following reasons:

▸ The *Bildungsstandards ignore Bildung* in the sense of personal growth, orientation, and reflection (see ch. 8.1.2).
▸ The *narrow focus* on functional communicative competences and testing is detrimental to intercultural and methodological goals.
▸ Competence comes with *little content* as if content was less relevant.
▸ The *descriptors and scales of language proficiency* are not always clear and distinct.
▸ *Average standards* (*Regelstandards*) should be changed to minimum standards (*Mindeststandards*, for weaker learners) and maximum standards (*Maximalstandards*, encouraging best performance).
▸ *Standardization* jars with individualization and differentiation.
▸ *Output orientation* neglects standards of good teaching and the insight into processes of language acquisition and learning.
▸ Output standards encourage *teaching to the test* (backwash).

Compare the overview of competences postulated in the CEF and the KMK competence framework outlined above (see figs. 1.5 and 1.6). List the major similarities and differences of the two and discuss the significance of what the KMK left out.

Download the curriculum for the level and type of school you want to teach at. Which goals, contents, and methods does the curriculum propose? How interesting do you find the content and the tasks? How can they contribute to developing communicative skills and intercultural competence? To what extent do the tasks contribute to general education, the development of learner strategies, and methodical competences addressed in the German educational standards?

Teacher education in Germany | 1.3

The KMK briefly defined **standards of teacher education** in Educational Studies (*Erziehungs- und Bildungswissenschaften*) and Psychology (2004, 2012a), and in modern foreign languages at secondary schools (2008: 36–37). In cooperation with other academic associations, the *Deutsche Anglistenverband* and the *Deutsche Gesellschaft für Amerikastudien* (2012) specified the competences – and above all, the content – of English and American studies and TEFL in greater detail. The KMK (2008/2014, 2012b) agreed on two basic stages of teacher education (see fig. 1.7):

Stages

▶ Stage 1: *studying at least two major subjects and Educational Studies* at university or at a college of education (*Pädagogische Hochschule*). The first stage concludes with the B. A., M. A., and/or the First State Examination, which consists of a final thesis as well as written and oral examinations in the major subjects studied, TEFL, and Educational Studies.

▶ Stage 2: *practical training* (*Referendariat*) at teacher seminars (*Studienseminare*) and assigned schools (*Ausbildungsschulen*). The practical training aims at interlinking competences in English Studies, in TEFL, and in Educational Studies (cf. KMK 2008/2014: 3–6, 36–37), ending with the Second State Examination.

Fig. 1.7 Teacher education in Germany		Stage 1	Stage 2
		▶ B.A.: 3–4 years + M.A.: 1–2 years ▶ First State Examination: 4–5 years	▶ Traineeship & Second State Examination: 1–2 years
	Forms of instruction	▶ Lecture ▶ Seminar ▶ Tutorial ▶ Practical language training ▶ Short-term practical training or student-teaching semester (*Praxissemester*)	▶ Seminar: theoretically informed reflection of teaching and learning ▶ Observation of teaching (*Hospitation*) ▶ Guided and independent teaching
	Content & competences	▶ English language ▶ Area & Cultural Studies ▶ Linguistics ▶ Literary Studies ▶ TEFL ▶ Educational Studies (socialization, motivation, learner psychology, counseling, conflict management, etc.)	▶ Planning, implementing, and reflecting processes of learning English (methods, learning processes, assessment, etc.) ▶ Institutional education, functions of professional teachers ▶ School development and educational research

In spite of the similar requirements, the education of language teachers within these two stages varies considerably across the German federal states with regard to the subjects of academic education and the link to practical teacher training. The academic education of teachers at primary schools may be separated from that of teachers at secondary schools. For example, Baden-Wuerttemberg offers programs for teaching English at primary schools and secondary schools at a college of education. Students of teaching English at the *Gymnasium* enroll at a university with more study time allotted to Cultural, Literary, and Linguistic Studies than to TEFL and Educational Studies compared to colleges of education. The federal states also offer a third stage of in-service teacher training (*Lehrerfortbildungen*), but it is less systematically structured and implemented than the first two stages.

The gap between English and American Studies as an academic subject and its teaching at school has generated a long debate. Recently, centers of teacher education (*Zentren für Lehrerbildung*) have been founded, in which academic scholars, teacher trainers, and administrators work on bridging the gap between university and school. Most federal states require university students to attend stints of practical training at schools, often supervised by experts from both the school and university (cf. Volkmann 2012: 474–75). It is true that academic subject knowledge – apart from TEFL – goes beyond what is needed at school. However, generating knowledge is a genuine function of a university, and it is often only a matter of time until academic content and methods filter into primary and secondary education: for example, linguistic research in language acquisition has influenced the methods and implementation of early EFL teaching. The focus on race/ethnicity, class, and gender in Cultural Studies has had a lasting impact on textbooks, such as the representation of women and minorities. The expansion of literary studies led to opening the canon to works from Africa and India, comics, and film adaptations. In turn, teachers' reflected practice is a valuable form of theorizing that has fed back into TEFL as an academic subject.

Bridging the gap

> Obtain information on the particular requirements in TEFL at your university or your school and the links to studying English as a subject.

As Zydatiß (2005: 312–20, 363–67) argues, educational standards and curricula are not sufficient in order to improve the quality of FL education. Among others, the following factors play a crucial role (see ch. 2):

- The *quantitative conditions* of the educational system (e. g., financing, staffing, and resources)
- The *quality of schools* (e. g., their management and focus)
- The *quality of teaching* in the classroom (e. g., the interaction between teachers and learners, the methods, and the use of media)

Crucial factors

It remains to be seen whether the European Profile for Language Teacher Education (Kelly et al. 2004) and the European Profiling Grid for Assessing Language Teacher Competences will in the future be an instrument used by the German federal states to support the professional development of their teaching staff. The Profile sets up standards of education, training, and qualifications of teachers with regard to communicative, intercultural, media, methodological, and administrative competences.

The research and effort that go into institutionalized language teaching has not escaped criticism. The educational and functional objectives of institutionalized language teaching aim at competences that work in real-life interaction, but it is difficult to implement activities that help to achieve these competences. For example, the gradual progression along language structures in textbooks is in conflict with demands for authentic language use, especially for beginners and intermediate learners. The simulation of real-life situations may founder on the rocks of missing vocabulary or pragmatic skills in the average classroom. The simulation of intercultural dialogs in English among speakers of German may be awkward and demotivating if one cannot express what one could easily do in the mother tongue. In a real-life situation where the FL is the only means of communication, language input may exceed one's level of skills, and one needs to solve problems of communication under time pressure in addition to fulfilling the task at hand. Media and the contact with native speakers help to integrate authentic discourse in the classroom. Ideally, the immersion into the FL during an extended stay in an English-speaking country should complement both the academic training of pre-service teachers and language learning at school – a demand Comenius introduced hundreds of years ago.

Recommended reading

Council of Europe (2001). *Common European Framework of Reference for Languages: Learning, Teaching, Assessment.* Cambridge: Cambridge University Press.

Gnutzmann, Claus & Frauke Intemann, eds. (2008). *The Globalisation of English and the English Language Classroom.* 2nd ed. Tuebingen: Francke.

Kultusministerkonferenz (2003). *Bildungsstandards für die erste Fremdsprache (Englisch/ Französisch) für den Mittleren Abschluss. http://www.iqb.hu-berlin.de/bista/subject* (15 July 2014).

Schneider, Edgar W. (2011). *English Around the World: An Introduction.* Cambridge et al.: Cambridge University Press.

Timm, Johannes-P., ed. (2006). *Fremdsprachenlernen und Fremdsprachenforschung: Kompetenzen, Standards, Lernformen, Evaluation.* Tuebingen: Narr.

Zydatiß, Wolfgang (2005). *Bildungsstandards und Kompetenzniveaus im Englischunterricht: Konzepte, Empirie, Kritik und Konsequenzen.* Frankfurt a. M. et al.: Lang.

Challenges of the teaching profession

Contents

This chapter provides a structured, yet complex answer to the question of what it means to be a good teacher. It will first discuss the general prerequisites for good teaching practice based on the reflective practice model of professional development. This chapter will then address the question of what is required to be(come) a professional teacher of English as a Foreign Language (EFL). It closes with a focus on the paradigm shift in 21st century education as well as the essential role of foreign language (FL) teacher professional development and school innovation.

Abstract

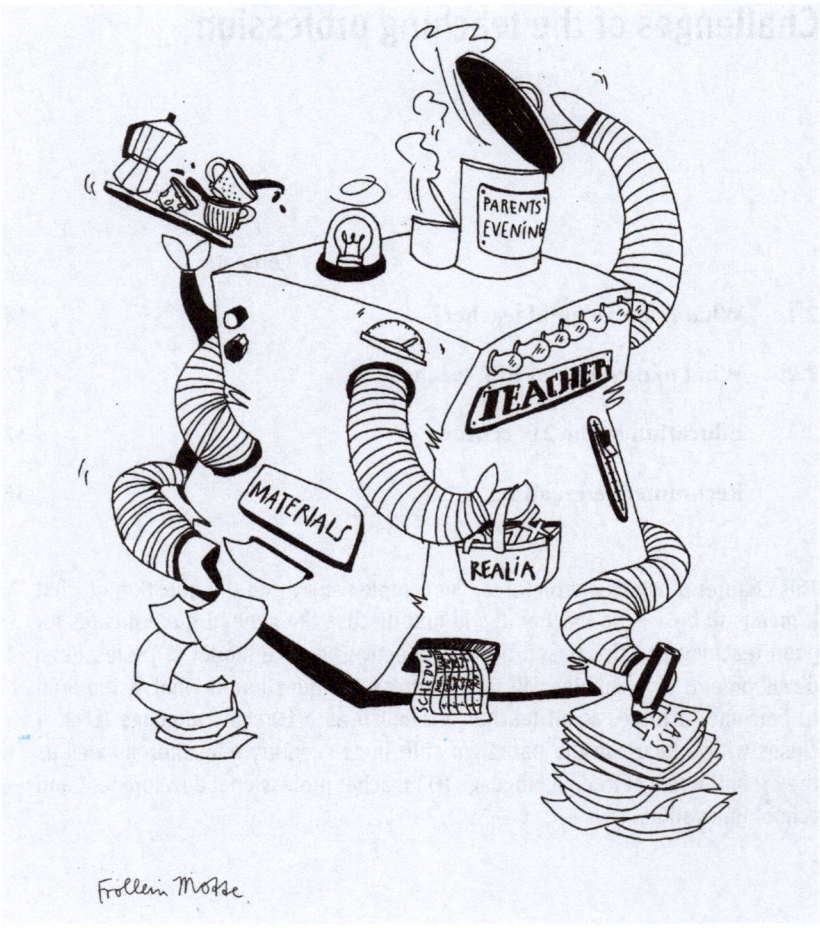

Frollein Motte

> Have a look at the cartoon. Think about the challenges teachers face today and the knowledge and competences teachers should have or develop to be able to cope with these challenges.

2.1 | What makes a good teacher?

Defining the *characteristics and knowledge base of good teachers* has spawned an extensive number of scholarly publications (cf. Shulman 1986, 1987, 1998; Heuer & Klippel 1987; Wallace 1991; Langer et al. 2003; Shulman & Shulman 2004; Richards & Farrell 2005; Lipowsky 2006; Helmke 2006; Hattie 2009, 2011; Schocker-von Ditfurth 2008; Hallet 2010; Baumert & Kunter 2011; Kunter et al. 2011; Bailey 2011; Jourdenais 2011). While the delineations in this chapter are informed by these sources, various definitions and overviews of teacher knowledge and competences outlined therein have been adapted to serve the focus of this chapter, which is *reflective practice* – specifically that of EFL teachers.

The reflective practice model of professional development

| 2.1.1

The *reflective practice model of professional development* (cf. Wallace 1991, Jourdenais 2011; see fig. 2.1) proves useful in providing orientation for pre- as well as in-service teachers with respect to what they bring to the teaching profession (*stage 1*), how this is modified and refined during their professional education (*stage 2*), and how continuous reflection then leads to professional competence (*goal*). It promotes a view of teachers as professionals competent to *teach, educate, evaluate, and innovate* (KMK 2004: 7–13; cf. Bauer 2006, Möllers 2011, Jantowski 2011) through reflecting upon educational policies, pursuing personal and professional growth, analyzing their practice and performance in lessons, and striving for creating a humane school environment.

As a reflective teacher, one should bring to the teaching profession the following reflective capabilities:

▶ *Multiple perspectives*: the ability to approach educational issues from a wide range of perspectives (e. g., personal, regional, national, global, socio-economic, philosophical)
▶ *Experiential learning*: the ability to reflect upon practical field experience and integrate this teaching experience into academic discourses in lectures and seminars

Who dares to teach must never cease to learn. –
John Cotton Dana

What one should bring to the teaching profession

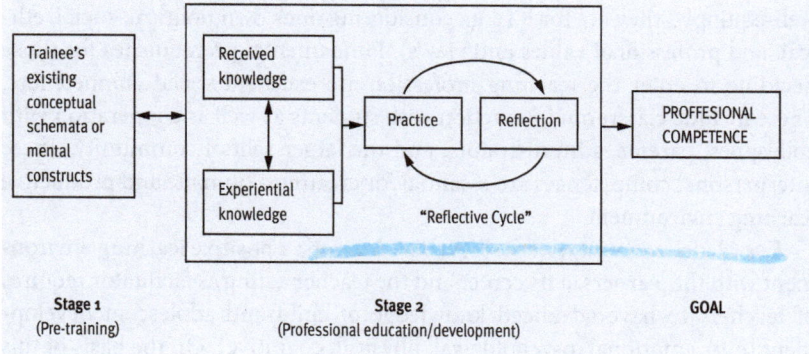

| Fig. 2.1
The reflective practice model of professional development (Wallace 1991: 94)

▶ *Construction of knowledge*: the ability to keep record of, diagnose, evaluate, and discuss one's personal and professional growth (e. g., portfolios, reports, presentations, general coursework, academic interaction)
▶ *Critical inquiry*: the ability to reflect on the impact of one's own teaching practice as well as general school settings and policies on students, their families, and the school community

Knowledge and competences of teachers

If the capabilities of reflective teachers are manifold, then – in light of their professional action competence (*professionelle Handlungskompetenz*, cf. Baumert & Kunter 2011) – the knowledge and competences reflective teachers need to master are equally wide-ranging (see fig. 2.2):

Fig. 2.2 | Knowledge and competences of reflective teachers

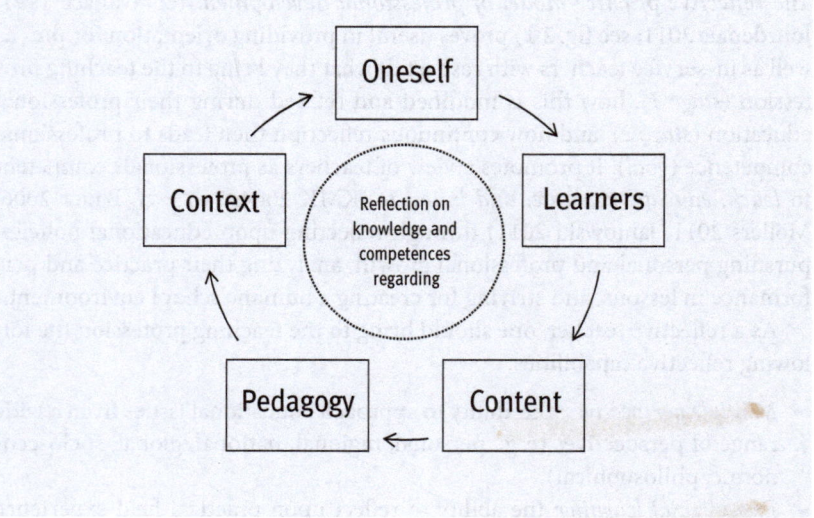

Oneself

Knowledge and competences regarding oneself: a sound knowledge of oneself is essential. Students entering university as pre-service teachers should already have honestly and critically reflected upon their future profession and how well-equipped they are for it (e. g., considering one's own political, social, ethical, and professional values and views). Fundamental prerequisites for those deciding to enter the teaching profession are excellent social competences. These include classroom interaction with students as well as cooperation with colleagues, parents, administrators, and the larger school community. These interpersonal competences are essential for creating a humane and productive learning environment.

Learners

Knowledge and competences regarding learners: a positive learning environment with the learners at its center and the teacher acting as facilitator requires of teachers to have advanced knowledge of child and adolescent development (e. g., emotional, psychological, physical, cognitive). On the basis of this knowledge, teachers should be able to diagnose developmental delays in students and provide support and counseling in cooperation with the parents, the school counselor, or therapists. Teachers today are also met with the challenge of increasingly heterogeneous and inclusive classes (see ch. 6.3). Teachers will encounter students with different learning histories from pre-school and primary education and are required to apply their knowledge of learning theories to the individual needs of their students. Teachers may also encounter a large

20

cultural diversity in their classrooms, and they might also teach children whose success in school may be negatively affected by a poor socio-economic background, where financial and/or parental support may be lacking.

Knowledge and competences regarding content: a sound knowledge of pre-school, primary and secondary school curricula and the general principles and objectives of education in these respective school settings will enable teachers to seek out interdisciplinary approaches to teaching and learning. A sound knowledge of the content of various school subjects as well as a mastery of their own subjects will help teachers understand, analyze, and incorporate multiple perspectives into their specific subjects.

Content

Knowledge and competences regarding pedagogy: a sound knowledge of modern pedagogy is essential for reflective teachers. It will help them reflect upon their teaching and their role in promoting a humane learning environment. It will also provide them with guidelines for developing lesson sequences based on their students' needs and interests. Such a student-centered approach must inevitably be informed by a variety of methods to facilitate learning processes, involve students, and assess them.

Pedagogy

Knowledge and competences regarding context: teachers need a sound knowledge of the larger educational context they find themselves in. Even if they teach at a specific school in a specific place, they need to know about other schools and school forms in the region. They need to know about the population of the region and specifically, the student populace of their school. Teachers should adjust their teaching to the specific teaching and learning conditions at their school.

Context

Personal characteristics

2.1.2

When one consults the academic discourse on *important characteristics of teachers* (cf. Hattie 2009: 108–28, 238–44; Shulman & Shulman 2004; Bailey 2011: 708–14), they are often described as *professionals who create an atmosphere of mutual respect in the classroom, the school, and beyond*. Characteristics frequently mentioned include the following (see fig. 2.3):

A good teacher can inspire hope, ignite the imagination, and instill a love of learning. – Brad Henry

Characteristic	Description	Check
Engaging	Teachers should facilitate interesting learning experiences, create interactive learning environments, and use a variety of materials and methods.	
Enthusiastic	Teachers should show their own enthusiasm for the subject matter at hand and explicitly invite students to share this enthusiasm.	
Intelligent	Teachers should be in command of the subject matter taught and demonstrate a sound basis of general knowledge.	
Well-organized	Teachers should invest time and effort into lesson preparation and make the course of teaching and learning transparent to their students.	

Fig. 2.3

Personal characteristics of teachers

Flexible	Teachers should be able to solve unexpected problems without getting panic-stricken in the face of challenges.
Fair	Teachers should refrain from cynicism of any kind as well as be sensitive and know when to criticize, correct, discipline, and when not.
Professional	Teachers should have high qualifications and show a professional attitude.
Reflective	Teachers should be willing to constantly evaluate their own teaching performance, adjust their own teaching methods, and sense what works and what does not in their own teaching.

The list is not meant to be understood as a ranking, but rather as a list of eight characteristics considered to be equally important for defining good teachers.

> Discuss why these characteristics are important. Choose three that you consider most important and elaborate on your choice. Tick the characteristics that you can honestly say apply to you.

2.1.3 | Principles of good teaching practice

Effective teaching is not the drilling and trilling of the less than willing. – John Hattie

Teachers who strive to develop or already possess most of the aforementioned characteristics of good teachers should be able to put into practice the ***principles of good teaching practice*** as provided by Meyer (2006, 2014; cf. Ditton 2000, Helmke 2006, Thompson 2009) in his helpful book *Was ist guter Unterricht?* (see fig. 2.4, see ch. 10):

Fig. 2.4 |

Principles of good teaching practice (Meyer 2006: 5–8, adapted)

Principle	Elements	Rank
Clear teaching structure	► Process clarity ► Clearly defined roles ► Agreement on rules, rituals, and what is permissible	
High amount of time-on-task	► Intelligent time management ► Punctuality ► Reduction of organizational work in the classroom	
Climate conducive to learning	► Mutual respect ► Rules that are adhered to ► Balancing of responsibility ► Equality and care for one another	
Content clarity	► Well-defined tasks ► Plausibility of thematic processes ► Clarity and continuity of retaining that which was taught	
Meaningful communication	► Participatory planning ► Discussions on the meaning of tasks ► Frequent mutual feedback	

Variety of instructional methods	▶ Multitude of teaching and learning patterns ▶ Balancing of individualized and collective learning, of self-regulated and guided learning	
Individual support	▶ Being patient with students and taking time for them ▶ Internal differentiation ▶ Individual learning analyses and individual learning plans ▶ Paying particular attention to at-risk students	
Intelligent exercises	▶ Making students aware of learning strategies ▶ Precise assignments for exercises ▶ Concerted support	
Clear description of goals to be achieved	▶ Learning situations fitted to the curricula and the capabilities of the students ▶ Punctual feedback on learning progress	
Well-prepared learning environment	▶ Well-organized, functional facilities ▶ Useable learning tools	

Take a critical look at the table above. Discuss how easy or difficult (1 = very easy, 2 = rather easy, 3 = rather difficult, 4 = very difficult) it would be to adhere to this code of conduct.

Both the characteristics of good teachers as well as the principles of good teaching practice can then be translated into *four pieces of practical advice* for teachers in the fields of instruction, diagnosis, learning environment, and professionalism (cf. Thompson 2009: 8–9):

Practice

▶ *Instruction*: design instruction that appeals to the various learning modalities of your students. Use educational standards to inform instruction. Differentiate instruction so that the individual needs of all learners are met. Use techniques that minimize the loss of time when disruption occurs. Use technology to enhance your instructional practices.
▶ *Diagnosis*: demonstrate knowledge of your students' development, skills, abilities, and aptitudes. Administer appropriate assessments to determine student mastery level. Help students to establish and achieve learning goals.
▶ *Learning environment*: understand how students learn and use that knowledge to reach your students. Use sound judgment about which teaching practices are suitable for your students. Use a variety of methods to motivate students to perform well in school both academically and behaviorally. Establish a positive relationship with every student. Establish a safe and productive classroom environment. Provide a risk-free and supportive learning environment. Treat all students with dignity and respect regardless of factors such as ethnicity, class, or gender.

23

▶ *Professionalism*: assume responsibility for your own professional growth. Work collaboratively with colleagues for the benefit of all staff members and students.

Know thy impact. –
John Hattie
In this context, one cannot but refer to Hattie's extensive meta-study *Visible Learning* (2009; cf. Hattie 2003, 2011), which has been lauded as "[r]esearch [that] reveals teaching's Holy Grail" (Mansell 2009: n. p., cf. Terhart 2011). In this study, the following *six items* regarding the *positive impact of teachers and their teaching on student achievement* are listed in the top ten (Hattie 2009: 297–300; cf. Lipowsky 2006, Maier 2012; see ch 4.7):

▶ *Providing formative evaluation*: feedback to teachers which draws on data- and evidence-based models (cf. ibid.: 181).
▶ *Microteaching*: short lessons that are videotaped, analyzed, and discussed with peers and mentors. Microteaching provides teachers with "an often intense under-the-microscope view of their teaching" (ibid.: 112).
▶ *Comprehensive interventions for learning disabled students*: beneficial inter-ventions include segmenting information, sequencing of tasks, controlling task difficulty, learning in small interactive groups, strategy training (cf. ibid.: 217–18).
▶ *Teacher clarity*: communicating the intentions of a lesson, organizing it, pro-viding clear explanations, guiding students' learning and assessing it (cf. ibid.: 125–26).
▶ *Reciprocal teaching*: a dialogic process between teachers and students with the aim to enable the latter to learn and apply cognitive strategies (e. g., pre-dicting, questioning, clarifying, summarizing; cf. ibid.: 203–04).
▶ *Feedback*: it "needs to be clear, purposeful, meaningful and compatible with students' prior knowledge, and to provide logical connections. It also needs to prompt active information processing on the part of the learner, have low task complexity, relate to specific and clear goals, and provide little threat to the person at the self level." (ibid.: 178)

2.1.4 | New technologies, new challenges

Regarding the knowledge to be mastered and the competences required of teachers today, the need for *technological knowledge and competences* has increased enormously. Without a doubt, the last decade especially "has wit-nessed vast changes accompanying the turn from an industrial to a technology-based information society, *yet in many classrooms around the world, teachers are still standing in front of a group of students with a piece of chalk in their hand*" (Van den Branden 2011: 659, emphasis added). Technological competences in connection with pedagogical competences regarding the reasonable and effec-tive use of technology in educational settings are among the *most important, yet still underrepresented fields of teacher professional development* (see chs. 9.1, 9.4).

Authored by Koehler and Mishra (2009) and based on Shulman's knowledge base categories (1987: 8), the *Technological Pedagogical Content Knowledge model* (TPACK, see fig. 2.5) depicts how essential it is for teachers to recognize the *interface between content knowledge, pedagogical knowledge, and technological knowledge*:

Content – pedagogy – technology

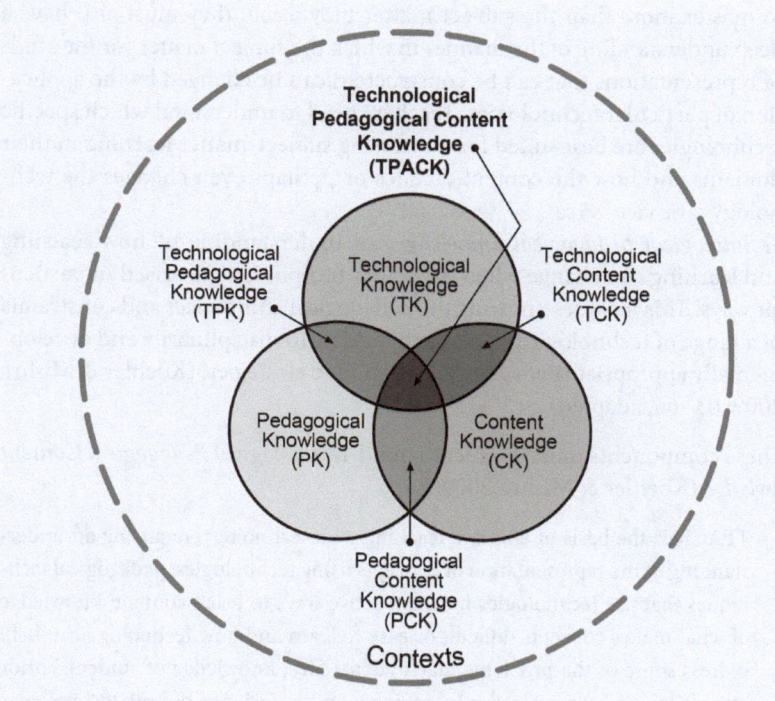

Fig. 2.5

The TPACK framework and its knowledge components (Koehler & Mishra 2009: 63)

- ▶ *Content knowledge*: teachers' knowledge about the subject matter to be learned or taught. [...] Knowledge and the nature of inquiry differ greatly between fields, and teachers should understand the deeper knowledge fundamentals of the disciplines in which they teach.
- ▶ *Pedagogical knowledge*: teachers' deep knowledge about the processes and practices or methods of teaching and learning. [...] A teacher with deep pedagogical knowledge understands how students construct knowledge and acquire skills and how they develop habits of mind and positive dispositions toward learning.
- ▶ *Pedagogical content knowledge*: the transformation of the subject matter for teaching. [...] [T]his transformation occurs as the teacher interprets the subject matter, finds multiple ways to represent it, and adapts and tailors the instructional materials to alternative conceptions and students' prior knowledge.

- *Technological knowledge*: requires a deeper, more essential understanding and mastery of information technology for information processing, communication, and problem solving than does the traditional definition of computer literacy.
- *Technological content knowledge*: an understanding of the manner in which technology and content influence and constrain one another. Teachers need to master more than the subject matter they teach; they must also have a deep understanding of the manner in which the subject matter (or the kinds of representations that can be constructed) can be changed by the application of particular technologies. Teachers need to understand which specific technologies are best suited for addressing subject-matter learning in their domains and how the content dictates or perhaps even changes the technology – or vice versa.
- *Technological pedagogical knowledge*: an understanding of how teaching and learning can change when particular technologies are used in particular ways. This includes knowing the pedagogical affordances and constraints of a range of technological tools as they relate to disciplinarily and developmentally appropriate pedagogical designs and strategies. (Koehler & Mishra 2009: 63–65, adapted)

All these components must interact to build *Technological Pedagogical Content Knowledge* (Koehler & Mishra 2009: 66):

> TPACK is the basis of effective teaching with technology, requiring an understanding of the representation of concepts using technologies; pedagogical techniques that use technologies in constructive ways to teach content; knowledge of what makes concepts difficult or easy to learn and how technology can help redress some of the problems that students face; knowledge of students' prior knowledge and theories of epistemology; and knowledge of how technologies can be used to build on existing knowledge to develop new epistemologies or strengthen old ones.

If teachers are expected to show *a mastery of this wide-ranging knowledge base*, then teacher education, school infrastructure, and in-service teacher training programs have to offer them expert technological as well as methodological training.

Imagine teaching an EFL lesson with an interactive whiteboard. Use the TPACK model to describe the knowledge and competences necessary to teach effectively using a whiteboard.

What makes a good EFL teacher?

In the attempt to boil down all of the delineations above to the central question of what makes a good EFL teacher, one should choose a differentiated approach that avoids homogenization. This is done for one particular reason:

> [The] development from students to teachers, from a state of expertise as learners through a novitiate as teachers exposes and highlights the complex bodies of knowledge and skills needed to function effectively as a teacher. The result is that error, success, and refinement – in a word, teacher knowledge growth – *are seen in high profile and in slow motion.* (Shulman 1987: 4, emphasis added)

The complex body of knowledge and competences that this section will depart from is based on the reflective practice model of professional development and the necessary knowledge and competences of reflective teachers introduced before.

Knowledge and competences regarding oneself

The reflection upon one's own values and views is essential for EFL teachers. This includes a reflection upon one's own views of teaching and inherent values of formal education. Personal values and views will also inform every teacher's choice of methods, activities, and classroom settings (see chs. 3.2, 4). A critical approach to one's own political, educational, and socio-cultural values and views is therefore important to, for example, reflect upon one's teaching of literature and target cultures. It is safe to assume that students who were subjected almost exclusively to the classical canon of literature and the two traditional target cultures (UK, USA) in their formative years at school will show a tendency to copy this approach. Therefore, pre-service and in-service teachers should always *look beyond traditional approaches to teaching.*

Teachers teach as they were taught, not as they were taught to teach. –
Howard B. Altman

A sound knowledge of oneself and how one is perceived by others will help teachers create a positive and productive FL learning environment, which is essential with respect to students' *effective second language acquisition* (SLA; see chs. 3.2.2, 4.5). Interpersonal skills are also important when cooperating with colleagues in order to carry out subject-specific or interdisciplinary study units. Teachers will increasingly be asked to take on *leadership roles in school innovation.* This will require of them to cooperate effectively with school administrators, curriculum planners, teacher trainers, and the parents of their students.

Case study 1

Staying in control of the classroom is the most important thing for Frank, who describes himself as a perfectionist. In fact, he hates it when things get out of control and do not run as smoothly as he planned at home when preparing his lessons. However, reflecting upon his English lessons today made him feel very uneasy. It struck him that his obsession with staying in control had affected his relationship with his students negatively. Sure, he was in control of the classroom, his students received good test results and he got his work done. The problem was that there was no humor, no enthusiasm, and no real motivation for learning English in the classroom. It just wasn't any fun for him or his students.

What is problematic about Frank's code of conduct in class? What should he change about himself and his perception of teaching and learning? What could help him to add fun, motivation, and enthusiasm to his English lessons?

2.2.2 | Knowledge and competences regarding learners

Prior knowledge and expectations

A sound knowledge of *child and adolescent development patterns and developmental stages* will help teachers understand student behavior and academic development. In the EFL classroom, knowledge of developmental patterns is essential: depending on the students' developmental stage, teachers will have to *adapt their teaching materials, adjust their teaching methods, as well as their classroom instruction and interaction* (see chs. 5.1.2, 10.2, 11.2).

Student behavior in classroom settings as well as their academic development will also depend on their *individual learning histories*. In pre-school or primary education, the ways and complexity of FL instruction differ immensely from that in secondary education. Especially at stages of transition, teachers will have to diagnose their students' FL competence levels (see ch. 4.5). In order to allow for *smooth transitions*, teachers need a sound knowledge of language learning theories and processes in pre-school, primary, and secondary education. Teachers will also have to take into consideration their students' *social status, ethnicity, and gender*. For example, while a multicultural classroom offers a wide range of opportunities for *intercultural learning*, it may also pose problems resulting from *critical incidents* in the classroom (see ch. 7.1.3). Also, *students' views of English as a school subject and the merits it holds for them* will have an impact on their individual success. Some students might hold the view that FL learning is bothersome and difficult, to some English might just not be their favorite subject, and others might simply love it. It is the teacher's task then to motivate students with a negative view of the subject by catering to different types of learners (e. g., by providing a wide range of language learning materials, varied activities and tasks).

Case study 2

> Driving home after a long day at school, Katharina was at the end of her rope. She felt that the high expectations she held for students were interfering with classroom interaction. All she had wished for her English lesson today was to have a good conversation with her students about a short story they had read the lesson before. But she ended up getting very angry at some of her students whose interpretations of the short story were totally off. Other students just would not talk at all. Instead of having a productive conversation about the short story and its meaning, conversation in class stalled.
>
> What is problematic about Katharina's expectations for this lesson on literature? What should she change about her approach in order to invite all students into the discussion?

Knowledge and competences regarding content

2.2.3

At the core of professional teaching lies *sound subject-specific content and curricular knowledge*. With the large amount of grammatical, lexical, cultural, and literary content to be taught to students, teachers will not only have to be proficient in a wide range of disciplines, but they will also have to use their own good judgment and pedagogical expertise to *select and adapt what and how they will actually present a specific topic to their students*. Ideally, these decisions should always be informed by the general principles of *liberal education*: empowering learners through providing them with transferable intellectual and practical competences, preparing them to deal with complexity, diversity, and change in the real world, and helping them to develop a sense of social responsibility.

It is also useful for teachers to know about other subject-specific curricula to initiate interdisciplinary projects. Interdisciplinary approaches have already been implemented in many German schools with *bilingual instruction* in specific subjects (e. g., in History, Geography, Social Studies; see ch. 4.4). But with a general cross-curricular view and interest, teachers may also team up with teachers of other subjects whenever their teaching focus in the EFL classroom *can be enriched and may even become more effective and productive through collaboration with colleagues* (e. g., during excursions, in project weeks).

It is less the content of curricula that is important than the strategies teachers use to implement the curriculum so that students progress upwards through the curricula content. – John Hattie

Case study 3

In order not to disappoint his mentor and make a good impression at the school, Mark made a point of moving through the topics exactly as they were outlined in the curriculum and scheduled in the in-school syllabus for grade eight. Recently, a couple of his students had suggested to discuss a popular song in one of his English lessons. While the students made a convincing case for discussing the song, Mark turned them down, telling them that the song did not fit in his overall plan and that there was simply no time to stray from the syllabus. The students were very disappointed, word got around, and, consequently, many of his students gave Mark the cold shoulder during the next couple of weeks.

Mark is obviously very focused on meeting what is required of him by the curriculum. This seems to interfere with his relationship with his students. How could he have handled the situation differently? Should teachers judge themselves or be judged by others solely on the basis of whether or not they manage to comply with curriculum requirements? Elaborate.

2.2.4 | Knowledge and competences regarding pedagogy

Positive learning environment and teacher-student relationships

A sound knowledge of pedagogy will help teachers to reflect on their own as well as on their students' classroom interaction. Reflection should focus on the *improvement of the general classroom atmosphere and learning environment*, on ways of giving oral and written feedback in classroom discourse, and on the balance between teacher talk time (TTT) and student talk time (STT, see ch. 10.4.1). In FL teaching and learning this may include differentiation in team-, group-, or project-work, peer assessment, the efficient use of media, as well as the engagement of students in decisions about, for example, what literary text to read, what song to listen to, or what film to watch. Teachers might also find that their *knowledge of a variety of methods* has a definite impact on how well their students learn, on enabling them to evaluate and adapt their own learning strategies, and on involving them in classroom discourse.

We need classes that develop the courage to err. –
John Hattie

While assessment is a necessity in formal education, FL teachers are advised *that it does not always need to take the form of a grade spelled as a number.* Other forms of assessment and feedback are possible, such as portfolios, learning diaries, etc. (see ch. 12.5.3). It is the teacher's task to select appropriate assessment methods for different teaching scenarios. *Transparent methods* of assessing students and their academic work lie at the heart of creating and managing an anxiety-free learning environment (see ch. 12.3).

Case study 4

In order to improve her students' oral skills, Stefanie had set presentation topics for her students to prepare and present. During the presentations, Stefanie noticed that many of them lacked structure and language accuracy. Some of her students even quoted directly from Wikipedia and others just read out their notes. After the presentation days, Stefanie realized that none of her students had received a good grade. In fact, most of the grades for the presentations were average or below. What was even worse, students were angry about Stefanie's grading and claimed that they did not know what was expected of them beforehand.

What should Stefanie have done differently? Make suggestions for improvement with regard to preparing students for presentations as well as making the grading process more transparent.

Knowledge and competences regarding context

| 2.2.5

Teachers are also required to have a sound knowledge of *school forms* (e. g., primary, secondary, vocational, special-needs) and their *educational principles*. They also need to acquaint themselves with the infrastructure, organization, management, colleagues, and student populace of the specific school they are or will be working at. For EFL teachers, it is especially important to know about any *special focus or field of expertise* that their school specializes in (e. g., the Arts, Music, Sports, the Sciences, Languages).

Teachers are also required to critically reflect upon the *purposes and conditions of formal education*. In FL teaching, this would include being aware that FL teaching is an *intercultural endeavor* which requires teachers to be interculturally aware and sensitive in their teaching of other cultures (cf. Kramsch 1994), being active in advancing FL learning environments, and pushing for better FL learning equipment (e. g., textbooks, school library, media, soft-/hardware).

It is school leaders who promote challenging goals, and then establish safe environments for teachers to critique, question, and support other teachers to reach these goals together that have most effect on student outcomes. – John Hattie

Case study 5

Marie works at a school that has recently begun to put the concept of inclusion into practice. While Marie is convinced of this concept, teaching English in one of her mixed-ability classes was becoming more and more difficult. The students in this class were just so heterogeneous and Marie's teaching methods did not reach all of them. In fact, too many students were falling behind. Sure, she did some pair and group work here and there, but in order to meet curriculum requirements most of her teaching was teacher-centered. She felt that her university education had not really prepared her for what it meant to teach mixed-ability classes; she just did not know what to do and felt completely left alone.

What could Marie do to improve her knowledge about teaching in mixed-ability classes? What should the school do to support its teachers? Which adjustments need to be made to teacher education, if teachers and schools are to meet the challenge of successfully integrating students with disabilities in mainstream schooling?

2.3 | Education in the 21st century

2.3.1 | Paradigm shift

What should education look like today and in the future?

Schools and teachers will do students disservice if they do not equip them with the knowledge and competences necessary in the 21st century (cf. The New London Group 2000, Trilling & Fadel 2009; see chs. 7.2, 9.1). The ways of teaching in 21st century classrooms have already changed immensely, *but still have to be further improved in light of the many challenges education is facing*: fast changes in society, technology, economy, and culture require open minds, flexibility, problem-solving skills, self-management, social skills, etc. These skills and competences go far beyond perceptions of the teaching profession, classroom settings, educational objectives, and approaches to teaching one generation ago. The following adjustments should be considered (see fig. 2.6):

Fig. 2.6 |
Paradigm shift

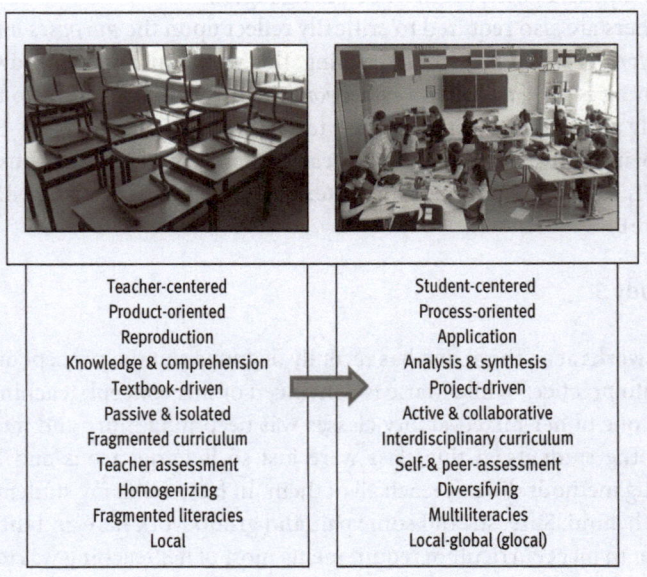

Teacher-centered	Student-centered
Product-oriented	Process-oriented
Reproduction	Application
Knowledge & comprehension	Analysis & synthesis
Textbook-driven	Project-driven
Passive & isolated	Active & collaborative
Fragmented curriculum	Interdisciplinary curriculum
Teacher assessment	Self-& peer-assessment
Homogenizing	Diversifying
Fragmented literacies	Multiliteracies
Local	Local-global (glocal)

▶ Education should be student-centered and process-oriented with the students at the center and the teacher as a *facilitator* of varied learning scenarios and a *learning coach* to students.

▶ It should focus on *students' application of knowledge and competences to new situations* and, consequently, needs to shift from the mere distribution of declarative knowledge and testing student comprehension to providing students with ample opportunities and time to analyze and synthesize knowledge (*procedural knowledge*).

▶ It should be project-driven instead of merely textbook-oriented to facilitate *active and collaborative learning as well as interdisciplinary approaches to teaching and learning.*

▶ It should make use of a *variety of assessment methods* that go beyond mere teacher assessments and involve, for example, language portfolios, peer assessment, and learning diaries.

▶ It should *differentiate* between students, their skills, needs, and interests instead of considering students as a homogenous mass.

▶ It should make students aware of the fact that they need to acquire a large amount of competences and literacies (*multiliteracies*) in order to *meet the global challenges of the 21st century.*

> Discuss the proposed changes and modifications to education with regard to, for example, questions of implementation, practicality, effectiveness, and long-term success.

Teacher professional development and action research

| 2.3.2

In this chapter, much space has been taken up to outline what teachers should know as well as how they should teach and act. However, one must be aware *that changes to education cannot be mandated, but must be implemented from the bottom up.* In other words, only individual teachers can implement the necessary adjustments and thus *play a fundamental role in school innovation.* Therefore, continuous professional development, starting during pre-service teacher education and continuing throughout in-service teaching over the years, is of utmost importance (see ch. 1.3).

If we are to have a revolution in education, it probably won't come from the top down but from the bottom up. – Sir Kenneth Robinson

What is *teacher professional development*, and why is it necessary? While it plays an important role for in-service teachers, the *willingness to improve on a personal, social, and professional level is a paramount prerequisite already during pre-service teacher training at university.* Professional development at its most basic level requires of both pre-service and in-service teachers to be able and willing to reflect on their teacher training, practical training, and teaching practice: "It [teacher development] serves a long-term goal and seeks to facilitate growth of teachers' understanding of teaching and of themselves as teachers."

(Richards & Farrell 2005: 4) *Goals of teacher professional development* include the following (ibid.):

► Understanding how the process of second language development occurs
► Understanding how our roles change according to the kind of learners we are teaching
► Understanding the kinds of decision making that occur during lessons
► Reviewing our own theories and principles of language teaching
► Developing an understanding of different styles of teaching
► Determining learners' perceptions of classroom activities

While teachers talk to their colleagues about curriculum, assessment, children, lack of time and resources, they rarely talk about their teaching. – John Hattie

Since it is not enough to simply tell teachers that they should strive for continuous professional development, teachers need *practical and applicable methods* to help them reflect on their teaching as well as develop and improve their teaching practice. There are many *instruments with which teachers can keep track of and judge their own performance*: classroom observations, surveys and questionnaires, portfolios, test results, checklists, interviews, visual recordings, journals or diaries, and evidence-based quantitative diagnostics (cf. Stiller 2006, Foord 2009, Helmke & Lenske 2013, Helmke et al. 2014). *Action research* (*Aktionsforschung, anwendungsbezogene Forschung*) has proven particularly helpful when teachers come across practical and recurring problems that they want to solve. Burns (2005: 61, adapted) delineates what action research involves:

► *Philosophical assumptions*: people within social situations can solve problems through self-study and intervention
► *Purpose*: to develop solutions to problems identified within one's own social environment
► *Main methods*: mainly qualitative, interpretive; cases studied reflectively through cyclical observational and non-observational means
► *Outcome*: action to effect change and improvement, and deeper understanding of one's own social situation
► *Criteria for judgment*: subjectivity, feasibility, trustworthiness, and resonance of research outcomes with those in the same or similar social situation

If teachers want to execute action research, they will have to act as researchers, following a concrete *plan of action* that usually involves four distinct phases (see fig. 2.7):

Phase	Action
Planning	A problem or issue is identified and a plan of action is developed in order to bring about improvements in specific areas of the research context.
Action	The plan is put into action over an agreed period of time.
Observation	The effects of the action are observed and data are collected.
Reflection	The effects of the action are evaluated and become the basis for further cycles of research.

Fig. 2.7

Phases of action research (Burns 2000: 6, adapted; cf. Kemmis & McTaggart 1988)

Teachers who are able to execute action research on their own teaching and who are convinced that all of us "have an obligation to raise standards in the interests of improvement and reform" (Shulman 1987: 20), will ultimately be the *change agents* putting into practice

Teachers as agents of change

> [i]nnovations aiming for the implementation of more communicative, functional language teaching methods […], [i]nnovations aiming for the introduction of modern technology in second/foreign language education […], [i]nnovations emphasizing the importance of measuring learner growth and assessing the output of language education […] (Van den Branden 2011: 659–60).

Without a question, teachers and schools will never be perfect, but we can all strive to make them so, thus catering to both student achievement as well as to the contentment and health of teachers (cf. Jantowski & Hartleib 2013).

Get a clearer idea of the teaching profession and assess whether your personality, experiences, and interests match a career in teaching: www.cct-germany.de.

Recommended reading

Foord, Duncan (2009). *The Developing Teacher: Practical Activities for Professional Development*. Surrey: Delta Publishing.

Hattie, John (2009). *Visible Learning: A Synthesis of Over 800 Meta-Analyses Relating to Achievement*. London et al.: Routledge.

Hattie, John (2011). *Visible Learning for Teachers: Maximizing Impact on Learning*. London et al.: Routledge.

Lipowsky, Frank (2006). Auf den Lehrer kommt es an: Empirische Evidenzen für Zusammenhänge zwischen Lehrerkompetenzen, Lehrerhandeln und dem Lernen der Schüler. In: Cristina Allemann-Ghionda & Ewald Terhart, eds. *Kompetenzen und Kompetenzentwicklung von Lehrerinnen und Lehrern: Ausbildung und Beruf*. Weinheim et al.: Beltz, 47–70.

Meyer, Hilbert (2014). *Was ist guter Unterricht?* 10th ed. Berlin: Cornelsen.

Richards, Jack C. & Thomas S. C. Farrell (2005). *Professional Development for Language Teachers: Strategies for Teacher Learning*. Cambridge et al.: Cambridge University Press.

TEFL as a transdisciplinary project

Contents

In order to teach successfully, one needs to understand how learning works in general and language learning as well as foreign language learning in particular. In addition, one needs to know what students should learn. In order to answer these fundamental questions, Teaching English as a Foreign Language (TEFL) draws on Educational Studies and English Linguistics, Literary Studies, and Cultural Studies. The wide conception of education encompasses the formation of an individual and social identity as well as participation in society, culture, and the economy. Various branches of Linguistics and Psychology explore how the first language (L1) and foreign languages (FL) are learned, which form the very basis of TEFL.

Abstract

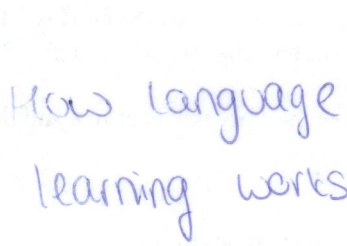

Chapter 3&4

How language
learning works

What does education mean to you? (1) Think about the roles of teachers and learners, and the processes of teaching and learning. Jot down your ideas related to the cartoon above. (2) Compare these ideas to the concepts of learning and teaching in this little story:

In Japan at the time of the Samurai, a boy leaves home in search of a teacher. After three days of walking in the hills, he finds a Zen master in his hermitage and politely asks whether the master would accept him as his disciple. The master remains silent, prepares tea, gives the boy a bowl, and pours the tea. He keeps on pouring when the bowl is full and the hot tea scalds the boy's fingers. 'Master, what are you doing?' 'This,' says the Zen master, 'is the first lesson.'

(3) Imagine how the story will continue and discuss your ideas with your peers.

3.1 | Definitions and link disciplines

TEFL is a sea of knowledge fed by many disciplines that provide useful approaches and principles:

Link disciplines ▶ *Educational Studies* (*Erziehungs- oder Bildungswissenschaften*) include, among other disciplines, Pedagogy (more like *Schulpädagogik* or *Allgemeine Didaktik*), Sociology, and Psychology. The boundaries between these disciplines are fuzzy, their interests overlap, and their approaches are often combined (e. g., in Developmental Psychology or Pedagogical Psychology). These studies reflect on education related to society, schools, and the goals, content, and processes of teaching and learning.

▶ *Linguistics* is concerned with language as a system, pragmatic communication, psychological and social phenomena, language acquisition, and intercultural communication.

▶ *Anglophone Literary Studies, Cultural Studies, and Media Studies* deal with understanding texts, media, and practices of all kinds in and across countries and cultures.

Not reflecting on basics of learning could lead one into the trap of ineffective teaching because "most teachers teach as they were taught" and "concentrate on the coverage of the material over retention of the material – that is, teaching over learning" (Straumanis 2012: n. p.). The approaches and ideas presented in the following serve as a challenge to make pre- and in-service teachers think about their own learning and future teaching.

Educational Studies cover general issues, specific types and levels of schools (e. g., *Grundschuldidaktik*), and individual subjects or skills (e. g., TEFL, literacy). They describe, analyze, and propose goals, ways, and contents of teaching and learning. Educational Studies conceive theoretical frameworks for educational practices, which feed back into theory and are analyzed in empirical research. The key question is: who should learn what in which way and through which means, with whom and from whom, and for what purpose? (cf. Jank & Meyer 2009: 16, 41–60)

Educational Studies

Education refers to both the process and the product of individual development in the context of institutions. Individual cultivation or *Bildung* is often associated with the following qualities (cf. Hentig 1996: 54, Bieri 2012: 229–40, Prisching 2012: 21–26, 44–53, Spaemann 2012: 224–27):

▶ *Personal growth*: the cultivation of language, values, aesthetic taste, and judgment; coping with complexity and uncertainty
▶ *Reflection* on and control of one's emotions, thoughts, and actions
▶ *Relativization of the self*, insight into one's limitations, being able to see the world through others' eyes, and valuing both self and other
▶ *Orientation*: insight into the systematic and historical relationships of social, cultural, economic, and historical phenomena
▶ *Action*: emancipation, independence, and responsibility

Learning can be considered as conceptual and behavioral change in cognitive, affective, and psychomotor skills:

▶ *Cognitive learning* aims at knowledge such as the acquisition, integration, and recall of information and skills of reasoning such as analysis, interpretation, and critical evaluation.

Goals and kinds of learning

▶ *Affective and ethical learning* means a change in feelings, attitudes, and disposition, for example developing empathy, self-confidence, and responsibility.

▶ *Acquiring psychomotor skills* goes beyond practical skills in the Arts or Physical Education and comprises attendance, participation, effort, etc., which contribute to efficient work habits (cf. Guskey 2013: 3–4).

Some of the competences outlined in the CEF and the national educational standards, such as sociocultural and intercultural competences, require the combination of several kinds of learning (see ch. 1.2). Contextual and individual factors of learning, such as aptitude and motivation, are dealt with after discussing approaches to language development and TEFL (see ch. 4.6).

3.2 | Language acquisition and learning in Psychology and Linguistics

Consider your beliefs about learning a language and mark your position on these sliding scales (see fig. 3.1) *before and after* reading this chapter and chapter 4 (in different marks or colors). If you think that both concepts are of equal importance, put your mark in the middle of the scale. Do not guess if you are not sure but tick the extra box on the right.

Fig. 3.1 |
Beliefs about learning
a language

What is language?

▶ System of rules ☐☐☐ Communicative practice   ☐ I don't know.
▶ Tool of thinking ☐☐☐ Form of behavior   ☐ I don't know.
▶ Languages share universal features ☐☐☐ Languages
  are different systems   ☐ I don't know.

How do we develop language skills?

▶ Instinct, human nature ☐☐☐ Input, nurture   ☐ I don't know.
▶ Imitation ☐☐☐ Individual construction   ☐ I don't know.
▶ Habitualization of patterns ☐☐☐ Negotiation of
  meaning with others   ☐ I don't know.
▶ Subconscious acquisition ☐☐☐ Conscious learning   ☐ I don't know.
▶ Cognitive process ☐☐☐ Holistic process
  (including emotions, social relations)   ☐ I don't know.

What are the teacher's and the learner's roles?

▶ Expert and novice ☐☐☐ Guide and partner   ☐ I don't know.
▶ Model and imitator ☐☐☐ Facilitator and
  autonomous individual   ☐ I don't know.

What do we teach and how do we teach English?

▸ Content ☐☐☐ Form   ☐ I don't know.
▸ Vocab, vocab, vocab ☐☐☐ Grammar rules   ☐ I don't know.
▸ Discrete items (e. g., use of articles) ☐☐☐
  Holistic language (e. g., phrases in situations)   ☐ I don't know.
▸ Listening, speaking ☐☐☐ Reading, writing   ☐ I don't know.
▸ Simplified input ☐☐☐ Authentic input   ☐ I don't know.
▸ Contrast between L1 and L2 ☐☐☐ L2 only   ☐ I don't know.
▸ Language skills ☐☐☐ Intercultural
  communicative competence   ☐ I don't know.
▸ Tolerating mistakes ☐☐☐ Correcting mistakes   ☐ I don't know.
▸ Declarative knowledge (what: explanations of rules)
  ☐☐☐ Procedural knowledge (how: use)   ☐ I don't know.
▸ Linear progression (from simple to complex)
  ☐☐☐ Cyclical approach (moving forward
  and repeating previous elements)   ☐ I don't know.

Psychologists and linguists have developed theories of first language acquisition (LA1, *Erstspracherwerb*), which often informed concepts of second language acquisition (LA2, SLA, *Zweitspracherwerb*). The term *language acqui-*
sition (Spracherwerb) is mainly used, as in this chapter, for *developing implicit*
knowledge in a subconscious way as opposed to language learning, which refers
to the explicit and conscious appropriation of language items and rules. Increasingly, language acquisition is used as a general term for all processes of developing language because often the question whether something has been acquired
or learned cannot be clearly answered.

First and second language acquisition

In spite of the parallels that some approaches establish between LA1 and
LA2, the difference between a natural and an instructional setting needs to be
taken into account (see fig. 3.2, adapted from Lightbown & Spada 2006: 110–12):

Differences

Natural setting	Instructional setting
▸ Socio-cultural context	▸ Educational institutions, classroom
▸ Contact with native speakers	▸ Often non-native teacher as model
▸ Exposure to varied, authentic, much input	▸ Usually modified, simplified, limited input
▸ Meaning before accuracy	▸ Meaning and/or accuracy
▸ Errors usually go uncorrected	▸ Feedback and correction
▸ Time pressure on production	▸ Time to learn and produce

Fig. 3.2
Second language acquisition: natural vs. instructional setting

In light of these differences, pertinent questions include (1) whether the classroom offers better opportunities for (language) learning than life, (2) whether
teaching should mirror the learning opportunities of a natural setting in the
classroom, or (3) whether teaching can combine advantages of the natural setting (the focus on meaningful, authentic input) and the instructional setting

(simplified input and time for learning through feedback). The answers to these questions depend upon the approach to SLA that one believes in.

Approaches to language acquisition Three basic approaches have been prominent in the research on language acquisition, stressing environmental influences, the learner's innate capacity, or the interaction between the learner and the environment:

- ▶ The *Empiricist Approach*, in particular the behaviorist one, assumes that learning is based on the experience and imitation of the language used in the learner's environment.
- ▶ The *Nativist Approach* proposes that a specific genetic or innate capacity enables language acquisition.
- ▶ *Cognitive, Social, or Radical Constructivist Approaches* maintain that language learning results from the individual's interaction with the world.

3.2.1 | Behaviorism: feeding the parrot

The environment as dominant force *Behaviorism*, a theory of learning from the early 20th century, believes in a blank mind without inherited capacities and in the environment as the dominant force in development. In other words, given the right stimuli, anybody can learn anything. Learning is based on *conditioning*, which offers the learner a stimulus and positively reinforces the correct response. For example, a dog can learn to stand on its hind legs and a parrot learns to repeat phrases if rewarded by food.

In the 1950s, the psychologist Skinner looked at the *habit formation* of language in childhood by imitation and practice. Skinner proposed that the "quality and quantity of the language the child hears, as well as the consistency of the reinforcement offered by others in the environment, would shape the child's language behavior" (Lightbown & Spada 2006: 10). According to the *Contrastive Hypothesis*, since different languages consist of contrasting structures in sound, word formation, and syntax, the FL learner needs to change his or her speech habits in order to produce the different target language structures. In educational settings, behaviorism takes the form of correct input (stimulus), repetition (response), and feedback as positive reinforcement or error correction in order to prevent the formation of wrong habits, the 'fossilization' of errors (see fig. 3.3).

Fig. 3.3 | The behaviorist model

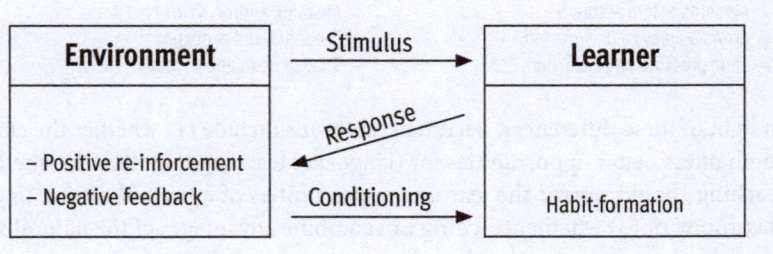

Behaviorism had a large impact on the *Audiolingual Method*, which was prom-   Discussion
inent from the 1950s to the 1960s. Behaviorism considered *pattern drills* as
effective for acquiring fluency and accuracy, and explicit grammar teaching as
detrimental to fluency. While empirical evidence reveals that very young children imitate frequent and basic language patterns, they do not simply parrot
input but select what they imitate (cf. ibid.: 11–12, 14–15). According to the
Contrastive Hypothesis, some errors can be attributed to interference from the
L1, which needs to be prevented (e. g., false friends, different adverb positions
in German and English). However, neither imitation nor interference can fully
explain that learners with different native languages display similar errors in
the beginning of SLA, such as not using the third-person -s (cf. ibid.: 93–95).
In sum, *Behaviorism over-estimates imitation and disregards factors such as apti-*
tude, insight, motivation, and comprehensive educational goals.

Nativism: genes, genes, genes | 3.2.2

The linguist Chomsky criticized that behaviorists cannot explain that *virtu-*   How do children
ally all children learn to speak their mother tongue competently in spite of vastly   acquire language?
different conditions. A generative process should explain this phenomenon:
"an infinite number of utterances are possible because of a limited number of
underlying linguistic principles. In other words, the linguistic system of a child
will develop beyond the input to which the child is exposed. This argument is
called the *poverty of the stimulus.*" (Whong 2011: 31, emphasis added). Children are frequently exposed to a limited amount and partly defective oral language (e. g., fragmentary sentences), but they can usually tell the difference
between a grammatically correct and an incorrect sentence (see ch. 5.1.2).
Therefore, Chomsky assumed that human beings have a genetic potential to
acquire language through what he termed the *Language Acquisition Device*
(LAD, *Spracherwerbsmechanismus*) on the basis of *Universal Grammar*, a fundamental set of principles that structures languages in general. Language learning happens if input activates certain structures in the LAD, for example the
distribution of English sounds in phonology (pat/pet/pit/pot/put), the combination of morphemes in word formation (re-consider-ation), or of lexical items
in syntax (SVO, see fig. 3.4).

Following Chomsky, nativists argued that the innate capacity needs to be   The role of age in SLA
activated in a *critical period* until puberty in order to master the L1 well. Concerning SLA, the evidence is mixed: in areas such as grammar, adolescent and
adult learners may advance faster than children because most of them have a
greater competence in abstract thinking and metalinguistic awareness. However, younger learners have motor organs that are still able to develop and learn
new sounds, and they may attain a better level of ultimate achievement (cf.
Lightbown & Spada 2006: 68–74, Whong 2011: 14).

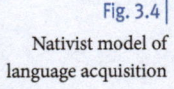

Fig. 3.4 |
Nativist model of
language acquisition

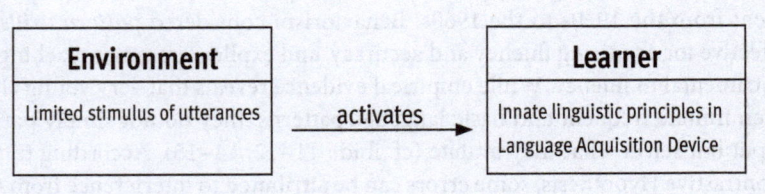

Translating Chomsky's idea of LA1 to LA2, Krashen and Terrell assume that LA2 mirrors LA1. This analogy is called *Identity Hypothesis*, motivating the *Natural Approach*. Krashen suggested five famous – if contested – hypotheses (cf. Lightbown & Spada 2006: 36–37, Whong 2011: 37, Spiro 2013: 13):

Hypotheses on
language learning

1. The *Acquisition-Learning Hypothesis*: meaning motivates acquisition. Students unconsciously acquire a FL rather than consciously learn it.
2. The *Natural Order Hypothesis*: students learn features of the L2 in the same order as in the L1, for example plural -s before the -s attached to verbs in the third person singular, or 'no+verb' (*'I no like.') in negation before 'auxiliary+negation+verb' ('I don't like.'). Listening to the FL promotes speaking skills and reading fosters writing skills.
3. The *Monitor Hypothesis*: the explicit learning of rules does not contribute to acquisition and only allows speakers to monitor or edit the accuracy of what they acquired before.
4. The *Comprehensible Input Hypothesis*: input needs to be comprehensible if somewhat challenging. Teachers should provide input a little above the level of the learners in order to offer them new language together with familiar material tailored to their needs. Learners need a silent period in order to process input.
5. The *Affective Filter Hypothesis*: a supportive and anxiety-free learning atmosphere and learner motivation are relevant because fear or boredom prevent input to get through to the student; in other words: negative affect clogs the filter of language input.

How would you teach English if you followed Krashen's hypotheses?

Discussion

Krashen and Terrell have influenced the turn from the teacher-centered Grammar-Translation and Audiolingual Methods toward learner-oriented Communicative Language Teaching (CLT) that focuses on meaning rather than form. Empirical evidence reveals that focusing on extensive comprehensible input, especially with beginners, yields good results both in listening comprehension and speaking. Psychological evidence has confirmed the relevance of a positive learning atmosphere and emotions (cf. Lightbown & Spada 2006:

145–49). However, nativists have come under fire: Chomsky has been criticized for ignoring the pragmatic and social use of language as well as for his disregard of differences between speakers of different native languages, who transfer some features from their L1 to the L2 rather than sharing one underlying structure (cf. Whong 2011: 65). Krashen's Acquisition-Learning Hypothesis mistakenly cuts a clear line between the import of conscious learning and subconscious acquisition. Children do acquire language subconsciously, but they also consciously memorize and reflect on language. In short, *comprehensible input is important but not sufficient to produce accurate and socially appropriate language.*

Cognitivism: the mind as processor

| 3.2.3

A third group of language acquisition theories roughly takes the middle position between external input feeding a virtually empty mind (nurture, behaviorism) and a capable mind with a language instinct (nature, nativism). *Cognitive or Constructivist Approaches* focus on learning processes on the level of the individual mind without assuming that there is a language acquisition device (cf. Lightbown & Spada 2006: 21–23). *Sociocultural Approaches* to language development concentrate on the function of interaction in social contexts. All of these theories are concerned with one major question: *how does the learner process which kind of input in which social situations?* Some scholars assume that the Sociocultural Approach is compatible with the large variety of Cognitive Approaches, which focus on information processing and skills learning, but others see a fundamental difference between the individual processing of input and the mutual construction of meaning in social interaction (cf. Myles 2013: 65).

A middle position between nurture and nature

The developmental psychologist Piaget postulated that children form *cognitive schemata* on the basis of their embodied experience of the world, moving from the concrete handling and thinking of objects to abstract thinking or generalization. If children discover something unknown to them, they form new schemata, and if they are confronted with something that does not make sense they try to modify their schemata in *bottom-up accommodation*: data provoke 'a change of mind.' In *top-down assimilation*, schemata inform the re-cognition of something as belonging to a familiar pattern: information is added and connected to previous conceptions (cf. Adey & Shayer 2013: 28–29; see fig. 3.6). These processes could be viewed as opposites: assimilation resists mental change and reduces new phenomena to existing concepts, whereas a new experience leads to new or revised concepts in accommodation (cf. Piaget 1977: 274). This opposition would correspond to a split personality: Mr. Stone sticks to stereotypes, but Mr. Water quickly changes his mind. However, it is more appropriate to regard these processes as complementary: each individual needs to find a balance between clinging to schemata and being open to

Schemata

experience, arriving at "a true equilibrium, that is, a harmony between internal organization and external experience" (ibid.: 277).

Ideally, *development leads to a growing formation, differentiation, and coordination of schemata that allow for a more sophisticated understanding of phenomena.* For example, a small child may apply the concept 'horse' to a donkey, a zebra, and a cow, assimilating all of these animals to the simple schema of head and tail, big size, and four legs. He/she will learn to differentiate and accommodate the concept 'horse', recognizing specific features and applying the concept more selectively to include different kinds of horses. In addition, the child forms new schemata of the other animals mentioned above and coordinates these under the shared schemata of mammals and quadrupeds: "if the schema is differentiated, it marks the start of new assimilations" (ibid.: 274).

Piaget regards social interaction as governed by the same mechanism as cognitive processing: the individual needs to accommodate or adjust his/her egocentric point of view to the totality of the perspectives of others, and, in turn, may influence others' perspectives, ideally in "the reciprocal formation of relationships of perspectives" that enables cooperation (ibid.: 294). The individual is part of society and dependent upon cognitive cooperation and the coordination of perspectives (cf. ibid.: 858): "It is by cooperation with another person that the mind arrives at verifying judgments [...]. [T]he interdependence of the search for truth and of socialization seems to us undeniable." (ibid.: 279). In sum, language serves as the symbolic representation of the interaction between the child's individual cognitive development and its material world, which is checked against social perspectives in interaction.

When a girl of two years boarded an airplane for the first time, she started weeping because 'the airplane was gone.' Her concept of an airplane only related to the external shape she could no longer see when on the plane. Being told that she was inside the airplane, to look at the wings visible through the windows, and her experience as a passenger made her accommodate her concept of an airplane to something like a flying bus ('airbus', see fig. 3.5). While the girl had no problems to assimilate unusual airport vehicles to her concept of 'truck', she initially assimilated the men and women in uniform to her schema of the police, but was told – and experienced – that these were flight attendants who serve food and drinks. So she accommodated her concept of uniform to cover different professions.

Fig. 3.5 |
Example 'airbus'

Impact on education
How are theories of cognitive development related to education? Education should intervene in and accelerate cognitive development less by explaining schemata than by *activating existent schemata, by stimulating the formation of new schemata, and by challenging learners to differentiate or alter schemata* (cf. Hallet 2006: 18–20). According to Piaget, "the mind develops in response to challenge, or to disequilibrium, so the intervention must provide some cognitive conflict" (qtd. in Adey & Shayer 2013: 29). However, students need to experience that puzzling information is not an annoyance but a problem they

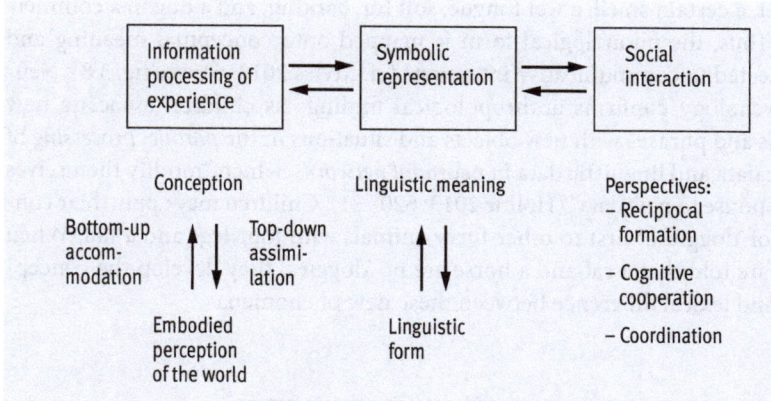

|Fig. 3.6
The Piagetian model of learning

may want to solve (cf. Piaget 1977: 275). The mind profits from "reflective abstraction, the mind's growing ability to become conscious of and so take control of its own processes, so the intervention must encourage students to be metacognitive"(ibid.). *The Cognitive Acceleration Method* also recognizes the social dimension of learning. The teacher supports the learners' mutual exploration and discussion of new concepts (ibid.), for example different meanings of the concepts 'friend' or 'woman' in various cultures. The results of empirical studies confirm that Piagetian approaches are among the most successful strategies to enhance academic achievement (cf. Hattie 2009: 299).

Some contemporary Cognitive Approaches in Psychology and Linguistics build on Piaget's interaction of top-down and bottom-up information processing but expand the factor of *situated communication* (the social dimension of language). In contrast to Chomsky, they do not see any special differences between general learning and language learning:

> [L]anguage is learned from participatory experience of processing input and producing language during interaction in social contexts where individually desired non-linguistic outcomes (a bank transfer, another cup of milk) are goals to be achieved (or not) by communicating intentions, concepts and meaning with others. (Robinson & Ellis 2008: 490)

The anthropologist Tomasello proposes that two *socio-cognitive mechanisms* form the basis of language acquisition: *pattern-finding ability* allows infants to find patterns in perceptual or linguistic input, while *intention-reading* allows them to connect linguistic forms with intended meanings. *Language emerges from usage*: the "child learns language from actual 'usage-events,' i. e. from particular utterances in particular contexts, and builds up increasingly complex and abstract linguistic representations from these" (Lieven & Tomasello 2008: 168, see fig. 3.7). Small children attend to the objects named and pointed out to them by their parents: they would associate the sound 'doggie' with the fam-

Basis of language acquisition

Speech has both an individual and a social side, and we cannot conceive of one without the other. – Ferdinand de Saussure

ily pet, a certain smell, a wet tongue, soft fur, barking, and a dog in a commercial. Thus, the phonological form is mapped onto conceptual meaning and connected to communicative intentions (cf. Myles 2013: 61; see fig. 3.8). Neuropsychology confirms anthropological findings as children associate new words and phrases with new objects and situations in the *parallel processing* of sense data and linguistic data *in neuronal networks*, which "modify themselves in response to new data" (Holme 2013: 620–21). Children may apply their concept of 'doggie' at first to other furry animals with four legs and a tail. When they are told that a cat and a horse are no 'doggies,' they develop the conceptual and lexical difference between these new phenomena.

Fig. 3.7 |

Socio-cognitive mechanisms of language acquisition

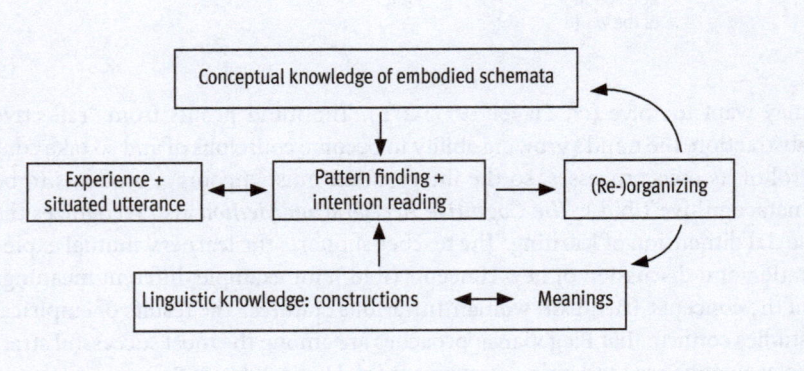

Fig. 3.8 |

Example 'doggie'

Teaching constraints

Frequent repetitions of perceived patterns strengthen neuronal associations and lead to *cumulative learning and appropriate usage* by "frequency-based associationist preferences" (Myles 2013: 61) rather than by activating innate structures or learning rules by rote. For example, learners understand and generalize the schematic meaning of transitive verbs as it emerges from frequent examples of phrases that use this pattern, such as agent+process+patient in 'She broke a jug' and 'He ate a banana' (cf. Holme 2013: 610). The relevance of insight into frequent and meaningful constructions confirms modified and consistent input in English textbooks, which frequently repeat certain lexical items and grammatical forms within units.

However, the question is whether learners are ready to process the input offered to them according to the (grammatical) gradation of the textbook syllabus. Regardless of age, LA2 – very much like LA1 – moves from simple to complex forms. For example, the processing of words precedes that of phrases and sentences. Certain forms of negation are acquired in a particular sequence without being able to skip stages, a fact that calls for the introduction of simple forms before complex ones (cf. Lightbown & Spada 2006: 85–86):

1. A simple 'no' is placed before the verb (*'I no like rice.')
2. 'No' may alternate with 'don't' (*'He no/don't like rice.')
3. The negation follows the auxiliary verb (*'He don't like rice.')
4. 'Do' is marked for tense, person, and number ('He doesn't like rice.')

This acquisition sequence from simple to complex forms is called *Processability Hierarchy,* which, in turn, puts constraints on teaching and leads to the *Teachability Hypothesis*: teaching cannot promote learning if learners are not developmentally ready for the form (Pienemann & Keßler 2012: 240–41). Cognitive approaches to teaching take into account the *limited processing capacity*: "what is processable by students at any time determines what is learnable, and thereby, what is teachable" in terms of understanding and producing language (Long 2011: 380; see ch. 5.1.2).

Understanding the Processability Hierarchy and the Teachability Hypothesis generates tolerance for beginners' typical errors. *Errors are a necessary part of* SLA and a basic feature of the learner's ever-developing *Interlanguage* (*Lernersprache, Interimssprache*), the changing level of constructing a language by mixing elements of L1 and L2, even inventing new forms (cf. Ortega 2011: 81). *'He have the ball getaked and to Sarah gethrowed' would be a perfectly comprehensible utterance at a German primary school.

> Identify and explain the errors in the utterance above, and suggest ways of developing the Interlanguage.

The utterance fails to mark the third-person -s, reveals interferences from L1 in tense, and overgeneralization in morphology. For constructivists, the learner does not know or feel the need to use the correct forms because they make sense to other learners and thus are *viable (passend)*. Cognitivists would explain the errors in the phrase above with the limits of processability: this learner may not yet be ready for the correct forms. Cognitive support could provide more input of similar form-function pairings, offering tasks that require learners to use these constructions, and of giving different forms of feedback on errors. *Dynamic feedback* becomes increasingly explicit if learners do not notice implicit feedback:

Different approaches to errors

- ▶ Implicit negative feedback in recasts: 'So, he took the ball and threw it to Sarah.'
- ▶ Clarification requests: 'What did he do with the ball?'
- ▶ Elicitation of the correct form by repetition and leaving a gap: 'He …'
- ▶ Explicit correction provides the correct form: 'You would say, he took the ball and threw it to Sarah.'
- ▶ Metalinguistic feedback does not give the correct form but comments on the type of error or the rule of using an item: 'In German, we often use the present perfect tense if we talk about something that happened in the past:

Er hat den Ball genommen. In English, a finished action is usually expressed in the simple past tense: He took the ball.' (cf. Lightbown & Spada 2006: 125–29; see chs. 5.1.2, 12.3).

Cognitive approaches *scaffold* (*unterstützen*) (1) meaningful language input, (2) increasingly complex tasks that stimulate cognitive processing, and (3) meta-linguistic as well as metacognitive reflection such as raising awareness of language and of learning processes (cf. Robinson & Ellis 2008: 496–97). Complex tasks demand authentic interaction, which involves the cognitive processing of verbal information, joint attention, reading the interlocutor's communicative and social intentions as well as pursuing one's own intentions (cf. Segalowitz & Trofimovich 2012: 187–88).

Empirical evidence
    Critics and defenders of cognitive approaches muster empirical evidence to support their arguments. For critics who hold the **non-interface position** (knowing how to communicate is unrelated to knowing rules), empirical evidence proves that implicit learning in the sense of high-frequency exposure is effective without the need of explicit (meta-)cognitive learning because of the learner's innate syllabus and the extensive subconscious processing of experience – unless problems are noticed (Bleyhl 2013: 35–37, van Patten 2012: 273–76). Others do not consider implicit learning alone to be sufficient for successful language learning and call for an *alternating focus on meaning and focus on form* (DeKeyser 2011: 129–30). For DeKeyser, it is evident that "no procedural, let alone automatized or implicit knowledge develop[s] in the absence of declarative knowledge, even after thousands of exposures" (2011: 127). Given that the goal of language learning is automatized processing and production, cognitive psychologists and SLA researchers are debating how explicit, declarative knowledge of vocabulary and grammar relates to procedural knowledge of interacting (cf. ibid.: 121).

Guided instruction
    In *focus on form* stages, explicit feedback and periods of guided instruction promote *noticing* (*Aufmerksamkeit*) the gap between input and one's own production, or the gap between one's own speech and declarative knowledge, which "is a handy crutch to lean on whenever our procedural knowledge is insufficient" (ibid: 130). Guided instruction does not necessarily mean teacher-centered explanation, but can take the shape of guiding the learners' discovery of meaningful form. *Structured input activities* "encourage learners to make form-meaning connections," such as identifying the subject in active and passive constructions via different cues rather than taking the first noun as the subject of a sentence according to the basic SVO-pattern (Barcroft & Wong 2013: 644–45). For example, in the sentence 'The car was searched by the policeman' the marker 'inanimate' helps learners decide that the first noun is not the subject: it is not the car or its driver that search a policeman.

Constructivism: the creative mind

| 3.2.4

While many cognitive models of learning propose a rather balanced interaction between the learner and the world, Constructivist Approaches attribute more weight to the *learner as a self-referential, autonomous system*. *Radical Constructivism* acknowledges the relevance of individual cognition and social interaction, but points out that no one has direct access to material reality and other people, which reveals skepticism toward Piaget's concepts of 'truth' and 'verification.' Experience cannot be matched against 'the world' as such and is not directly accessible to others. No one can 'find' meaningful information in the world but people literally 'make sense' of experience. Noticing difference is important, but difference is not meaningful in itself. The individual mind does not mirror the world but actively 'constructs' models of the world on the basis of sense data (cf. Wendt 2002: 25–26). There is no objective truth outside the observer or a reality as such, but the only reality is the one 'realized.' Subjective truths need to be tested in interaction with others in order to become intersubjective truths, but interlocutors do not co-construct the *same* knowledge (cf. von Glasersfeld 1995: 142). Individuals do not talk about the same concepts but aim at compatible or *viable concepts* that work. People *do not find meaning in words* but attribute meaning to them and test it. For example, they need to perceive the difference between the sound of a burp and that of a word, but the difference does not make sense unless they attribute sense to the sound as a bodily function or lexical item. Consequently, "[e]very learner of a language must construct his or her word meanings out of elements of individual experience and then adapt these meanings by trial, error, and hanging on to what seems to work in the linguistic interactions with others" (von Glasersfeld 1995: 137). In turn, a

> piece of language directs the receiver to build up a conceptual structure, but there is no direct transmission of the meaning the speaker or writer intended. The only building blocks available to the interpreter are his or her own subjective conceptualizations and re-presentations. (ibid.: 141)

The mind does not mirror the world but creates meaning

In the constructivist view, learning does not simply mean processing input in linear progression (Wendt 2002: 27). On the contrary, experience triggers cognitive constructions, which develop in leaps (the so-called *Aha-Erlebnis*). Learning is motivated by interaction and through *perturbation* (*Erwartungswiderspruch, Verstörung*), the confrontation with cognitive problems that need to be negotiated in order to modify schemata. In simple terms, one needs to change schemata and behavior upon noticing that what one has done does not work, what one has read does not make sense, or what one has said is not understood. If individuals ignore rather than face the challenge, learning does not take place. *Learning means adapting actions, concepts, and language in order to make them viable.* In the classroom, teachers can prepare food for thought,

Learning through perturbation

Fig. 3.9 |
You can lead a horse
to water, but you
can't make it drink.

but it is up to the learners to 'eat and digest' it. Teachers cannot teach anybody anything in the sense of handing down knowledge (see fig. 3.9). They rather need to offer authentic material, tasks, and support that may trigger individual perturbation and reflection – if you are not confused, you haven't understood anything. Facing a complex task, a novice uses trial and error and aims at processing data, whereas the more advanced learner searches for strategies that work and aims at interpretation (cf. Hattie 2009: 30). However, too much complexity and uncertainty may frustrate learners, and may provoke resistance rather than personal interest and effort.

Reich's *Interactionist Approach to Constructivist Pedagogy* (*systemisch-konstruktive Pädagogik*) tries to find a balance between the social quality and the individual process of learning. Learners are rarely left alone with making sense of raw experience. Social or Interactionist Constructivism recognizes that language is acquired in situated communication, which suggests intersubjective connections between forms and meanings in social and cultural contexts. The social level of interaction in terms of the relationship among the interlocutors, the expression of one's own attitude, and the appeal to others form the basis of communication on the content level (cf. Timm 2013: 45–46). The sheer quantity of reconstructing social models of reality far surpasses that of directly constructing reality from individual experience. Thus, testing social against individual constructions, and vice versa, is a central process of understanding; and learning takes place at three levels (cf. Hallet 2006: 17, Timm 2013: 45–46; see fig. 3.10):

Levels of learning

▶ *Constructing individual models* of reality based on experience
▶ *Reconstructing social models* of reality in interaction with others and in relation to the learner's own models
▶ *Critically deconstructing social models* of reality in order to reconstruct more comprehensive and complex concepts

Fig. 3.10 |
Social Constructivist
model of learning

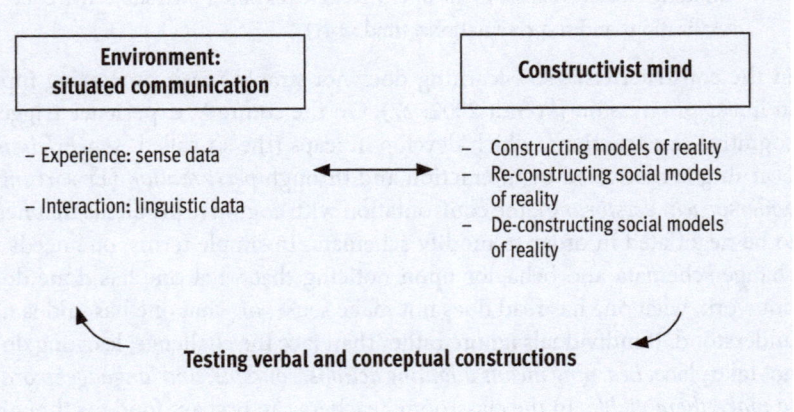

**Environment:
situated communication**

Constructivist mind

– Experience: sense data

– Interaction: linguistic data

– Constructing models of reality
– Re-constructing social models of reality
– De-constructing social models of reality

Testing verbal and conceptual constructions

Constructivist teaching favors learner-centered, holistic, and action-based methods (*handlungsorientierter Unterricht*) with an emphasis on *autonomy, attention, discovery, learning by doing, involvement, meaningful interaction, negotiation, and reflection* in order to raise awareness of language, learning, and culture (cf. Reinfried 2002: 29–30, 40–44; Overmann 2002: 88–98; Timm 2013: 54–59).

Constructivists take some of the burden of being responsible for learning off the teachers' shoulders. In turn, the question arises whether learners can shoulder the load of being responsible for their own learning, especially if they have difficulties. In addition, both teachers and learners have to cope with the problem of testing cognitive and linguistic achievement because viability is a fairly open concept and allows for various individual responses to a communicative task.

> How would a constructivist explain the process of learning and teaching in the story of the boy and the Zen master at the beginning of this chapter?

Sociolinguistic, Sociocultural, and Interactionist Approaches: the social agent

| 3.2.5

Shifting the perspective of Cognitive Linguistics on language as "a reflection of general cognitive processes [...] grounded in lived human experience with the real world" (Tyler 2008: 459), *Sociolinguistic, Sociocultural, and Interactionist Approaches* assume that *social interaction in cultural contexts is the most important factor in LA1 and LA2*: "human thinking is mediated by culturally organized and transmitted symbolic meaning" (Lantolf 2012: 57). Social Approaches to SLA in general conceive of the learner as a social agent and of learning a language as socialization and enculturation through participant observation and negotiating meanings or co-constructing knowledge in social interaction (see fig. 3.11).

Language is a social art. – Quine

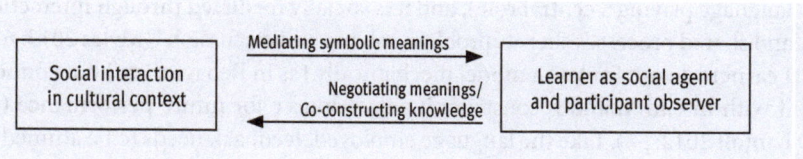

| Fig. 3.11
Sociocultural model of language development in social interaction

In contrast to the rather narrow function of language as a communicative instrument, *Sociolinguistics envisions a larger learning agenda of developing voice, agency, empathy, and respect*, which ties in with the goal of political emancipation favored in some branches of Educational Studies (cf. Jank & Meyer 2009: 282–85). The sociolinguistic perspective on the connection

Larger learning agenda

between language, society, ideology, and power regards teaching normative standards as ambivalent. Teaching one standard language as a global tool of empowerment neglects the values and communicative functions of different varieties and registers of languages representing different groups and identities in a multicultural world (see ch. 1.1). The recognition and teaching of linguistic diversity would help the mutual understanding of and mediating between various groups (cf. Stroud & Heugh 2011: 424–29). In addition to class and ethnicity, sociolinguistic perspectives also take gender into consideration. For example, men tend to interrupt women more often than other men, while women tend to hedge their utterances ('I think,' 'I believe'), which men mistakenly identify as a sign of uncertainty. Recognizing and teaching diversity can take the forms of listening comprehension exercises with recordings of speakers from different social and ethnic backgrounds, of presenting social issues from different perspectives in the textbook, or of reading about intercultural encounters in literature.

From infant to autonomous social agent

Sociocultural Approaches to SLA are concerned with the gradual development of the learner from a dependent infant to an autonomous social agent. The psychologist Vygotsky contended that *language emerges in social interaction* between caretakers and children and that *thinking is internalized, dialogic speech* (cf. Lightbown & Spada 2006: 20). In the private sphere, mothers speak to young children in a simplified and highly repetitive language and at a slower pace (*motherese*), a practice that teachers have adopted in the role of caretakers of early and intermediate learners (*teacherese*), scaffolding their language and their support according to learners' needs (cf. Spiro 2013: 15). Adapting Vygotsky's observation, involving children in personal interaction would be much more effective than simply making them watch media that transmit information. In a communicative situation that challenges the learners a little above their current level (*zone of proximal development*), they solve problems with a teacher or a more advanced peer and "co-construct knowledge in collaboration with an interlocutor" (Lightbown & Spada 2006: 47). Thus, learning "is mediated both through learners developing use and control of mental tools (with language playing a central role), and it is socially mediated through interaction and shared processes such as problem solving and discussion" (Myles 2013: 68). Learners do not imitate a model mechanically (as in Behaviorism) but connect it with intention and reconstruct it as a resource for future performance (cf. Lantolf 2012: 58). Like the language employed, feedback needs to be attuned to learner ability in order to gradually build up learner agency from dependency on explicit feedback to independent self-correction (cf. Lantolf 2012: 60–63).

Involvement, agency, responsibility

Working within the zone of proximal development is particularly effective if learners themselves create and manage situations that organize assistance to make them perform better (cf. Ohta 2013: 667–68) – in other words, if they assume responsibility and agency on the way to learner autonomy. Involvement, agency, and responsibility are relevant as goals of education and motivation in general and as factors of learning and communication in particular. Social interactionists look at specific ways of achieving mutual comprehension among speakers of different language levels. Long's *Interactionist Hypothesis* states that in case of comprehension problems learners and L2 speakers need to negotiate meaning in order to achieve mutual understanding. *Negotiation of meaning* (*Bedeutungsaushandung*) means that both interlocutors need to express, comprehend, and adjust utterances in order to offer and receive comprehensible input (cf. Mayo & Soler 2013: 209–13). Both the more and the less proficient participant can *modify interaction* through gesture, checking comprehension, paraphrasing, and requesting clarification. Since input needs to be comprehensible in order to be processed and become intake, teachers should give learners the opportunity to modify interaction in order to avoid Krashen's problem of finding the right level of input (Input Hypothesis).

While Krashen focuses on input, Swain contests that producing *comprehensible output* also furthers language development since learners have to focus on content *and* form in order to be understood. Being required to produce output, learners may *notice the gap* between what they want to say and how to say it or to express it accurately, a fact that motivates them to reflect on language and learn more in order to communicate better (cf. Mayo & Soler 2013: 217–19). More advanced speakers should give *corrective feedback*, recasting the incorrect phrase implicitly by repeating it in the correct form or explicitly by commenting on the accurate use of language. Empirical evidence suggests that collaborative expert-novice interaction with corrective feedback is of particular value, whether between teacher and learner or among more and less advanced peers (cf. Lightbown & Spada 2006: 151–56). Sociocultural, Sociolinguistic, and Interactionist Approaches stipulate that communicative language skills are learned through communication – as an end and a means, which is the hallmark of CLT.

Challenge: content and form

The theories of language acquisition discussed in this chapter suggest methods and proceedings on a sliding scale between the extreme poles of instructivism and constructivism. Teachers who believe that learners need controlled input and practice tend toward an instructivist model of teaching, in which they take the role of the model speaker and the sage on the stage. The instructivist teacher assumes the role of the authority, passes on knowledge, and gives explanations in the shape of explicit and declarative knowledge of rules or structures. The standard sequence of instruction is the teacher's *initiation* of speech and the learner's *response*, followed by the teacher's *evaluation* of the response (IRE): accuracy is of paramount importance. However, instructivism meets with limitations: "*learners, not teachers, have most control over their language development*" (Long 2011: 378, see fig. 3.12).

Between instructivism and constructivism

According to some cognitivists and most constructivists, a strictly controlled gradual progression of language input would not respect individual learners' needs and differences (cf. Decke-Cornill & Küster 2010: 33–36, Long

Fig. 3.12 |

Bettina Winkler: Teaching and learning as mountaineering

2011: 382). Learners need rich, varied, and challenging input as well as plenty of time for individual intake (*incubation period*). The teacher acts as the guide by the side and the facilitator, providing opportunities for individual learning processes and interaction. Authentic input is as important as the experience of perturbation. Because the viability of concepts *and* language are at stake, negotiating meaning *and* focus on form when needed are on the agenda (cf. Long 2011: 380–81). Hattie criticizes the opposition of instructivist and constructivist teaching because developing teaching in response to the perspective of the learner requires educators not only to facilitate learning in constructivist ways but also to activate processes of learning in instructivist ways (cf. Hattie 2009: 26, 243–44; see cartoon at the beginning of ch. 4).

Fig. 3.13 |

Overview of approaches (cf. Wolff 2002: 19–24, Wendt 2002: 25–28, Overmann 2002: 88–90)

	Concept of language	Teacher and student	Teaching and learning
Instructivist Approaches	▶ System of rules, skills	T ▶ Sage, expert, model in lecture hall	T ▶ Direct instruction, controlled, linear progression ▶ PPP, IRE
		S ▶ Novice	S ▶ Imitation, reproduction, habitualization ▶ Input becomes intake and output
Cognitive and Constructivist Approaches	▶ Patterns of form-meaning pairings ▶ Symbolic representation of cognitive concepts	T ▶ Facilitator of rich learning environment	T ▶ Stimulating cyclical, reflexive cognitive and meta-cognitive processes through challenging input
		S ▶ Cognitive processor ▶ Autonomous, self-referential individual	S ▶ Form-meaning mappings ▶ (Re-)constructing schemata

Sociocultural and Interaction-ist Approaches	▶ Mediation in social interaction ▶ Internalized speech	T ▶ Guide, interlocutor in market place	T ▶ Guidance, scaffolding, dialog
		S ▶ Social agent, sharer of meaning	S ▶ Internalization of dialog, appropriation of forms and meanings, negotiation of meaning ▶ Participation, socialization, individuation

Which approach fits which classroom situation depicted in the cartoon at the beginning of the chapter?

Recommended reading

Gass, Susan M. & Alison Mackey, eds. (2012). *The Routledge Handbook of Second Language Acquisition.* London et al.: Routledge.

Hattie, John (2009). *Visible Learning: A Synthesis of over 800 Meta-Analyses Relating to Achievement.* London et al.: Routledge.

Lightbown, Patsy M. & Nina Spada (2006). *How Languages Are Learned.* 3rd ed. Oxford et al.: Oxford University Press.

Roche, Jörg (2013). *Fremdsprachenerwerb – Fremdsprachendidaktik.* 3rd ed. Tuebingen et al.: Francke.

From methods to principles

Contents

The present chapter delineates major methods of teaching English, many of which are clearly based on psychological and linguistic approaches to second language acquisition (SLA, see ch. 3). The discussion of advantages and disadvantages of diverse methods as general recipes for teaching will lead to considerations of individual differences in learning and effective principles of teaching and learning that have been validated in empirical research.

Abstract

Take a close look at the cartoon and spell out the problems of learning and teaching English at the beginner level. Find similarities and differences between the situation in the cartoon and your most enjoyable and successful experience of learning English. Could your experience serve as a model for learning and teaching English?

4.1 | Approach – method – technique

From approach to technique

Many books offer long lists of 'great ideas' for the classroom as a random collection of techniques, which complement the mandatory course materials but do not offer a rationale that clearly explains the psycholinguistic reasoning for their implementation. A teaching *technique* (*Inszenierungstechnik*) is only the smallest step in the ordered sequence of a *procedure* (*Vorgehen, Verlauf*) in the classroom. The procedure is the result of a design or a *method* (*Methode, Verfahren*), which defines the roles of teachers and learners, the content, material, and types of activities as systematized in a curriculum. In turn, the method may be based on an *approach* (*Ansatz*), a theory about the principles and functions of language, learning, and education (cf. Harmer 2011: 62). Considered from top to bottom, *an approach provides you with reasons why you should use a method, which then tells you how to plan and implement classroom procedures as a systematic sequence of techniques.*

Why do teachers love using the song "Head, Shoulders, Knees and Toes" (see YouTube) to help primary students learn vocabulary about the body? One possible procedure would involve six techniques: (1) The teacher slowly plays or sings the whole song and (2) touches the parts of his/her body he/she mentions, then (3) encourages a small group of fast learners to touch their own bodies while he/she repeats the song, and (4) signals that their peers should observe and imitate the performance. (5) The teacher repeatedly sings the song line by line with those who are ready in the class, (6) who, in turn, exhort more peers to sing along. The method behind this procedure, *Total Physical Response* (TPR, developed in the 1960s), stipulates that teachers serve as models and guides, who involve students in imitative acquisition rather than conscious learning. Teachers demonstrate vocabulary by enacting what they say and have learners perform the actions without having to speak. Learners are allowed to remain silent and start to speak when they are ready to do so in order to take pressure off them, reduce anxiety, and facilitate intake (cf. Larsen-Freeman & Anderson 2011: 103–14). Total Physical Response appeals especially to very young learners.

Example: why choose which technique?

Knowing about diverse approaches and methods helps pre-service and in-service teachers notice many aspects of teaching and learning and encourages them to reflect on their own beliefs and practices (see ch. 2.1.1). Some teachers adhere to the one and only method they find convincing and feel comfortable with, others select different methods appropriate to particular learners, levels, or goals (cf. ibid.: 226–30). Approaches and methods aim at finding general principles of learning and teaching and therefore tend to neglect individual differences among students and specific learning scenarios. Good teaching needs to arrive at a fit between principles, goals, methods, and content, as well as the context and individuals involved in teaching and learning.

Deliberate choices

Teacher-orientation

4.2

Teacher-oriented methods follow an instructivist approach (see fig. 3.13). The teacher takes the position of the sage on the stage, who directs and monitors learning step by step in linear progression toward a goal defined by the curriculum.

Grammar-Translation Method: the knowledge of rules

4.2.1

The time-honored *Grammar-Translation Method* (17th–20th centuries) introduces vocabulary and grammar through explicit and teacher-fronted instruction. The teacher assumes the role of the master, the students the role of apprentices. The comparison and contrast of the first language (L1) and the second

Focus on vocabulary and grammar

(L2) highlights the particular *structures* of the native and the target languages. *Declarative knowledge* and *accuracy* are important: rules and patterns are explicitly taught and memorized. Translating discrete written samples that display models of good language serves to prepare learners to read texts from the target culture. 'Imitating' these texts through writing compositions increases the learners' grasp of the target language and culture. Reading canonical literary or philosophical texts serves the cultivation of the individual (*Persönlichkeitsbildung*).

> Pick a very short passage from a literary or cultural text as a translation exercise for your peers. Translate it yourself to check whether it is a challenge your peers could master. Find comprehension questions. Elaborate on the cultural and educational value of the passage. Identify a few words or phrases you would single out for exercises on rules of word formation and grammar and provide these rules for yourself (cf. ibid.: 23).
> Work in pairs. (1) Translate the passage. (2) Answer the comprehension questions. (3) Apply the grammar rule given to you and complete the exercise. (4) Reflect on your learning process and the result.

Discussing the method

The aims of accuracy, cultural knowledge, and cultivation make sense, but the method requires learners to first master lists of vocabulary and grammar rules before they get to ideas of interest – if they are interested in elite culture. Studying grammatical rules does not automatically result in correct spoken or written language production. The instruction in the mother tongue supports the understanding of the structure and content of texts, but this focus neglects listening and speaking relevant to everyday communicative practice. This method was later abandoned in favor of monolingual teaching. However, recently, advocates of '*enlightened monolingualism*' (*aufgeklärte Einsprachigkeit*) have stressed that the intermittent use of German as the linguistic and conceptual knowledge base – the comparative foil – and the language of explanation is more 'natural' and efficient than the 'direct method' of monolingual immersion (cf. Butzkamm 2012: 95–114). In a few cases, beginners and intermediate learners find it easier and faster to translate and learn about certain English constructions in contrast with German equivalents (*cross-lingual analysis*) rather than getting explanations of English grammar in English.

4.2.2 | Direct Method: situated listening and speaking

Focus on oral communication skills

Advocates of the *Direct Method* are critical of the fact that the Grammar-Translation Method does not provide training in what foreign language learners actually need: oral communication skills for interaction with native speakers in specific situations. The Direct Method was developed by the Berlitz School in the late 19th century and is still being implemented at this institution today.

The Direct Method claims to be more 'natural' since it 'directly' uses the target language as a medium of instruction. Objects, pictures, or demonstrations help to connect words directly with meaning, i. e. without recourse to the learners' mother tongue. Vocabulary is taught and learned through chunks and sentences rather than by teaching discrete items and learning them by heart from word lists. Grammar is not a central concern, and explanations – if necessary at all – move from the language sample to the rule in an *inductive* way. The imitation of the (near-)native model and the immediate correction of errors are intended to guarantee accuracy. Learners need to communicate with the teacher and among each other in the target language. The practice of oral skills is embedded in everyday situations and is connected to contextual knowledge speakers of the target culture would take for granted (e. g., greetings or ordering dishes at a restaurant).

The teacher (T) says the following to intermediate learners, who already know English terms for food and basics about eating out (grade 8): 'Let's suppose we are in New York City and have heard about delicious Southern food at *Sylvia's Soul Food* in Harlem. Let's have a look at what's on the menu and make a reservation for the weekend.' Students (S) google the restaurant and read the online menu. The S ask the T to help them out with the kind of food on offer (or check the list of 'soul food' and dishes on Wikipedia). S talk about which dishes they might like or dislike. Individual S, sitting with their back to the T, simulate a phone call to place a reservation, get online directions about the location, and discuss the best way of getting there. Subsequently, S do a role play on ordering their meals, practicing conventional expressions (e. g., 'I will have …,' 'I think I will go for …,' 'I would like to order …').

Example

The practicing of everyday language and typical situations in the Direct Method addresses regular ways of processing information, a proceeding that complies with insights of cognitive psychology: people organize their knowledge of life in terms of conceptual schemata, which provide the structure of situations and scripts that define roles (cf. Mandler 1985). However, the Direct Method ignores the linguistic and cultural frames existent in the L1 as a means to create awareness of frames in L2. Furthermore, it seems difficult to impart more complex meanings or grammar issues without explaining them in a deductive and comparative way.

Discussing the method

Audiolingual/Audiovisual Method: habit formation

| 4.2.3

The *Audiolingual Method* (1950s-60s) draws upon the idea of *habit formation* from Behaviorism (see ch. 3.2.1) and of language as a formal system of sounds, words, and sentences from structural linguistics. The term 'audiolin-

Focus on speech habits

gual' reveals that listening and speaking in dialogs is preferred to reading and writing. Learners need to imitate and practice step by step the different sounds, words, and syntactic patterns of English in order to use these as habitually as their L1. Monolingual teaching is valued because the L1 should not interfere with habit formation in the L2. Positive feedback for correct usage reinforces 'good habits,' and the immediate correction of mistakes prevents the formation of 'wrong habits.' Instruction proceeds in the sequence of *stimulus – response – reinforcement* (*Reiz – Antwort – Verstärkung*; cf. Harmer 2011: 64): the teacher as a language model or the audio file in the language laboratory offer input, usually in the form of a dialog, which learners repeat and practice in order to produce correct sounds and structures (see fig. 4.1). The major aim is not understanding how language works but intuitive response in L2 dialogs. Rote learning (*Auswendiglernen*), repetition drills (*Wiederholungsdrills*), transformation exercises (*Umformungsübungen*), and substitution drills (*Satzschalttafeln*) are some of the preferred methods of practicing (cf. Larsen-Freeman & Anderson 2011: 47–48):

Methods of practicing

- ▶ *Repetition drills* require individual students or the class to repeat the teacher's model in chorus.
- ▶ *Chain drills* require learners one-by-one to use a minimal speech pattern the teacher can closely monitor (e. g., 'My name is Tom. How are you?' – 'I'm fine. My name is Susan. How are you?').
- ▶ *Transformation drills* ask students to transform sentence patterns (e. g., an affirmative into a negative, an active into a passive sentence pattern).
- ▶ *Single-slot substitution drills* practice the use of words or phrases in certain positions in sentences. The teacher presents a line followed by a word or phrase, called a cue, which the students adapt when they repeat the line.

Identify the kind of drills and explain their functions in this lesson for early beginners:

- ▶ After an introduction to animals on a farm, the teacher (T) plays the song "The Farmer Takes a Wife" to the students (S).
- ▶ T sings the song line by line and all the S repeat the lines.
- ▶ T sings the song line by line and individual S repeat the line one-by-one.
- ▶ T sings the song line by line but leaves out the object of the first line and later the subject of the following line and has the class fill in the words: 'The farmer takes a […]. The […] takes a […].' T says: 'I like horses. I don't like rats.' T asks an individual S which animals he/she likes and dislikes. S responds and asks the same question of the S beside her. This continues until all S have had the opportunity both to respond and to ask their neighbor the question.

The Audiolingual Method maximizes time for practicing and quickly produces results for beginners, especially with pronunciation, intonation, vocabulary, and syntactic patterns. However, the focus on memory and drill ignores the learners' cognitive and emotional needs. Wrong output is only seen as a need for more practice and not an indication of the learners' ever-developing *Interlanguage* (see chs. 3.2.3, 5.1.2). The close control of learner behavior leaves little room for flexibility and cultural knowledge needed in real conversations.

Discussing the method

The *Audiovisual Method* (1960s) added to the Audiolingual one by visualizing and contextualizing the dialog in a situation through visual media. The visual support takes the form of a sequence of pictures illustrating utterances. The typical proceeding is as follows (cf. Reinfried 2004: 61–64):

Focus on dialogic situations

▶ The *presentation* of a sequence of pictures one-by-one before the corresponding utterances are played
▶ *Explanation*, aiming at a global understanding of the dialog through pointing, imitation, and paraphrasing in dialog with learners
▶ The *imitation* of recorded utterances in order to practice pronunciation and phrases
▶ The *exploitation* of the input through questions and answers as well as role play
▶ The learners' *transposition* of the dialog to a new topic or situation

The Audiovisual Method inspired the use of more visualized and situated dialogs, but it fell short of serving motivational and practical needs due to its rigid proceeding, its neglect of reading and writing, and its failure to develop language awareness. Still, the Audiolingual and Audiovisual Methods are part and parcel of current commercial language learning software, which uses imitation and pattern drills, complemented by tutoring functions.

Discussing the method

The teacher-centered methods outlined above attribute authority and close control over input and output to the teacher: he/she manages in detail the learners' exposure to and practice of language. The gradual, step-by-step progression allows for the easy monitoring and testing of discrete items or patterns. The premium on accuracy ignores the relevance of the learners' Interlanguage development. The practice of phrases and patterns in these methods quickly yields results that may work in stereotypical situations but does not lead to the flexibility necessary to cope with limitations and unexpected turns in communication (cf. Lightbown & Spada 2006: 142–43). Successful communication tolerates certain mistakes, such as the missing third-person -s, but not the violation of sociolinguistic rules, such as forms of politeness and turn-taking, which Communicative Language Teaching (CLT) pays attention to.

Summary: teacher-centered methods

4.3 | Student-orientation

Student-oriented methods have shifted attention from teaching to learning, inspired by the turn from Structural Linguistics to Pragmatic Linguistics and Sociolinguistics, as well as from Behaviorist to Cognitive, Constructivist, and Sociocultural Approaches. In order to communicate successfully, learners need forms and functions, but meaning and fluency come before accuracy. Practicing communication requires a move away from the didactic teacher-learner communication and a focus on authentic interaction among learners, which requires picking topics of interest to them.

4.3.1 | Communicative Language Teaching: authentic communication

Focus on meaningful communication

CLT (1970s) inverts the structural idea of mastering an abstract system as a basis of accurate language use. It aims at meaningful and appropriate communication, which requires more flexibility and awareness of pragmatic and social contexts than the reproduction of patterns practiced in the Direct, Audiolingual, and Audiovisual Methods. Fluency and comprehensibility are more important than accuracy.

Pragmatic linguists, sociolinguists, and sociologists served as 'midwives' of CLT with their definition of *communicative competence* as the ability to interact in meaningful ways and to express one's intentions in a socially appropriate form in specific situations as well as within a framework of cultural norms. In order to do so, speakers need linguistic (or grammatical) competence, sociolinguistic competence, discourse competence, and strategic competence (cf. Council of Europe 2001: 11–14, 101–09; Hedge 2007: 45–56; see fig. 4.2):

Fig. 4.2 |
Model of communicative competence
(based on Canale &
Swain 1980, Canale
2013)

Linguistic competence	Sociolinguistic competence
Knowledge of the language code	Knowledge of sociocultural rules of language use
▸ Vocabulary ▸ Word formation ▸ Sentence formation ▸ Pronounciation and spelling ▸ Semantics	▸ Appropriateness in sociolinguistic contexts depending on status of participants, purposes of interaction, norms/conventions of interaction (e.g., politeness, formality, directness) ▸ Awareness of culture-specific aspects of language (e.g., idioms, expressions, cultural references)

Communicative competence

Mastery of verbal and non-verbal communication strategies	Mastery of how to combine grammatical forms and meanings to achieve a unified spoken or written text in different genres
▸ To compensate for breakdowns in communication (e.g. through paraphrasing) ▸ To enhance the effectiveness of communication (e.g., through deliberate choices such as slow and soft speech for rhetorical effect)	▸ Cohesion in form (e.g., through the use of cohesion devices such as pronouns, ellipses, synonyms, etc.) ▸ Coherence in meaning (e.g., through repetition, progression, non-contradiction, relevance)
Strategic competence	**Discourse competence**

In several models of CLT, fluency is considered the fifth competence, i. e. to process language and to respond in 'real time' (cf. Hedge 2007: 56). These competences have been expanded to include intercultural communicative competence (see ch. 7).

Communicative competence

CLT comes in many shapes and forms, which share basic principles (cf. Hedge 2007: 57–58):

Basic principles of CLT

▶ Communication is the means to and the purpose of language learning.
▶ Conveying meaning is the aim of communication.
▶ Meaning should be negotiated among learners with little intervention by teachers.

Adherents of the method have debated whether the focus should be on meaningful communication alone or on teaching forms to practice communication. The so-called 'strong' version of CLT uses communication as the means of learning how to communicate, and the 'weak' or 'balanced' version teaches the linguistic means of communication in order to facilitate communication (cf. Ellis 2012: 196).

'Strong' and 'weak' CLT

In the strong version, teachers contrive contexts and interactions which require particular forms to communicate effectively, such as reading a dialog covering shopping as a topic and then performing a role play, which demands forms of politeness and requests as well as positive and negative responses. The "idea is that if learners put the language to appropriate use, they will be able to infer a knowledge of the code that enables them to do it" (Widdowson 2012: 9). However, communication is to some extent possible by using non-standard, unconventional forms, and learners would not necessarily notice errors if 'it works' and fulfils the criterion of viability (see ch. 3.2.4). According to Spada (2007: 275), the strong version has given rise to five misleading assumptions that CLT means (1) focusing on meaning only, (2) providing no corrective feedback, (3) offering pure learner-orientation, (4) focusing on listening and speaking only, and (5) strictly adhering to the principles of monolingual teaching. Due to the limitations implied in these myths, most teachers avoid the strong version and tend to follow the *weak version of CLT, which clearly introduces and reflects on means of communication before learners are expected to read texts or produce output*: for example, by offering learners notions and functions to express intentions, such as the notion of possibility ('may') needed to express predictions (function) about the future ('I may go to university.') or politeness in order to achieve intentions ('May I borrow your pen, please?'). The 'strong' version of CLT does not explicitly introduce notions but expects students to learn them through trial and error.

Differences

Often, CLT moves from simplified, comprehensible input with a sharp focus on a particular new structure to more authentic input. It gives learners plenty of time for practicing authentic communication and negotiating meaning in interaction. It is essential to address the learners' needs in order to get

Proceeding

them interested in talking or writing about a relevant topic rather than having them interact as part of a didactic exercise to practice correct forms of English. However, it is not always easy to cater to each learner's interest and simulate authentic sociocultural situations and interactions, which vary according to generation, gender, ethnicity, and class in different cultures. Textbooks have to select characters, situations, and topics, but the focus is on a majority of young male and female white middle-class characters, and a minority of 'Black British', Asian, African, or lower-class characters, a fact that may alienate less privileged learners. Media, such as interviews, literature, or movies, may help learners observe authentic communication and step into the shoes of others. A typical textbook pattern conforms to the following sequence:

Typical textbook pattern

▶ *Presentation*: the introduction of a topic with pictures and texts that may frequently display specific forms and speech functions
▶ *Practice*: exercises that focus on language form
▶ *Production*: tasks that address specific skills and aim at using specific functions in situated communication
▶ *Metacognitive reflection* on communicative or learning strategies
▶ *Further practice and differentiation* with additional material or tasks

Compare and evaluate the units on a topic of your choice, such as pets, friends, or sports, in two textbooks for grade 5 from different publishers: how do they address the learners' interests? Is the input appropriate or inappropriate, didactic or authentic? Which vocabulary, speech functions, and communicative competences would you need to express yourself in the situated tasks? Do the tasks promote both the practice of relevant speech functions and authentic communication at the same time? Which of the material and activities would you select if you were to teach the unit? Would you adapt material and tasks or add others?

'Mind the gap': theory and actual practice

In spite of the fact that many practitioners endorse the principles of CLT, their practice often lags behind their aims because they talk most of the time and favor teacher-centered patterns of initiation-response-evaluation (IRE) rather than stimulating genuine interaction among learners (cf. Spiro 2013: 8–9, 32).

4.3.2 | Task-based Language Teaching: problem-solving

Focus on communicative tasks

Task-based Language Teaching or *Learning* (TBLT or TBLL, 1980s, *aufgabenorientierter Unterricht*) is often considered a strong version of CLT, which mainly prefers authentic and 'natural' language learning to learning discrete items, and learner-driven interaction to intervention by teachers (cf. Ellis 2012: 196–97). In spite of many similarities between CLT and TBLT, TBLT tends to avoid the practice of specific forms to learn discrete speech functions and opts for more comprehensive and holistic tasks to practice communication. The focus of a task is on meaningful and appropriate interaction as well as process- and product-oriented performance as the means and goals of learning (cf. Bach & Timm 2013: 12–15). Learners employ their linguistic and cognitive resources to retrieve and exchange information or to discuss opinions in order to achieve an outcome that is not primarily of a linguistic nature (e. g., arriving at a decision on how to travel to New York, where to stay, and what to do there within a week; cf. Ellis 2012: 198).

TBLT and its German cousin, ***Holistic and Action-based Language Teaching*** (*ganzheitlicher und handlungsorientierter Unterricht*), relate to Cognitive, Sociocultural, and Interactionist Approaches (see ch. 3.2.3–5): the learner is seen as a social agent, who wants to communicate, solve problems, and achieve goals in particular situations. TBLT conforms to the aim of holistic and humanistic language teaching, which is to unfold "the students' full potential for growth by acknowledging the importance of the affective dimension in learning as well as the cognitive" (Ellis 2003: 31). The teacher creates opportunities for authentic interaction. *Interaction in the pursuit of tasks* advances

Learners as social agents

- ▶ *Incidental acquisition:* e. g., picking up the stress and intonation of a word
- ▶ *Explicit language learning:* e. g., looking up a word and memorizing it
- ▶ *Peer feedback in collaborative scaffolding* and the *cognitive processing of input*: e. g., through comments on the content and form of each other's contributions
- ▶ *Modified output*

Thus, while TBLT primarily aims at *negotiation of meaning* and *problem solving*, form is by no means neglected but integrated through clarifying feedback and consciousness-raising activities stimulated by teachers and peers (cf. Ellis 2012: 267–68).

A ***task as a work plan*** (see fig. 4.3) focuses on tasks comparable to those in the real world with a clearly defined communicative outcome (cf. Ellis 2003: 10–11). The famous airport project for intermediate learners aims at coping with information and communication in English in the context of international travel. At the next international airport, groups of learners look for and sample English texts (e. g., announcements, menus), interview passengers in English about their country of origin and their destination, record these, later locate their itineraries on a map, present the most interesting results to their peers, and reflect upon the results. They practice organizing teamwork, reading, interaction (e. g., listening comprehension, forms of politeness, paraphrasing), presentation, and reflection (Legutke 2013: 104–106). The task as a work plan differs from ***task as a process***, the actual activities learners perform according to their interpretation of the task.

Definition: work plan versus process

In TBLT, teachers may use the *textbook* and its media package *as a resource*, which may already contain appropriate tasks or may need to be complemented

Textbook as resource

by complex tasks that involve learners in cognitive, social, interactive, and practical activities. However, complex tasks present a challenge to both teachers and students because the difficulties for learners as well as the process and outcome are less predictable than in tightly sequenced and monitored lessons. Consequently, teachers need to reflect on the complexity of input, the required cognitive and interactive processes, the output, and to collaborate with learners to make them recognize the diagnostic value of tasks (see fig. 4.3; cf. Ellis 2003: 21, 276; Müller-Hartmann & Schocker-von Ditfurth 2011: 94–101, 108–17, 163–65, 191–96; Ellis 2012: 200; Hallet 2012: 14–18; Bach & Timm 2013: 17–21).

Task as a work plan: three steps

Fig. 4.3 |
Methodology and principles of the task as work plan (adapted from Ellis 2003: 244, 257–58, 276–78; Ellis 2012: 200–2; Keller 2013: 77)

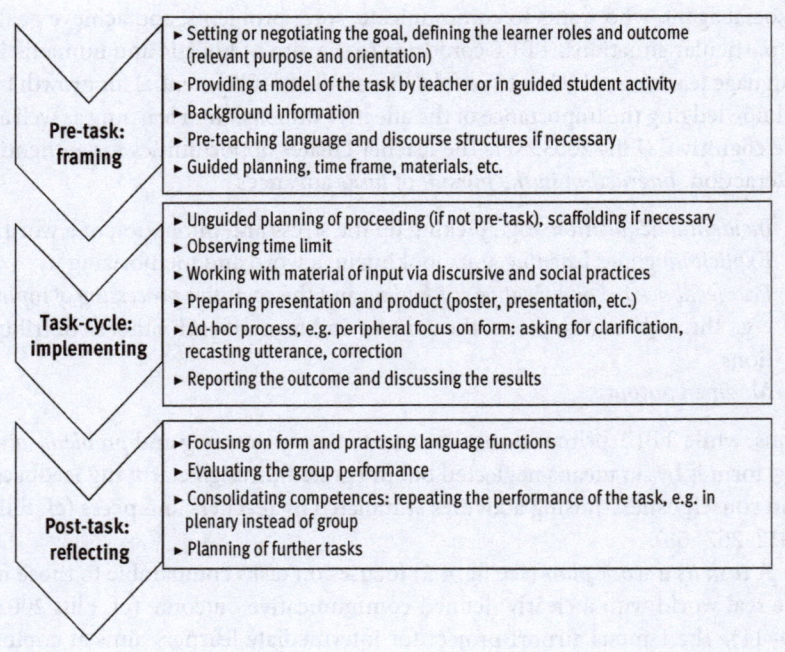

Pre-task: framing
- Setting or negotiating the goal, defining the learner roles and outcome (relevant purpose and orientation)
- Providing a model of the task by teacher or in guided student activity
- Background information
- Pre-teaching language and discourse structures if necessary
- Guided planning, time frame, materials, etc.

Task-cycle: implementing
- Unguided planning of proceeding (if not pre-task), scaffolding if necessary
- Observing time limit
- Working with material of input via discursive and social practices
- Preparing presentation and product (poster, presentation, etc.)
- Ad-hoc process, e.g. peripheral focus on form: asking for clarification, recasting utterance, correction
- Reporting the outcome and discussing the results

Post-task: reflecting
- Focusing on form and practising language functions
- Evaluating the group performance
- Consolidating competences: repeating the performance of the task, e.g. in plenary instead of group
- Planning of further tasks

Team work central to TBLT

Since teamwork is of crucial importance for solving problems, special attention should be given to its functions and implementation. *Team work gives more speaking time, agency, and responsibility to learners* in comparison to their responsive role in teacher-centered lessons. However, the fairly open proceeding and outcome of teamwork may lead to poor results if tasks are too complex, collaboration is inefficient, and scaffolding insufficient to meet learners' abilities and needs. Teachers should offer clear orientation and specify the product, appeal to individual responsibility and accountability, foster collaborative skills of how to negotiate meaning effectively, maintain the same groups to keep positive interdependence among learners, monitor and scaffold the process, and insert phases of focus on form (cf. Ellis 2003: 266–72).

Genetsch et al. (2012: 100–05) give an example of how to use the textbook   Example
as a resource and develop motivating and challenging tasks. In the textbook
Red Line 3 for grade 7 (Haß 2008: 62–63), a magazine report on child labor in
India appears under the headline "Cheap Children," which serves as a starting
point for tasks that aim at the following learning goals: (1) topical and ethical
global knowledge, understanding, and evaluation, related to the learners' situation (their own jobs and position as privileged consumers); (2) coping with
a social and transcultural topic through participating in reflexive social thinking and action. A conventional task is to read and scan the core text for relevant information to find out about the child's life. An information grid serves
as a means of scaffolding for below-average learners. For the sake of differentiation and for more advanced learners, sophisticated tasks include (1) finding
out about, presenting to each other, and discussing further cases of child labor
on the basis of pre-selected, accessible websites or a WebQuest, (2) discussing
whether rules for child labor should be drawn up with reference to children's
rights, or (3) designing a poster and preparing a short talk at a (simulated) conference on child labor concerning economic, social, ethical, and cultural issues.

Critics raise objections to TBLT, claiming that it does not define precisely   Discussion of the
what a task is, nor does it lead to rapid acquisition of relevant vocabulary and   method
chunks necessary to build up language skills, especially those of beginners. In
addition, it takes a lot of time, accuracy is neglected, and it is difficult to assess.
According to critics, TBLT should complement rather than replace a structural
syllabus (cf. Harmer 2011: 73). However, this criticism has been largely countered: tasks are flexible patterns that serve the acquisition of relevant competences. Topical, authentic, complex tasks pose problems similar to those in the
real world. They demand and develop the combination of various language
competences, cognitive and pragmatic problem-solving strategies, as well as
interactive and socio-cultural competences (cf. Hallet 2012: 12–13).

TBLT works with beginners, too, because tasks can vary a lot in complex-   TBLT and beginners
ity, addressing only one skill or several, doing something familiar or transferring competences to a new situation. For example, the teacher can introduce
the topic of giving directions by telling learners where something is located
and asking individuals to fetch it. Then peers can direct an individual learner,
who has been waiting outside the classroom, to the hiding place of an object
in the classroom. Next, learners can discuss how to furnish a little toy house
they are drawing or building in class, or tell each other how to get from school
to their homes with the help of maps that they are asked to draw. Learners can
also show and tell each other where to go on a map. More advanced learners
can give directions (without demonstrating them), which their partners trace
with a pencil on the map (information gap), and discuss whether the partner
followed the directions and whether alternative routes might be better (opinion gap, comparing, problem-solving). Time is a relative issue, because quickly
acquired vocabulary and language functions do not help if learners cannot

retrieve and use these in situated communication, which is practiced best via meaningful tasks.

TBLT and errors

The focus on meaning may risk the fossilization of errors (or: stabilization of Interlanguage), which can be prevented by a ***proactive focus on form***, i. e. anticipating learners' errors and providing input that creates awareness of problems before output, or ***reactive focus on form*** after learner output, which can take place in an intermittent way while learners interact or in a retrospective way after a task (cf. Ellis 2012: 227–28, 303–05; see ch. 5.2.1).

TBLT and assessment

Assessment remains an issue (see ch. 12): discrete-item tests of linguistic units and errors, such as testing prepositions or tenses in multiple-choice tests, are 'objective' and reliable but do not measure performance in tasks. Evaluating task performance, for example in the form of an interview or locating a place in a city, connects the learning experience in the lessons, the form of assessment, and real-life challenges (cf. Ellis 2003: 279). "In TBA [task-based assessment], language ability is measured in relation to some subject content" (Ellis 2003: 309) and requires a multi-dimensional assessment in order to be reliable and valid, or it should be complemented by discrete-item tests.

4.3.3 | Collaborative and Participatory Methods: social and critical agency

> What are the benefits and problems of group work? Consider the potential effects on cognitive, social, and language learning. What is your preferred role in groups (e. g., leader, questioner, or mediator)? How do you support others, and what do you learn from them? What is necessary to improve the cognitive, social, and linguistic effects of group work?

Focus on collaboration and participation

Collaborative (also known as Cooperative) and Participatory Methods recognize the fundamentally social dimension of human life, learning, and language. In the ***Collaborative Method***, *interaction, controversy, and cooperation are central means to and goals of learning,* and are based on findings in Social Psychology, as well as Socio- and Psycholinguistics. The social focus of the Collaborative Method fully complies with the democratic agenda of the CEF (see ch. 1.2.1).

Cooperation before competition

The education system relies heavily on individual competition (see ch. 12) and needs to be complemented (or replaced – in the 'strong' form) by team-based cooperation for pedagogic and pragmatic reasons. If learners are to "become citizens capable of making reasoned judgments about the complex problems facing society, they must learn to use the higher-level reasoning and critical thinking processes involved in effective [and collaborative] problem solving" (Johnson & Johnson 1994: 71). Where competitive, individualistic learning is concerned, debate often foregrounds a dualist either/or, right or wrong, and leads to winners and losers. Open discussions among individuals tend to generate relativist positions beyond mutual understanding or agreement. In cooperative, social learning in teams, privileging harmony is detrimental to achievement since it may result in outcomes of the lowest common denominator. However, *structured controversy* negotiates pros and cons to arrive at a more integrative argument or a more complex solution to a problem. Respectful but challenging controversy tends to involve learners and to stimulate cognitive processing and social skills through an exchange of divergent arguments and perspectives. It "tends to result in greater mastery and retention of the subject matter being studied as well as greater ability to generalize the principles learned to a wider variety of situations" (ibid.).

In terms of socio- and psycholinguistic factors of language learning, *social interaction* in groups surpasses other classroom activities in maximizing the opportunity and time for comprehensible input and output in a low-anxiety atmosphere, in providing practice in turn-taking, active listening, sharing of information and perspectives, as well as in negotiating meaning and interaction strategies. The Collaborative Method uses teamwork not only intermittently, as CLT does, but as the core of all lessons. It allocates four heterogeneous learners each to a base team over a longer period, for example a whole school year or more, in order to build stable and supportive relationships that foster cognitive and social development. In addition to these '*home groups*,' learners work in different '*ad hoc groups*' on a particular assignment for a limited period of time (e. g., in expert groups) and return to their home groups to teach the newly won expertise to each other (jigsaw peer-tutoring technique; cf. Bejarano 1994: 195–99, 202–04).

Team work as core of the lesson

Learners need clear tasks and objectives for efficient group work. Most importantly, they need to internalize *cooperative principles* of successful teamwork (cf. Johnson & Johnson 1994: 58–59):

▶ *Positive interdependence*: 'one for all, all for one'; insight into boosting learning through sharing individual resources and mutual support to enhance individual and group achievement (e. g., bonus points in a test if all group members achieve a high score)

Principles of teamwork

▶ *Face-to-face promotive interaction*: helping each other with cognitive learning of concepts and problem-solving strategies, and encouraging each other in non-verbal and verbal responses

▶ *Individual accountability*: an individual learner's achievement represents that of the group if her product or test score is taken as the result of a joint effort, which makes the group take care of individual progress, and vice versa

▶ *Social skills*: teaching social skills is as important as teaching academic skills (e. g., arriving at decisions, building trust, managing conflicts, leading a team)

► *Group processing*: reflecting on the quality of group work in order to improve the planning and implementation of successful cognitive and social processes

Discussing the method

While empirical evidence proves the efficiency of mutual feedback and reciprocal teaching (Hattie 2012: 269–70), it may be difficult to implement cooperative principles, to contain the competitive mode, and to maintain structured collaborative work in the face of heterogeneous learners. Critics may contend that the Collaborative Method as defined above can be simply employed to make learners work more on pre-defined topics and in a prescribed way rather than starting at the preliminary level and letting learners participate in the selection of aims, topics, and activities. In addition, taking group work as the dominant form of learning may frustrate learners who are more inclined to work on their own and those who prefer to get a lot of feedback from the teacher as an authority figure.

Focus on critical agency

The ***Participatory or Critical Method*** is based on insights from ***Critical Pedagogy*** into the politics of power, language, and knowledge (cf. Crookes 2011: 598–602, Janks 2010, Larsen-Freeman & Anderson 2011: 167–77; see ch. 8.2.3). Participation is the method and the aim: learners participate in determining the topics of education in order to participate in improving their living conditions and society. Critical Pedagogy aims at raising awareness of social injustice and economic discrepancies. Its intention is to *empower learners* to raise their voices in a bid to change inequality and discrimination rather than reproducing the status quo. Since language is not neutral but inflected with social and cultural norms and values, learners need to develop critical thinking and critical literacy through *critical discourse analysis*, which uncovers how bias is often implied in language use for the purpose of manipulation and domination (e. g., race, class, gender, generation): for example, 'human capital' does not mean using capital for humanitarian purposes, but reduces employees to the factors of cost and profit. The stereotypical discourse about the 'problem of migrants' insinuates that migrants are the problem and often ignores that the policy of containment, which may harbor racist or xenophobic sentiment, creates problems for migrants, who could actually contribute to solving the problem of aging societies. Topics are not picked by the teacher (or the textbook), but developed together with the learners, who are encouraged to talk about their lives. The teacher formulates the problems suggested by the learners' experiences and supplies the language needed to discuss these. Problems of mutual interest are cooperatively discussed in class, which guarantees relevance for life and motivation in learning the language.

Discussing the method

Given that many classes are multicultural, the method should generate numerous opportunities to discuss problems with divergent sociocultural norms and values embedded in different languages. However, teachers must be as willing and ready as learners to talk about critical incidents and touchy

issues, for example conflicts due to differences in politeness, respect, relationships across boundaries of gender or generation. Needless to say, opening up
presupposes trusting teachers and peers, and the hope that sharing the problem will help to solve it. Critics who are more or less happy with the status quo
may find fault with the progressive political agenda of the method. Teachers
who feel the need to be in control of the class and who believe that learners
need graded input might object to the focus on learner issues rather than language functions.

Subject-orientation: Bilingual Teaching or Content and Language Integrated Learning | 4.4

Bilingual Teaching (*bilingualer Sachfachunterricht*) or its relative, **Content and Language Integrated Learning** (CLIL), primarily follow subject-orientation rather than teacher- or learner-orientation. A *bilingual speaker* is able to use two languages, but it is a matter of debate to which extent this speaker needs to be proficient in both of these. An ordinary bilingual speaker, who masters *basic interpersonal communicative skills* (BICS), could hardly be expected to write a technical report about a chemical experiment, which requires *cognitive academic language proficiency* (CALP). In ordinary life as in academic discourse, people describe things (what) or processes, analyze and explain these (how), give reasons for or against something, and evaluate it (why), but academic concepts and discourses are more precise, objective, and systematic (cf. Zydatiß 2010: 261–62).

> Teaching other subjects through English

CLT aims at bilingualism as well (BICS), but a bilingual program teaches an academic subject in a L2 (CALP). However, the term 'bilingual teaching' is misleading since instruction mainly takes place in the L2 even if it is neces-sary to learn the concepts as well as the subject-specific discourse in both the native and the target language. Cognitive linguistics alerts us to the fact that learners have acquired numerous concepts and words in their L1, which may interfere with their development of concepts in the L2 if they simply translate words and are not made aware of divergent categorizations. Consequently, Nie-meier (2005: 24–28, 37–40) argues that bilingual teaching needs to be literally bilingual and raise awareness of different conceptual mappings in different lan-guages. For example, the prototypical bird that first comes to mind would be the sparrow in Germany and the robin in Great Britain. Americans are quick to call someone a 'friend' in cases where Germans would use the word 'acquaint-ance.' However, it would be wrong to conclude that Americans are superficial because their concept is broader than that of the German '*Freund*,' which is more like the American 'close friend.'

> 'Two for the price of one'?

Bilingual Teaching or CLIL are umbrella terms that include programs that range from short-term intensive exposure to long-term immersion programs. The Canadian model of immersion makes students plunge into a 'language

> Different programs: major aims

bath.' Canada introduced immersion in the 1960s, teaching all non-language subjects in French in order to make monolingual English speakers, who comprised the majority of the population, learn the other of the two official national languages, and to promote mutual understanding and recognition. The motivation to introduce CLIL in Europe was influenced by political interest in advancing intercultural understanding, and by economic interest in applied knowledge in foreign languages on the part of companies and increasingly mobile individuals. In addition, educators were interested in boosting language skills through increasing input and motivating learners by making foreign languages immediately useful in developing content knowledge.

Implementation in Germany   There is a great variety of bilingual programs at German pre-schools and schools (cf. Niemeier 2005: 32–34, Elsner & Keßler 2013: 18–22, Keßler & Schlemminger 2013: 15–26): while several hundred kindergartens employ an immersive approach, predominantly using English as a L2, only a few primary schools do so. Many secondary schools do not go the whole way to immersion but offer bilingual courses or modules in a few subjects. The distribution and diversity of the programs makes continuity and transition a problem (*Übergangsproblematik*). At secondary schools, two major types of CLIL have been established, following more intensive language classes in grades 5 and 6: (1) the continuous teaching of several subjects in the L2 from grade 7 until the end of school (*bilingualer Zug*), or (2) the modular type (*bilinguale Module*), which alternates teaching topics in the L1 or L2 in one subject (e. g., 'the British Empire' in English and 'Fascism' in German). Modules at primary school may deal with the topics of 'animals and pets,' 'the seasons,' 'my home and town,' thus addressing the learners' personal interests: for example, in drawing their rooms, homes, and towns (art), and learning to talk about their features and functions (language and *Sachkunde*; cf. Dausend 2013, Mehisto et al. 2008: 34–45). At secondary school, Geography, History, and Social Studies are privileged subjects of CLIL because they invite inter- and transcultural perspectives. However, Mathematics, Science, and the Arts are gaining ground because they use numerical and visual signs as well as hands-on work, which complement language.

CLIL principles   A single coherent method does not exist due to different academic discourses taught in CLIL, but there is a consensus about a set of preferred *principles concerning content, cognition, communication, and culture* (cf. Mehisto et al. 2008: 29, 69, 138–71):

- ▶ *Double focus* on academic and language learning
- ▶ *Cross-curricular topics and projects*
- ▶ *Language across the curriculum*
- ▶ *Active, co-operative, task-based, and holistic learning*
- ▶ *Scaffolding* (building on learners' existing experience and knowledge; clarifying goals, expectations, and processes; modeling and rehearsing a task; supporting learners to cope with particular problems)

▶ *Development of concepts and skills in specific subjects* (describing, analyzing, judging, evaluating; performing practical and social tasks and roles)
▶ *Comprehensible input and output*, negotiation of meaning, routine discourse
▶ *Authenticity* in communication and materials
▶ *Message before accuracy*
▶ *Media literacy*
▶ *Learner strategies* to advance learner autonomy
▶ *Raising awareness* of language, cultural differences, and transcultural connections

Research British online newspapers, British and German historical sources on the Great War (*Erster Weltkrieg*), and watch the episode *Blackadder Goes Forth* from the British satire in order to come up with arguments for and against the British celebrations of the beginning (!) of the Great War in 2014. Select and critically reflect on material that highlights different perspectives *within* Great Britain and between British and German views of the Great War. Reflect on the difference between this comparative approach and the idea of a modular concept that teaches one topic in one language and from 'one' cultural point of view. With regard to the principles mentioned above, suggest tasks and materials for working on the topic in grades 11 or 12.

Sceptics have raised four objections to CLIL: (1) the L1 may suffer from bilingual education because language development may lag behind that of monolingual speakers. (2) Either the content knowledge or the L2 suffers from the double focus. Knowledge in the subject taught in the L2 may turn out to be shallower than that of peers taught in the L1. (3) Only an elite of learners benefits from CLIL. (4) Bilingual classes are more demanding on teachers, who may not master the necessary academic English and may lack appropriate material.

The first three objections have been largely defeated (cf. Heine 2010: 209–11, Lamsfuß-Schenk 2010: 224–25, Zydatiß 2010: 268, Poarch 2013: 9–15):

(1) Young bilingual learners may have a smaller vocabulary than monolingual speakers, but the combined vocabulary is larger. The variations in language development are considerable among monolingual learners, too. Bilingual learners mix languages and switch codes, but so do adult bilinguals. Subject-specific discourse may be introduced in the L1 along with the L2. (2) Evidence suggests that sufficient proficiency due to early and extensive exposure to the L2 has a positive effect on cognitive development. In comparison to classes taught in the L1 only, the greater effort of finding appropriate concepts and words in the L2 leads to greater cognitive depth of processing. And the more careful negotiation of meaning in L2 classes accounts for the fact that achievement in subject knowledge is often comparable, if not better, in CLIL-classes, and this is in spite of, or even because of, deficits in the L2. Fluency increases considerably over the years, but accuracy may lag behind if content is foregrounded. Phases

Discussing the method

of focus on form help repair errors – as in regular English classes. (3) Immigrant children, who are often at a disadvantage in German, start at the same level as their German peers. If learners are given a choice between classes in their L1 and in the L2, the potential problems of learners with low aptitude will be avoided.

(4) However, the education of teachers and the development of appropriate materials are a problematic subject. Many teachers have not had training in Bilingual Teaching. Knowing an L2 and a subject does not mean having expertise in the specific discourse in the L2. Methods and goals of teaching English and the subject need to be coordinated. English material is not tailored to meet L2 learners' demands and needs to be adapted, or teachers need to create materials of their own (see ch. 11; cf. Montijano Cabrera 2012: 124–40). For example, English and American textbooks in Political or Social Studies often move inductively from anecdotes or case studies to abstract principles in the tradition of pragmatism, whereas German textbooks often proceed in a deductive way from explaining the system to an example: an American textbook would tell the story of the Watergate scandal, the Republican President Nixon's illegal tapping of the phones of Democrats and members of his own administration, the discovery of the scandal by journalists, and the legal proceeding against Nixon as an intriguing case study to explain how US-American politics and the media work. German textbooks present the system of the US-American government and the media, and, if learners are lucky, Watergate as a short example. In terms of assessment, the question may be whether language problems impede the display of the learners' cognitive skills and knowledge, an issue that can be solved by using both languages in tests. Yet the potential disadvantages pale in comparison to the gains in terms of increased language awareness concerning both L1 and L2, advancement of language skills through intensive and extensive exposure, competence in subject knowledge in the L2, and motivation through authentic communication.

4.5 | Age and stage: early language learning and transition

Complementing the teacher-centered, learner-centered, and subject-oriented perspectives presented above, early language learning and transition take heed of the fact that learners at a certain age and stage of development have particular abilities and needs.

'The earlier, the better'? In light of children's great capacity to acquire languages and the European goal of plurilingualism, German federal states introduced English in grades 1 or 3 of primary school (*Fremdsprachenfrühbeginn*). Optimists believe that first language acquisition (LA1) is easy within the early critical period and that LA2 works like LA1. However, most early learners only receive one to three hours of English per week, and thus have a fraction of exposure to the L2 and little practice in an institutional context in comparison to LA1 (cf. Mindt & Wagner 2009: 9–16). Empirical evidence has not confirmed fixed limits for a critical period in LA2 (as opposed to LA1). Many children are clearly at an advantage concerning pronunciation if they are immersed in the foreign language, but adolescent and adult learners display a better mastery of learning lexis, morphology, and syntax (cf. Grotjahn & Schlak 2010: 254–56).

Secondary school teachers often complain that they have to start all over again because the children only play and do not learn anything of use in primary school (e. g., language structures, reading and writing skills). Primary school teachers respond that teachers and the linear curriculum in secondary school neglect learner-orientation, motivation, and the knowledge acquired so far (cf. Wagner 2009: 17–24, 123–25, 327–30). The issue of transition returns between school and university (e. g., when professors wonder what students learned at school) and between university and school (e. g., when pre-service teachers are told that academic knowledge from university is of no use at school). The 'gap' is an issue for learners and teachers alike, albeit of a different kind in each case. Learners need to face a change of school, peer groups, teachers, methods, subjects, and expectations concerning their performance, but quite a few are excited about moving on and cope quite well with the new challenges (cf. ibid.). Teachers should know about the goals, methods, and the content of both primary and secondary schools in order to ease the transition phase for learners.

Facilitating smooth transitions: communication between teachers needed

The primary school pursues the following major goals in English (cf. Schmid-Schönbein 2008: 37–61, Mayer 2013: 89):

► *Stimulating a positive attitude* toward and awareness of the target language and culture
► *Promoting basic communication skills* to cope with very simple everyday situations
► *Developing learning strategies*
► *Strengthening confidence and self-efficacy*

Goals in primary schools

The following principles and techniques of teaching beginners address the *goals* above (cf. Burmeister 2006, Edelenbos et al. 2006, Keßler 2006b, Christiani et al. 2008, Schmid-Schönbein 2008, Mindt & Wagner 2009, Wagner 2009, Böttger 2012):

► *Motivation* through topics of interest to children, situated in meaningful contexts
► *Comprehensible input* through teacherese, expressive non-verbal interaction and pantomime
► *Rich input*, appealing to all senses with objects and authentic audio/visual media
► *Qualifying L2 communication* only if necessary
► *Addressing prior knowledge*: English words learners know as used in German
► *Metalinguistic knowledge* from learners' first languages to reflect on English
► *Creative Interlanguage*, e. g., motivating the formation of hypotheses

Teaching principles and techniques in primary school

▶ *Accurate pronunciation* but *tolerating structural errors*
▶ *Alternating proceedings* through discovery learning, explicit teaching of skills, and guided practice
▶ *Authentic speech production* in playful and holistic tasks
▶ *A positive atmosphere* to lower the affective filter

Comparison of primary and secondary schools

A closer look at the curricula, methods, and contents of primary and secondary schooling reveals many similarities: the aims of communicative competence, appropriate topics of interest to learners, language awareness, intercultural awareness, learner strategies, and many of the related principles and techniques of teaching and learning (as listed above). The major differences are listed in figure 4.4 (cf. Wagner 2009: 19, 92–117; Jäger 2012).

Fig. 4.4 |

Differences in teaching English at primary and secondary school

Primary school	Secondary school
▶ Modular: topics and processes	▶ Linear: structural curriculum
▶ Primarily implicit acquisition	▶ Acquisition and learning
▶ German only if necessary	▶ Mediation as a skill
▶ Multisensory and holistic learning	▶ More cognitive learning
▶ Accuracy in pronunciation	▶ More accuracy in grammar
▶ Oral skills, supported by reading and writing	▶ Oral skills and literacy
▶ Mainly receptive media literacy	▶ Receptive and productive media literacy
▶ Intercultural awareness	▶ Intercultural communicative competence
▶ Little or no homework and testing	▶ Regular homework and relevant assessment

Transition: a sensitive issue

If there are as many similarities as differences, the question is why the issue of transition continues to provoke discussions regarding steps teachers can take to narrow the gap. Many reasons account for the tensions concerning transition: secondary school teachers' negative beliefs and misguided expectations of what learners can do, the difference between what is stipulated in curricula and in current teachers' handbooks in comparison to what teachers and learners actually do in the classroom.

Beginners' textbooks

A look at beginners' textbooks does not necessarily help. The grammatical progression of many textbooks for both primary and secondary school violates the psycholinguistic sequence of LA2, a problem which calls for the alignment of *processability*, learning to express communicative intentions, and the introduction of grammar (cf. Keßler 2006a: 119–24, see ch. 5.2). Most beginners are not yet ready for some of the grammatical functions in the curriculum and the textbooks (e. g., the third-person -s, accurate forms of negation or questions; cf. Keßler 2006a: 278–82). Still, many secondary school teachers expect learners to master these language structures (as do Mindt & Wagner 2009: 90–98). Reading and writing are not among the core skills for beginners. Thus, they cannot be expected to perform well in reading and writing at the point of transition. Beginners may not have been offered rich input and the opportunity to produce (rather than reproduce) language, which is why they may not be able to cope well with simple communicative situations.

What can teachers do to narrow the gap? Primary school teachers can pre-
pare children for transition by focusing more on language production and
learner strategies. They can document learners' performance in portfolios to
inform secondary school teachers about their individual competences. In turn,
secondary school teachers can elicit previous knowledge and skills in order
to know where to start, and implement holistic activities learners are familiar
with (cf. Schwarz 2006: 7). In addition, they can diagnose grammatical competence at the beginning of secondary school in order to manage continuity and
transition (cf. Keßler 2006a: 143–48). Keßler (2006a: 228–32) established an
empirical transition profile, which reveals that most children certainly acquire
stages 1 and 2 (and some stage 3) of the processability hierarchy (see chs. 3.2.3,
5.1.2) in two years of primary school: this means that most learners can use a
number of words and formulae (stage 1, possessive -s, plural -s), past -ed, continuous -ing, and SVO in declarative sentences, questions (rising intonation)
and negations (*'He no eat apples', *'He don't eat apples'; stage 2). The testing
of learners would reveal individual differences (heterogeneity), which is related
to many factors and will be dealt with further below.

Solutions: narrowing
the gap

> Compare the example of TPR at the beginning of this chapter and a 'spot
> the difference' task from a current primary school textbook with the goals,
> principles, and expectations of early language learning.

Individual differences and factors

| 4.6

The basic assumption underlying most curricula, textbooks, and teaching until
recently has been that learners of roughly the same age form a fairly homogenous group in spite of evidence to the contrary in every class. At primary
school, *heterogeneity* is probably greater than at secondary school. However,
the policy of *inclusion* has increased individual differences at all school types
(see ch. 6.3). In addition to the curriculum, the methods, and the materials,
learning is subject to numerous influences (cf. Hattie 2009: 33–36, 62–70, 247;
Riemer 2010: 168–70):

▶ *Sociocultural background* (socio-psychological environment at home, the
   parents' knowledge of schooling, expectations and aspirations)
▶ *Experience* (achievement, self-concept, self-efficacy: 'can do')
▶ *Attitude* toward the target language and culture
▶ *Quantity and quality of teaching*
▶ *Situation and conditions of learning*
▶ *Classroom climate* and culture of trust, caring, and safety related to (1) peer
   behavior and influence, and (2) the teacher's expectations, clarity, openness,
   and engagement of learners

We should focus on the greatest source of variance that can make the difference – the teacher. –
John Hattie

Empirical studies undermine some of the *dearly held beliefs* about impact factors on academic achievement. The structural features of schools, such as the financing of schools, class size, and the streaming of children (as in the three-tiered system in Germany) do not seem to have a major beneficial influence on individual achievement. Neither do more discipline and more homework (Hattie 2009: 33, 2009b). If, for example, the class size is halved, but teaching follows the traditional pattern of transmitting knowledge to passive learners, it is unlikely that achievement increases. The attribution of reasons for achievement to structural conditions or the individual learner deflects the responsibility for achievement *away from the teacher* and his or her teaching: "The greatest danger in individual difference research is characterizing learners as 'types' who are either able or not able to take advantage of language instruction." (Ellis 2012: 333)

Student achievement: interrelated factors

Successful learning is dependent upon the interaction of many factors. Aptitude and motivation, the 'big two' of learning, used to be considered as stable, individual properties, which made it easy for the teacher to attribute failure to the learner rather than the ways of teaching and learning (cf. Hattie 2009: 253). However, Educational, Social, and Cognitive Psychology maintain that *cognition, motivation, and affect* are interrelated in complex and dynamic ways with social contexts and educational processes.

Cognition – motivation – affect

For the sake of clarity, factors of individual differences can be separated (see fig. 4.5, adapted from Dörnyei & Skehan 2003: 619, Dörnyei 2010: 249, Schlak 2010: 258, Ellis 2012: 308–16):

Fig. 4.5 |
Individual learner differences

Cognition	Language aptitude (*Sprachlerneignung*): ▶ Phonemic coding: noticing and identifying new sounds ▶ Semantic processing: connecting sounds and meanings ▶ Language analysis: comparing input with mental grammar, inferring grammatical rules and integrating new features Working memory: ▶ Directing processes of attention, encoding, storing, and retrieving ▶ Various components: storing acoustic, verbal, visual, kinesthetic information, parallel processing, and an 'episodic buffer' that combines different information in stories ▶ Rehearsing elements from input Long-term memory: ▶ Accessing stored knowledge to process input and output
Motivation	▶ Integrative: displaying an interest in the other social culture ▶ Instrumental: focusing on the use of skills for particular purposes (e. g., job, travel) ▶ Intrinsic: pleasure and pride in being able to communicate ▶ Extrinsic: interest in reward and grades
Affect	▶ Trait anxiety as a personality feature ▶ Situation-specific anxiety ▶ State anxiety as apprehension in response to a specific moment in a situation

82

Recall particularly motivating and demotivating learning experiences. Reflect on individual and contextual factors of influence. Establish a list of recommendations of what to do and what to avoid as a learner and a teacher to stimulate and maintain motivation.

Psychology and LA2 research have turned from the "*individual differences myth*" to the "*cognition/motivation interface*" (Dörnyei 2010: 259; emphasis added). Aptitude, cognition, motivation, and affect have been recognized as intertwined, situated, and dynamic (see fig. 4.6). Emotions facilitate or impede attention and cognitive involvement due to the *affective appraisal* (*affektive Wertung*) of stimuli according to "novelty, pleasantness, goal significance, self and social image, and coping potential" (Dewaele 2011: 24; cf. Arnold 2011: 13). Aptitude or talent ('can do') does not explain why someone is motivated to invest time and energy in order to learn something ('will do'). *Cognition sets goals, but affect makes people work toward goals.* For example, high motivation can drive cognitive effort. In turn, high achievement due to cognitive ability can be motivating. However, motivation, involvement, time on task, and teaching that addresses individual needs can all compensate for low aptitude: "Motivation is less a trait than fluid play, an ever-changing one that emerges from the processes of interaction of many agents, internal and external, in the ever-changing complex world of the learner" (Ellis & Larsen-Freeman in Dörnyei 2010: 253).

Among the internal agents, the self and *possible selves* can play a significant role in SLA. The acquisition of communicative, social, and cultural knowledge, values, and skills suggests that foreign language learners assume something like a 'foreign language identity'. Individual learners' identities are related to possible selves, the idea of what learners might become, what they would like to become as ideal selves, and what they are afraid of becoming. Possible selves serve as guides, motivating learners "to reduce the discrepancy between our actual and our ideal selves" (Dörnyei 2010: 265). The ideal self motivates the real learner to 'integrate' with his or her ideal self (rather than with 'the target culture,' as in the traditional definition of integrative motivation, which simplifies the link between the target language and a particular culture rather than cultures; cf. Ushioda & Chen 2011: 45). Individuals can imagine who they would be, how they would feel, and what they would think and do as ideal selves, connecting cognition, emotion, motivation, and action. The motivating force of an ideal self can take effect if it is plausible and in harmony with expectations of relevant others, if it incurs clear negative consequences in case of failure, if it is vivid and regularly activated, and if it is "accompanied by relevant and effective *procedural strategies* that act as a *roadmap* towards the goal" (Dörnyei 2010: 257).

Discussion of the impact of different factors

Imagine your ideal self as a teacher of English in detail. What do you look like? How do you feel? What motivates you? What do you think and do? What can you achieve? How do you work with and relate to learners, colleagues, and parents? How would you motivate your students? Imagine a movie or write a story that takes you step by step from your present self to your ideal self as an English teacher. Include what the emotional and motivational consequences of failing your ideal self as a teacher are in the form of a nightmare.

Motivation: a dynamic system

The relationships within the system do not simply follow cause and effect but vary according to the relative strength of one particular factor in the network of multiple other factors. The sociocultural context influences – but does not determine – the learning opportunities on offer and communication in the classroom. On the level of the individual, a talented learner may not be motivated to accomplish a task if it does not seem worth the effort or if peer pressure sanctions high achievement. A learner with a low sense of self-efficacy and extrinsic motivation may decide to work hard if the demands are reasonable and good grades clearly within reach.

Motivation is a system and a process. The evaluation of achievement may have an impact on future choice motivation and the performance of a task. If good achievement is attributed to effort and strategies rather than luck, motivation, positive affect, and self-efficacy will increase. If a student attributes poor performance to little effort, he or she may be motivated to study harder, if to low aptitude, he or she may no longer make any effort because of a low self-concept as a learner. The positive evaluation of the performance may also affect the teacher's and the peers' expectations of future achievements, the current atmosphere, and communication in class.

Look at every item in the dynamic system of motivation (see fig. 4.6): reflect on your strengths and your weaknesses and mark these. Think about what you can do to improve your own cognition/motivation. Work on your three most important weaknesses and monitor your progress. Discuss with your peers which topics and activities would stimulate your motivation.

4.7 | Postmethod principles in a nutshell

The pros and cons of methods

Many teachers appreciate the orientation and guidance methods offer. Nevertheless, the differences in models of LA2, teaching methods, in the age, stage, and individuality of learners render a decision of how to teach difficult. This dilemma has resulted in the turn from a rivalry over the 'best recipe' to a set of postmethod principles. In spite of conceptual differences, alternative methods often propose similar procedures, and abstract strategies give way to on-the-

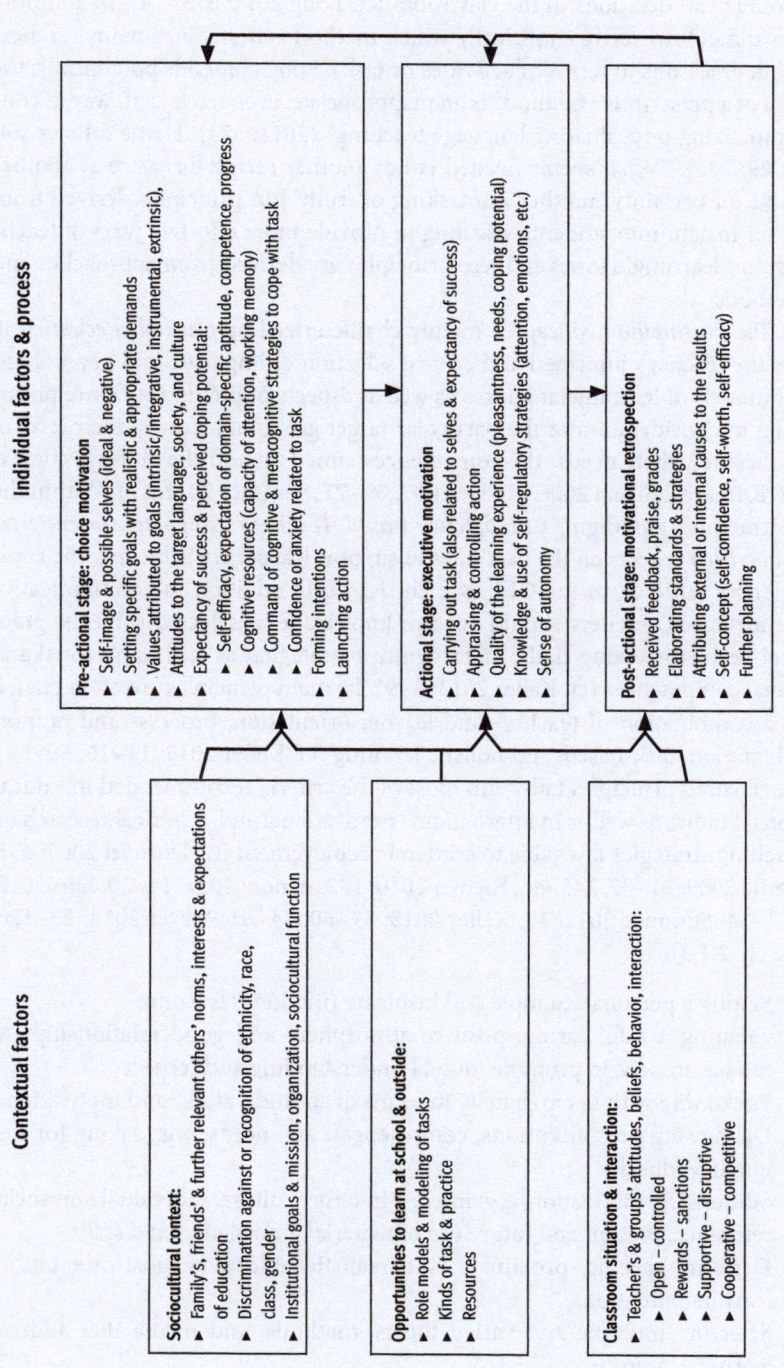

| Fig. 4.6

Dynamic system of
motivation (adapted
from Dörnyei &
Skehan 2003: 619;
Dörnyei 2004:
429–30; Riemer
2010: 171)

Individual factors & process

Pre-actional stage: choice motivation
▲ Self-image & possible selves (ideal & negative)
▲ Setting specific goals with realistic & appropriate demands
▲ Values attributed to goals (intrinsic/integrative, instrumental, extrinsic,
    Attitudes to the target language, society, and culture
▲ Expectancy of success & perceived coping potential:
    ▲ Self-efficacy, expectation of domain-specific aptitude, competence, progress
    ▲ Cognitive resources (capacity of attention, working memory)
    ▲ Command of cognitive & metacognitive strategies to cope with task
    ▲ Confidence or anxiety related to task
    ▲ Forming intentions
    ▲ Launching action

Actional stage: executive motivation
▲ Carrying out task (also related to selves & expectancy of success)
▲ Appraising & controlling action
▲ Quality of the learning experience (pleasantness, needs, coping potential)
▲ Knowledge & use of self-regulatory strategies (attention, emotions, etc.)
▲ Sense of autonomy

Post-actional stage: motivational retrospection
▲ Received feedback, praise, grades
▲ Elaborating standards & strategies
▲ Attributing external or internal causes to the results
▲ Self-concept (self-confidence, self-worth, self-efficacy)
▲ Further planning

Contextual factors

Sociocultural context:
▲ Family's, friends' & further relevant others' norms, interests & expectations
    of education
▲ Discrimination against or recognition of ethnicity, race,
    class, gender
▲ Institutional goals & mission, organization, sociocultural function

Opportunities to learn at school & outside:
▲ Role models & modeling of tasks
▲ Kinds of task & practice
▲ Resources

Classroom situation & interaction:
▲ Teacher's & groups' attitudes, beliefs, behavior, interaction:
    ▲ Open – controlled
    ▲ Rewards – sanctions
    ▲ Supportive – disruptive
    ▲ Cooperative – competitive

spot tactical decisions in the classroom (cf. Long 2011: 373–74). In addition, it is difficult to verify empirically which method is best. Since many teachers think of lessons in terms of activities or tasks, Long contends polemically, the idea of a prescriptive method "is an inappropriate, even irrelevant, way of conceptualizing or evaluating language teaching" (2011: 374). Hattie follows suit (2009: 237): "What seems needed is not another recipe for success, another quest for certainty, another unmasking of truth" but principles derived from better insight into students' learning to provide more effective ways of teaching and learning. However, these principles are derived from approaches and methods.

It is up to the teacher! — *The postmethod concept* is mainly characterized by *principled eclecticism*, i.e. the teacher's informed and critical selection of linguistic and psychological models of learning languages as well as aspects of methods that are promising in consideration of the particular target group of learners, their level of proficiency, their needs, the competences aimed at, and the cultural context (cf. Kumaravadivelu 2006, Hedge 2007: 69–71, Summer 2012: 11). Within the postmethod paradigm, *Competence-Based Teaching* (*kompetenzorientierter Unterricht*) reflects on the best ways to support learners in achieving the competences outlined in the CEF (see ch. 1.2.1). In addition to communicative competences, learners should acquire knowledge in selected subjects, practical problem-solving skills, metacognitive strategies, as well as personal and social competences (cf. Keller 2013: 8–9). Its main principles are often related to a combination of teacher- and learner-orientation, process- and output-orientation, task-based, and holistic learning (cf. Keller 2013: 14–16, 59–60). The favored principles tally with most of the criteria recommended in Educational Studies as well as in international motivational and empirical research on teaching strategies favorable to academic achievement (cf. Dörnyei 2004: 431, Hattie 2009: 31–37, 245–46, Riemer 2010: 172, Arnold 2011: 14–20, Ellis 2012: 327–34, Summer 2012: 12, Keller 2013: 59–60, 74–81, Meyer 2014: 23–126; see ch. 2.1.3):

Pedagogical principles that facilitate student achievement

▶ Setting a personal example and inspiring (life-long) learning
▶ Creating a safe, caring, positive atmosphere and good relationships to reduce anxiety, to promote mutual understanding and respect
▶ Reckoning with heterogeneity in terms of aptitude, skills, and motivation
▶ Diagnosing preconceptions, competences, and needs, e. g., asking for frequent feedback
▶ Stimulating motivation, e. g. interest in target culture, individual and social relevance, present and future use of material, knowledge, and skills
▶ Defining specific, proximate, and realistic objectives: goal-orientation, learning intentions
▶ Selecting multiple and varied topics, methods, and media that address learners' interests

- Clearly structuring the process of lessons, e.g., rules, roles, tasks, time, and actions
- Providing comprehensible, contextualized, and salient input to stimulate attention and noticing
- Designing clear, activating, and challenging tasks for discovery and holistic learning to appeal to cognitive, affective, motivational, and psychomotor factors
- Offering choices and helping students pursue individual goals and strategies of problem solving, learning, self-evaluation, and self-regulation (from scaffolding toward autonomy)
- Providing much time on task and multiple opportunities of negotiated interaction and the deliberate practice of integrated skills
- Fostering confidence, responsibility, autonomy, and cooperation (e.g., peer interaction, reciprocal teaching)
- Making learners observe peer models of successful learning and reflect on language, culture, and strategies (awareness and meta-cognitive competences)
- Giving feedback that connects progress to effort and builds self-confidence
- Providing clear success criteria and developing appropriate tests
- Supporting remedial learning

Method	Aims: competences	Roles of teacher and learner	Proceeding of teaching and learning
Grammar-Translation	▸ Knowledge of language system, literature, culture ▸ Reading and writing ▸ Cultivation	T ▸ Master, authority S ▸ Disciple, apprentice	▸ Top-down communication ▸ Deductive: move from rule to example ▸ Comparison L2–L1 ▸ Translation, memorizing, reading, writing
Direct	▸ Everyday oral skills in situated cultural interaction	T ▸ Language model S ▸ Imitator	▸ Direct association of meaning with target language ▸ Oral conversation in simulated everyday situations
Audiolingual, Audiovisual	▸ Correct oral reception and production: sentence and sound patterns	T ▸ Instructor, drill master S ▸ Trainee, imitator	▸ Habit formation ▸ Pattern drills ▸ PPP: Presentation – Practice – Production

Fig. 4.7

Table of basic methods (adapted from Larson-Freeman & Anderson 2011: 222–23). TBLT, Cooperative and Participatory Approaches share the tenets of CLT but add specific goals, roles, and methods, which is why they are depicted in one section.

CLT	▶ Linguistically, socially, culturally appropriate interation	T ▶ Facilitator, guide	▶ Communication, negoti-ating meaning ▶ IRE: Initiation – Response – Evaluation
TBLT	▶ Real world problem-solving	S ▶ Social agent ▶ Practically capable individual	▶ Group work, role play ▶ Problem-solving in sit-uated tasks: goal-ori-ented learning by doing
Cooperative LT & Partici-patory LT	▶ Social cooperation ▶ Socio-political insight, emancipation and empowerment	▶ Team-worker ▶ Socio-political agent	▶ Training social skills ▶ Critical discourse anal-ysis ▶ Dialog with learners on solving learners' prob-lems

Recommended reading

Bach, Gerhard & Johannes-P. Timm, eds. (2013). *Englischunterricht: Grundlagen und Metho-den einer handlungsorientierten Unterrichtspraxis.* 5th ed. Tuebingen: Francke.

Hallet, Wolfgang & Frank G. Königs, eds. (2010). *Handbuch Fremdsprachendidaktik.* Seelze-Velber: Klett/Kallmeyer.

Hattie, John (2012). *Visible Learning for Teachers: Maximizing Impact on Learning.* London et al.: Routledge.

Larsen-Freeman, Diane & Marti Anderson (2011). *Techniques & Principles in Language Teaching.* 3rd ed. Oxford: Oxford University Press.

Grammar and vocabulary

Contents

The role and methods of introducing grammar and vocabulary have been discussed intensively. This debate will be addressed throughout this chapter together with fundamental linguistic findings relevant for teachers. The chapter will then present effective methods of teaching grammar and vocabulary with an emphasis on activities, learning strategies, categorizing errors, and evaluating textbooks.

Abstract

Mindmap 1:
Chapter 5 & 6

"How learning
works"

"How vocabulary
learning works /
the mental lexicon
works" (s. 104)

Have a look at the cartoon. Recapitulate how grammar and vocabulary were taught in your own school days. Discuss the place the teaching of grammar and vocabulary should have in the foreign language classroom and how it should be taught.

5.1 | Communication and competence

5.1.1 | Today's consensus

Und wenn es auch gelänge, ihm die beste Grammatik und das umfassendste Wörterbuch in den Kopf zu schaffen, so hätte er noch immer keine Sprache gelernt. –
Wilhelm Viëtor

If *communicative competence* is seen as the paramount goal of *Communicative Language Teaching* (CLT; cf. Piepho 1974, Council of Europe 2001, Brandl 2008), teaching grammar and vocabulary must be integrated into the *model of communicative competence* (see ch. 4.3.1, fig. 4.2). Keßler and Plesser (2011: 47) contest that "the mere focus on communication that stresses the role of message as always being more important than the role of accuracy may be a little short-sighted and may lead to a simplified (Tarzan-like) use of the target language". However, Savignon (2002: 7) clarifies that CLT does not regard the role of grammar or the attention to language structures as obsolete:

> While involvement in communicative events is seen as central to language development [in CLT], this involvement necessarily requires attention to form. Communication cannot take place in the absence of structure, or grammar, a set of shared assumptions about how language works, along with a willingness of participants to cooperate in the negotiation of meaning.

For example, a learner utterance such as 'Don't be so sensible!' (*a false friend*) in response to another student being sad or angry about something requires attention to form (*semantic mistake*) and, possibly, correction in the form of a recast or clarification request in order to avoid misunderstandings in communication. This utterance should also call for attention to form regarding the *rules of politeness in conversations*, especially in intercultural communication (see chs. 1.2.1, 6.1.4, 7.1.3). A rather straightforward utterance like this might be perceived as rude by a native speaker of English.

Speech production and Interlanguage

| 5.1.2

Some preliminary remarks on the mechanisms of speech production and on *Interlanguage* (Interimssprache, IL) seem apt for reasons of knowing *when* to teach *what*, *why* learners make *which* kinds of errors and mistakes, and *how* to adapt textbook content to learner needs (cf. Keßler & Plesser 2011: 138). To understand the complexity of second language acquisition (SLA), one might start with a look at how speech production works. Levelt's *psycholinguistic model of speech production* (see fig. 5.1) shows that language processing works like programming, involving complex processes of encoding and decoding.

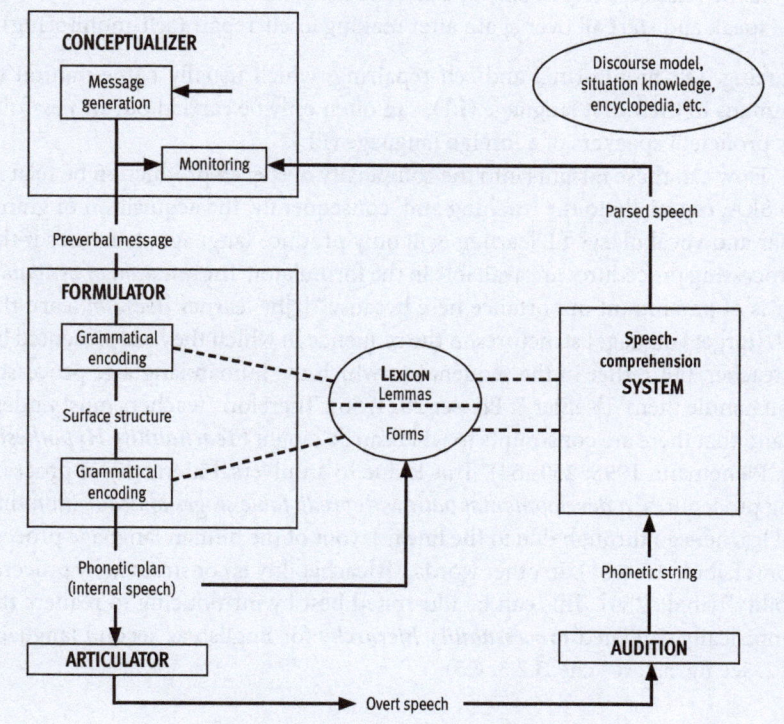

| Fig. 5.1

Psycholinguistic model of speech production (Levelt 1994: 91)

Speech production   A simple sentence such as 'I went to the movie theater yesterday' would involve the following processes (cf. Levelt 1994: 90–92):

▶ *Conceptualizer*: the speaker conceives of his/her communicative intention. He/she wants to share information about where he/she went yesterday.
▶ *Formulator*: for this message to be uttered, the speaker needs to cast it in a linguistic form. This means that he/she has to select appropriate words (lemmas) and word forms from the lexicon (e.g., past tense of irregular verb 'go,' retrieving the right word for '*Kino*'). Then, the speaker has to put them into a correct syntactic order (e.g., SVO, time adverbial at the end of the sentence). At the end of this sub-process, the speaker arrives at a surface structure of his/her utterance, which then needs to be encoded phonologically (internal speech).
▶ *Articulator*: the articulatory system (lungs, larynx, tongue, lips, etc.) transforms internal speech into audible speech (overt speech).
▶ *Audition*: the speaker listens to his/her own speech.
▶ *Speech comprehension system*: if the speech comprehension system detects speech errors or mistakes in the phonetic string the speaker parses his utterance (parsed speech). This means, he/she analyzes his/her utterance by breaking it down into smaller parts of speech and checking grammar, syntactic relations, etc. In case of a serious error, the speaker may even stop to speak and start all over again after making a self-repair (self-monitoring).

Parsing, self-monitoring, and self-repairing, which usually come natural to humans in their first language (L1), can often only be carried out successfully by proficient speakers of a foreign language (FL).

Processability and   How can these insights into the complexity of speech production be related
teachability   to SLA, especially to the teaching and, consequently, the acquisition of grammar and vocabulary? FL learners will only produce language structures if the processing procedures are available in the formulator. The *question of availability* is of paramount importance here because "[t]he learner *does not* learn the TL [target language] structures in the sequence in which they are presented by a teacher, but rather in the sequence in which the human language processor can handle them" (Keßler & Plesser 2011: 86). Therefore, teachers must understand that there are constraints to what can be taught (*Teachability Hypothesis*, cf. Pienemann 1998: 250–64). This is due to a universal hierarchy of processing procedures, *a developmental path with predictable stages of acquisition* that all learners go through due to the linear layout of the human language processor (cf. ibid.: 169–81). In other words, "[t]eachability is constrained by processability" (ibid.: 250). This can be illustrated best by introducing to readers the empirically validated *processability hierarchy* for English as second language (L2, see fig. 5.2; see chs. 3.2.3, 4.5):

Processing procedure	Universal L2 process	English Morphology	English Syntax
6 **Subordinate clause procedure**	Main and sub-ordinate clause		▶ *Neg/auxiliary-2nd?* Why ***doesn't*** he go home? ▶ *Cancel inversion:* I wonder why he sold the car.
5 **Sentence proce-dure**	Interphrasal information exchange	▶ *Interphrasal mor-phemes (e. g., subject-verb-agreement):* ***He*** get***s*** up at six o'clock.	▶ *Passive construction:* The ball was kicked by Peter. ▶ *Wh-auxiliary-2nd:* Why ***did*** he sell the car? ▶ *Wh-copula inversion:* Where ***has*** he gone?
4 **Verb phrase pro-cedure**	Interphrasal information exchange		▶ *Yes/no inversion:* ***Has*** he seen you? ▶ *Wh-copula:* ***Where is*** John? ▶ *Copula inversion:* ***Is*** John at home?
3 **Phrasal procedure**	Phrasal infor-mation exchange	▶ *Phrasal mor-phemes (e. g., noun phrase agreement):* ***two*** boys ▶ *Neg + verb:* *Me ***no*** go home.	▶ *Adverb first:* ****In the morning,*** he drink coffee. ▶ *Do-fronting:* ***Do*** you like it? ****Do*** he go home? ▶ *Wh-SVO-?* ****Why*** he go home? ▶ *Aux-SVO-?* ***Can*** he go home?
2 **Category procedure**	Lexical mor-phemes	▶ *Plural:* boy***s*** ▶ *Past -ed:* Walk***ed***	▶ *Canonical order (SVO)-Ques-tion:* *He go home? ▶ *Canonical order (SVO):* *He go home.
1 **Word / lemma**	'Words' / for-mulae	*Various lexical items (e. g., finite verbs, short sentences), which are stored as one unit in the learner's mind. No creative use of those items.* Hi. / How are you? / What's your name?	

Fig. 5.2

Processability hierar-chy for English as L2 from advanced (6) to beginners (1) (Piene-mann in Keßler & Plesser 2011: 86–87, adapted)

It is important that this developmental path is understood as a *hierarchical order* in the sense that (1) no stage can be skipped; (2) learners need to master one stage before they can enter the next; (3) with each stage, the morphologi-cal as well as syntactical structures – and thus the challenges for the language learner – become more complex, and, most importantly; (4) the developmen-tal path cannot be altered or sped up by classroom instruction. Consequently, *grammar instruction will be ineffective if the developmental state of individual learners is not diagnosed or simply ignored.* One useful diagnostic tool is Rapid Profile (cf. Keßler 2006, Keßler & Liebner 2011).

The third-person -s: Why do learners omit it?

One famous example that runs through the secondary literature on SLA is that of the *third-person -s* (see ch. 3.2.3), which is taught in the first year of English language teaching. According to the processability hierarchy, the third-person -s is only acquired at *stage five*. Teachers, who have always wondered why students just do not internalize the mnemonic verse '*he/she/it – s muss mit!*' and fail to attach the third-person -s to the verb, might be relieved to find the answer to this phenomenon in SLA research: "[T]he processes required for this attachment are complex [...]. Subject-verb agreement happens across phrase boundaries and is, thus, a more complex task for the human mind than to achieve agreement within one and the same phrase." (Keßler & Plesser 2011: 89, cf. Ellis 2006: 88) Producing the third-person -s requires of learners to match number (value: singular), person (value: 3), tense (value: present), and aspect (value: non-continuous; cf. Pienemann 2008: 19, Keßler & Plesser 2011: 89–90).

The processabiliy hierarchy also provides insights into **learner errors** (see chs. 3.2.3, 12.6). Learners, as they go through the various stages of the developmental path, cannot and will not speak 'proper English' right away in the sense that their language production will be free of errors and mistakes. Teachers must understand and accept the fact that *learner errors are a natural part of SLA* (cf. Ellis 2002). They are, in fact, an *indicator* of the "learner's current level of processing" (Pienemann 2005: 48), which Selinker (1972) termed '*Interlanguage*':

Interlanguage

> IL posits that learners are involved in a continual process of hypothesis formulation and testing. As new elements of L2 are acquired, language is tested and assessed. L2 items are also constructed through analogy with items and rules already known. This may be carried out subconsciously, along with the processing of feedback and how this may or may not change the IL as the learner moves along the continuum. The changes may bring the IL closer to the desired L2 form, but not necessarily. (Cherrington 2000: 307)

According to Selinker (1972: 215–20), IL utterances result from the following *five cognitive processes* at work in the learner's mind:

▶ *Language transfer*: interference from the L1, often identifiable in German learners by their overuse of the present perfect instead of simple past
▶ *Transfer-of-training*: items of the L2 language training procedures; for example, if a teacher repeatedly provides activities in which the third-person -s is trained exclusively by using the pronoun 'he,' then students might produce 'he' for both 'she' and 'it'
▶ *Strategies of L2 learning*: approaches by the learner to the material to be learned such as, for example, reducing the TL to simpler norms
▶ *Strategies of L2 communication*: approaches by the learner to communicate with native speakers of the TL
▶ *Overgeneralization of TL linguistic material*: rules and semantic features (see fig. 5.3)

| Fig. 5.3
Example of overgen-
eralization (Light-
bown & Spada 2006:
16)

The boy in the picture has acquired the simple past tense of regular verbs. However, he has not yet acquired the difference between regular and irregular verb
inflection. He simply attaches the regular past-tense suffix '-ed' to the irregular
verb 'put' and thus overgeneralizes a previously acquired grammatical structure. The conversational recast (*korrigierendes Rückkopplungssignal*) provided
by the adult goes unnoticed because "the boy does not see the mother's correction to be a morphological one (*putted vs. put) but a semantic one (I vs. you)"
(Keßler & Plesser 2011: 44).

Teachers must understand that many of the errors learners make are due   Errors and mistakes
to the stage they find themselves in on the developmental path. This requires
teachers to make use of their *diagnostic skills* in order to discern where each
individual learner is at in his/her IL development. Learners will benefit from
classroom instruction and language learning material that exposes them to
"structures from 'the next stage'" (Pienemann 1998: 250), which are *structures
they are close to acquiring*. This, of course, is easier said than done because
teachers will encounter great variation in the pace of IL development across
increasingly heterogeneous learner groups. Heterogeneity calls for differentiation in terms of teaching methods, instructional material, activities, etc. (see
chs. 4.3, 6.3, 10.3.2). Should teachers then simply ignore errors and mistakes?
To answer this question, one must distinguish between *developmental errors
and variational mistakes* (cf. Keßler & Plesser 2011: 110–13).

▶ *Developmental error*: if a learner makes an error because he/she has not yet
  reached the specific stage in the processability hierarchy, correction will be
  ineffective for this individual learner. However, it might be beneficial for
  others who have already advanced further along the developmental path

and have thus already entered this stage. Salient examples of developmental errors include, for example, the omission of plural -s, the omission of third-person -s, the overuse of the article 'the' (and corresponding under-use of 'a'), the double comparative (e. g., *'more faster'), resumptive pronouns in relative clauses (e. g., *'The man who my sister had married him'), and process verbs (e. g., *'The size was increased greatly'; cf. Ellis 2002: 22).

▶ *Variational mistake*: if a learner makes a mistake although he/she has already entered the respective developmental stage, this mistake must receive corrective feedback. This is vital for the student not only to help him/her along the developmental path and prepare him/her for the next stage, but also to avoid the fossilization of a simplified IL version.

Helpful books on common learner errors and mistakes are *The Mistakes Clinic for German-speaking Learners of English* (Parkes 2003), the *Longman Dictionary of Common Errors* (Turton & Heaton 2004), and *Learner English: A Teacher's Guide to Interference and Other Problems* (Swan & Smith 2013).

> Recapitulate and reflect on what has been stated in this section about (1) processability and teachability, (2) Interlanguage theory, and (3) learner errors.

5.2 | Teaching and learning grammar

5.2.1 | Choices and approaches

Deductive and inductive grammar teaching

In instructional settings as well as in secondary literature on grammar teaching, a basic distinction is usually made between *deductive and inductive approaches* to teaching grammar (cf. Larsen-Freeman 2011, Timmis 2012). In the *deductive approach*, a grammar rule is presented by the teacher, then practiced by the learners, and often tested at the end of the grammar teaching sequence. *Inductive approaches* provide rich input in which a grammatical structure is repeated several times so that students can discover the rule on their own. While the deductive approach is usually more explicit in its treatment of grammatical rules, it would be wrong to assume that the inductive approach treats grammar rules only implicitly:

> In inductive learning the teacher first presents a couple of examples and the learners are supposed to discover the rules from the examples. This inductive approach to grammar teaching, however, is not an implicit but an explicit one. Inductive and implicit learning of language rules hardly ever takes place in foreign language but is rather a feature of first language acquisition as it is learning from the full and rich input of the target language without any providing of grammar rules. (Keßler & Plesser 2011: 28)

Consequently, teachers are required to take "an informed and principled approach to grammar teaching" (Timmis 2012: 119). They need to consider it from many *different angles* to come to an informed conclusion as to how to teach grammar and to be able to *combine different approaches* in order to address different learner groups and types (see ch. 6.2.2). For example, some learners may profit from inductive, less explicit grammar teaching, while others may prefer a deductive, more explicit introduction to new grammatical structures.

The historical account of FL teaching methodology has already drawn attention to the fact that the role of grammar is a different one in the respective methods and *remains disputed to this day* (cf. Timmis 2012: 119; see chs. 1.1, 3.2, 4.2). The *Grammar-Translation Method* was based on rote learning of grammatical rules and language features, deductive teaching of prescriptive grammar rules and a detailed meta-analysis of grammar, as well as on strict adherence to grammatical accuracy. With the advent of the *Direct Method*, inductive teaching of grammar was introduced, and the focus shifted from grammar to lexical items and chunks important to everyday communication. The *Audiolingual and Audiovisual Methods* sought to arrive at grammatical accuracy through pattern drills and rigid error correction with little or no explicit grammar instruction. Against the background of today's *communicative approach to FL teaching*, knowledge of grammar is considered a part of communicative competence. However, while we might have arrived at a communicative approach to FL teaching theoretically, in day-to-day teaching practices, the remnants of teaching methods, such as pattern drills, gap-fill exercises, etc., appear ever so often.

The role of grammar in different methods

Grammar teaching still meets criticism: Ellis notes that "problems of selection probably explain why grammatical syllabuses are so similar and have changed so little over the years; it is safer to follow what has been done before" (2006: 89). Grammar teaching still tends to favor form over meaning and neglects teaching English as it is spoken in actual use. It treats grammatical structures in isolation, usually follows along the way grammar is presented in the textbook, and exposes students to inauthentic language material, which is tailor-made to teach a single grammatical structure. Regarding grammar in textbooks, Lenzing (2008: 221) contests that "crucial insights into how learners acquire a language have not been considered in the design of curricula and textbooks" and, consequently, calls into question "*whether the learning goals that are promoted in the textbooks are realistic ones*" (ibid., emphasis added):

The trouble with teaching grammar

▶ Grammar progression in textbooks is said to progress from simple to complex structures. *However, this claim lacks a theoretical rationale*. As can be deduced from the example of the third-person -s, textbooks very often run counter to SLA research and findings (*processability*).
▶ The *density* of grammatical structures presented in textbooks as well as the *pace of grammatical progression* is often overwhelming. For example, the

textbook *English G 21: A1* (Schwarz 2013) for grade 5 covers personal pronouns + be, can/can't, imperatives, have got/has got, there's/there are, simple present statements, the plural of nouns, possessive determiners, the s-genitive, simple present questions, the present progressive, the simple past, word order in subordinate clauses, and the going to-future.

▶ Large sections of textbooks are apportioned to grammar exercises and the explanation of grammatical rules in the grammar file. However, it remains questionable whether this explicit treatment of rules helps students in their *IL development* and in how far it aids the transfer of *declarative into procedural knowledge*.

What is more, in isolated lessons on grammar, the classroom atmosphere often does not encourage learners to become *active participators in meaningful communication* (cf. Bleyhl & Timm 2007: 270). Consequently, grammar teaching – more often than not – still 'produces' learners who might do well in isolated test formats (see ch. 12.4.3), but who fail to perform well in communicative situations.

> Look at current textbooks and discuss how grammar is presented in them.

5.2.2 | Selected approaches

Explicit and implicit knowledge

Acknowledging that "research is some way from being able to offer conclusive evidence in favour of particular approaches or positions" (Timmis 2012: 119), a **weak interface position**, which suggests that explicit and implicit knowledge "can work cooperatively in any given instance" (Gass 2013: 286, cf. Ellis 2006), should be favored. Ellis (2007: 20) explains *the role that explicit knowledge plays in SLA*:

> [E]xplicit knowledge plays various roles (1) in the perception of, and selective attending to, L2 form by facilitating the processes of 'noticing' (i. e. paying attention to specific linguistic features of the input), (2) by 'noticing the gap' (i. e. comparing the noticed features with those the learner typically produces in output), and (3) in output, with explicit knowledge coaching practice, particularly in initial stages, with this controlled use of declarative knowledge guiding the proceduralization and eventual automatization of language processing, as it does in the acquisition of other cognitive skills.

Relying on SLA research, Keßler and Plesser (2011: 60) conclude "that an adequate focus on form in the L2 classroom can be conducive to the SLA process". However, teachers should *avoid teaching grammar as linear textbook progression and abandon the idea of learner grammar as developing in a linear way*. SLA "is a gradual, cumulative, [and] often non-linear process" (Long 2005: 3).

If the power of teachers regarding grammar instruction is limited, *should or can grammar be taught at all?* Keßler and Plesser (2011: 35–36, adapted) make a strong case for teaching grammar:

► Any use of language (spoken or written) *is grammar*; grammar can be seen as the *backbone not only of language but also of literature*: without being able to change the syntax, we would always have to stick to the same sentence pattern and thus make communication rather monotonous.
► Grammar is a system of finite rules that can generate *an infinite number of utterances*; teaching grammar can help us understand that system in more detail and put learners into the position of having a choice between different ways of expressing something.
► Quite a number of grammar rules can be transferred from one language into another; teaching grammar concepts (e. g., nouns, verbs, number, gender, tenses, aspect) in both the L1 and the FL supports *successful language use by native and non-native speakers.*

In the following, *three approaches* to teaching grammar in the EFL classroom are outlined. The examples presented are not meant as templates but as suggestions, for "*any 'ready-made' recipes do not cater for individual classroom situations and individual leaners' needs*" (Keßler & Plesser 2011: 170–71, emphasis added). Teachers are encouraged to follow an approach that Timmis (2012: 128) calls "principled eclecticism," resulting in the challenge "to match the approach with the type of learner and the type of language structure" (ibid.): "[W]hat is important is to recognize what options are available, what the theoretical rationales for these options are, and what the problems are with these rationales. This is the starting point for developing *a personal theory of grammar teaching.*" (Ellis 2006: 103, emphasis added)

Focus on form

Focus on form (FonF, Long 1991) must not be confused with *Focus on formS* (FonS): "[F]ocus on form *entails* a focus on formal elements of language, whereas focus on formS is *limited* to such a focus" (Doughty & Williams 1998: 4). The latter often creates questionable teaching scenarios "where students spend much of their time working on isolated linguistic structures in a sequence predetermined externally and imposed on them by a syllabus designer or textbook writer, in conflict with the learner's internal syllabus" (Doughty & Long 2003: 64).

Within the context of FonF methodology, students *noticing* a grammatical feature and then being able to integrate it into their IL can be explained as follows (Keßler & Plesser 2011: 152, adapted):

- ▸ *Noticing*: the learner registers a particular linguistic form in communication or instructional material.
- ▸ *Comparing – noticing the gap*: the learner compares the linguistic feature noticed in the input with his/her own mental grammar, registering to what extent there is a 'gap' between the input and his/her IL.
- ▸ *Integrating*: the learner integrates a representation of the new linguistic feature into his/her IL.

For a grammatical feature to be noticed by students, teachers should make use of implicit and explicit **Input Enhancement techniques** (see fig. 5.4):

Fig. 5.4		Feedback (Teacher)	Material
Input Enhancement techniques (based on Keßler & Plesser 2011: 153, adapted)	**Implicit**	▸ *Recasts:* S: 'I want read.' T: 'Oh, you want to read?' ▸ *Clarification requests:* S: 'What the woman do?' T: 'I don't understand. What do you mean?' ▸ *Oral equivalent of textual enhancement through stress, intonation, gestures:* S: 'I have seen her yesterday.' T: 'You saw her yesterday?'	▸ *Visual textual enhancement via typographical alterations*: italicizing, boldface type, color coding, etc. ▸ *Input flooding:* T (wants to introduce the use of the preposition 'on' and provides many examples of its use): 'My books are on the table. You are sitting on your chairs. The answers are on the blackboard. There is a stain on my shirt.' ▸ *Task-essential language*: requires a learner to use a target structure in order to complete a given activity
	Explicit	▸ *Metalinguistic feedback:* S: 'Where he is study?' T: 'Well, watch out for your grammar. You need to use the -ing-form after auxiliary verbs to indicate the present progressive. And you need to reverse the place of auxiliary and subject – Where is he studying?' ▸ *Negative evidence through overt error correction:* S: 'Last weekend I go shopping and do homework.' T: 'No, that's not exactly how we would say that. Remember that you are talking about the past. The correct sentence is – Last weekend I went shopping and did my homework.'	▸ *Processing instruction:* T provides a sample sentence with a grammatical structure; the learners have to understand the underlying grammatical structure in order to capture the meaning of the sentence.

Input Enhancement can help learners to '*notice the gap*' and facilitates SLA. With FonF, teachers can select from two options: (1) *proactive FonF* (teachers prepare instructional materials that facilitate the elicitation of a grammatical structure) and (2) *reactive FonF* (a grammatical structure comes into focus only if the need arises). An example of proactive FonF is provided in figure 5.5.

Input Enhancement activity	T provides enriched material: S listen to a dialog between two individuals talking about their last holiday.
Production activity	Pair work: T asks S to talk to each other about their last holiday.
Main task	Picture description task: S are given a picture sequence which shows an individual carrying out different activities. The title says that these pictures refer to a past event. S are asked to describe the pictures.

| Fig. 5.5

Proactive FonF
focusing on past -ed
(Keßler & Plesser
2011: 150, adapted)

Task-based Language Teaching

| 5.2.2.2

Task-based Language Teaching (TBLT, see ch. 4.3.2) focuses more on meaning than on form. It draws on *learner-learner interaction* by posing tasks:

> Classroom tasks should facilitate meaningful interaction and offer the learner ample opportunity to process meaningful input and produce meaningful output in order to reach relevant and obtainable goals. In other words, tasks invite the learner to act primarily as a language *user*, and not as a language *learner*. (Van den Branden 2006: 6–9)

Tasks in TBLT

TBLT draws attention to the *process* of working on a given task: there is a distinct focus on how students work on the task(s) and on the process by which they arrive at results. Tasks in TBLT should adhere to a *well-structured framework* (see ch. 4, fig. 4.2). The *teacher's role* in TBLT is mainly that of a motivator, advisor, and facilitator in the pre-task phase, of a monitor and supporter during the task cycle, and of moderator, exemplifier, and evaluator in the post-task phase (see fig. 5.6).

Pre-task
► *Aim*: to introduce the topic of celebrations and to give S exposure to language related to them.
► *Activation*: T shows S pictures of a celebration (e. g., a family celebrating Christmas or someone's birthday). T tells S how the celebration went. T uses the pictures to provide as many details as possible.
► *Pre-activity*: T distributes a card with the following questions and has S answer them. When was your last family celebration? Which are some of the special occasions you celebrate with family or friends? What is your favorite celebration with friends or family? What was the last celebration you had with your family or friends? How was it? What details make a celebration a success? Do you remember an especially happy celebration with friends or family? What happened?

| Fig. 5.6

Example of TBLT
(Rodríguez-Bonces
& Rodríguez-Bonces
2010: 172–74,
adapted)

Task cycle		
Task	**Planning**	**Report**
► T tells S (in groups of four) that they will plan a celebration including all aspects around it like invitation cards or a newspaper article to report all the facts about the celebration. ► The groups discuss possibilities for a celebration and brainstorm vocabulary (e. g., kinds of celebrations, objects used for certain celebrations). ► T provides grading schemes so that S know how they will be assessed. ► T monitors and answers questions.	► S (in groups) plan their celebration (e. g., Christmas, Halloween, birthday, 4ᵗʰ of July). T provides a task card which explains the process and requirements. ► S prepare to report. ► T checks how roles and assignments are distributed within the group (all S should be involved). ► T provides language feedback.	► The classroom is divided. Each group is assigned a place in the classroom to decorate the environment for their celebration. ► S present, classmates listen and participate in the celebration. They can ask questions after the presentation. ► T gives feedback on the content and comments on it briefly. ► S vote and choose the best presentation.

Post-task: language focus	
Analysis	**Practice**
► T writes selected sentences uttered by S on the board. ► T highlights language structures that need to be addressed. ► S review phrases in context and take notes of the language they need.	► Option A (in the classroom): each S asks two questions about one of the celebrations. ► Option B (at home): T assigns homework to practice new words or structures.

Evaluation
► S complete a task evaluation form ► T completes grading schemes

5.2.2.3 | Acquisition-based Method

The Acquisition-based Method (ABM, *erwerbsorientier Grammatikunterricht*; Ziegésar & Ziegésar 2007, 2009) suggests teaching grammar *inductively within authentic communicative situations* (see fig. 5.7). Ziegésar and Ziegésar (2007: 292–97, 2009: 9–23) propose that teachers proceed through the following five phases:

Phases
1. *Demonstration*: the teacher presents the grammatical structure in a typical communicative context, which provides rich, holistic, and lively input. The grammatical structure is repeated up to 15 times.
2. *Understanding and reacting*: the students show their understanding of the structure by reacting to, for example, questions by the teacher with language structures they have already acquired.

102

3. *Reproduction*: the students use the grammatical structure for the first time in a guided teacher-student dialog.
4. *Clarification and focusing*: the teacher engages students in a classroom discussion through which students should discover the grammatical rule. An explanation of the rule follows.
5. *Production*: the students apply the structure in meaningful ways in team or partner practice (e. g., information gap tasks).

Demonstration

T: You all know quite a lot of English now. One day you'll speak it so well that you'll be able to go to Britain for a holiday. If you go to Britain you'll need a passport or identity card, of course. If you don't have these documents they won't let you into the country (*T shows S his/her own passport*). Now let's think about how you'll get there. How could you travel?

S: Fly or by train and ferry.

T: (*shows S a travel brochure and air connections on a transparency*) You can fly from Stuttgart to Heathrow. That takes just over an hour. Can you find Heathrow on the map? Or from Frankfurt to Manchester. It will be faster if you fly. But if you fly you won't see very much, will you? You'll see much more if you go by train and ferry.

T: (*shows S a timetable with ferry connections*) Let's see which way you can go. If you go this way, through Belgium, you'll get to Ostend (*S mark travel routes and connections on a map*). If you get on a ferry in Ostend you'll arrive at Ramsgate. Who can show us the Ostend-Ramsgate route on the map? That's a long way. If you go from Ostend you'll be on the ferry for about four and a half hours. So let's find a different route (*to be continued with more alternative routes*). Now, let's say you've arrived in Britain and you haven't been seasick. Let's think about what you're going to do. If you go to London you'll see lots of famous sights. But then you won't see much of the rest of the country if you stay there all the time, will you? What would you like to see in Britain? (*S comment*)

Understanding and reacting

T: (*prepares copies of traffic signs, prohibition signs, notices*) When you arrive in Britain you'll probably see some of these notices. Let's see if you can understand them all. Listen. Which notice am I talking about? 1. They won't let you into the country if you haven't got one.

S: Passports.

T: That's right. Can you go on? Which notice is this? (*to be continued with more false statements by T and corrections by S*)

Reproduction

T: (*challenges students with false statements about British customs and conventions and writes statements with highlighted words on the blackboard*) Let's imagine you're going to Britain on holiday. Let's see if you know everything you'll need to know. Tell me if this is right: You **won't** need a passport if you **go** to Britain.

S: That's wrong. You **will** need a passport if you **go** to Britain (*to be continued with more false statements by T and corrections by S*).

Clarification and focusing

T asks students for regularities. S should recognize and explain the underlying grammatical structure of Conditional I (simple present in conditional subordinate clause, will-future in main clause).

Production

T provides student pairs with tandem sheets with tips for going to Britain that differ on each of the two sheets. S1 has to ask S2 for tips and vice versa (information gap exercise).

Fig. 5.7

Example of ABM (Ziegésar & Ziegésar 2007: 292–98, adapted)

Mindmap 1

How learning

vocabulary

works

Discuss possible advantages and disadvantages of these three approaches to grammar teaching. Consider, for example, (1) the relation between meaning and form, (2) the explicitness/implicitness of the approach, (3) the time and material needed.

5.3 | Teaching and learning vocabulary

5.3.1 | Psycholinguistic basics

mental lexicon

How words are presented in our minds = Storage

Referring back to Levelt's model of speech production (see fig. 5.1), speech production only works if the *mental lexicon* feeds words into the formulator so that they can be grammatically encoded. Structured like a *network*, the mental lexicon contains *a myriad of information about lexical items and their connections to each other*: "Our lexical knowledge includes information about a word's spelling, its pronunciation (including numerous variants), its word-class, its possible meanings, its derivations, its reference to synonyms, antonyms and collocations, its register and numerous connotations." (Hutz 2012: 106) To illustrate this, one may look at the lexical complexity of the simple word 'bird' (in extracts):

What is behind a word?

- ▶ *Pronunciation*: /bɜ ː (ɹ)d/
- ▶ *Spelling*: bird
- ▶ *Morphology*: substantive (word class), birds (plural)
- ▶ *Syntax*: subject or object
- ▶ *Conceptual meaning*: a two-legged creature with feathers and wings, which lays eggs and can usually fly
- ▶ *Referential meaning*: 'bird' (British slang: a girl or a young woman), 'for the birds' (slang: useless or worthless, not to be taken seriously), 'a rare, odd, clever bird' (informal: denoting a person), 'to kill two birds with one stone' (idiom: to accomplish two things with one action), 'birds of a feather' (idiom: people with the same ideas or interests), 'the birds and the bees' (idiom: basic information about sex and reproduction), etc.

The above list is far from complete, for the word 'bird' is also used as a verb: 'to bird' (catching or shooting birds). The list goes on with back-formation lexemes such as 'to bird-watch' (identifying wild birds and observing them in their natural habitat) and 'to bird-nest' (plundering bird nests). Furthermore, in sports, 'bird' can also denote a clay pigeon or shuttlecock and in informal use, an aircraft, a spacecraft, or a guided missile.

To know a word

A synonym is a word you use when you can't spell the other one. –
Baltasar Gracián

According to the *Common European Framework of Reference for Languages* (CEF), "[l]*exical competence*, knowledge of, and ability to use, the vocabulary of a language, consists of lexical elements and grammatical elements" (Council of Europe 2001: 110, emphasis added). Thus, complete knowledge of a word means to be able to *recognize and perform* the following (see fig. 5.8):

Form	
Spoken	▸ *Receptive*: what does the word sound like? ▸ *Productive*: how is the word pronounced?
Written	▸ *Receptive*: what does the word look like? ▸ *Productive*: how is the word written and spelled?
Position	
Grammatical patterns	▸ *Receptive*: in what patterns does the word occur? ▸ *Productive*: in what patterns must we use the word?
Collocations	▸ *Receptive*: what words or types of words can be expected before or after the word? ▸ *Productive*: what words or types of words must we use with this word?
Function	
Frequency	▸ *Receptive*: how common is the word? ▸ *Productive*: how often should the word be used?
Appropriateness	▸ *Receptive*: where would we expect to meet this word? ▸ *Productive*: where can this word be used?
Meaning	
Concept	▸ *Receptive*: what does the word mean? ▸ *Productive*: what word should be used to express this meaning?
Associations	▸ *Receptive*: what other words does this word make us think of? ▸ *Productive*: what other words could we use instead of this one?

Fig. 5.8

Lexical competence
(Nation 1990: 31, adapted)

How does the mental lexicon store this enormous amount of information? In order for words to be retrieved in milliseconds, the mental lexicon is *craftily organized*:

Organization of the mental lexicon

▸ Lexical items which are semantically related seem to be stored together. *Syntagmatic relations*, such as *synonymy* (e.g., 'to start'/'to begin', 'furious'/'angry'/'enraged', 'deep'/'profound'), *antonymy* (e.g., 'fast'/'slow', 'rich'/'poor') or *hyponymy* (e.g., 'flower' – 'daisy', 'furniture' – 'table') seem to play an important role in connecting words in the mind. In this case, words that belong to the same *word class* (e.g., adjectives) are strongly associated with each other.
▸ Lexical items which often co-occur in the same context seem to be stored together. These so-called *paradigmatic relations* (e.g., collocational links such as 'to ride a bicycle', 'to quench one's thirst', 'to make hay', 'a juvenile delinquent', 'a burning/keen/passionate/strong/unfulfilled desire') consist of adjective-noun pairs or verb-noun pairs that are frequently used together.
▸ Lexical items which have a *similar sound structure* seem to be stored together. Such '*clang associations*' can be found, for example, in word pairs such as 'consolation' and 'compensation' or 'merry' and 'Mary'. (Hutz 2012: 106, adapted)

Word retrieval

Considering that "[i]n normal fluent speech, we retrieve words at a rate of two or three per second" and usually "hit the appropriate words, sure as a gun, in a huge lexicon containing several tens of thousands of items" (Levelt 1994: 96), *speaking* is truly a fascinating capability. However, sometimes the way our mental lexicon organizes words along the structures delineated above gets in the way and speakers produce unwittingly hilarious utterances: 'perple' (blend of people/person, intended: 'people'), 'I must let the house out of the cat' (syntactic misordering, intended: 'I must let the cat out of the house'), 'foon speeding' (phonological speech error, intended: 'spoon feeding').

The relationship between the L1 and L2 lexicons

Of what nature is the relationship between the L1 and L2 lexicons? SLA research offers differing theories on this, but what has come to be called the **Subset Hypothesis** (*lexical items of the L1 and L2 are stored in the mental lexicon as different sub-sets with close connections*) is credited the most. The Subset Hypothesis accounts for L1 interference and code switching (cf. Hutz 2012: 110). Due to the *restricted quality and quantity of lexical input* learners receive in the FL classroom, the L2 lexicon will never cover as many lexical items as the L1 lexicon. The depth of knowledge about these items in terms of form, meaning, and use is often incomplete.

> With your knowledge about word retrieval, the organization of the mental lexicon, and the relation between the L1 and L2 lexicons, explain what went wrong in the following utterances:
> 1) 'He hit me so hardly that it gave me a black eye.'
> 2) 'I love to color eggs for Christmas.'
> 3) 'The accident I witnessed yesterday was torrible.'

Which words to know and how many?

The good news is that – once acquired – *"lexical knowledge is very stable"* (De Bot 2000: 410, emphasis added). While native speakers are estimated to have a vocabulary of *20,000* word families (that is a *passive lexicon* of around *75,000* words and an *active lexicon* of about *30,000* words), FL learners "will be lucky to have acquired *5,000* word families even after several years of study" (Thornbury 2002: 20, emphasis added). Nation and Chung (2011: 543) state that for FL learners "it takes at least a year, and usually much longer, to increase vocabulary size by a thousand words". An estimated *400 to 700* words are supposed to be taught in an average school year (depending on the learner group, a maximum of 10 to 20 new words per lesson; cf. Reinisch 2013: 102). However, *teaching vocabulary does not necessarily result in vocabulary acquisition.* Therefore, working on extending vocabulary size is as much the responsibility of teachers as it is that of students. If *meaningful communication* is to take place in the FL classroom as soon as possible, then "[t]here is a strong argument [...] for equipping learners with a core vocabulary of *2,000* words as soon as possible" (Thornbury 2002: 21, emphasis added). These **high-frequency words** can be found in the classic *General Service List of English Words* (GSL, West 1953) and, as an updated version, in the *New General Service List* (NGSL, Browne et al. 2013; www.newgeneralservicelist.org). This core vocabulary accounts for most of the words occurring in normal conversations and "cover[s] between 80 % and 90 % of the running words in a text" (Nation & Chung 2011: 545). These 2,000 words should be considered the *threshold level*. Thornbury (2002: 21) recommends a basic vocabulary of *3,000* and, for more specialized needs, *5,000* word families. For learners wanting to pursue academic studies in English, Nation and Chung (2011: 545) recommend the *Academic Word List* (AWL, Coxhead 2010; www.victoria.ac.nz/lals/resources/academicwordlist). The CEF, too, recommends "to follow *lexico-statistical principles* selecting the highest frequency words in large general word-counts or those undertaken for restricted thematic areas" (Council of Europe 2001: 151, emphasis added). However, the CEF also points out *other options of lexical selection*:

▶ To select key words and phrases 1) in thematic areas required for the achievement of *communicative tasks relevant to learner needs*, 2) which embody *cultural difference and/or significant values and beliefs* shared by the social group(s) whose language is being learned

▶ To select (authentic) *spoken and written texts* and learn/teach whatever words they contain

▶ Not to pre-plan vocabulary development, but to allow it to *develop organically* in response to learner demand when engaged in communicative tasks (ibid.: 150–51, adapted)

> Have a look at the vocabulary file in a current textbook and assess according to which principle(s) lexical selection has been made. Discuss your findings.

'Words', he said, 'is oh such a twitch-tickling problem to me all my life. So you must simply try to be patient and stop squibbling. As I am telling you before, I know exactly what words I am wanting to say, but somehow or other they is always getting squiff-squiddled around.' – Roald Dahl

Structuring vocabulary lessons

| 5.3.2

Just as with grammar, one needs to *differentiate* between vocabulary teaching and vocabulary acquisition. While the teaching of vocabulary is an *externally controlled process*, the actual acquisition of vocabulary is largely a *self-regulated process* carried out by learners in order to consolidate and increase their vocabulary size (cf. Stork 2003: 39).

With *beginners*, teachers should use a ***systematic approach*** (Doyé 1985, Neveling 2010: 333–34) with four phases:

Introducing vocabulary to beginners: a systematic approach

1. *Presentation* (*Darbietungsphase*): words are introduced in a multichannel fashion (see fig. 5.9) in order to appeal to as many senses as possible (auditory, visual, olfactory, gustatory, and tactile). Words should be introduced in meaningful contexts that clarify their meaning and use in the TL. Correct pronunciation is trained. While the written form may be introduced, correct spelling is of secondary importance in this phase.

2. *Practicing (Übungsphase)*: the integration of the words into the mental lexicon is facilitated by different exercises and activities. The form of these exercises needs to cater to the inherent structure of the mental lexicon (syntagmatic, paradigmatic). It is also important to link these words to vocabulary
previously learned. Pronunciation and spelling are practiced, as are a variety of learning techniques and strategies that help students file, structure,
and learn vocabulary in systematic ways.

3. *Application (Integrationsphase)*: this phase is more communicative in nature
than phase two. In other words, the lexical items need to be embedded in
meaningful communication in order to help students understand and practice syntagmatic connections (e. g., syntax, collocations).

4. *Assessment (Überprüfungsphase)*: the testing of lexical knowledge should
mirror the ways in which lexical items were introduced by the teacher. This
means that the multichannel way of vocabulary introduction in the presentation phase should reappear in test formats. This, in turn, means that
vocabulary testing "should go beyond knowledge of decontextualized items"
(Laufer & Goldstein 2004: 401) and instead "incorporate communicative
competence in addition to the knowledge of discrete items" (ibid.).

Ways of introducing
and explaining new
vocabulary

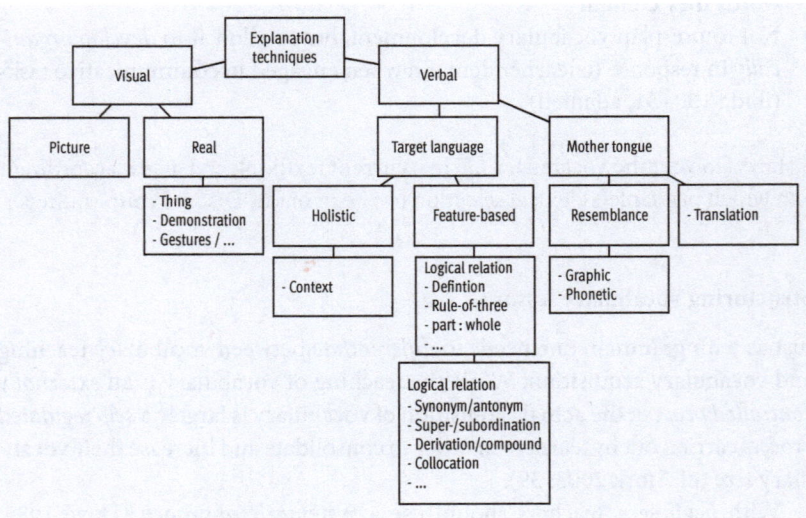

Fig. 5.9 |

Explanation tech-
niques (Quetz 2007:
277, adapted)

A closer look at the
presentation phase

The presentation phase should also involve a *negotiation of meaning* between
the teacher and the students, as in the following example (Quetz 2007: 281,
adapted):

T: Now our next word is 'to smell.' Now watch me and look at me. Now I'm smell-
ing. (*T schnüffelt*) Hmmmm. The smell is OK in here. It's not too bad. ... Now –
when you smell, what do you smell with? (*S schnüffeln*)

S1: Er – with my nose.

T: That's right. Yeah, you smell with your nose. And sometimes things also smell. And they can smell good, or they can smell …

S: (*mehrere murmeln*) … bad.

T: Right. … My socks, for example, smell terrible.

S2: (*leise*) Müllabfuhr …

While with beginners, the introduction of vocabulary proceeds in a rather systematic way, it should move in the direction of a more self-regulated process with intermediate and advanced students. The teaching activities as well as the learning strategies introduced in the next two sections should facilitate this.

> Practice presentation. How would you introduce and explain the following words/word fields:
> 1) to shout (verb)
> 2) tall (adjective)
> 3) handy (adjective)
> 3) vegetables (word field)
> 4) hobbies (word field)
> 5) hurricane (noun)
> 6) global warming (noun)

Teaching activities | 5.3.3

For the successful acquisition of vocabulary, teachers need to provide students with *repeated encounters* with words, create *communicative situations* in which students can use the words in various contexts to facilitate cognitive and affective depth, give them time for *vocabulary rehearsal*, and introduce *learning strategies* to use in the classroom and at home. Above all, teachers should remind students that increasing vocabulary size is a *lifelong undertaking that requires constant attention*: "As a teacher […], you should share your sense of the excitement and fascination of words with your students. Vocabulary learning never stops, even long after the grammar system is firmly in place." (Thornbury 2002: 160) The activities presented in the following should make for interesting vocabulary lessons (cf. Thornbury 2002: 145–59, Quetz 2007: 283–90, Nation 2012: 96–99, Hutz 2012: 112–13, Reinisch 2013: 104–15):

▶ *Structuring vocabulary:* word forks (see fig. 5.10), word ladders (see fig. 5.11), antonym/synonym-pairs, etc. all help to establish connections between words and increase vocabulary size and depth.

▶ *Guessing the category:* based on a list of ten words, students have to find one superordinate term that covers the ten words. This also works the other way around with students having to name words that fit into a general category

Fig. 5.10 |
Word fork (Hutz
2012: 115)

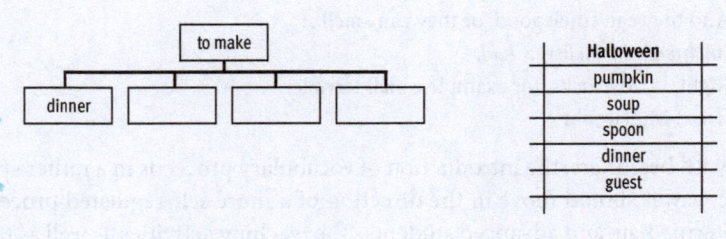

Fig. 5.11 |
Word ladder (Hutz
2012: 112)

(hyponymy/hyperonomy). Either way, these approaches also work very well when set up as a competition between students or student groups.

▸ *Word thieves*: while the teacher is reading out a text, students have to 'steal' words from it that fit into a general category provided by the teacher. For example, the teachers reads out a text about his/her Easter holidays and the learners have to detect and 'steal' words related to Easter (e. g., Easter egg, Easter bunny, Easter basket).

▸ *Word clouds*: using Internet tools such as Wordle (www.wordle.net) or Tagxedo (www.tagxedo.com), teachers create word clouds with lexical items that students then need to categorize into meaningful categories (see ch. 11.3).

▸ *Finding collocations*: the teacher provides students with a choice of words and students have to find suitable collocations.

▸ *Word cards*: originally a learning technique for vocabulary repetition, students' sets of word cards can also be employed fruitfully in the classroom. For example, students can teach each other words that they do not share in their set of word cards, students try to create a coherent sentence using two words from a word card set, etc. A useful digital tool to create and use word cards digitally is Quizlet (quizlet.com).

▸ *Vocabulary guesswork*: the teacher creates sentences with nonsense words and students have to guess the right word from the context provided by the sentence.

▸ *Associations*: words which students can combine with certain feelings and emotions help to enter their long-term memory. This can be achieved by presenting/drawing memorable pictures, employing/writing rhymes, or embedding words into funny or nonsense stories.

▸ *False friends*: Germans have a tendency to use English words in wrong ways (e. g., 'handy', 'public viewing') and are masters of inventing words that do not exist in English (e. g., 'smoking island' instead of 'smoking area', 'baby body' instead of 'onesie'). Working with lists of false friends is one way to draw students' attention to this phenomenon. Instead of merely using lists, however, three ingenious collections of German translation blunders by Robert Tonks (see fig. 5.12) are recommended here for classroom use: *It Is*

110

Not All English What Shines (2011), *Denglisch in Pool Position* (2012), *The Denglisch Doosh Reader* (2013). This may even motivate students and teachers to go on their own hunt for 'Denglish' in their neighborhood.

 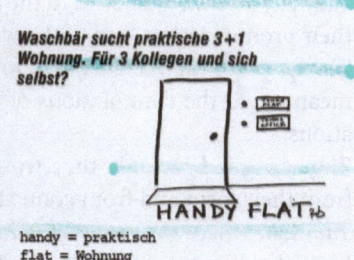

Fig. 5.12
Hilarious 'Denglish'
(Tonks 2012: 2; www.
robert-tonks.de)

► *Using dictionaries*: it goes without saying that teachers should train students in the basic skills of working with (online) dictionaries/thesauri (e. g., finding words fast; finding synonyms, antonyms; finding out about pronunciation, register, connotations, collocations, idioms). Working with dictionaries can also involve negotiation of meaning, as in the following example: teachers hand out copies with a text that contains a number of unfamiliar words. Individually, students make a shortlist of five words that they are allowed to look up in the dictionary. Students then compare their lists in pairs (and then in successively larger groups). This gives students the chance to explain the meaning of words that they do not have on their respective lists to each other. Finally, a class vote is executed and a final five-word list is created.
► *Vocabulary games*: integrating vocabulary games into the EFL classroom makes for refreshing learning scenarios. There are a number of board games and other (online) games such as Scrabble, Memory, and many more.
► *LearningApps*: this platform (learningapps.org) offers a wide range of motivating vocabulary learning and memorization activities, including matching exercises, quizzes, games such as the Millionaire game, grids, crosswords, etc. (see ch. 11.3)
► *Extensive reading*: reading texts suitable for students (e. g., graded readers) will help them improve their vocabulary size by taking up lexical items incidentally. It also trains them in decoding words from context.

The above list of teaching activities is far from complete. There are many more activities provided in books and online (cf. Nation 2008, Jentges 2009, Kilp 2010, Grimm & Riecken 2014).

From the activities listed above, choose three that you like most and three you do not really like. Discuss the choices made and the reasons for them. Collect more activities for motivating vocabulary lessons.

Mindmap 1

5.3.4 | Learning strategies

Successful learners

How voca...

learning ...

With regard to learning vocabulary and extending vocabulary size, successful learners apply the following *strategies* (Thornbury 2002: 144–45, adapted):

▶ *They pay attention to form*: to the constituents of words, to their spelling, to their pronunciation, and to the way they are stressed.
▶ *They pay attention to meaning*: to the way words are similar or different in meaning, to the connotations of words, to their style, and to their associations.
▶ *They are good guessers*: they work out the meanings of unfamiliar words from their form and from contextual clues.
▶ *They take risks and are not afraid of making mistakes*: they make the most of limited resources, and they adopt strategies to cope when the right words simply do not come forth.
▶ *They know how to organize their own learning*: by, for example, keeping a systematic record of new words, using dictionaries and other study aids resourcefully, using memorizing techniques, and putting time aside for the 'spade work' in language learning, such as repetitive practice.

In view of successful vocabulary learning and acquisition, teachers should familiarize students with *learning techniques*, such as (cf. Haß et al. 2008: 121–24, Nation 2008):

▶ Using pictures to memorize the meaning of words
▶ Picturing words in one's mind
▶ Connecting words to personal experiences
▶ Connecting new words to synonyms, antonyms
▶ Grouping words together in grids, mind maps, etc. that show their semantic relations
▶ Paraphrasing the meaning of words
▶ Guessing from context
▶ Listening to words
▶ Acting out words
▶ Making up a story using new words
▶ Putting English labels on physical objects
▶ Engaging actively with English-language media (literature, songs, movies)
▶ Using learning software, online word games, and tests

The presentation of vocabulary in textbooks

Finally, a few remarks seem apt about the presentation and treatment of vocabulary in contemporary textbooks. Unquestionably, textbooks have made considerable headway when it comes to presenting lexical items in memorable ways and thus supporting vocabulary acquisition. Different ways of structuring lexical items and techniques of learning vocabulary are integrated both in the textbook proper as well as in separate *skill sections*. However, the vocabulary

112

file that students usually learn their words from is still presented in the form of rather *unstructured lists of isolated lexical items occurring in a unit*. While these lists nowadays feature sample sentences, pictures, and mnemonic verses, they still contain the *traditional English-German translation in two separate columns*. This results in *two major problems*: (1) learning from vocabulary lists may lead to success in the short run (e.g., in announced vocabulary tests), but it does not help students to enter words in their mental lexicon in the long run and to be able to retrieve them from long-term memory. (2) Learning from vocabulary lists may result in a backwash effect in that students understand vocabulary lists as the one and only means to structure vocabulary. As a result, they will write down lexical items in the form of lists even in their own vocabulary notebooks. To counteract this tendency, it is important that teachers integrate into EFL lessons teaching foci on learning strategies (see ch. 6.2.1).

Recommended reading

Ellis, Rod (2006). Current Issues in the Teaching of Grammar: An SLA Perspective. In: *TESOL Quarterly* 40.1, 83–107.

Hutz, Matthias (2012). Storing Words in the Mind: The Mental Lexicon and Vocabulary Learning. In: Maria Eisenmann & Theresa Summer, eds. *Basic Issues in EFL Teaching and Learning*. Heidelberg: Winter, 105–17.

Keßler, Jörg-U. & Anja Plesser (2011). *Teaching Grammar*. Paderborn: Schöningh.

Keßler, Jörg-U. & Mathias Liebner (2011). Diagnosing L2 Development: Rapid Profile. In: Manfred Pienemann & Jörg-U. Keßler, eds. *Studying Processability Theory: An Introductory Textbook*. Amsterdam: John Benjamins, 133–47.

Nation, Paul (2008). *Teaching Vocabulary: Strategies and Techniques*. Boston, MA et al.: Heinle.

Pienemann, Manfred (2008). A Brief Introduction to Processability Theory. In: Jörg-U. Keßler, ed. *Processability Approaches to Second Language Development and Second Language Learning*. Newcastle upon Tyne: Cambridge Scholars, 9–29.

Language competences, learning strategies, and the individual learner

Contents	

Using an integrative and interactive model, this chapter delineates how the key language skills of reading, listening, writing, and speaking as well as mediation and intercultural communicative competence can be developed together with relevant learning strategies. Moreover, general foreign language learning strategies and types of foreign language learners are taken into account to respond to differences, diversity, and individual learners. Specifically, the issues of dealing with heterogeneous learner groups and working in an inclusive classroom are addressed.

Abstract

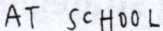

Look at the cartoon and consider the question of how students acquire foreign language skills inside and outside the classroom.

Key competences and skills

This chapter uses the term 'skill' with regard to the traditional four language skills – reading, writing, speaking, and listening. The term 'competence' is used to imply broader, procedural, and less easily categorizable skills (see ch. 1.2.1).

An integrative approach

Learning to speak a foreign language (FL) requires much more than knowing its grammatical rules and having a good command of its vocabulary (see chs. 4, 5). Learners also need to become competent in expressing themselves *fluently* and *appropriately* in interpersonal exchanges. They need to acquire skills in understanding written and spoken English in various contexts. Furthermore, *competence development* entails an increasing awareness and active command of verbal and non-verbal cues, cultural nuances and connotations. The development of such a complex set of interrelated competences cannot be fostered through the teaching and learning of isolated skills. Rather, receptive skills (listening, reading) and productive skills (speaking, writing) as well as mediation and other language-related skills (particularly non-verbal as well as intercultural competences) must be learned and taught in accordance with an ***integrative or interactive model***, which forms the basis of the *Common European Framework of Reference for Languages* (CEF).

> Integrating various skills and competences

This chapter follows the categorization and descriptions of key language competences used in the CEF and corroborates the CEF's stance that FL teaching first and foremost needs to be concerned with language in actual use. Furthermore, this chapter stresses the importance of teaching learning strategies and taking different learner types into consideration. It specifies some of the concerns of the CEF about differentiation by suggesting methods to teach English as a Foreign Language (EFL) in *heterogeneous and mixed-ability* learner groups. Moreover, the issue of *inclusion* (integrating and including students with various physical or mental handicaps) is addressed by suggesting a number of teaching and learning methods which can help teachers handle challenging situations in mixed-ability classes and/or with physically or mentally challenged students.

However, when following the basic concept of the CEF, two *serious drawbacks* of the CEF model need to be pointed out (see ch. 1.2.1): (1) It is exactly the focus on *teachable, testable, and comparable practical skills* featured in the CEF which has created a utilitarian neglect of general goals such as those in the fields of education, ethics, aesthetics, and literature since these areas are notoriously difficult to itemize according to *testable categories* and 'can do-descriptors' (cf. Hallet & Müller-Hartmann 2006). (2) In the wake of the PISA shock and in accordance with official documents such as the CEF, the drive toward

> Standardization vs. differentiation: focus on the individual learner

standardization and compatible teaching and learning targets has gained fresh momentum. The demand for differentiation and inclusion runs absolutely counter to the prioritization of standardization and competence testing. This is clearly a contradiction in terms and one of the great challenges of teaching: finding a practical and flexible solution to these *diametrically opposite demands*.

As a foundation for describing the various skills, competences, learning strategies, and learner types, as well as the need for differentiation and inclusion, it seems important to stress *five basic assumptions* about competence development in the EFL classroom (cf. Rivers 1981: 165, O'Malley & Chamot 1996: 217, Council of Europe 2001: 5, Haß 2008, Eisenmann 2012):

Competence & skill development

▶ Language learning involves *highly complex cognitive skills* that have properties in common with other complex skills in terms of information storage and learning.
▶ Language learning must be viewed as a *stage-wise progression*: it starts with initial awareness and the active forging of language skills as a tool. It then involves greater and greater skills until using the tool becomes a natural and increasingly automatic activity.
▶ Language learning is, on the one hand, "a *life-long task* to be promoted and facilitated throughout educational systems, from pre-school to adult education" (Council of Europe 2001: 5, emphasis added).
▶ Language learning is, on the other hand, also about *autonomous learning*: empowering individuals to acquire and fine-tune the 'language tool' themselves.
▶ Therefore, learners need to acquire manifold learning strategies, which have the potential to influence their *individual learning outcomes* in a positive manner.

In the CEF, the acquisition of the key language skills of reading, writing, speaking, and listening (and mediation) is clearly *interrelated* with the need to acquire general learning strategies as well as competence-related strategies.

Consider the following passages from the CEF. They sum up the interrelationship of language competences and learning strategies. Look for suggestions for furthering strategies of learning and language use when reading this chapter.

In interaction at least two individuals participate in an oral and/or written exchange in which production and reception alternate and may in fact overlap in oral communication. Not only may two interlocutors be speaking and yet listening to each other simultaneously. Even where turn-taking is strictly respected, the listener is generally already forecasting the remainder of the speaker's message and preparing a response. Learning to interact thus involves more than learning to receive and to produce utterances. High importance is generally attributed to interaction in language use and learning in view of its central role in communication.

Language use, embracing language learning, comprises the actions performed by persons who as individuals and as social agents develop a range of competences, both general and in particular communicative language competences. They draw on the competences at their disposal in various contexts under various conditions and under various constraints to engage in language activities involving language processes to produce and/or receive texts in relation to themes in specific domains, activating those strategies which seem most appropriate for carrying out the tasks to be accomplished. The monitoring of these actions by the participants leads to the reinforcement or modification of their competences. (ibid: 14, 9)

In the CEF, progression in skill development is described in terms of 'can do-descriptors' in detailed lists for all skills and all six levels of competence (see ch. 1). As an introduction to this *skill-based model of categorization*, a look at the descriptive tables for overall language skills is useful. For instance, teachers at the beginning of each new school year could assess which level their student group in general and individual students in particular are on. A differentiated *skill assessment* according to all four skill categories could ensue for a more thorough evaluation. To take one example, the description for the A1-level (basic user) reads as follows (see fig. 6.1, ibid.: 66):

CEF: a skill-based model

Listening	Can follow speech which is very slow and carefully articulated, with long pauses for him/her to assimilate meaning.
Reading	Can understand very short, simple texts a single phrase at a time, picking up familiar names, words and basic phrases and rereading as required.
Spoken interaction	Can interact in a simple way but communication is totally dependent on repetition at a slower rate of speech, rephrasing and repair. Can ask and answer simple questions, initiate and respond to simple statements in areas of immediate need or on very familiar topics.
Written interaction	Can write simple isolated phrases and sentences.

Fig. 6.1
Skill description for the A1-level

In accordance with the CEF's six proficiency levels (A1-C2), skill-based definitions of competences are described as developing as a *vertical progression* (see ch. 1). The individual skills grow and widen from step to step. The CEF has more than 50 lists categorizing and describing areas concerning skills and subskills for each of the four traditional skills as well as for mediation. Using just a part of one such list, fig. 6.2 shows how one of the skills (oral production) progresses from A1 to B1 (ibid.: 58):

Fig. 6.2	B1	Can reasonably fluently sustain a straightforward description of one of a variety of subjects within her/his field of interest, presenting it as a linear sequence of points.
Oral production – progression from A1 to B1	A2	Can give a simple description or presentation of people, living or working conditions, daily routines, likes/dislikes, etc. as a short series of simple phrases or sentences linked into a list.
	A1	Can produce simple mainly isolated phrases about people and places.

In the CEF, as in other publications on the topic of language skills and learning strategies, there is a clear link between *communication strategies* and *metacognitive strategies* (cf. ibid.: 222): "The use of communication strategies can be seen as the application of the metacognitive principles: *Pre-planning, Execution, Monitoring*, and *Repair Action* to the different kinds of communicative activity: Reception, Interaction, Production and Mediation." (ibid.: 57)

Three-phase model

In many German publications a *different terminology* is used: the strategies are often aligned with *pre-, while- (=during), and post-phases* of activities (see ch. 4.3.2) that are geared toward working with various text types or engaging in various tasks. Below, skill-specific activities will be explained in more detail. In general, the development of skills and learning strategies should not be viewed merely as a 'disability model,' compensating for deficient language proficiency (cf. ibid.: 57). Native speakers, too, regularly employ the strategies outlined below. In the following the basic functions of the three *activity phases* are explained (cf. ibid.: 90–91; O'Malley & Chamot 1996: 44–46, 137–39; Weskamp 2001: 118–19).

If we go to a restaurant we store the experience in our restaurant schema, if we attend a party, our party schema, and so on. –
Nila Banton Smith

Pre-activities: for implementing pre-activities it seems crucial to take into account the concept of **mental schemata** (see ch. 3.2.3). The mental image or concept individuals have of certain words, combination of words, speech acts, or 'scripts' is (1) 'habitualized,' (2) culturally conditioned, and (3) reflected in prototypical language or speech items or utterances. For example, a word like 'tree' triggers different associations in individuals, some visualizing it as a palm tree, others as an apple tree, or a fir tree. Similarly, the 'scripts' of a telephone conversation or a political speech follow certain routines, as do literary or filmic genres (sonnet or thriller). Schemata make us "engage in predictions and ask questions which will be answered in our interaction with the real world," and are therefore *a basic precondition for teaching* "effective listening, speaking, writing, and reading in the EFL classroom" (Weskamp 2001: 119, our trans.). In the pre-activity phase, the schemata which will be used or encountered in the activity phase can be triggered, augmented, changed, and focused upon. Also in the pre-activity phase, the following representative strategies can be employed (see fig. 6.3, based on O'Malley & Chamot 1996: 44–46):

Selective attention & planning	Planning	
▶ Students focus on special aspects of a learning task, as in planning to listen for key words or phrases. ▶ Students decide in advance which aspects to focus on and to ignore irrelevant information or distractors (e. g., as in scanning a text later on for information).	▶ Students plan for the organization of either written or spoken discourse (e. g., they can write cue cards with expressions they want to use later on; they learn about the overall composition of a response in a letter). ▶ Students structure their expected activity according to expectations regarding a certain topic, proposing strategies for handling an upcoming task. ▶ Students generate a plan for details of handling a task, planning for and rehearsing linguistic items necessary to carry out an upcoming task.	Fig. 6.3 Pre-activity phase strategies

(While-)activities: the principles of execution, but also monitoring and repair action can be regarded as coming to the fore in the phase of engaging in activities such as reading a text or interacting in a discussion. The following *representative strategies* can be employed in the EFL classroom (see fig. 6.4):

Execution, monitoring, and repair action	
▶ Reviewing attention to a task ▶ Ignoring irrelevant information ▶ Checking one's comprehension during the task ▶ Inferencing (e. g., guessing meaning from linguistic clues) ▶ Using linguistic, pragmatic, and strategic competences ▶ Checking the accuracy or appropriateness of one's language production while it is taking place	Fig. 6.4 Activity-phase strategies

Post-activities: This does not just include 'repair action' but also the elements of self-evaluation and self-management. *Representative strategies* are shown in fig. 6.5:

Self-management and self-monitoring	Self-evaluation	
▶ Understanding the conditions that help one learn or engage in the activity used and set up those conditions ▶ Checking one's comprehension or command of the skill after the activity and learning from that	▶ Checking the outcomes of one's own language learning or command against a standard after it has been completed ▶ Evaluating language production and learning how to improve it	Fig. 6.5 Post-activity strategies

Most situations involve a *mixture of strategy and activity types*. In a typical EFL lesson, students may be required to listen to the teacher's input or an audio file at the beginning, comment on a visual impulse, read a text (silently or aloud), interact with fellow students in pairs, in group or project work, respond to the input or a text by writing something into a file. For teachers, it seems advisable to check intermittently whether they emphasize skill development in *all four areas* and in an *integrative manner* or whether they tend to neglect skill devel-

'Balanced' skill development

121

opment in a certain area. While historically, writing and reading skills were favored, the CEF has drawn special attention to furthering listening, audio-visual, and interactive speaking skills.

6.1.2 | Receptive skills: reading and listening

Crucially, *reception strategies* involve working with the concept of schemata – those of the students and those of the 'text' (written or spoken). Teachers need to consider the 'horizons of expectation' or the prior knowledge of their learners with regard to the text and its linguistic, contextual, or generic challenges. Schemata should be activated with a task prefiguring the encounter with the text, thus facilitating text reception before exposure. During the reception process, expectations are compared with the actual encounter: "Through a process of successive approximation, apparent and possible gaps in the message are filled in order to flesh out the representation of meaning, and the significance of the message and of its constituent parts are worked out (*Inferring*)." (Council of Europe 2001: 72) Students constantly check actual text items against textual schemata with regard to how they fit into their own schemata. They *revise hypotheses* and re-interpret incoming clues.

Get the task right!   Such '*negotiation of schemata*' can be quite challenging under time pressure. If, as in many scenarios, students are asked explicitly or implicitly to understand everything, authentic materials can discourage students and daunt them. It is therefore recommended that, when authentic language is used, students should be encouraged to learn how to read or listen selectively, for gist or for basic information: "Instead of simplifying the language of the text, simplify the task that is demanded of the student." (Field 2002: 244)

Reading

People learn to read by reading, not by doing exercises. – William Grabe   The CEF (2001: 69–70) differentiates between *several types of reading activities*. *Different ways of reading* may be applied such as reading for gist (*general understanding, skimming*), for specific information (*scanning*), for *detailed understanding*, for *implications*, etc. Reading skills have come into the public focus since the 'PISA shock' (see chs. 1.2, 10.1) and the general discontent concerning *waning reading skills*. The decline in readings skills has been widely lamented, and debates about fostering reading skills often revolve around the following arguments: (1) there are *fewer reading role models* in families and society, (2) *allegedly fewer people read* and reading no longer appears as a key competence, and (3) other competences like 'media competence' or '*multiliteracies*' are increasingly in demand in the age of the *digital revolution* (cf. Küster 2014; see ch. 9). (4) There is a vicious circle, with students finding reading difficult or boring because they have not learned to read effectively and thus sooner or later make less of an effort to gain reading competences and thus increasingly employ *avoidance strategies* (Weskamp 2001: 129). Obviously, FL classes have to contribute to fostering a 'culture of reading' (cf. Henseler & Surkamp 2007), following these two hypotheses: (1) a certain degree of language proficiency is needed in order to be able to read and enjoy FL texts (**Linguistic Threshold Hypothesis**) and (2) reading strategies and habits acquired in the mother tongue are applied to those in the FL (**Linguistic Interdependence Hypothesis**) (cf. Grabe 2011: 447–52). Solutions galore have been suggested for remedying the general reading malaise: for example, favoring silent reading periods (also in class), allowing students to select meaningful, interesting, and adequate reading material, choosing a wider range of literary texts than ever before such as young adult fiction and picture books, and encouraging extended periods of reading longer texts (cf. Bland 2012).

Like listening, reading can be described as an interaction of two processes (cf. Hermes 2007: 229–30): (1) the *bottom-up process* of recognizing letters, words, sentences, etc., and (2) the *top-down process* of comparing one's own schemata with those of the text. If, for instance, the reader knows that a text is a sonnet (and has read a sonnet before), certain expectations are created with regard to form and content. If a reader is told that the text is from a left-wing magazine about the topic of globalization, a certain line of argumentation or certain key words may be encountered in the reading process. These processes can be exploited for *pre-reading activities*, helping students to make predictions about a text, to find these confirmed later on or not, and to correct expectations in the reading process.

Bottom-up & top-down processes

Reading has been described as a highly complex activity, requiring "a number of processing subskills and linguistic knowledge bases" (Grabe 2011: 441; cf. Hattie 2009: 129). This includes *visual skills* (perceiving the written text), *orthographic skills* (recognizing the script), *linguistic/syntactic skills* (identifying the order), *semantic skills* (understanding the basic meaning), and *cognitive skills* (analyzing and interpreting). Techniques to improve reading skills are summed up in fig. 6.6 (based on Weskamp 2001: 133–34, Grabe 2011: 455–56):

Pre-reading	Reading	Post-reading
▶ Brainstorming about the topic, genre, author (activating prior knowledge) ▶ Inferring from title, poster, other visuals ▶ Making hypotheses about possible content, style, language, etc. ▶ A quick first look at the text: what could this text be about?	▶ Using various ways of reading from skimming to scanning ▶ Clarifying linguistic and semantic meaning (guessing from context); using annotations and dictionaries ▶ Making further predictions and clarifying meaning with others ▶ Re-reading, if necessary	▶ Reflecting on how what has been read fits into the schemata ▶ Reflecting on what the readers have learned, how they can use this text, how it appeals to them ▶ Underlining key passages, summing up, responding to the text in various ways ▶ Reviewing and discussing a text in context

Fig. 6.6
Improving reading skills

A number of *metacognitive, cognitive, social, and affective strategies* can be taught to develop reading skills (cf. O'Malley & Chamot 1996: 6, 137, 179, 211; also cf. Hattie 2009: 129–141):

Strategies to develop reading skills

▶ Getting into reading routines (e. g., reading English language texts on a regular basis)
▶ Finding suitable and interesting reading material
▶ Identifying reading strategies in L1, then applying the same strategies to L2
▶ Elaboration of prior knowledge
▶ Selective attention to scan for specific information
▶ Making inferences about meanings of new words through their immediate or extended context
▶ Using known grammar or word formation rules to identify unknown word forms
▶ Checking, verifying, and correcting one's understanding
▶ Taking notes, underlining key passages, key words, etc.
▶ Producing summaries of the main argument
▶ Questioning for clarification and verification of meaning
▶ Evaluation of one's own comprehension
▶ Using reference material (e. g., dictionary, annotations)
▶ Working with others to understand texts

In an article on 'getting rid' of worn-out and outdated teaching methods in the EFL classroom, Arendt (1999: 402–03) suggests that when teaching reading skills, teachers should no longer (1) have students read out a text; (2) couple reading tasks with tasks focusing on understanding, interpreting, or analyzing; and (3) they should scrap comprehension questions completely. In Arendt's opinion, all these methods run counter to 'natural' practices of reading.
What is your opinion? Should these time-honored classroom practices be dropped completely, continued, or modified?

Listening

Listening – 'the Cinderella skill'?

Listening has been called "the Cinderella skill in foreign language learning" (Nunan 2002: 238). And indeed, even the CEF contains little information and elaboration on listening skills, 'aural reception,' or listening activities used by the language learner as a listener who receives and processes spoken input produced by one or more speakers (Council of Europe 2001: 65). This is all the more regrettable as in EFL classroom scenarios there is a *dearth of opportunities* to interact with native speakers, which, in turn, creates an urgent need to expose learners to various kinds of scenarios where native-speaker input can be taken in. This need can be met by audiovisual materials such as CDs, audio files, videos, films, and TV material including genres such as documentaries,

124

newscasts, or even soap operas (see ch. 9.1). This material can provide *attractive and informative content* and raise *student motivation*. It can be used to expose learners to a wide range of authentic language use with different registers, accents, intonation, rhythms, and stresses. And it can provide examples of language in actual use, thus adding relevance to the learning of English (cf. Shumin 2002: 209).

The *Cinderella status* of listening may be exacerbated by two established practices of teaching listening skills in the EFL classroom: (1) listening tends to be *tested rather than taught*: "We tend to judge successful listening simplistically in terms of correct answers to comprehension questions and tasks." (Field 2002: 246) (2) Both teaching and testing tend to present rather *artificial listening scenarios* which often do not cover the kind of listening that takes place in real life. Instead, artificially articulated exchanges are presented, marked by slow pace and close connection to the textbook. Generally, comprehension exercises tend to focus on the product of listening rather than on the *complex process* of listening. The latter needs to be thoroughly understood by teachers so that they can help students to be more successful in developing listening skills. This includes taking into consideration the types of listening that can be defined and then practiced with adequate listening tasks, the *mental processes* taking place in listening activities, and, finally, the listening strategies and techniques that should be taught and practiced.

Listening activities include listening to various types of listening material including public announcements (e.g., information, instructions, warnings), listening to media (e.g., radio, TV, recordings, DVDs, which also includes audiovisual reception, *Hör-Seh-Verstehen*). *Audiovisual activities* (Shumin 2002: 209) can be based on a variety of material, ranging from pictorial aids and visual imagery to videos, music video clips to feature films. Visual input creates an additional *sensory impact* and allows for the extension of situational contexts through which students can focus on or gain help in understanding through non-verbal behavior, interpersonal exchanges, gesture, mime, etc.

Listening activities can also include taking part in live events (e.g., theater productions, public meetings, public lectures, entertainments, which may demand a more elaborate pre-listening preparation, see below), or engaging in a conversation and using interactive skills. The types of listening scenarios can be further differentiated according to the *degree of information content* (high information content can be found in a news bulletin, low information content in casual exchanges between friends); the semantic and acoustic complexity of the exchange (often depending on the number of speakers involved); the difficulty of the topic, accents, the quality of the recording, etc. Moreover, the question of whether the listener is required to take part in an interaction ('reciprocal listening') needs to be considered. This *degree of difficulty* is connected to problems EFL learners may encounter when exposed to listening tasks:

Teaching listening skills: wrong approaches?

Listening scenarios

▶ Words once spoken cannot be repeated or listened to for a second time

▶ Oral communication is frequently fast (up to 10 phonemes per second). Phonemes can influence each other or be contracted, and there are few pauses between words or sentences

▶ Problems of audibility depending on the quality of a recording, background noise, etc.

▶ Problems with colloquialisms, slang, non-standard English, dialects, varieties, etc.

Most importantly, the *purpose* of listening needs to be considered as different listening processes and strategies need to be involved depending on whether one is *listening for specific information, for gist, or for implications or clues* which need to be taken up in a written or oral response.

'One hears what one knows.' As with reading, *two views of listening* have influenced FL teaching since the 1980s (cf. Nunan 2002: 239, Vandergrift & Goh 2011: 399–402). Both must be seen as being reciprocal processes influencing listening: (1) the *bottom-up processing* perspective focuses on listening as a step-by-step, linear process of decoding the sounds that one hears from the smallest meaningful units (phonemes) to words, phrases to sentences, and finally whole 'texts.' This perspective has been called the 'tape recorder view' of listening "because it assumes that the listener takes in and stores messages sequentially, in much the same way as a tape recorder" (Nunan 2002: 239). (2) The complementary, *top-down perspective* holds that the listener decodes the meaning using incoming sounds as clues and assimilating what is heard into his/her prior knowledge of the context or situation. This is where the listener's (cultural) schemata come into play (i.e., previous knowledge of the world, events, people, countries, and the FL).

The *interrelatedness* of the bottom-up and top-down processes has implications for teaching listening skills:

> In developing courses, materials, and lessons, it is important to teach not only bottom-up processing skills, such as the ability to discriminate between minimal pairs, but also to help learners use what they already know to understand what they hear. If teachers suspect that there are gaps in their learners' knowledge, the listening itself can be preceded by schema-building activities to prepare learners for the listening task to come. (Nunan 2002: 239)

Students therefore need *systematic training* in the following areas:

Training listening skills
▶ Learning to *distinguish* between key sounds, intonation patterns, different accents, etc. This can be achieved by 'remedial exercises' or 'microlistening activities' (e. g., students listen to differences between voiced and unvoiced consonants)

▶ Listening to material containing parts and passages *unknown* to students

126

▶ Listening to material incorporating *different features* of spoken language (e. g., gender, different accents, different tones of voice: angry vs. excited)
▶ Being prepared for situations where listeners will *not have a full understanding* of what they hear (e. g., background noise, unknown vocabulary, dialect)
▶ *Different types and purposes* of listening, from listening selectively to listening for gist

It goes without saying that such training should focus on the kind of language and situations students are most likely to encounter in *real life*. Likewise, training should not work with the assumption that learners will identify most of the words they hear. Instead, lessons should be modelled most closely to the kind of process "that takes place in a real-life situation where understanding of what is said is less than perfect" (Field 2002: 246). Techniques used to further listening skills are listed in fig. 6.7 (cf. Weskamp 2001: 124, Field 2002: 242–45, Vandergrift & Goh 2011: 402–05):

Pre-listening	Listening	Post-listening
▶ Activating students' prior knowledge about the topic(s) to be featured in the listening activity (e. g., building hypotheses about topics, possible vocabulary and grammar) ▶ Pre-teaching new vocabulary items of the recording and/or basic context/content ▶ Giving hints as to understanding unknown accents, dialects, etc. ▶ Creating motivation ▶ Establishing objectives of listening activity ▶ Establishing the type of listening activity (selective listening or detailed understanding) ▶ Giving a number of attention pointers beforehand	▶ Using various listening types from detailed understanding to listening for gist ▶ Inferring meaning ▶ Dealing with pre-set task(s) ▶ Checking answers and comparing hypotheses with actual content ▶ Predicting what will be communicated next ▶ Taking notes ▶ Paying attention to linguistic markers that signal main ideas, details, or discourse structure	▶ Reflecting on how what has been listened to fits into the schemata ▶ Reflecting on what has been learned, how this can be used ▶ Analyzing language ▶ Repeating ▶ Checking and comparing answers and understanding ▶ Pooling the information received, then presenting it in oral or written summaries ▶ Responding to recording in various ways

Fig. 6.7
Improving listening skills

Arendt (1999: 404–05) argues against using listening comprehensions featuring listening for discrete items (discrimination tasks) and uninteresting topics. Most importantly, Arendt surmises, listening tasks should not have several repetitions of the recording. These practices run counter to listening scenarios in real life.

What is your opinion, especially regarding the suggestion that recordings should be played only once?

6.1.3 | **Productive skills: writing and speaking**

With regard to productive skills, the CEF distinguishes between *productive/transactional* and *interactive* activities and skills. Production and transaction can be seen to take place when somebody writes something creative, follows a certain narrative and rhetorical pattern (e. g., a report, an essay) or engages in a sustained monolog (e. g., putting a case to an audience, delivering a speech, giving a public announcement). Interaction in writing includes different types of correspondences (e. g., notes, messages, forms which will be responded to).

Writing

Writing is the geometry of the soul. – Plato

A written text is produced to be received by readers. Writing includes completing forms and questionnaires; writing contributions for (online) newspapers, newsletters, forums, etc.; producing posters for display; writing reports, essays, etc.; taking notes in class; making notes for future reference; creative and imaginative writing; writing personal or professional letters, etc. As with reading, L1 approaches and insights into developing writing skills need to be regarded (cf. Hattie 2009: 141–43). There appears to be a *strong link* between writing skills in the L1 and the FL, which indicates that negative results in writing tasks are not necessarily related to a lack of FL proficiency. Writing in any language requires *composition proficiency*, which needs to be fostered. However, in FL writing learners tend to stay closer to the text or text model their writing responds to or is based on. They need to be encouraged to develop their own ideas and develop both *language and argumentative skills* which enable them to refrain from sticking closely to the original text. Similarly, typical expressions, chunks, and rhetorical strategies used in a certain text genre need to be introduced and practiced (e. g., 'to sum up', 'in a nutshell').

Writing as a complex process

Most significantly, writing needs to be considered as a *process*. The **process approach** to teaching writing does not mean that writing is completely dissociated from the written product but to "construct process-oriented writing instructions that will affect performance" (Freedman et al. in Seow 2002: 316; cf. Polio & Williams 2011: 490–91). The writing process may be seen as comprising four interrelated phases of *planning, drafting, revising*, and *editing*. However, the phases are not necessarily sequential or orderly; rather, they may take place in an exploratory, recursive, and non-linear manner. When teaching process writing, in contrast, teachers usually follow a highly structured and orderly phasing. For advanced learners, though, such a 'formulaic' approach needs to be expanded to cover free variations of writing stages. In the following, the four phases will be briefly discussed (cf. Seow 2002: 316–17, Polio & Williams 2011: 490–96).

Phases of writing

Planning: students are encouraged to write. Methods and strategies include the following:

- Generating ideas (e. g., through brainstorming, think-pair-share activities, establishing clusters of ideas)
- Getting into the mood or habit of writing: individual students jot down freely and quickly (rapid free writing) their ideas about a topic, a time limit is given, ideas and phrases are compared
- Ideas and phrases are *structured and selected*, the topic or task is focused on
- *Wh-questions*: students generate who, why, what, where, when, and how questions about a topic. This is elaborated on by adding more questions consecutively
- *Ideas about writing* can be gleaned from other texts, multimedia sources, etc.

Drafting: having collected sufficient ideas on a topic, the *first attempt* at writing can proceed. This involves a focus on the fluency of writing down ideas, getting them into a linear order, considering the *implied reader* or audience. Both the overall composition of what will be written needs to be kept in mind as well as the arrangement of single ideas or phrases. Additionally, the *text genre* needs to be observed. Students could be encouraged to experiment with different draft versions, ranging from just writing down key ideas in bullet-point fashion to composing a complete first draft already including more elaborate parts.

Writing: writing itself is a *complex activity*. It includes keeping both the overall and paragraph composition in mind, considering style, grammar, lexis, etc. It also involves *constant reflection* on how to formulate and revise while in the process of writing, adding or modifying aspects, as well as restructuring. The formulation component, to focus on one important element, "takes the output from the planning component and assembles it into linguistic form. This involves lexical, grammatical, phonological (and in the case of writing, orthographic) processes" (Council of Europe 2001: 91).

Revising and editing: revising does not just mean checking for language errors and mistakes, but also *re-examining* parts of the text or the whole text with regard to how meaning is most effectively communicated to the reader. Revision may also build on *responses or assessments* by peers or the teacher. Editing takes place both after the drafting phase and after a product has been evaluated and assessed by peers or the teacher. Editing is done for grammar, spelling, punctuation, diction, sentence structure, development of argument and the like. Teachers should issue a *simple checklist* (based on Seow 2002: 318):

- Have you used the verbs in the correct form and the correct tense (past tense vs. present perfect)?
- Have you used the correct articles, pronouns, and prepositions?
- Is your choice and use of adjectives, adverbs, and nouns correct?
- Is your syntax correct and are your sentences complete?

► Have you linked your sentences and ideas through adverbs, fixed phrases, etc.?

► Is your line of argumentation coherent?

Meaningful writing scenarios

Writing should not take place in a cultural vacuum but rather in a certain (inter-)cultural context where it becomes clear to students that they *generate meaning in writing* – meaning which will be responded to by other readers. Therefore, writing activities must be fashioned as meaningful, personal, and imaginative scenarios (cf. Hattie 2009: 142), where the genre of the text to be written, its content, its addressee and mode (from speech to report) need to be observed from the beginning of the writing process to its end (cf. Polio & Williams 2011: 496–98). Responses to postings on the Internet or participating in online discussions of global issues (e.g., concerning the environment) are among such student-oriented writing activities with a high degree of *real-world relevance*. Post-writing activities include sharing a complete piece of writing (or several of them) by publishing it, reading it with others, reading aloud, acting it out, or displaying it:

> The post-writing stage is a platform for recognising students' work as important and worthwhile. It may be used as a motivation for writing as well as to hedge against students finding excuses for not writing. Students must be made to feel that they are writing for a very real purpose. (Seow 2002: 319)

Arendt (1999: 407) suggests that writing skills should never be practiced with rigid and patterned activities such as writing 'model dialogs' but rather by focusing on real-life and creative forms of writing. Think of ways to make writing more creative, with students writing responses resembling real-life situations.

Speaking

Transaction and interaction

The functions of spoken language are both *transactional and interactive*. Generally, the main goal of the former is to convey *information and ideas*, while that of the latter consists of *maintaining social relationships* (cf. Shumin 2002: 208). This differentiation should have an effect on the teaching of oral skills, since most of our daily communication is interactional: "Therefore, language instructors should provide learners with opportunities for meaningful communicative behavior about relevant topics by using learner-learner interaction as the key to teaching language for communication" (ibid.). Crucially, this can be supported and stimulated through *extensive exposure* to interesting and meaningful authentic language material. *Interactive activities* based on or stimulated by such authentic material should (1) be structured in a way that learners can *manipulate and play* with certain specific features of language (i.e., not pattern drills, but playing out real-life scenarios with unexpected or unknown elements), (2) allow learners to rehearse communicative skills they need *outside* of the classroom, and (3) encourage them to learn and practice more *autonomously*.

As with listening, speaking – specifically as part of an *interactive task* – needs to be seen as a process consisting of four main phases: conceptualizing, formulating, articulating, repair/self-control (cf. Bygate 2011: 419–20). When using a FL, speakers are influenced in each phase by the phonological, grammatical, and lexical system of their mother tongue, and, in general, by the schemata and scripts of their own culture. These schemata are especially influential in the phase of conceptualization (see ch. 5.1): here, speakers become aware of their communicative needs and intentions and structure these according to what has already been communicated and according to their cultural or intercultural schemata. When formulating a word and utterances, words are provided to formulate sentence structures including components of phonology and prosody. This leads to articulation, the execution of 'inner speech' by means of the organs of speech. Finally, while articulating, the speaker monitors him- or herself constantly and makes use of repair mechanisms.

Speaking as a process

Interaction encompasses both receptive and productive skills. Since real oral communication is based on some kind of commonly shared cultural and situational context and two or more interlocutors can be seen as 'negotiating' a process of creating meaning or common ground, there are a number of skills involved: soft skills, *communicative skills*, intercultural skills – mainly involving the skill of knowing how to interact in a specific situation (cf. Schubert 2006). In other words, grammatical, discourse, sociolinguistic, and strategic competences (see ch. 4.3.1) are all components of interactive communication skills. Teaching and learning interaction can feature the following activities and development of sub-skills:

Speaking as interacting

Planning or framing: speakers activate cultural and language *schemata*. They envision – sometimes in split seconds – what would be the possible and probable forthcoming activity. They identify what is *expected from them*, what options they have, and prepare possible moves in interchanges. Similar pre-activities can be practiced as in listening tasks. In addition, speech routines and certain speech acts can be practiced in role plays – again, with an emphasis on practical applicability and flexibility. Activities preparing for the process of exchanges should be featured. They include (cf. Bygate 2011: 419–20):

Interaction skills

▶ *Initiating and maintaining conversation*: this includes the routines of greeting and establishing contact and rapport, routines of small talk, avoiding problematic topics, finding common ground and mutual understanding, staying focused on a certain subject, cooperating, using politeness routines, specifically 'face-work' (e. g., apologies and praise)
▶ *Turn-taking strategies and taking the floor*: this includes routines used to

respond, verbally and non-verbally, to signal understanding, affirmation, confirmation, etc.; polite ways of disagreeing, defending one's position; staying with a subject, and changing the subject of a conversation
► *Monitoring and repair work*: asking for assistance in formulating something; clarifying miscomprehension or ambiguities; if necessary, re-establishing communication and clearing up misunderstandings (communication repair on the levels of linguistics, politeness, intercultural understanding, etc.)

Interactional activities in the classroom should be characterized by (1) *intrinsic motivation* through relevant topics, (2) an *anxiety-free atmosphere* with students knowing that the communicative phase is based on the principle of *fluency before accuracy*, (3) the teacher providing *additional support* such as linguistic help, visual or textual support (e. g., a map of London if the lesson is about finding one's way), (4) the class feeling *no need to seek* one-to-one equivalences for words, avoiding artificial language and slipping into the mother tongue, (5) a sense of *achievement* and as many students as possible being *involved*, and (6) topics which are made *relevant* or 'spiced up' through interesting tasks.

Learning speaking through speaking

Examples of *effective speaking activities* include the following (based on Weskamp 2001: 128–29):

► *Mini-debates*: following the example of debating societies, speakers take on contrary opinions and defend them.
► *Interviews*: interviews can be with experts or non-experts, structured or not, and may be done inside and outside the classroom. Typical examples are media interviews (e. g., simulating an interview with a famous person), job interviews, or real interviews where there is a reason to conduct them in English (e. g., at the airport, with international companies, online interviews via Skype).
► *Think-pair-share and similar scenarios*: here students are asked to think alone first, then share ideas with partners, then respond to all members of the class. Similar arrangements are ball-bearing (inner and outer circle, students move on one chair to talk to the next person) or fish-bowl discussions (two or three discuss in the middle, the others seated around them may join in).
► *Discussions on a topic in small groups, expert groups, panel discussions*: these discussions can include the participation of the whole group at one point and/or allow contributions aided by notes.
► *Responses to literature/film*: students discuss their responses to literary or filmic texts (see chs. 8, 9). This may involve teacher participation, especially with the teacher as an expert on analyzing literary texts.
► *Role playing*: students perform their own script, based on a text or an original script.

▶ *Storytelling*: students present their own texts and the emphasis, again, is on pronunciation and prosody.
▶ *Formal speeches and illustrated talks*: with or without the help of media (e.g., PowerPoint presentations) and notes, students present a short or long talk. Eye contact, pauses, intonation, pitch, etc. are taken into consideration. A talk could also be accompanied by an interactive part (e.g., a question and answer session).

Finally, a note on teachers as *role models for oral skills* (cf. Rivers 1981: 33): non-fluent teachers may be advised to hone their own skills with the help of audio files and tapes used in class, and pay careful attention to articulation and into-nation compared with native speakers on recordings. They should carefully watch themselves for inhibitions about speaking the FL since this will create an atmosphere where students are quite unwilling to speak the FL themselves. It seems advisable to use techniques which encourage students to use the FL as much as possible, and to be patient and persevere in improving one's own oral skills (e.g., by watching TV shows or series in original language versions in one's spare time).

> Arendt (1999: 405–06) suggests that frontal teaching is one of the main obstacles to students' developing speaking or interaction skills. Think of ways to decrease teacher talk time. Compare with suggestions in chapter 10.4.2.

Mediation and intercultural competence | 6.1.4

The skill of mediation may at first appear like a *revamping* of time-honored and much-maligned activities of (literal and exact) translating and interpreting. However, a revived interest in 'mediating' between the mother tongue and the FL can be attributed to insights into what happens in *real-life situations*. Various forms of acting as an *intermediary* between two or more languages may be required, such as in the following scenarios:

Real-life mediation

▶ *Summing up* a FL text in one's own language to present information required for a certain activity later on – particularly for others who do not speak the FL or do not understand certain technical terms
▶ Being asked to interpret, *not verbatim*, but by paraphrasing a text the other person does not understand (e.g., the content of an inscription, basics of a manual)
▶ Being asked to translate simultaneously at a meeting (e.g., for a foreign vis-itor to one's country, to native speakers when abroad)
▶ *Negotiating meaning* in non-native-speaker to non-native-speaker contexts, where some speakers speak English, while others do not

Elements of *plurilingualism* and *interculturality* are important in mediation activities:

> The linguistic and cultural competences in respect of each language are modified by knowledge of the other and contribute to intercultural awareness, skills and know-how. They enable the individual to develop an enriched, more complex personality and an enhanced capacity for further language learning and greater openness to new cultural experiences. (Council of Europe 2001: 91)

Mediation activities can be structured according to the pre-activity, activity, and post-activity pattern described for listening and reading activities above. In addition, *mediation-specific skills* such as the following need to be developed:

- ▶ Being able to take the communicative need of the partner(s) into account
- ▶ Being able to do things simultaneously by anticipating what will be communicated next while interpreting
- ▶ Being aware of 'untranslatable' or culturally different expressions
- ▶ Bridging gaps and finding impromptu repair mechanisms and equivalents (e. g., if a word is unknown)
- ▶ Being able to repair by using reference works efficiently
- ▶ Using knowledge of other languages and their syntax, vocabulary, etc. (e. g., French, Spanish, Turkish, Latin) for the purpose of communicating with native and non-native speakers

> Think of possible scenarios where students would use mediation skills, especially on the Internet. Make a list and consider ways of preparing students for such scenarios.

All language skills, including mediation, must be regarded as being inextricably intertwined with intercultural competence (cf. Byram 1997, see ch. 7.2.2).

Politeness skills
Frequently, intercultural competence boils down to adhering wisely to politeness conventions of the target culture or of the individuals one encounters. Basically, this means *avoiding frankness and bluntness*, using 'please' and 'thank you' appropriately, and knowing the difference in the use of positive and negative politeness (cf. Schubert 2006). While 'positive politeness' implies showing interest in the other person's well-being by establishing rapport, expressing admiration, affection, and gratitude, 'negative politeness' strategies aim at avoiding 'face-threatening behavior' (e. g., direct orders, corrections, prohibitions). In intercultural situations, politeness is often connected with *non-verbal communication*, and there is great need for highlighting these elements in the EFL classroom:

> Because of the influence or interference of their own cultural norms, it is hard for non-native speakers to choose the forms appropriate for certain situations. For instance, in Chinese culture, paying a compliment to someone obliges that per-

son to give a negative answer (such as 'No. It is not so good.') in order to show 'modesty', whereas in North American culture such a response might be both inappropriate and embarrassing. (Shumin 2002: 206)

There is an enormous variation across cultures and languages in how people express themselves with mime, gesture, and body language (cf. Oomen-Welke 2004). Learners often do not know how to *interpret non-verbal messages*. In intercultural encounters, this creates misunderstandings as described in the following example from a US-American setting:

> One day, when a Chinese student heard 'Let's get together for lunch sometime.' he immediately responded by proposing to fix a specific date without noticing the speaker's indifferent facial expression. Undoubtedly, he was puzzled when his interlocutor left without giving him an expected answer. (Shumin 2002: 206)

It is obvious that the Chinese student had *different concepts of politeness* and, on top of that, did not understand the *non-verbal cue*. In the following, a number of activities aimed at fostering students communicative, intercultural, and non-verbal skills are suggested. These take into account the categories of non-verbal signals as described by Argyle (1975, cf. Oomen-Welke 2004): bodily contact, proximity, orientation, appearance, posture, head-nods, facial expressions, gestures, and looking. In addition, they alert us to the functions of non-verbal signs in intercultural contexts: to manage the immediate social situation, to sustain verbal communication, and/or to replace verbal communication.

Non-verbal messages

Read the following suggestions for practicing non-verbal communication skills. Try some of them in your class.

Activity	Description
Observe the teacher/student	Teachers or students act out everyday situations in front of students (without words); they read out a text using gestures; students observe, comment, and imitate
What's the meaning?	This is an activity about understanding sign language across cultures: students interpret several typical gestures (V-sign with index and middle fingers and how they differ across cultures (e. g., displayed on a transparency)
Acting out small scenes	This could start with textbook dialogs and go on to scenes from (mini-)dramas or scenes composed by the students: the focus is on non-verbal communication and how it can underline or contradict verbal messages
Analyzing literature	Students discuss the use of non-verbal communication in literary texts, ranging from drama to conversations in novels
Describing pictures	One student explains a picture the other student cannot see; the other student draws; then they discuss the use of gestures

| Fig. 6.8

Teaching non-verbal communication – activities raising awareness

Playing 'Activity'	Cards with terms or phrases are prepared and need to be explained without words (e. g., 'spiral staircase,' 'blackout,' 'stage fright')
Watching (scenes from) a film	This is done with the sound off: what can be inferred just from non-verbal communication? Alternatively, scenes from a silent movie can be worked with
Intelligent guessing	Gestures and non-verbal aspects of communication are shown visually: students are asked to infer the mood of the person shown
Role play: using sign language	A scenario is set where, in a foreign country, the students do not speak the language. They are asked to think of ways to express needs like: 'I'm hungry,' 'I'm looking for the bathroom,' etc. Alternatively, students are asked to reflect on how they communicate in situations where words cannot be used (e. g., across the classroom, at a concert)
Discussing non-verbal language with non-German guests, exchange students, etc.	Students are asked to consider specific gestures, eye contact, proximity, etc.: how close, for instance, would you stand to another person in a line waiting for the bus? How long would you look into the eyes of another person (same sex, different sex) in certain situations?

6.1.5 | Authentic communicative tasks and activities

Similar to the tasks for raising awareness about the importance of non-verbal communication suggested above, there are tasks and activities which aim at *making communication in the classroom similar to communication in real life* by juxtaposing it with oral practices in traditional classroom settings (cf. Nunan 2002). Figure 6.9 shows on the left-hand side more traditional classroom activities, on the right-hand side *authentic communicative activities* or tasks (The Examinations Office for TELC 2002: 6.03–07, abridged).

Fig. 6.9		(Oral) practice in the classroom	(Oral) practice outside the classroom
Traditional classroom discourse vs. authentic communicative activities	*What: content of communication*	Content or topic are decided by the teacher, textbook, etc. Content is highly predictable.	Speakers express their own ideas, wishes, opinions, attitudes, etc. The exact meaning of any speaker's message is unpredictable.
	Why: reason for communication	Learners speak in order to practice speaking or because the teacher tells them to.	Speakers have a social or personal reason to speak. There is an information gap to be filled or an area of uncertainty to be made clear. What is said is potentially interesting or useful to the participants.
	Why: result of communication	The foreign language is spoken, the teacher corrects or accepts what is said; a grade is given (extrinsic motivation).	Speakers achieve their aims: they get what they wanted, an information gap is filled, a problem is solved, a decision is reached or a social contract is made. The result is of intrinsic interest or value to the participants.

Who: participants in communication	A large group in which not everyone is facing the speakers or interested in what they say, except perhaps for one person, the teacher, who pays less attention to what they say than to how correctly they say it.	Two or more people, facing each other, pay attention and respond to what is said rather than to how correctly it is said.
How: means of communication	Language from teacher or medium is very closely adapted to learners' level. All speech is as accurate as possible, and usually in complete sentences. Learners are corrected if their speech deviates from standard forms, whether or not their meaning is clear.	Little consideration is paid to the general language level of the speaker. If there are problems, compensation strategies are used. The interlocutor helps to ensure that the content is correct.

In other words, for the classroom to change and to be as *authentic* as possible, classroom activities should be designed in accordance with the criteria of process- and product-orientation, with verbal (a 'text') or non-verbal (a solution, a decision) elements.

Communicative activities: learning reading *through* reading, writing *through* writing, speaking *through* speaking, listening *through* listening

Suggest more activities that would entail the features described on the left-hand side. Write them into the right-hand column.

Feature of activity	Typical activities	Other activities
Has an end/result/end product	Designing a poster, displaying it in class, discussing it; writing a CV for an application	
Participants are interested in achieving the aim/result	Writing an application for being in a chat-show, or for an appearance in a TV series; students have to follow a written instruction to assemble something	
The participants can make use of their own ideas, needs, experiences, views, etc.	Responding to literature, films, videos	
They have an information and/or opinion gap	A specialist in class reports on sports; students watch live television coverage of an important event	
There is a reason for speaking/writing and for reading/listening	The issue at hand is of global concern and the debate is on a global level, with English as lingua franca (e. g. writing to ATTAC, Amnesty International, a politician in another country)	

| Fig. 6.10

Communicative activities

Language behavior is as authentic as possible, i. e. no simplifications, no unnaturally slow speech, but use of compensation strategies, spontaneous speech	Inviting a guest to class; skyping with an English-speaking person about an important and significant issue
There is a reason for interaction, production and/or reception	Being invited to present a speech in English; having to organize a trip to another country

6.2 | Learning strategies and learner types

6.2.1 | Learning strategies

Der Unterricht ist "auf die Mittelköpfe" ausgerichtet (Tillmann 2007: 2) – Teaching only to the 'average' student?

The fostering of learning strategies, enabling learners progressively to become more autonomous, has already been an integral part of the delineations above. Such learning strategies involve taking into account *different learner types* (for an introduction cf. Haudeck 2007, Haß 2008, Viebrock 2010, Eisenmann 2012; a critical discussion can be found in Hattie 2009: 195–99, 236, 244–47). Which strategies learners use and how they use them have been referred to in the vital fields of listening, reading, writing, and speaking, as well as in coterminous and related fields such as conversation skills, politeness and conversation routines, mediation, non-verbal communication, and intercultural skills. To illustrate the *applicability of strategies* with regard to concrete learning goals, a condition (IF) is linked to one or more action clauses (THEN) (O'Malley & Chamot 1996: 52, adapted):

Applying strategies

▶ IF the goal is to comprehend an oral or written text, and I am unable to identify the word's meaning, THEN I will try to infer the meaning from the context.
▶ IF the goal is to comprehend a concept in a written text, and I know the concept is not at the beginning, THEN I will scan through the text to locate the concept.
▶ IF the goal is to comprehend and remember an oral passage and I have heard a complete passage or thought expressed, THEN I will summarize the passage to ensure I understand it.

Express in three lines, using IF and THEN constructions, goals and strategies for the following contexts:

▶ Initiate a conversation
▶ Sound like a native speaker
▶ Use grammatically correct English
▶ Avoid intercultural blunders
▶ Understand every detail of a recording
▶ Understand a political speech

138

Defined as "specific actions, behaviors, steps, or techniques that students (often intentionally) use to improve their progress in developing L2 skills," learning strategies "can facilitate the internalization, storage, retrieval, or use of the new language" (Oxford 2002: 124; for concrete learning techniques cf. Rampillon 1985, 1991). *Learning how to learn* appears as a vital skill with life-long implications, promising more effective language learning and use. Research (Oxford 1990, Friedrich & Mandl 1992, O'Malley & Chamot 1996: 196, Cohen 1998, Oxford 2002: 124–37, Haß 2008, Viebrock 2010, Eisenmann 2012; see ch. 5.3.4) has suggested that the following should be considered in the EFL classroom:

▶ Effective FL learners are *aware* of the strategies they use and why they employ them.
▶ Mentally active learners are better learners, especially when *linking* new knowledge to existing knowledge and organizing new information accordingly.
▶ Strategies need to be regularly trained and should form an *integral part* of regular classroom events.
▶ Strategy training *takes time* and regular honing. It needs to be "planned, deliberate, and explicit" (Hattie 2009: 160). Strategy instructions should be incorporated in *meaningful communicative contexts*.
▶ Teachers should provide *explicit explanation* and modelling of strategy use and provide ample opportunities for practice.
▶ Students should be taught how to identify and analyze the learning strategies which are most useful for them *individually*. This can be done through action research but also by means of learning diaries and learning journals as well as through reflecting on one's own preferences.
▶ Learning strategies can be *transferred to new tasks*, where students, once accustomed to using certain strategies, can apply their skills to tasks similar to the ones they initially were trained to fulfil.

Learning strategies are usually differentiated into the categories of *metacognitive, cognitive,* and *social/affective strategies* (O'Malley & Chamot 1996: 197, Oxford 2002: 121, Hattie 2009: 190). With regard to FL learning, the following definitions and important strategies can be discerned (see fig. 6.11):

Metacognitive strategies	Cognitive strategies	Social/affective strategies
▶ Planning one's learning, comprehension, and production ▶ Evaluating one's progress	▶ Learning to interact with the material to be learned by manipulating it mentally or physically (e. g., using vocabulary cards)	▶ Interacting with others to assist learning, cooperating ▶ Asking for clarification ▶ Using affective control to assist a learning task

Definition: learning strategies

Categories

Fig. 6.11

Learning strategies

▶ Developing a plan to monitor progress (e. g., a learning diary), comparing with goals and other learners ▶ Focusing on task (e. g., planning to listen for key words or phrases) ▶ Planning the organization of written or oral task	▶ Using memory-enhancing strategies to help remember new words (e. g., visuals, keyword method) ▶ Learning inferencing and summarizing techniques	▶ Comparing notes with others ▶ Seeking feedback ▶ Developing a positive attitude toward target cultures ▶ Seeking chances to practice the FL

6.2.2 | Learner types

Factors influencing learners

A number of factors strongly influence how students of foreign languages choose and use learning styles: these factors include motivation, attitude (such as openness toward new experiences, persons, ideas, beliefs, etc.); career/academic specialization, sex, cultural background, age, personality (introversion or extroversion); proficiency or stage in language learning, and nature of tasks. Motivation appears as an important factor, since motivated FL learners generally use more strategies than less motivated learners (Council of Europe 2001: 176, Oxford 2002: 127).

Learner types

Within the wider context of the discussion of learning strategies certain *learner styles* or *learner types* have also been identified (for details, see chs. 4.6, 5.3.4). Teachers, however, should refrain from pigeon-holing learners or from believing that catering to different learner types serves as the one-size-fits all approach for all teaching or learning problems. There are, indeed, conflicting opinions in the literature on learner types: "The claim is that teaching is more effective when these learning preferences are taken into account – although others have claimed the opposite: that we should be teaching students the learning styles they do not have" (Hattie 2009: 195). Moreover, most students are *not solely* one specific learner type such as the visual, the auditory, or the kinesthetic type. These well-known '*VAK-types*' are often differentiated as follows according to the way information is taken in, stored, and recalled (Rosenberg 2013: 7, 16–18):

VAK learner types

▶ *Visual learner type*: he/she likes everything written down, marks materials with colors, likes visual stimulation and handouts and needs to take material 'off' the page, rewrite it, rearrange it, learn it again.
▶ *Auditory learner type*: they need to listen or speak to remember information. They often sub-vocalize when reading, move in rhythm, or learn best with music in the background. They love class discussions and listening to stories or telling stories.
▶ *Kinesthetic learner type*: (1) The emotional learner type needs to feel comfortable in a group, needs positive experiences and personalized learning material. (2) The motoric learner type needs to try out everything for him- or herself. He/she learns by doing and by real-life experiences. This type

enjoys moving about, often having problems staying put for a longer time. He/she is more concerned with a whole experience than with details. At home he/she may find that learning new vocabulary needs to be supported by walking about simultaneously.

Other learner types have also been identified (cf. Rosenberg 2013: 7, Viebrock 2012). Often opposite 'types' are defined such as the *global vs. the analytic* learner, the *abstract vs. the concrete* thinker, the *systematic vs. the non-systematic* way of processing and organizing information. However, students generally do not just fall into one category but tend to have certain preferences or penchants. Being aware of the fact that they have to teach different learner types, establishing what preferences individual learners have, and finding differentiated ideas and activities according to learner preferences can be an important teaching 'tool' (Rosenberg 2013: 7).

Heterogeneous groups and inclusion | 6.3

Heterogeneous groups | 6.3.1

Since teachers increasingly need to cater to the *diverse needs and abilities of learners*, the following pages will first focus on *learner types*, then *mixed-ability classes*, and finally on including learners who are physically or mentally handicapped ('*inclusion*'). In the broader sense, the following suggestions focus on taking individual learners seriously, adapting activities for different learners while keeping this in balance with standardization and competence orientation – which can be an extremely *demanding task*, indeed.

Diversity, heterogeneity, individuality

> We want to satisfy the many different students in front of us, teaching to their individual strengths with activities designed to produce the best results for each of them, yet we also want to address our teaching to the group as a whole. (Harmer in Rosenberg 2013: 12)

First of all, teachers need to recognize and/or diagnose how students in their class are 'different': from others in the class and also from what the curriculum or textbooks presuppose as the 'average' learner – if there ever was such a person.

The following five categories help to define *learning style dimensions* (cf. Felder & Henriques 1995: 12, Rosenberg 2013: 27–28):

▶ What is the preferred type of *information intake and processing* of the student: sensory (sights, sounds, physical sensations) or intuitive (memories, ideas, insights)?
▶ How is *sensory information* most effectively used: visual (pictures, diagrams, graphs, demonstrations) or verbal (written and spoken words, formulas)?
▶ How does the student *prefer to process* information: actively (engagement in physical activity or discussion) or reflectively (introspection)?

▶ How does the student *progress* toward understanding: sequentially (logical progression of small incremental steps) or globally (large jumps, holistically)?

▶ With which *organization* of information is the student most comfortable: inductive (facts and observations are given, underlying principles are inferred) or deductive (principles are given, consequences and applications are deduced)?

It may seem like an enormous task to explore and identify the different styles and types of learners in a class. Yet *beginning to notice how individual learners learn best* can be both an enjoyable and rewarding experience for teachers and learners alike: "By encouraging learners to develop those strategies [which are best for them and] which will make them more autonomous in how they approach and work on material, we can help them to become life-long learners." (Rosenberg 2013: 14)

Multistyle approaches   The *practical implementations* of the concept of different learner styles in the classroom can begin with offering teaching and learning scenarios which appeal to a *great variety of learner types*. Teachers need to make students aware of how they learn and communicate. They should encourage them and offer tasks which support their individual learning styles. Here is a list of teaching suggestions for 'multi-style learning and teaching' (based on Felder & Henriques 1995: 28–29; numerous other suggestions can be found in Börner et al. 2010, Eisenmann 2012):

▶ *Motivating classroom atmosphere*: new material is presented in true-to-life situations and students can relate their personal experience and anticipation about their lives.

▶ *Balancing concrete information* appealing to sensory perception and conceptual information (cognitive, deductive) according to the needs of learners, with an emphasis on concrete information in beginner classes.

▶ *Balancing structured teaching approaches* such as formal training with more open-ended unstructured activities (communicative phases).

▶ *Frequent use of visuals*, e. g., films, photographs, drawings, sketches, and cartoons to illustrate and reinforce the meanings of words, to focus on cultural issues, and to foster media competence.

▶ *Avoiding too much lecturing and writing on the board*. Providing intervals for students to take in information, including brief writing exercises (reflective); posing questions and problems to be dealt with by students in small groups, and enacting dialogs and mini-dramas.

▶ Giving students the *option of cooperating* with homework assignments and encouraging interaction. "All students participate in respectful work." (Eisenmann 2012: 300)

▶ *Balancing inductive and deductive presentation* of course material, leaving options for their own approaches, especially with more advanced learners.

For *heterogeneous learner groups* or *mixed-ability* classes teachers may use different textbooks in the same class. However, this may have a stigmatizing effect on students and, therefore, material and activities should be chosen satisfying both those with above-average and below-average skills. Such a *multilevel approach* is based on a few basic *principles* (cf. Bowler & Parminter 2002: 59, Klippert 2010, Müller 2012, Eisenmann 2012: 300):

Multilevel approach to heterogeneity

▸ It is not necessary for every student to understand every item of the material presented or worked with. Rather, success is measured by how individual students complete the task that is set for them as members of a group or even as individuals.
▸ Success and student ability can be measured according to a simple equation: 'text level of challenge + task level or support = student success.'
▸ In other words, a difficult and long text can be coupled with a simple task that makes reading it (scanning it, skimming it, looking for key words, etc.) achievable for weaker students. On the other hand, a short and simple text can be accompanied by a demanding task (e. g., finding the political symbolism in a fable).

For mixed-ability classes '*tiered tasks*' and '*biased tasks*' can be used to cater to different learner levels (cf. Bowler & Parminter 2002: 59). Using the *example* of students having to respond to a written text, a *tiered task* would have a set of three different tasks: below-average students are provided with support for answers on the task sheet (e. g., more information) and the task is relatively simple (e. g., matching activities, multiple-choice options). Average students get less (or no) additional information, but an option of several correct or incorrect answers in matching exercises. Above-average students would not get any extra support, but possibly more abstract and demanding questions. An *example* for a *biased* task would have a set of increasingly different tasks: below-average students just answer basic comprehension questions. Average students are asked to answer more detailed questions or questions including text analysis. Above-average students are asked to present an interpretation of the text with reference to certain passages. Outstanding students may be asked to interpret the text without any specific pointers or tasks given.

Tiered and biased tasks

> Devise biased and tiered tasks for below-average, average, and above-average students for (1) interpreting a scene from a film, (2) giving a short oral presentation on what students did during a school trip to London, (3) practicing a grammatical structure.

Some textbooks provide several task types, appealing to weaker and stronger learners, but also to different learning styles. However, it remains the task of the teacher to refrain from sending out *discriminatory signals* by habitually allotting simple tasks to weak students and more demanding tasks to strong students. There should be an element of *free choice* involved and different activities and skill applications require re-allocation of tasks and learners.

6.3.2 | Inclusion

> Discuss the following statement with regard to the challenge of 'inclusion':
> "From the first day of school our school system aims at securing the fiction
> of homogeneous learner groups." (Tillmann 2007: 7, our trans.)

Inclusion as a 'revolution'?

In 1994, the World Conference on Special Needs Education, which took place in Spain, issued the so-called *Salamanca Statement*, which addressed the problem of millions of children all over the world being excluded from the regular educational system. The principles outlined in this document formed the framework for the *UNESCO Guidelines for Inclusion: Ensuring Access to Education for All* (2005). There is a particular concern with the *identification and removal of barriers* to mainstream educational processes:

> Inclusion is seen as a process of addressing and responding to the diversity of needs of all learners through increasing participation in learning, cultures and communities, and reducing exclusion within and from education. It involves changes and modifications in content, approaches, structures and strategies, with a common vision which covers all children of the appropriate age range and a conviction that it is the responsibility of the regular system to educate all children. (UNESCO 2005: 13)

UNESCO guidelines

Governments, especially in Europe, while subscribing to the principles and recognizing the appeal for concrete actions, have been either slow (Germany) or fast (England) in starting to implement (some of) the proposed inclusive educational principles. In England, for example, the DfES (Department for Education and Skills) decreed a *Special Educational Needs and Disability Act* and published an "Index for Inclusion" to be used for all English schools (Booth & Ainscow 2002). Lagging behind, Germany ratified the *UN Disability Rights Convention (Behindertenrechtskonvention)* in 2009. In 2011, the *Bundesministerium für Arbeit und Soziales* issued an action plan entitled *Unser Weg in eine inklusive Gesellschaft*. While most of the projects listed in this document are mere declarations of intent, increasingly *concrete steps to implement inclusion* have been demanded. The federal states responsible for introducing inclusive principles into their educational systems have gradually begun practical implementations.

In 2012, a leading article in a major German newspaper put the problem or challenge of implementing inclusion principles into a nutshell by stating that "inclusion is not a reform but rather a revolution for the classroom" (Osel 2012: n. p., our trans.). And indeed, there are *manifold problems* which should not be swept under the carpet when finding solutions to how inclusion can be implemented:

▶ Inclusion entails a break with *traditional concepts deeply ingrained* in the educational system with several tiers, governed by the principles of *selection, competition, and achievement* – including special needs schools (*Förderschulen*).

Challenges

▶ Inclusion means a rift with traditional concepts of an *ability-based pedagogy* by advocating different goals.

Exclusion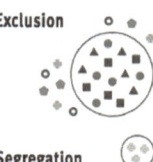

▶ Inclusion is advocated by many and is seen as the 'politically correct' approach. Yet, time and again there have been news reports on parents and pedagogues being extremely concerned about and opposed to concrete cases of inclusion *if their own children are involved.*

Segregation

▶ Inclusion, without a doubt, *cannot be implemented for free*: it will create additional costs for more staff, special classroom equipment, pre- and in-service teacher training, cooperation, etc.

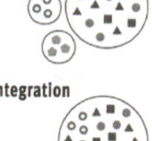

▶ There seems to be disagreement about what the term *'inclusion'* should cover, with a broader concept including all individuals (including categories such as sex, gender, ethnicity, or 'being different' in any way) or a more concrete definition of being physically or mentally handicapped.

Integration

▶ When using the narrow definition, there is still a *wide variety* of 'handicapped individuals', and an across-the-board suggestion for how to deal with 'inclusion of handicapped people' in the EFL classroom would be useless at best, counter-productive at worst. For example, there are at least ten types of dyslexia; and there is a tremendous difference between a blind person in the EFL classroom and a deaf person, a person with a speech impediment and a person who is slightly mentally challenged.

Inclusion

Fig. 6.12
Exclusion, segregation, integration, inclusion

▶ Finally, given the fact there are *no one-size-fits-all suggestions* for implementing inclusion in the EFL classroom, there is also very little published material helping EFL teachers (cf. Dam & Legenhausen 2013, Bartosch & Rohde 2014).

> Discuss the issue of 'inclusion' with friends, parents, children, and your peers. Do you know of instances of 'inclusion'? What is your personal position? Think of how teaching and learning methods need to be changed in general and for the EFL classroom in particular.

The idea of inclusion is closely connected with the concept of integration. However, there is a *crucial difference*:

From integration to inclusion

> Integrative schools did not see the need to change their organizational structure and their traditional teaching methods. The concept of integration implied that children with learning impairments and/or disabilities were either transferred from special needs schools, or were just placed in mainstream schools

where they were then given special attention according to their particular form of impairment and/or disability; it was a question of integrating individual learners into an existing system. This exempted the mainstream practitioners from the responsibility of adapting their 'normal' teaching to the needs of these children. This meant, in other words, that the mainstream approach as such was not challenged in integrative schools. Inclusion, by contrast, implies a change in terms of organization and approach. The system as such needs to be reconceptualised and adapted so that it can accommodate all learners. (Dam & Legenhausen 2013: 116–17; see fig. 6.13)

No body is disabled but every body has different ables. – Nolan Byrnes

Fig. 6.13 |

Differences between integration and inclusion (based on Damm & Legenhausen 2013)

	Integration	Inclusion
Teaching, goals, assessment	▸ Traditional concepts, based on 'bell curve thinking' (see ch. 12.3.1) ▸ Teaching goal: academic achievement, based on competitive spirit, selection and distribution of chances	▸ Encompasses all learners, avoiding or negating 'bell-curve thinking': all individuals have certain abilities, talents, qualities, etc. for a community to learn from ▸ Holistic teaching goals: empathy, tolerance, cooperation ▸ Diversity as an enriching experience
Teaching methods	▸ Traditional teaching methods	▸ Focus on multiple and learner-oriented methods
Selective processes	▸ Segregation through special needs schools ▸ Or: special attention to individual learners who are integrated into existing structures and systems	▸ Inclusion as a reciprocal process: structures and systems need to be changed to incorporate all individuals
Approach to 'otherness'	No need for adaptation for mainstream pedagogy and teaching practices; different learners are 'labelled': (1) *Handicapped people are handicapped because society constructs them as handicapped.* This creates barriers and limits opportunities for equal participation. (2) Disruptive students, for example, are seen as a problem of individuals not playing by the rules of society and therefore having to change.	Mainstream needs to make participation possible, become flexible, change teaching goals, question standardization drives: (1) *It is not the handicapped person who is handicapped, but society is 'handicapped' by constructing the individual as handicapped.* Concepts of 'normalcy' are questioned. (2) Disruptive students could help to change and improve classroom rules.

To summarize, inclusion requires a different approach to 'difference' and finally a *change in attitude* toward the educational goals of the school system. Often two *interrelated arguments* are brought forth *against* inclusive classrooms: (1)

that special needs children fare worse in inclusive classrooms as opposed to special needs schools where certain learning difficulties are considered from the outset, (2) that in inclusive classrooms the gifted learners are impeded in their progress through the presence of less gifted learners, who would get special attention. While there is still need for more detailed research, empirical evidence gathered in Great Britain suggests that both concerns cannot be verified through the data collected in longitudinal studies. It appears that the advantages of special needs pedagogy are negligible. Also, there is "no evidence of a correlation of inclusion and achievement or progress either way" (ibid.: 119). Instead, there is a clear possibility of learners *profiting* from inclusive teaching methodologies, such as less teacher-centeredness, more autonomous learning, etc. (Dam 1995, Eisenmann 2012, Dam & Legenhausen 2013).

Dam and Legenhausen (2013: 122–28) present an interesting *case study* to illustrate how inclusion can be put into practice with special focus on fostering learner autonomy. In a longitudinal study, students of a Danish *folkeskole* class (a comprehensive school with mixed-ability classes for students six to fifteen years of age) were observed with a special focus on different abilities. A learner named Dennis, who had serious problems in reading and writing and presented a constant source of unrest and disruption, was assisted by (1) sitting and *working together* with a *highly gifted learner* and, crucially, (2) was encouraged to choose an *acting-out activity*, where he was involved in producing and presenting a play, (3) closely *working together with classmates*: he was cast as "Dennis the Menace" and quite enjoyed this role. A fellow student commented in her logbook: "*See a play called Denis menase, It was a very good play because they have practiced very much. Dennis was very good to play Dennis menase. I have never heard hem say so much. They play very well.*" (ibid: 127, original orthography) Another student, Susan, a severe dyslexic, was allowed to *cooperate* with fellow students in activities, finding other students who would help her with her spelling; and she was allowed to draw in simple vocabulary tests on objects, etc. The bottom line was: "Susan ended her schooling in the 10th grade at Karlslunde school with one of the top marks in her English oral state exam." (ibid.) However, Dam and Legenhausen add the following *words of caution*:

The inclusive classroom: case studies

> It has to be emphasized, of course, that neither Dennis nor Susan needed or were provided with additional teacher support, which perhaps more severe learning difficulties or impairments might have necessitated. [...] [T]he problem arises of where inclusive pedagogy reaches its limits. It will probably not be feasible, for example, to include autistic learners with aggressive potential within a mainstream system without a support teacher. (ibid.: 128)

What, then, are *practical methodological principles* for inclusive pedagogy and the inclusive EFL classroom? In general, there needs to be a shift toward a learning scenario where rich and sufficient learning opportunities are pre-

Principles

sented to everyone for all learners to participate in learning (cf. Eisenmann 2012). This entails:

► *Work choice*: learners have more options to learn how, where, and with whom they want to learn.
► *Peer tutoring*: the inclusive classroom is a step toward students teaching students.
► *Activities for all*: it seems helpful to introduce and design activity types which everybody can participate in. This means that these activities do not presuppose a certain level of competency; students can start out from their existing knowledge and tackle tasks according to their preferences.
► *Material choice*: students can choose the material best suited for them.
► *Clear structures*: learners are provided with a clear and transparent organizational framework; especially for those with special learning difficulties or other impairments, clear instructions and adhering to procedural routines seems an urgent need.

Helping students to gain and keep self-esteem

In general, the principles of ***autonomous learning***, ***differentiation***, and ***dealing with heterogeneity*** can be advocated for the inclusive classroom. "The focus should not be on how to remove or reduce weaknesses but on how to enhance students' strengths." (Eisenmann 2012: 307) Specifically, teachers should be encouraged to plan and design their lessons with the goal of furthering their students' self-esteem. The following elements are part and parcel of such a student-oriented objective (cf. Borras et al. 2009):

► *Security*, fostered by a climate of mutual respect and trust which makes the learner feel safe, respected and valued: 'I can feel safe.'
► *Belonging*, meaning the learner can be authentic and feels that the interests and needs of all learners are respected and valued: 'I belong to a group and they support me.'
► *Identity*, feeling rooted in oneself and being able to refer to one's own personal experience; feeling that learning contributes to personality development: 'I am special.'
► *Purpose*, by being presented structured learning tasks and clear instructions; developing an awareness of what language learning requires; becoming involved in the learning process: 'I know what to do. I know my goals.'
► *Competence*, including the capacity for self-evaluation and a determination to become better: 'I am capable of doing things.'

Consider how principles used for different learner styles can be employed in the inclusive EFL classroom. Consider the crucial concepts of fostering autonomous learning and supporting the individual learner's self-esteem.

148

Recommended reading

Arendt, Manfred (1999). Entrümpelung des Methodenrepertoires. In: *Fremdsprachenun-terricht* 43.52, 401–08.

Börner, Otfried; Christoph Edelhoff & Christa Lohmann, eds. (2010). *Individualisierung und Differenzierung im kommunikativen Englischunterricht*. Braunschweig: Diesterweg.

Dam, Leni & Lienhard Legenhausen (2013). Learner Autonomy – A Possible Answer to Inclusion. In: Maria Eisenmann; Margit Hempel & Christian Ludwig, eds. *Medien und Interkulturalität im Fremdsprachenunterricht: Zwischen Autonomie, Kollaboration und Konstruktion*. Duisburg: Universitätsverlag Rhein-Ruhr, 115–32.

Eisenmann, Maria (2012). Introduction: Heterogeneity and Differentiation. In: Maria Eisenmann & Theresa Summer, eds. *Basic Issues in EFL Teaching and Learning*. Heidelberg: Winter, 297–311.

Klippert, Heinz (2010). *Heterogenität im Klassenzimmer: Wie Lehrkräfte effektiv und zeitsparend damit umgehen können*. Weinheim et al.: Beltz.

O'Malley, J. Michael & Anna Uhl Chamot (1996). *Learning Strategies in Second Language Acquisition*. Cambridge: Cambridge University Press.

Oxford, Rebecca L. (1990). *Language Learning Strategies: What Every Teacher Should Know*. Boston, MA: Heinle & Heinle.

Intercultural and transcultural learning

Contents

Abstract

This chapter will introduce one of the vital issues of teaching a foreign language (FL). Language and communicative skills are always interrelated with 'intercultural skills.' *Landeskunde* (area studies/regional studies) was strongly influential for many decades after 1945, focusing on the target cultures' life and institutions, providing facts and figures and prioritizing the teaching and learning of 'culture with a capital C.' However, in the last decades, Cultural Studies (*Kulturwissenschaft*) and intercultural learning have changed concepts of learning about cultures. Increasingly, the perspective has widened concerning the target cultures in the EFL classroom, with everyday life, popular culture, minority cultures, globalizing cultures, and different English-speaking cultures than the UK and USA vying for attention. This chapter offers a survey of this shift from *Landeskunde* to intercultural and, finally, transcultural concepts, models, and practices of TEFL.

Consider the introductory cartoon for this chapter together with the following statement: "If you get the present perfect and the simple past wrong you may lose marks; if you get the culture wrong you may lose face, money or even life." (Gibson 1994: 127) Discuss why the intercultural encounter depicted in the cartoon goes wrong. Which assumptions lead to particular perspectives and problems, and how could one avoid the blunders shown in the cartoon?

From *Landeskunde* to intercultural learning | 7.1

Culture and language | 7.1.1

> Consider the following two sentences: 'It was at the end of November.
> Grandpa brought the bird to the table.' Imagine the scene and discuss how
> the story would continue.

A closer look at these inconspicuous-sounding two sentences sheds a reveal- Language creates
ing light on the perennial issue of how *language and culture are interconnected*. mental images
Graphemes and phonemes in any language, here English, trigger different
images in the minds of individuals – and these are clearly *culturally inflected*.
Of the manifold possible images of this scenario created in the minds of individuals, only three can be singled out here. (1) The first one would spring to the
mind of advanced FL learners, who would grasp that for most US-Americans
the association immediately created would be that of a Thanksgiving dinner
(the traditional meal of stuffed turkey, mashed potatoes, beans, etc.), celebrated
in American homes on the fourth Thursday of November. (2) In a more international context of English language use, for example in China, 'bird' could be
associated with a singing bird, a canary for example, to be exhibited proudly to
the rest of the family. (3) In yet another context, this could have rather dubi-
ous implications, with 'bird' being a slang expression for a young lady in Britain (see ch. 5.3.1) and 'grandpa' either a 'dirty old man' or a 'sexy senior citizen.'
Again, the two attributes for 'grandpa' used here show how different linguistic
expressions create different mental images.

Just how close language and culture are linked has been the subject of long
debates. *Do languages create different realities?* The so-called **Sapir-Whorf
Hypothesis**, influential since the 1920s, explicitly presupposes the *formative
power of words or languages* on how individuals construct their environment.
Famously, Inuits supposedly have dozens of different expressions for 'snow' and
the Hanunov tribe of the Philippines uses 92 different words for 'rice' (Jandt
1998: 131). Nowadays, the idea that languages 'determine' concepts of reality is
considered to be too extreme, and scholars favor more complex models of how
reality is created by and in languages.

There are, however, practically minded approaches to teaching foreign lan- Teaching language
guages without reference to their cultural contexts. Such approaches basically without culture?
hold that intercultural communication is possible without specific cultural
knowledge – that we are all 'the same under the skin.' Here language becomes a
vehicle for the expression of similar values and the enactment of similar objectives. In separating the linguistic from the cultural context, the idea is to teach
a few general rules of politeness and conversation strategies. At most, students
are equipped with a list of *Do's and Don'ts* with reference to the different cultures of the world where English is used by native speakers or as a lingua franca.

This might be called the *lingua franca-approach* to TEFL, as for example practiced by the influential commercial Berlitz school, which favors a rather culture-neutral concept of communicative competence.

However, FL teaching and learning in an educational context always implies more comprehensive *educational goals* than just a focus on communicative skills. In addition, most EFL scholars today would agree that language and communication are always *embedded* in a culture or cultures. In other words, language and communication are always inflected not only by national identities, but also by regions, ethnicities, social classes, and the like. As Byram states: "[A]bove all, learners need to reflect on their own social identities and their own cultures in order to better understand those of other people and the impact their perceptions of each other have on the success of intercultural communication." (2000: 15)

Language and culture

Here are a few examples of how *language and culture* are closely related.

> Consider the following examples and think about the cultural differences and peculiarities demonstrated here (hints for interpretation are given right after the task):
>
> ▶ If a British student asks for a 'rubber', why is his American fellow student irritated?
> ▶ Why is the following line in a song by John Lennon extremely difficult to translate: 'Imagine there's no heaven, above us only skies.'
> ▶ Is a 'friend' on Facebook really what you would consider a '*Freund*' in Germany?
> ▶ On the streets of Delhi, India, you see signs for a 'hotel.' Does this mean you can actually stay there overnight?
> ▶ Why are Americans taken aback if you ask for the 'toilet'?
> ▶ What is a 'black eye'?
> ▶ How would you translate '*gemütlich*' into English?
> ▶ What do Americans and Europeans associate with the term 'capitalism'?
> ▶ What is a 'liberal person' in America and in Europe?
> ▶ Can you use the expression 'negro' for an African American?

To speak a language is to take on a world, a culture. –
Franz Fanon

Suggestions for answers:

▶ In American English a rubber is a colloquial expression for a condom (AE: eraser).
▶ Heaven and sky for *Himmel*: polysemantic meaning of English expression.
▶ 'Friend' in English, especially in American English, would often be translated by *Bekannter* in German. In this case, culturally different concepts of relationships shape the use of words.
▶ In India, a 'hotel' is actually a food stall (see fig. 7.1).

▶ The term 'toilet' is a taboo word. Instead, expressions like 'I need to wash my hands' or 'I need to go to the ladies / gents room' are used. In polite conversation, in most English-speaking countries euphemisms are used for taboo areas such as death, sexuality, or sanitary matters.

▶ A 'black' eye is a bruised eye (*blaues Auge*). *Mit einem blauen Auge davonkommen*: to be saved / to escape by the skin of one's teeth. Metaphors and sayings are frequently culturally inflected.

▶ *Gemütlich* is a very German concept, and sometimes used as a loan word in English – it implies feeling cozy, comfortable, at home.

▶ For many Americans, 'capitalism' has positive connotations: freedom, independence, chances, individualism. For Europeans, it can imply a rampant, dog-eat-dog, laissez-faire economy.

▶ A liberal person in the USA is an open-minded, progressive person. In mainland Europe, this person would be politically in favor of less state interference.

▶ 'Negro' may be acceptable, but 'African American' is preferred; however, 'nigger' is a taboo word – sometimes referred to as 'the n-word' and only used in slang by African Americans among themselves.

Fig. 7.1
Indian food stall

From *Landeskunde* to Cultural Studies and intercultural competence

7.1.2

In German-speaking countries, a sea change in cultural learning happened in the 1980s when intercultural-learning approaches began to replace concepts of *area studies, regional studies or background studies* (also sometimes called 'Life and Institutions' of the target culture; all these terms are roughly encapsulated in the concept of *Landeskunde*, 1950s to 1980s). *Landeskunde* was partly conceived as a rational reaction to the pre-1945 approaches of *Kultur- und Wesenskunde*. Culminating negatively in the *Wesenskunde* of the Hitler regime, *Kulturkunde* since its beginnings in the late 19th century had aimed at teaching the 'spirit of a nation' (*Geist oder Wesen einer Nation*), implying that, most crucially, the English national psyche could be understood by reading the works of Britain's greatest writer William Shakespeare. *Kulturkunde* based its concepts on focusing on cultural and national contrasts, with the Nazis using the teaching of British and US-American culture increasingly as negative contrastive foils to the preferred Arian model of Germany. After 1945, a break with irrational, militant, and essentialist concepts of cultural learning was needed (Volkmann 2010: 45–46, see ch. 1.1.3).

The concept of area studies was marred from the beginning. Especially in university courses, it was often considered an *ancillary area or discipline*, which provided background knowledge for understanding great works of art. Its political or educative agenda remained vague, generally aiming at reducing national stereotypes and at creating 'international or universal understanding' (*Völkerverständigung*) by conveying instructive knowledge. Implicitly, it intended to

Area/background studies (*Landeskunde*): a problematic concept propagate *concepts of democratic societies and their institutions* as role models for a post-war generation of learners of English. Frequently, it offered a sort of sophisticated 'tourist kit' for future tourist travels to London, assorted British tourist spots, and the major sights of the USA – hence it was sometimes dubbed a '**tourist-kit approach**.' It often provided *idealized social images*, such as the complete nuclear family or the tension-free multicultural neighborhood. The target cultures – usually presented either in neutral or positive terms – were clearly defined as Great Britain (often focusing on England) and the USA, with occasional foci on areas of the Commonwealth (especially Australia). In addition, culture was defined as '***culture with a capital C***'; and knowledge transfer implied learning about *facts and figures*: typically, about the British Parliament and the American elections. Essential areas covered the following cultural phenomena:

▶ *The uses of language* in the context of literature (canonized texts): *Landeskunde* was seen as carrying the information needed to understand linguistic and literary phenomena
▶ *History*: timelines and significant historical dates ('1066 and all that …'), epochs
▶ *Art*: music, painting, art galleries
▶ *Science*: great scientific achievements
▶ *Economics*: industry, industrial relations, the financial sector, distribution of wealth, poverty
▶ *Social structure*: class systems, ethnic minorities, gender roles
▶ *Political institutions*: for example, 'checks and balances' in the USA
▶ *Religion, ideologies, and 'creeds'*: for example, 'the American creed', 'the melting pot', the American Dream
▶ *Minorities*: regional, ethnic
▶ *Geography, regionalism*
▶ *Codes of behavior*: for example, the gentleman ideal

Such a list of cultural elements cannot be completely abandoned when teaching and learning (inter-)cultural competence. However, already during the heyday of *Landeskunde* (between the 1960s and 1970s), there was a growing sense of discontent, culminating in various suggestions to conceptualize a *Landeskunde plus* that would go beyond the mere teaching of facts and figures. In this context, two often unrelated influences brought about the *forceful shift* from *Landeskunde* to *Cultural Studies* and *intercultural learning* in the 1980s.

Cultural Studies & intercultural learning

Both concepts – Cultural Studies and intercultural learning – introduced far-reaching *changes* in the perception of what culture is and how cultures or individuals interact (cf. Teske 2006). Both reflect the notion of culture as being more than merely a normative system. They do not understand national culture as creating a fixed national identity finding its most valuable and typical expression in great works of art or literature. Rather, culture is seen as *open*, *wide-ranging, shifting, and flexible*; nations are constantly being constructed as *'imagined communities'* (cf. Anderson 1983). In a reciprocal process, culture and cultural phenomena both shape the life of humans (humans as consumers, objects of culture) and are shaped by them (humans as active agents, being empowered by their choice of cultural elements). Furthermore, elitist notions are rejected in favor of an inclusive concept of culture (*culture as a way of life*), in which popular and everyday cultural practices ('*small-c culture*') as well as media-shaped practices are also recognized as valuable cultural experiences. Finally, the perspective on what used to be clearly defined target cultures has utterly changed. Intercultural exchanges have been foregrounded. The focus is not merely on native speakers of the 'core countries' UK and USA, but on other Anglophone countries and areas such as Australia, India, New Zealand, South Africa, Jamaica, and Canada. Finally, international exchanges in English as a lingua franca in so-called non-native-speaker to non-native-speaker communication have become increasingly important.

Since about the turn of the millennium, Cultural Studies, as an established academic discipline, has evolved with a *dynamic set of theoretical perspectives* with its own histories, methods, and agendas (cf. Delanoy & Volkmann 2006, Assmann 2006). It was first introduced in the 1960s and 1970s by the British scholars Raymond Williams, Richard Hoggart, and E. P. Thompson, who initially propagated a rather *socialist perspective* for the cultural empowerment of the working classes and, later, for ethnic minority groups. It aimed at developing a *counter-hegemonic perspective* which would benefit students in the interest of a more equitable society and has repeatedly been linked to political intervention in the interest of specific gender issues and social as well as ethnic groups such as the working class or indigenous communities. Its focus shifted from literature to films as well as to products of popular culture (e. g., soap operas, pop songs), and directed attention to the production, composition, reception, and circulation of cultural practices. While Anglo-Saxon approaches tend to move against elitist concepts of culture and their principally negative attitude to the popular, German proponents of Cultural Studies often view such practices as ambivalent phenomena – not so much as a source of individual and collective empowerment but rather as ideological manipulation of what the Frankfurt school (Horkheimer, Adorno) dubbed the manipulative 'Culture Industry' (*Kulturindustrie*).

While Cultural Studies is frequently linked to concepts of *emancipation, egalitarianism,* and *critical thinking* or carries *ideological implications*, the field of intercultural learning lacks such ambitious theoretical underpinnings or political concepts. Originating in multicultural societies such as the USA, intercultural learning or intercultural competence was first conceptualized in the 1960s as intracultural learning, i. e., learning to live together in multicultural and multiethnic communities. Learning about habits, norms, values, taboos, etc. of other immigrant groups has remained one of the driving forces behind

Cultural Studies as cultural counter-discourse

Pragmatic intercultural learning

intercultural learning programs. In the international business community, culminating in Hofstede's concepts of *'cultural norms'* (cf. Jandt 1998, Gibson 2000, Thomas 2005), the goals were less educational or political, but rather practical and utilitarian: to make business communication in the increasingly globalizing world more effective and friction-free as well as to avoid social blunders and detrimental faux pas (see the cartoon at the beginning of this chapter). Soon, handbooks of cultural *Do's and Don'ts* were published galore, with plentiful suggestions of how to express politeness, what norms and values to obey, and how to exhibit adequate communicative behavior, verbally and nonverbally (cf. Gibson 2000).

Intercultural learning
in the EFL classroom
Intercultural learning scenarios, as part of English lessons at school, need to focus on certain parameters: (1) they have to be linked to and become an *integral part* of FL learning, starting with beginners who, for example, learn that Christmas is celebrated differently in other parts of the world, what to expect for breakfast there, and that, simply put, it can be helpful to add a 'please' to a demand. (2) Since the EFL classroom does not cover one or two target cultures only, intercultural learning could and should focus on conversation routines and language use with English as a linguistic tool in various contexts, where different rules and routines of politeness and conversation apply. (3) While the classroom should not be overburdened with political or ideological critique (as in Cultural Studies), nor be devoid of educational goals as in intercultural learning programs for managers, the *educational objectives* of *tolerance, understanding* other cultures, and *solidarity* with suppressed and discriminated against individuals and groups cannot be neglected.

Fremdverstehen
Bredella's concept of **Fremdverstehen** offers a philosophical depth to the frequently merely pragmatic concepts of intercultural learning (Bredella 2010). Building on a hermeneutic notion of cultural exchanges as a 'melting of horizons' of two perspectives (*Horizontverschmelzung*), *Fremdverstehen* defines those involved in intercultural understanding as highly complex entities, engaging in an ongoing cross-cultural **'negotiation of meaning'** (*Bedeutungsaushandlung*). Such a perspective requires a redefinition of cultural learning. Since understanding cultures is dependent on preconceptions, a shift here is needed toward *intercultural* processes of meaning creation. Moreover, learners should no longer be seen as mere 'receptacles' to be filled with factual information. Instead, they are invited to become personally involved in the exploration of English-speaking cultures as self-reflective co-constructors of cultural meanings. Crucially, an intercultural experience aims at unfolding several perspectives, asking participants to see the world through the eyes of the other person (the 'Other'), compare this world view with their own and negotiate the two (*Perspektivenwechsel, Perspektivenkoordination*), leading to an ongoing comparison of horizons of expectation rather than to a blending of such horizons.

Bredella (2010) and others (e. g., Freese 2002, Volkmann, Gehring & Stier-storfer 2002, Hallet 2002, Delanony 2005, 2015) have stressed the crucial role of literature, but also of films and cultural artefacts in furthering intercultural understanding, as they presuppose active reader participation and an exploratory approach to *cultural texts*, inviting readers to identify with characters and slip into the role of the culturally Other. Literature invites its readers to see the foreign world through the eyes of the other, to get an 'inside perspective' (see ch. 8.2). Participation in the secondary world of fiction can "help readers to develop empathy with and solidarity for the characters portrayed. Thus, such an aesthetic response also has a strong ethical dimension" (Delanoy 2005: 57).

The role of literature

Concepts of intercultural competence

| 7.1.3

In foreign language education, researchers have stressed the significance of the *communicative act* in intercultural exchanges (cf. Byram 1997), as the continuous negotiation of meanings takes place in concrete, symbolically mediated interaction processes. From such a perspective, language and culture are closely interrelated, thus asking for **intercultural communicative competence**. Accordingly, intercultural communicative competence can be defined as consisting of (Freese 2002: 15, slightly adapted):

- *Critical awareness and reflexivity*: the critical awareness of one's own cultural pre-conditioning and of the various cultural conditionings of others
- *Tolerance, openness, respect*, and the willingness to accept members of other cultures on their own terms
- The *readiness to meet with others* in the interstices between two cultures that form what Claire Kramsch (1998) and others have described as a **third place**, 'a culture of a third kind,' constituting an intercultural 'field of interchange.'
- The ability to develop *intercultural communicative action competence (Handlungskompetenz)*, i. e., to engage in communicative acts while being aware of unwritten rules and norms shaping intercultural encounters and using this awareness in a mutually beneficial manner.

Intercultural communicative competence

A model frequently used to describe how culture-bound frames or scripts of perception work is the so-called '*iceberg model*' (see fig. 7.2). Culture, accordingly, resembles an iceberg, with only a *small part* of the iceberg, the tip, displaying tangible or visible expressions of culture(s). Below the surface, one finds the underlying attitudes, beliefs, values, norms, and meanings. These shape and form the *tangible cultural phenomena* like food, clothing, music, and art in the mind of each individual. National cultures 'produce' different cultural icebergs, which in turn shape and form the individual's mind-set (cf. Gibson 2000: 16).

Culture as an iceberg

Fig. 7.2

The iceberg model of culture (Gibson 2000: 16, adapted)

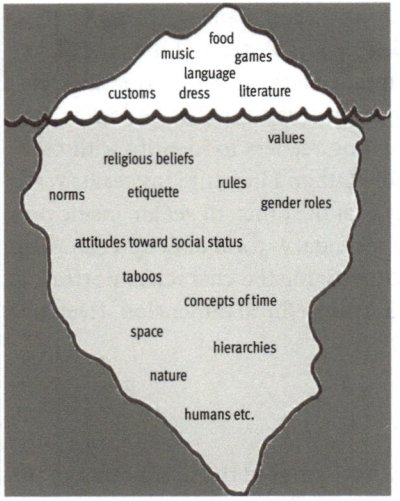

It must be stated that such *cultural conditioning* differs from culture to culture and person to person. Overgeneralizations can be just as detrimental to intercultural exchanges as the disregard of the other person's cultural conditioning.

Basically, the iceberg model of culture is a semiotic one. All *cultural phenomena* are seen as '*signs*' which are laden with meaning through their cultures. Here are a few examples: pork is forbidden in most Muslim societies, because it is considered 'dirty', unhealthy and unclean; carp, while appreciated in Germany, is usually not eaten in Anglo-Saxon countries, because it is considered as an inferior 'water swine'. Eye contact between a male stranger and a female on the streets of India or most parts of Asia is strictly avoided. Why is this so? Because the attitude behind it is that this would be an invitation by the female. If she reciprocated the

Cultural phenomena

male gaze, many Asians would consider her a prostitute. This attitude or taboo is rooted in different gender roles and perceptions of masculinity and femininity in Asian societies. Tangible cultural expressions can also be found among subcultures: for instance, baseball caps worn backward (in the USA, but also increasingly in global cultures) imply that the wearer wants to appear 'different' and 'cool'. *Cultural signs* can also *change meaning* and be appropriated by other cultural communities. One such sign is the Marlboro man, who was originally considered a symbol of traditional hypermasculinity and then turned into an icon of the gay community. Another one is the cross, which in secularized societies is turned from an indication of the wearer's faith to a mere fashion statement.

Dimensions of culture

The Dutch researcher Hofstede devised a structure of the lower part of the cultural iceberg by identifying four dimensions of national culture (cf. Harris & Moran 1993: 83). National cultures and, consequently, individuals can be categorized according to the following criteria:

▶ *Power distance*: defined as the degree to which a society accepts that social power is distributed unequally (e. g., laissez-faire capitalism vs. Soviet-style socialism)
▶ *Uncertainty avoidance*: defined as the extent to which a society feels threatened by uncertainty or ambiguous situations (e. g., risk-taking vs. risk-averse society)
▶ *Individualism vs. collectivism*: defined as the social framework and how people are meant to take care of themselves, how individual responsibility for

oneself (in the USA higher than in Germany) compares to the responsibility of society to support individuals (in Germany higher than in the USA)

▶ *Masculinity vs. femininity*: this juxtaposition works with (allegedly) male values such as assertiveness, appreciation of money and power vs. (allegedly) female interests such as caring for others, quality of life, etc.

Such different *cultural dimensions* impinge on a wide range of fields: the perception of time, space, hierarchies, gender, work, friendship, spirituality, etc. In the area of **intercultural business communication** (*Interkulturelle Wirtschaftskommunikation*) such – and more complex – grids have been used to prepare for intercultural exchanges (cf. Straub, Nothnagel & Weidemann 2010: 19). Cultural dimensions as attitudes, norms, and values are reflected in culturally different (verbal) behavior. If different cultural codes 'collide' in intercultural exchanges, friction may be the result – leading to misunderstandings and, possibly, a breakdown of communication. To train for real-life intercultural encounters, the method of working with '*critical incidents*' has established itself as a most beneficial preparation.

A critical incident becomes more vivid in the EFL classroom through the usage of a short role play, text, movie clip, or other media presenting intercultural misunderstandings. As a first learning step, students can simply describe what went wrong (*surface phenomena*). Then they can analyze the different cultural beliefs and attitudes and discuss ways of avoiding cultural conflict. Again, a role play or some kind of simulation can follow in which an alternative, better way of approaching the scenario is presented. Such critical incidents can also be presented through films which feature an array of such intercultural misunderstandings: one truly hilarious example is the movie *Outsourced* (2006, see fig. 7.3), featuring an American businessman who instructs Indian workers in a call center in how to sound more American on the telephone when selling American products from India.

Critical incidents

Fig. 7.3

Outsourced – movie poster

> Ask students to search the Internet for a collection/list of Do's and Don'ts for Germany: ask them to compile a list of tips and present them in class. Discuss if they are true and what they tell you about the writer's cultural background.

A standard handbook for intercultural competence offers the following 'case study' of a critical incident involving a German manager and his Thai secretary:

> A German manager working in Thailand is unhappy that his secretary arrives at work at least 30 minutes, and sometimes as much as one hour, late for work. He knows that the traffic in Bangkok is bad but this is getting ridiculous – one morning when she arrives he explodes in front of the others in the busy office, and then takes her aside and tells her that if she can't get to work on time she may risk losing her job. She hands in her resignation. (Gibson 2000: 43)

Using critical
incidents for
classroom discussion

It seems worthwhile to consider the *surface problems* of this *intercultural conflict* first: for unknown reasons, the secretary is late for work. The German manager severely threatens his secretary's 'face' (her image) in front of other employees (through the strict application of Western norms). The Thai secretary resigns. Behind this mini-drama there are, of course, *differing cultural norms*, which – in a presentation of this and similar instances – can be analyzed in terms of different attitudes toward time and punctuality, different sentiments with regard to being exposed in front of one's peers and, finally, just plain insensitivity on the side of the German manager, who is more achievement- than people-oriented (as they would call it in business circles). Closer to young learners' real world are activities which aim at teaching learners *politeness* by means of a gap-filling activity such as this one (Volkmann 2010: 182):

Task for intermediate
learners

Situation: Your friend invites you to her house for the first time.
Friend: Why don't you come in?
You: Thanks. (After looking around) .... house you have.
(Possible answers: What a great/wonderful/beautiful)

National stereotypes

Doubtlessly, such ***awareness-raising activities*** can be very advantageous. However, they also carry with them the danger of *perpetuating national stereotypes*. Such 'images of the mind' are "necessary overgeneralizations and oversimplifications that are rigid, resistant to change, undependable in their actual content, produced without logical reasoning" (Lippmann in Hammer 2012: 23). While they may help cognitively to pre-structure any intercultural encounter, stereotypes often mar such exchanges, leading to misunderstandings and the breakdown of communication. Even more detrimental to intercultural understanding are racial stereotypes or prejudices with their negativism and denial of equality, which can seriously prevent interpersonal exchanges.

Consider the following intercultural questions. Discuss them with learners, also from another cultural background. In addition, discuss the attitudes behind cultural or communicative practices.
In your culture or when in a certain country …

▶ Is it considered correct to interrupt someone who is speaking and, if so, when is it permissible?
▶ How do you begin a conversation with someone you have never met before?
▶ How long do you maintain eye contact when talking with or listening to someone?
▶ What is the body distance you feel comfortable with when talking to someone you do not know?

Toward transcultural competence

| 7.2

Global issues and global education

| 7.2.1

Global issues, global education, and *transcultural learning* all take two conditions of a globalizing world as their point of departure: (1) all social, cultural, economic, and ecological issues are increasingly *interconnected* and there is no such thing as an isolated, merely local issue. (2) Globalization and hybridization affect all cultures and cultural phenomena. There are no pure, homogeneous, unchanging elements of culture and this affects the life of all individuals and social groups (cf. Welsch 1999). Global learning takes on a transcultural perspective and aims "to enable learners to effectively acquire a foreign or second language while empowering them with the knowledge, skills and commitment required by world citizens to solve global problems" (Cates 2002: n. p.; cf. The New London Group 2000). Here, local problems, challenges, and solutions are always seen as inextricably intertwined with global issues. The list of these 'real issues' seems to be "depressingly long" (Hammer 2012: 62): global warming; acid rain; high population growth; the spread of global diseases; violence against, exploitation, and suppression of women and children in the production of clothing; genocide in Syria and famines in Somalia causing the growing number of refugees and asylum seekers, etc. The subject matter of *global issues* entails the areas of social and economic development, their interrelated political and cultural aspects, and the interconnectedness of local life worlds and global concerns (cf. Volkmann et al. 2010). What could be called '*global competence*' can be developed by focusing on twelve obviously interrelated and overlapping thematic fields as presented in the following list (cf. Volkmann 2010: 195–96, Hammer 2012: 75):

Tolerance, intercultural dialogue and respect for diversity are more essential than ever in a world where peoples are becoming more and more closely interconnected. – Kofi Annan

Key global issues

▶ *Demographic aspects:* mobility, dissolution of space, spatial 'shrinking', processes of migration, settlement, mass migration, according to countries, cultures, social groups, etc., the politics of migration and immigration
▶ *Social aspects:* religion, living together in multicultural societies, integration and 'parallel societies'
▶ *Aspects of peace education and non-violence:* violence and war, racism, armament, refugees, terrorism
▶ *Social aspects:* human rights, gender issues, child rights, social commitment (e. g., ATTAC, Amnesty International, Terre des Femmes)
▶ *Political aspects and human rights education:* human rights, global governance, immigration laws, politics of assimilation, multiculturalism, integration
▶ *Ecological aspects and environmental education:* environmental pollution, deforestation, animal rights, recycling, natural catastrophes, climate change
▶ *Cultural aspects:* global pop culture, McDonaldization, globalization and localization (local and global interconnections)

163

▶ *Socio-economic aspects:* poverty, unequal distribution of wealth, consumer societies, commercialism, financial systems, market economies, fair trade
▶ *Technical aspects:* traffic, mobility, digitalization
▶ *Media aspects:* media use, Internet, social networks, global communication, smart phones
▶ *Health education:* drugs, fighting AIDS and other global diseases, food (fast food vs. balanced diet)
▶ *Language-related aspects:* language imperialism (English as 'killer language'), communication problems, English as a lingua franca, business communication (see ch. 1.1)

Teaching goals can be broadly defined according to the Project LINGUAPAX, initiated by UNESCO, which suggests the following guidelines for "teaching foreign languages and literature for peace and international understanding" (Hammer 2012: 63–64):

▶ Be aware of your responsibility to further international understanding through your teaching.
▶ Increase language teaching effectiveness so as to enhance mutual respect, peaceful coexistence, and cooperation among nations.
▶ Exploit extracurricular activities such as pen-pal programs, video exchanges, and overseas excursions to develop international understanding.
▶ Lay the basis for international cooperation through classroom cooperation using language-teaching approaches responsive to students' interests and needs.

Problems of transcultural learning and global education in EFL
As important as it certainly appears for the EFL classroom, the approach of transcultural learning and global education carries a number of *problematic aspects*: (1) The loss of clearly defined target cultures and key issues connected with theses cultures – as with *Landeskunde* – also carries with it a sense of bewilderment as to what to teach and where to find a focus that is not merely transdisciplinary, across all school subjects, but one that is germane to English as a school subject. (2) Classes might tend merely to scratch the surface of problems when too many topics are highlighted without specific national, regional, or historical foci. (3) English might lose its content as a school subject, becoming a sort of meta-subject in advanced classes without a clear agenda. Such detrimental tendencies can be countered if, first, in English classes, the *intercultural perspective* remains an integral part of any discussion of global issues, e. g., when the learner culture perspective is compared with that of a different culture. Second, language aspects should not be neglected. Rather, the specific terminology, discourse patterns, and discursive strategies used in the English language can be highlighted when dealing with global issues.

Ecodidactics
Of the global issues discussed above, one pressing concern deserves special attention. It has brought about a specific branch of pedagogy called *ecodi-*

dactics (cf. Mayer & Wilson 2006). What needs to be considered here is clearly the idea of 'sustainability', as already defined in a 1987 document by the World Commission on Environment and Development (Hammer 2012: 60), connecting economic with ecological issues:

> 'Sustainability' is the key political goal for the 21st century. It means that future generations should have the same chance of leading a fulfilled life as we have had. At the same time, the opportunity to live a good life must be more fairly distributed around the world for the people alive today. Sustainable development combines economic progress with social justice and conservation of the natural environment.

Ecodidactic approaches aim at creating ecological knowledge, furthering a deeper and broader understanding of sustaining natural resources and the environment (cf. Mayer & Wilson 2006). Thus, individual agents should be empowered to deal with nature and natural resources more carefully and responsibly to detect, assess, and prevent threats and dangers to nature. The ecological approach does not merely aim at a change of mind, but moreover, aims at a *change in consumer habits*, less materialism and exploitation of natural resources both by social groups as well as individuals. It stresses (1) the net-like interconnectedness of all human and non-human phenomena, (2) and favors approaches in the spirit of wholeness, sustainability, and diversity. (3) It questions the Western creed of technology as the major means of progress, and (4) it stresses the complexity of biosystems and the fragile, problematic position of humans, whose invasion of natural systems causes severe negative repercussions.

The following poem by Julia Damassa, entitled "Green" (1989), nicely points at the inconsistencies and ironic contradictions consumers have to live with. Without a clear marker of its specific cultural context, the poem – through its use of language – highlights a number of transcultural, global issues (qtd. in Volkmann 2012: 405, cf. Volkmann 2011a, b, 2014):

Task for intermediate and advanced learners

> Outside the supermarket
> sign the petition
> 'SAVE OUR EARTH'.
> Feel a momentary
> sense of achievement
> as you turn the ignition.

First, try to describe the contradiction presented here and why this is not a single, isolated incident. Then think of how it could be exemplary of similar double-bind situations we all are faced with. Consider possible ways of getting out of this double-bind. Then consider how you would present this poem. How can you get students to write similar poems – and how can they discuss possible strategies of escaping the double bind?

7.2.2 | **Assessing and evaluating inter- and transcultural competence**

The most frequently referred to model of *assessing and evaluating intercultural communicative competence* is a model by British scholar Michael Byram (see fig. 7.4, cf. Coperías-Aguilar 2007, Volkmann 2010: 165, Hammer 2012: 57, Blell & Doff 2014: 84). According to Byram (1997: 49–55), intercultural communicative competence can be defined in terms of the following *objectives*:

▶ *Knowledge* of social groups, their identities and perspectives, and the process of intercultural interaction
▶ *Skills* to compare, interpret, and relate perspectives from different cultures
▶ The ability to *discover and interact* with different cultural practices
▶ The attitude of *openness and readiness* to understand other people
▶ A *critical cultural awareness* of one's own culturally inflected values and how they shape intercultural encounters

These different *savoirs* can be acquired by individuals through direct exposure to foreigners or foreign-language media. However, if they are learned and taught within an educational context, they are embedded in a broader framework of educational objectives. The figure features the framework of *political education*, which depends on a country's or state's overall education policy. In German-speaking countries, the combination of intercultural communicative competence and political education would crucially aim at developing the learner's *critical awareness* and creating *responsible citizens* who show tolerance toward those with other political or religious convictions.

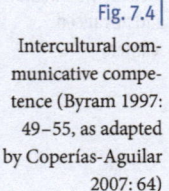

Fig. 7.4 |
Intercultural communicative competence (Byram 1997: 49–55, as adapted by Coperías-Aguilar 2007: 64)

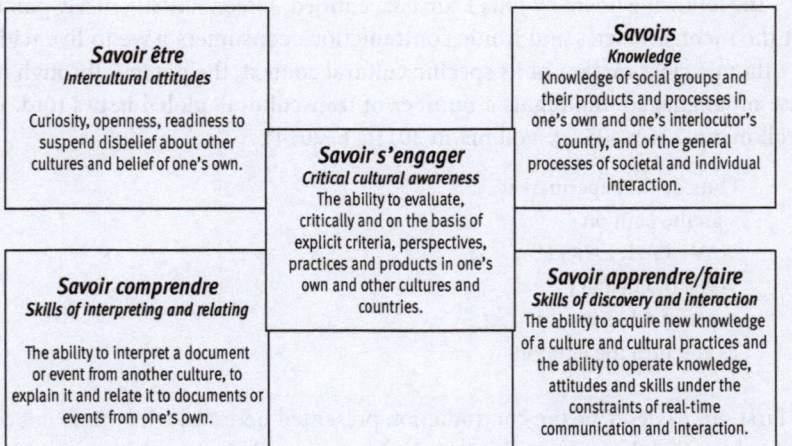

Savoir être
Intercultural attitudes

Curiosity, openness, readiness to suspend disbelief about other cultures and belief of one's own.

Savoir s'engager
Critical cultural awareness
The ability to evaluate, critically and on the basis of explicit criteria, perspectives, practices and products in one's own and other cultures and countries.

Savoirs
Knowledge
Knowledge of social groups and their products and processes in one's own and one's interlocutor's country, and of the general processes of societal and individual interaction.

Savoir comprendre
Skills of interpreting and relating

The ability to interpret a document or event from another culture, to explain it and relate it to documents or events from one's own.

Savoir apprendre/faire
Skills of discovery and interaction
The ability to acquire new knowledge of a culture and cultural practices and the ability to operate knowledge, attitudes and skills under the constraints of real-time communication and interaction.

Taking into consideration what has been outlined above about the objectives of *Landeskunde*, Cultural Studies, and inter-/transcultural learning, a definition of *teaching/learning objectives* can be itemized as follows (based on Byram's model):

Knowledge: Students know of

Teaching/learning objectives

▶ target cultures and their sub-cultures, their local and global importance, see problems, challenges, and opportunities
▶ the historical and social background and possible solutions of cultural phenomena; how they differ from those known to them and how they relate to them

Skills: Students can

▶ identify and explain cultural phenomena, critically reflect on them, and apply their skills to similar topics
▶ relate to problems and challenges presented to them cognitively, can tackle them in a creative, cooperative way and weigh possibilities of solving problems or crises; they can weigh issues considering several perspectives, and they can assess culture-specific and transcultural elements

Attitudes: Students are

▶ motivated to find out more about the target culture(s) and the issues presented
▶ aware of the problems and chances inherent in the issue at hand
▶ aware of their own and other approaches to defining the cultural phenomenon under discussion and ready to compare them
▶ more open toward the other culture, respect fairness, social justice, diversity, complexity, ambiguity, and develop empathy
▶ they are encouraged to act (verbally) according to the principle of 'think globally, act locally'

As to the issue of *testability*, it must be stated that knowledge (facts and figures, as in *Landeskunde* concepts) seems fairly easily testable, even in multiple choice tests. In addition to that, skills such as problem solving can be tested in oral exams or with less patterned forms of testing (essay questions). *Attitudes*, however, are notoriously difficult to test, for students can easily answer in socially acceptable formulaic utterances while acting in a completely different manner outside the classroom. Intercultural communicative competence in the form of tolerance and the willingness to accept others is certainly a lifelong and interdisciplinary learning challenge where good teaching can serve as an initiation or support.

Testing intercultural competence

Look again at the cartoon at the beginning of this chapter. Then try to define the teaching and learning objectives according to Byram with regard to the dialog presented in the cartoon. What knowledge, skills, and attitudes can students acquire? What overall educational objective would you aim at?

7.3 | Ten principles

In the following, ten principles or guidelines for inter- and transculturally effective teaching and learning are briefly delineated (cf. Nünning & Nünning 2000, Teske 2006, Volkmann 2010). They incorporate the changes from *Landeskunde* to inter- and transcultural learning, from concepts of 'culture with a capital C' to cultures as semiotic constructs, and the role of individual perspectives in intercultural negotiation described above.

1. From knowledge transfer to acquiring cultural competence

Acquiring intercultural competence is much more than merely being in command of declarative, comprehensive, and Wikipedia information. However, there seems to be a trend to throw the baby out with the bathwater. It seems dangerous to do without all factual knowledge (e. g., knowing the names of rivers or cities or of famous artists of a target culture) or the knowledge of core ideas and values and solely appreciate *procedural knowledge* learned for the purpose of using it in communication. Teachers and learners alike need to consider which form of knowledge is required to be learned and taught in culture-oriented classrooms. What are the procedural knowledge and skills needed in concrete communicative situations *and* needed for orientation in a complex global environment (*Orientierungswissen*)?

2. From canonical knowledge to exemplary learning

Given the abundance of target cultures, including those where English is used as a lingua franca, and the ever-changing set of topics that seem of relevance for the EFL classroom, any topic and learning arrangement can and must of necessity be *exemplary*: the classroom must offer *case studies*. For example, if the focus is on ethnic minorities in the USA, not all ethnic minorities can be dealt with equally, and there has to be a focus on a limited number of ethnic minorities. It certainly is not enough to provide just factual information about the selected example, such as an outline of history and social issues, but to provide lively, actual stories students can relate to. If this is done in an exemplary manner, issues such as ethnic minorities, migration, and immigration can be broadened to include other global areas and one's own society.

3. From the outside perspective to a multiperspectival approach

An essential part of intercultural learning is the ability and willingness to *change perspectives* and to learn to perceive problems and topics through the eyes of the cultural Other. Two opposite poles need to be avoided: while the egocentric or ethnocentric perspective merely regards one's own perspective as the true and valuable option, a complete adaptation of the foreign perspective might be just as limited. It is not the aim of the EFL classroom to turn learners into perfectly assimilated Anglo-Saxons, but rather to educate *reflec-*

tive agents in cultural exchanges. In contrast to the focus on 'objective' factual knowledge, approaches are needed in which the interaction between the self and the other is central, where the ongoing construction and negotiation of meaning feature prominently. Crucially, the learner's own cultural perspective is considered by discussing *similarities and differences* when it comes to dealing with other cultures.

4. From the concept of a 'neutral' learner to a focus on learner identity

Intercultural learning tends to conceptualize learners which resemble a gender-, age- and ethnic-neutral person. Teachers need to take into consideration *individual learners* and learner group identities. Topics as well as approaches need to regard issues of gender, ethnicity, nationality, age, and peer group interests. A classroom of multicultural learners and issues is an *asset* with regard to tackling cultural issues from a variety of perspectives.

Consequently, new strategies must be developed through which learners can connect factual information with personal experience, and learn to identify cultural differences, infer and foresee cultural problems, and cope with misunderstandings and communication breakdowns.

5. From culture to cultures

One of the main objectives of any intercultural learning is certainly to establish that a homogeneous, fixed, and unchangeable cultural entity is a myth. Culture is constructed, shifting, and subject to *sociocultural forces of change.* Learners need to experience the heterogeneity of British and American cultures as well as the other English-speaking nations around the world and their various regional cultures and sub-cultures, with their hybrid and globalizing tendencies. Teachers should present youth culture, popular culture, and everyday culture as well as insights into how cultural or national identities are formed. A beneficial activity could be that of discussing diverse 'cultural icons,' from geography and architecture (Big Ben, the Golden Gate Bridge, Ayer's Rock) to individuals (Mahatma Ghandi, Nelson Mandela, Martin Luther King).

| Fig. 7.5
Bengali sign to
the temple Hoolka
Dadka Guryaha
Deggan (London)

6. Finding the right cultural mix

Any presentation of another culture is in *danger of transmitting a biased image.* For example, when dealing with the USA, Germans tend to focus on gun-happy Americans, the repression of minorities, and gory aspects of the death sentence. Such proclivities are, of course, just as one-sided as praising American democracy and American-style capitalism. Demanding that teachers be neutral in their presentation of another culture is certainly utopian; yet, misrepresentations and presentations that foster one-sided *prejudices and negative stereotypes need to be avoided.* For instance, teachers could choose topics such as 'pioneering environmental ideas in the USA' or how citizens spend free time to solve inner-city problems (see the US Embassy project "Going Green": www.goinggreen2014.org). Scenarios should include a number of cultural texts from various perspectives and media. In any case, an 'at home everything is better' attitude needs to be avoided. Rather, a certain curiosity might be created with regard to the issue of how other nations or cultures could teach us to find new ways of tackling social, political, or ecological challenges.

7. Toward a holistic approach: integrating culture and language learning

The cultural information implicitly provided in textbooks frequently offers a vision of everyday life in assorted target cultures, often still starting with life in Great Britain for beginners. Only rarely do teachers find material to create intercultural awareness. In contrast, factual cultural information is still often reduced to teachable and memorizable chunks, which are mostly taught in an abstract way focusing on cognition (cf. Teske 2006). Even the format given to cultural information is different, as textbooks frequently use boxes to mark off the 'value added content,' some of them presenting this information in German. Thus, students have little chance of applying or transferring the information received, or of consolidating and integrating their knowledge through habitual or emotional processes. Additionally, cultural aspects tend to remain isolated, as progression in the teaching of cultural knowledge seems more difficult than defining progression of grammatical knowledge. It is therefore of pivotal importance that teachers find additional material and ways of highlighting the interconnectedness of culture and language in *integrative classroom formats*. Using critical incidents to create intercultural awareness could be a first, much needed step.

Task for beginners

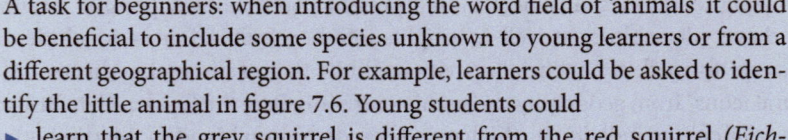

A task for beginners: when introducing the word field of 'animals' it could be beneficial to include some species unknown to young learners or from a different geographical region. For example, learners could be asked to identify the little animal in figure 7.6. Young students could

- learn that the grey squirrel is different from the red squirrel *(Eichhörnchen)*
- learn that it has its natural habitat in North America
- practice the difficult pronunciation of the word
- learn that English speakers have similar problems pronouncing the word *Eichhörnchen* (cf. YouTube videos, keywords 'Eichhörnchen – squirrel')
- learn about the spread of the grey squirrel in GB and find out about conservation projects such as Save Our Squirrels (www.saveoursquirrels.org.uk)
- discuss issues of wildlife preservation

Fig. 7.6 |
Picture of an American squirrel (California)

8. Representing cultures via various texts and media

Representing a cultural topic merely by using just one text creates one-dimensional images in two ways: (1) Every medium creates its own reality. Media specialist Marshall McLuhan famously stated: 'The medium is the message,' that is, the medium shapes the reception process to a great degree. (2) Presentation through just one text per se offers only a limited perspective. Using various media in a *'textual interplay'* (cf. Hallet 2002), where perspectives contradict and supplement one another, creates a more complex, multidimensional approach. Moreover, it furthers media competence in offering learning chances as to genre and media differences (how each medium constructs or encodes different realities and how they can be decoded and used respectively, see ch. 9.2). A typical sequence on a cultural topic would thus entail various media, an overall structure with regard to *how these media are related*, and appropriate tasks, relating these media in a meaningful way. Media range from *realia* (e. g., coins, menus, tickets, food, clothes) to real or virtual contact with native or non-native speakers (e. g., e-mail projects, chats) to verbal, visual, or oral presentations (e. g., films, pictures, speeches, dialogs), from print media to the Internet. As a hybrid medium, the Internet offers access to all the written, visual, and oral media referred to above and to a combination of all.

9. Considering balanced representations

Representations should ideally aim at presenting a *multi-facetted, sometimes controversial image* of a cultural topic that engages students *cognitively and emotionally* and that they can relate to their own experiences or future plans. 'Neutral' representations of another culture are impossible, and attempts at a totally balanced presentation would be rather boring. Multidimensional representations can be aimed at by using various media and by juxtaposing different voices on a topic. Students should be encouraged to reflect critically on different stances and make up their own minds. Ideally, the learning environment is shaped by a spirit of tolerance, empathy, and learning about the other without applying judgmental culture-bound opinions. However, dissident opinions cannot and should not be silenced or hushed over, but need to be part of a *culture of dialog.*

10. Toward student-centeredness

New concepts of teaching Cultural Studies or intercultural learning have discarded the idea of the teacher as the knowledgeable expert on English-speaking countries. Given the wide field of global English and global topics, teachers cannot be specialists on all the 'new English cultures' (cf. Eisenmann et al. 2010). In fact, it is a challenge to stay informed about more than one or two of the many target cultures, which should be visited regularly. Moreover, students' expertise regarding other cultures should be integrated actively into classroom activities. It goes without saying that understanding another culture is a *life-long process* and that teaching methods should thus aim at process- and action-orientation. Tasks and task-cycles should also be product-oriented, with students presenting their findings through individually or collaboratively produced posters, written, oral, and visual presentations, Wikis or other digital media.

Recommended reading

Byram, Michael (1997). *Teaching and Assessing Intercultural Communicative Competence.* Clevedon et al.: Multilingual Matters.

Eisenmann, Maria; Nancy Grimm & Laurenz Volkmann, eds. (2010). *Teaching the New English Cultures and Literatures.* Heidelberg: Winter.

Hammer, Julia (2012). *Die Auswirkungen der Globalisierung auf den modernen Fremdsprachenunterricht: Globale Herausforderungen als Lernziele und Inhalte des fortgeschrittenen Englischunterrichts – Are We Facing the Future?* Heidelberg: Winter.

Kramsch, Claire (1998). *Language and Culture.* Oxford et al.: Oxford University Press.

Teske, Doris (2006). Cultural Studies: Key Issues and Approaches. In: Werner Delanoy & Laurenz Volkmann, eds. *Cultural Studies in the EFL Classroom.* Heidelberg: Winter, 23–33.

Volkmann, Laurenz (2010). *Fachdidaktik Englisch: Kultur und Sprache.* Tuebingen: Narr.

Volkmann, Laurenz (2014). Die Abkehr vom Differenzdenken: Transkulturelles Lernen und *global education.* In: Frauke Matz; Michael Rogge & Philipp Siepmann, eds. *Transkulturelles Lernen im Fremdsprachenunterricht: Theorie und Praxis.* Frankfurt a. M.: Lang: 37–51.

Literature matters

Contents

Literature can contribute to linguistic, social, and intercultural competences as well as to general education in the sense of personal growth, creativity, and expression. Traditional approaches to teaching literature, including typical comprehension questions posed by teachers, will be scrutinized for underlying assumptions about reading and teaching literature. These will be juxtaposed to modern approaches to literature in the EFL classroom. Suggestions for teaching literary classics and alternative texts will round off this chapter.

Abstract

Reflect on the pleasures of reading: which was your favorite book of fiction and most rewarding reading (or listening) experience as a child and as an adolescent? What is your favorite literary text in English now? Why do you read literature, why not? Consider the images above to come up with statements such as this: 'To me, reading is like day-dreaming.' You may also want to draw alternative cartoons of your own. Then consider: what did you like and what did you dislike about dealing with literature at school?

174

Functions of literature | 8.1

Personal interest | 8.1.1

Reading popular literature extensively and for pleasure is often vastly differ-   Edutainment?
ent from reading literary classics intensively for educational purposes. However, both entertainment and education have been part and parcel of reading
and teaching literature. Parents – and primary school teachers – select picture
books that are both *entertaining and educational*. One such example is Carle's
picture book *The Very Hungry Caterpillar* (1969), which is attractive to children because of its bright and colorful drawings, its invitation to act (winding
the little toy caterpillar through the holes in the pages), its surprising storyline
(the change from larvae to butterfly), and its teaching of names for food, numbers, and days of the week. Another prominent example is the fairy tale, which
often comes in the form of a movie adaptation: melodramatic and funny Disney movies that address family values are certainly popular among the young.
However, Disney movies often convey rather conservative opinions on race,
class, and gender, which deserve critical analyses, for example through comparison with the parody *Shrek*.

    Children and teenagers who appreciate literature often read fiction that
serves as a *'mirror' of reality*, articulating conflicts, thoughts, values, and feelings they can relate to and take as a means of vicarious *problem solving and
orientation*. Realist literature invites *armchair travelling* to foreign countries
and comparing one's own culture to others. Romance and fantasy open doors
to *alternative worlds*, which invite the *imaginary participation* in exciting and
emotional adventures beyond the routine of ordinary life. The criticism of
escapism levelled at romance and fantasy is not always justified since these
unrealistic worlds can reveal familiar issues in an unfamiliar shape that may
motivate readers to think about the real world (e. g., issues with authorities,
relationships, ethical choices, racism, or the ecosystem). *Harry Potter* and *Twi-
light* can be read as entertainment, as educational *coming-of-age stories*, or as
comments on British or US-American culture. In other words, many genres
offer food for the soul and food for thought. The interest in identification makes
for gendered reading: girls tend to read books about human interest, but also
adventure stories. In general, boys read considerably less than girls and tend
to prefer titles of adventure, science fiction, or crime fiction, characterized by
strong male agents and fast-paced action (cf. Hesse 2009: 13–15). At school,
different interests call for the selection of books that straddle – or question –
the gendered gap: books selected should offer protagonists of either sex, plots
of general interest, male and female characters who may comply with or resist
gender boundaries. Teachers could stack book boxes for extensive reading with
'light books' and non-fiction for divergent readers' interests (cf. Hermes 2009:
12–20, Hesse 2009: 15, 116–18; Lütge 2013: 204–05).

8.1.2 | Institutional interest

Literature and competences

The *Common European Framework of Reference for Languages* (CEF) mentions that it is important "to develop students' aesthetic appreciation of literature" (Council of Europe 2001: 144), but it does not bridge the gap between enjoying reading in private and reading in an educational institution. The CEF devotes only one paragraph (in a text of 260 pages) to aesthetic literature, in which it pays lip service to the key role of literature as a "major contribution to the European cultural heritage" (ibid.: 56) that transports sociocultural values, beliefs, and attitudes: "Literary studies serve many more educational purposes – intellectual, moral and emotional, linguistic and cultural – than the purely aesthetic" (ibid.). The CEF suggests a few productive tasks and creative classroom activities, such as the following: "retelling and rewriting stories, [...] writing and speaking imaginative texts (stories, rhymes, etc.) including audiovisual texts, cartoons, picture stories, [...] performing scripted or unscripted plays, etc." (ibid.). In sum, the CEF conceptualizes literature as a linguistic or multimodal, aesthetic artefact and cultural product with social, moral, emotional, and cognitive dimensions, but it does not specify how these contribute to the multiple educational purposes of literature, let alone the pleasure of reading.

Unfortunately, the German educational standards as well as the examination requirements (*Einheitliche Prüfungsanforderungen in der Abiturprüfung*, EPA) issued by the *Kultusministerkonferenz* (KMK) reproduce the marginalization of literature because they focus on testable output in the areas of communicative, intercultural, and methodical competences; in particular, reproducing and understanding content, re-organizing and analyzing texts, and evaluating and producing texts (Burwitz-Melzer 2007: 127–36; Hollm 2009, Kimes-Link 2013: 69–77).

Literature and *Bildung*

However, reading literature in general can contribute to *individual cultivation* or *Bildung* as envisioned by educators and philosophers. Literature can offer its readers the opportunity to see the world from a different perspective, motivate the subjective identification with others while supporting the appreciation of both the self and others. Literature may trigger reflection on the reader's own emotions, thoughts, and actions. It may provoke thought on language and values, ambiguity and complexity, challenging judgment and cultivating aesthetic taste. Discussion in context provides useful insight into the systematic and historical relationships of social, cultural, and economic phenomena (cf. von Hentig 1996: 54, Hellwig 2005: 74–77, Bieri 2012: 229–40, Spaemann 2012: 224–27). In addition, teaching *literature in English can support the development of vocabulary, reading strategies, critical literacy, media literacy, and intercultural competence* (cf. Bredella 2004a: 85–127, 139–58; Hellwig 2005, Nünning & Surkamp 2006: 12–38, Hallet 2007a: 41–44, Hallet 2007b, Thaler 2008: 47–75, Volkmann 2009: 27–35, Bredella 2010: 18–54, Ahrens 2013: 183,

Surkamp 2012: 77–90, Kimes-Link 2013: 70–71, Hallet et al. 2014, Volkmann 2015: 50–56).

Burwitz-Melzer (2007: 137–55), Lütge (2013: 194–99), and Steininger (2014: 350–415) condense concepts from political frameworks, curricula, Philosophy, Pedagogy, and Literary Studies into dimensions of *literary competence*, which are interrelated with each other:

1. *Cognitive understanding* and *co-creation of meaning*: forming of mental models, filling gaps, forming hypotheses
2. Application and development of *linguistic-discursive competence* in interaction with literary reading, follow-up communication, and negotiation of meaning
3. *Motivation and orientation* as the ability to get involved in a text, to find pleasure in reading, to recognize the relevance of literature for life
4. *Subjective response to and participation in interpersonal and intercultural perspectives* of others (identification or resistance)
5. *Reflection on and critical judgment of moral values and actions* in literature and life
6. *Cognitive-aesthetic understanding and evaluation* of aesthetic structuring, contextual readings, textual impact and functions
7. *Methodological competences and creative production* through (re-)writing literary texts (media literacy, narrative, performative, and poetic competence)

It is noticeable that motivation is considered as something to be acquired rather than given (see ch. 4.6). Motivation needs to be stimulated through appropriate pre-reading activities and an adequate choice of texts, especially, but not exclusively, for reluctant readers (cf. Hesse 2009: 114–18).

Approaches to teaching literature | 8.2

Considerations regarding which literature to select, how to teach it, and for which reasons are based on underlying concepts from literary studies and literary pedagogy. Approaches to teaching English and the particular conditions at the school must also be taken into consideration. Furthermore, the learners' levels and interests should also play a role in the selection of primary and secondary material.

The old school type of teaching literature followed the teacher-centered pattern of initiation – response – evaluation (IRE, see ch. 3.2.5), and an analytical approach to literature in the sequence of the description and summary of content (what), the formal analysis of style and aesthetic structure (how), and the comment on 'the author's intention' or 'the message' about personal and social issues (why). This traditional proceeding from analysis to comment will be contrasted with modern analytical, subjective, cultural, and creative approaches.

8.2.1 | Analytical approaches: nothing but the text

In terms of content, *answering the questions of who, what, when, where, and why* aims at the basic understanding of nonfictional (expository, factual) and fictional texts. In the classroom, this takes the shape of writing or providing short summaries, describing and analyzing characters, actions, and circumstances, i. e. the specific spatiotemporal setting and atmosphere in their literal and symbolic meanings. However, *communication* always means that someone talks to someone about something: so, it is important to look at the speaker and the addressee as well as the manner and motivation of communication, and not only at the content (see fig. 8.1). In fictional – as opposed to factual – communication, the author usually does not speak as his/her 'real self', whatever this is, but through the voices and perspectives of fictional narrators and characters.

Fig. 8.1 |
Simplified model of
literature as commu-
nication (cf. Meyer
2011: 26, 68, 115)

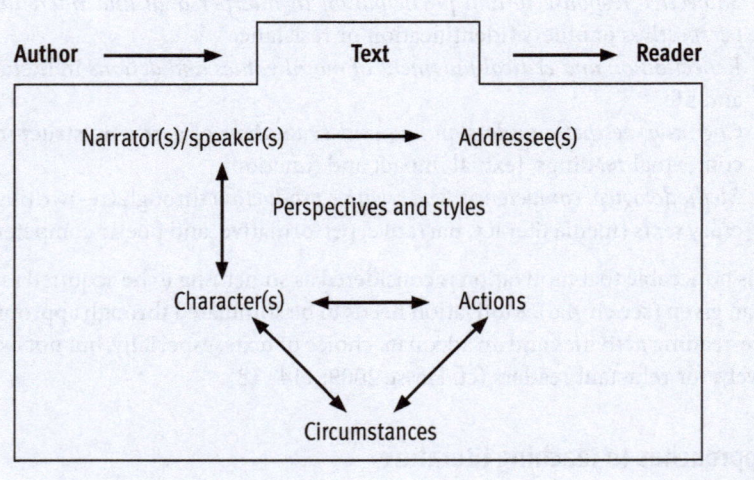

The particular ways in which voice and style are shaped in language and structure depend upon the framework of the chosen *genre*. These are distinguished by *historically changing conventions*. In poetry, a speaker usually talks in the present, and the style is marked by rhythm and repetition, but not necessarily in the shape of rhyme. Drama is a script written for live performance, which primarily conveys meaning through verbal and bodily interaction; here, a narrator is the exception rather than the rule. Narratives of all kinds derive meaning from the narrator's perspective on and shaping of past events in stories. In addition to voices and perspectives, imagery and the plot (the structure of situated actions and events) shape meanings in each of these genres. There are numerous accessible guides to the concepts and proceedings of analyzing or teaching literature (cf. Nünning & Surkamp 2006, Brosch 2007, Thaler 2008, Meyer 2010, 2011, Mays 2013, Nünning & Nünning 2014).

The ***intrinsic analytical approach*** (e. g., New Criticism), which concentrates on the text itself, holds that the *literary work is a timeless artefact* apart from its author and historical context. The *artefact needs to be analyzed in **intensive, close readings** in order to appreciate its complex artistic form as a perfect mold of the content.* For example, a typical task for a Shakespearean sonnet could be the following: 'Identify the rhyme scheme and the rhetorical features of the poem.' Simply identifying patterns in a poem is a mechanical and didactic exercise, 'counting beans' for the sake of demonstrating basic analytical skills. It is more helpful to start by inviting the learners' responses to the literary text at hand, eliciting, for example, what they understand, like or dislike, and what they find puzzling ('perturbation,' see ch. 3.2.4). After doing that, teachers can proceed to take a closer look at how *form shapes meaning* to stimulate familiar or new semantic associations – drawing attention to literary devices, such as metaphor and metonymy, where necessary for 'deeper' insight. Since the form-content nexus may yield different meanings to various learners, teachers should refrain from accepting only one interpretation. Teachers should rather make productive use of the opinion gap as a stimulation of authentic communication about the significance of the text to various readers.

> Questions: content and form

> *Great literature is simply language charged with meaning to the utmost possible degree. – Ezra Pound*

After analyzing the text, teachers often proceed toward questions about the author's intention and 'the message' of the text. The author's life and intention are often taken to be the sources of meanings, which can take the form of a positivist search for biographical facts as an 'explanation' of the text. Literature, however, should not be understood as a logical consequence of life but an imaginative transformation of experience: literature may function as speech therapy, compensation, or escapist fantasy. The question 'What did the author try to tell us?' impels the reader to look 'behind the text,' and has been denounced as an ***intentional fallacy*** (cf. Meyer 2011: 163). Literature is by no means a personal letter to the reader that directly communicates intentions. Readers who talk about the author's intention usually speak about the significance of the text to themselves. Teachers use this question to delimit the learners' subjective understandings and avoid open-ended discussions. Unless authors explicitly commented on their intentions, which they rarely do, readers are left with their own understanding. However, interpretation is not completely arbitrary. *Students should be encouraged to develop individual perspectives and to back up their readings with significant evidence from the text.*

> The pitfall of intention

While the question regarding the author's intention is directed at the 'origin' of the text, the question for 'the message' aims at the usefulness of the text to the reader. This question implies that a work of literature has a single meaning, like a brief SMS or a tweet. It is true that some fables, fairy tales, and openly political (agitprop) texts sport an explicit message, but this is the exception rather than the rule. In most cases, the question for 'the message' asks learners to dig for the 'essential meaning' as if for a hidden treasure in the wood of words, or to depend on the teacher for he/she will provide the 'right' answer sooner or

> The problem of 'the message'

later. Teachers who tend to closely control classes often use the 'author's intention,' 'the form' of the text, and 'the message' to reduce the number of learner's interpretations to one only, usually his or her own (or the one proposed in the teacher's manual; cf. Delanoy 2002: 28, Grimm & Hammer 2015: 324). This strategy of prescribing meaning frustrates learners and violates the processes of aesthetic reading and negotiating meaning (cf. Hesse 2009: 85–86).

Fictional literature is ambiguous and therefore *open to various interpretations* that depend upon the readers' prior knowledge. If one were able to tell what a whole book means in one sentence, why read the book and not the interpretation readily available on the Internet? In other words, if *Hamlet* only meant 'You shall not murder' or 'You shall not covet your neighbor's (here: your brother's) wife,' why would anyone bother to read or watch the whole play? The tragedy fascinates through its intense drama of inner and outer conflicts, stimulating feelings and thought. Reading works of fiction for a single 'moral message' would reduce much of literature to the ten commandments, which many readers know already, and so render reading a waste of time.

> Discuss which competences the teacher-centered and analytical approach promotes.

Discussion   The analytical approach in its intrinsic variety has its benefits because it *raises awareness of forms and functions of language and discourse* with respect to shaping or manipulating content, such as imagery, syntactic structures, registers, discourses, and narrative patterns. It may enhance *cognitive competences, aesthetic sensibility, and taste* due to more insights into the art of literature. To a limited extent, it may support reflection and judgment. However, the analytical approach implies that the reader 'only' retrieves what the text objectively contains as if it were a nut to crack.

8.2.2 | Making sense: subjective response and dialog

Fig. 8.2 |
Individual use of literature

In *efferent reading* (*sinnentnehmendes Lesen*) of factual texts, each reader should be able to retrieve the same information. The value of **aesthetic reading**, Felski contends, lies in its manifold meanings for individual readers and their "vast terrain of practices, expectations, emotions, hopes, dreams, and interpretations" (2008: 8). It is logically and didactically more convincing that readers actively 'make sense' of a text rather than 'find' meaning in the text, because then every reader would arrive at the same meaning provided that he/she carefully searched for it (cf. Reichl 2009: 16–17). In the *dynamic interaction between reader and text*, the text both stimulates and directs the reader's associations and ideas, which, in turn, infuse the words and socio-cultural schemata with subjective mental images and interpretations (cf. Meyer 2011: 202–03, Rosenblatt & Iser in Naylor & Wood 2012: 16–19). Aesthetic reading brings 'dead'

180

words on the page to life in the reader's imagination if the reader is willing to get involved in the experience of other minds and worlds, which requires playing along the game as if fiction was real. Scholars appropriated the balanced model of a dialog with the text from philosophy (such as hermeneutics) and reader-response theories (*Rezeptionsästhetik*) for a **learner-centered approach** to English literature (cf. Bredella & Burwitz-Melzer 2004, Kimes-Link 2013).

Cognitive models focus on the reader's information processing as an interaction between the reader's top-down knowledge (schemata) and bottom-up information (text). For example, mental models of a fictional character result from the interaction of cultural categories of 'character' and textual information that confirms or qualifies these categories (see chs. 3.2.3, 6.1.2; cf. Bredella 2007: 55, Reichl 2009: 31–50, Meyer 2011: 203–04, Schneider 2013: 122–25, Strasen 2013: 43–46).

Cognitive processing

> Discuss which competences approaches to individual reading processes promote and which they neglect.

Aesthetic reading means sharing the perspectives of fictional narrators and characters, predicting future developments, and appreciating the artfulness of the text (cf. Donnerstag & Wolff 2007: 150–55). In cognitive terms, the processing of fictional worlds goes along with *fiction emotion* (e. g., suspense), and the processing of the aesthetic quality with *artefact emotion* (e. g., the pleasure of realizing how well the text is made; cf. Reichl 2009: 105). The sharing and coordination of diverse perspectives in literature trigger processes of empathy, sympathy, and recognition – or resistance. *This process of adopting and changing perspectives (in terms of overt and covert assumptions) helps to make sense of oneself and others in complex social situations and across cultural boundaries.* Therefore, literature, especially about intercultural encounters and misunderstandings in so-called critical incidents, is of particular importance to developing intercultural and transcultural competence (see ch. 7.2.2–7.3, cf. Bredella 2004b: 139–58, Burwitz-Melzer 2003: 81–94, Felski 2008: 33, 54, 76, Delanoy 2002: 9–10, Nünning 2007, Eisenmann 2015: 221–23, Volkmann 2015: 53–61).

Aesthetic reading

Minds are like parachutes. They only function when they are open. –
Sir Dewar (attributed)

Bredella pleads to view literary texts as 'friends' rather than as objects or even 'suspects' (2004c: 59), preferring aesthetic appreciation to critical scrutiny. Bredella's conception of the reader's fundamental roles implies a proceeding for teaching literature (ibid.: 36–42):

Readers' roles

1. The *involved participant* uses his/her imaginative, emotional, and ethical resources.
2. The *detached spectator* relates reading to his/her literary and cultural experience.
3. The *literary critic* reflects on the aesthetic making of the text as a condition of his/her response.

Reading logs

Individual reading journals or logs (*Lesetagebuch*) can be used to record *subjective responses to literature* and serve as a basis for work in the classroom. Learners use a notebook (or a mobile device) to jot down spontaneous reactions, questions, memorable quotes, predictions, vocabulary in mind maps, add diagrams, sketches, multimodal clippings, and web links (e. g., concerning background information or film adaptations, which can be complemented by analytical and critical comments, as well as creative re-writings). The journals can be used for direct comments by peers or the teacher, given there is a trusting relationship, and as a collection of ideas that will be elaborated in a classroom discussion or an essay. The advantage of mobile devices is that learners can easily copy their log, omit certain responses they do not want others to read, and pass it on to others for discussion (cf. Fliethmann 2002: 270–73, Hesse 2009: 102–03). A modern-day alternative to reading journals includes blogs and learning platforms, which support both peer feedback and the negotiation of meaning (cf. Klemm & Grimm 2013). In sum, *the dialog with the text generates a learner text (subjective response) that ideally leads to an open dialog in class as an authentic follow-up communication to negotiate meaning with others (reflection).* Teachers should work with differences between individual readings in order to generate authentic communication and awareness of interpretation as an individual and social process.

8.2.3 | Context and culture as conditions of meaning

The strange mirror

Another approach to reading literature primarily searches for meaning in the relationship between *text and context*, rejecting the idea of the autonomous object (as in the analytical approach) or the subjective response (as in the reader-response approach) as too limited. Context can be understood as the 'real' material, mental, and social conditions of the time, or as the 'intertextual' network of cultural discourses in which literature is embedded. These concepts tie in with the teaching of intercultural communicative competence (see ch. 7.1.3).

Literature is news that STAYS news. – Ezra Pound

The idea of literature as *imitation or mimesis of reality* does not mean that it is an objective representation or a 'neutral mirror' of reality. Firstly, a mirror as such means little without an observer and his or her interpretive gaze. Secondly, the reading of literature for information disrespects the fictional quality of literature and its aesthetic experience (cf. Rosenblatt in Naylor & Wood 2012: 17). Literature is not a mere source of information: it does not claim to represent factual truth like a history book but transforms information and interprets experience. Literature is both 'referential' in a non-factual way and self-referential in the sense that it creates a fictional world of its own. A realistic novel invents characters and action but is more context-bound than a work of fantasy or romance. Literature is a *product or reflection of culture and a reflection on culture*, drawing on and exposing beliefs, values, attitudes, and forms of verbal and non-verbal behavior. As non-factual reflection of and on culture, literature is free from the pressure of practical decisions and actions. It can thus unfold a model of the world in a much more complex way to readers, who in real life would often feel the need to resort to schematic thinking and acting. Thus, reading literature may give pause to reflect on personal habits and schemata, and help to refine these.

Literature puts the whole range of *language use on display*: characteristics and differences of individuals, generations, gender, race, class, periods, regions, and nations in speaking, feeling, and thinking; diverse genres, such as diary entries, letters, reports, public speeches, advertisement, or the news; and finally different discourses, such as psychology, education, medicine, or the law. Soaking up and appropriating the potential wealth of language in literature can boost both *receptive and productive language skills*. In opposition to factual texts about other cultures, the literary reflection of and on English language and Anglophone cultures grants a privileged access to sociocultural communication because it allows the reader to both imaginatively participate in the fictional creation of another world and observe it from a detached point of view. Since literature thrives on change and conflicts of attitudes, beliefs, values, relationships, status, and situations, readers are introduced to the nexus between mental, social, and material culture (cf. Nünning & Surkamp 2006: 34).

Sociocultural interaction

Reading literature in the EFL classroom has been considered as a gateway to a third place, better: a virtual third space, where the learner moves to a *position between cultures, mediating between 'us' and 'them'* (see above, cf. Kramsch 1998, Matos 2012: 9–20). In other words, the EFL classroom would turn into a *contact zone* and a *hybrid third space* between the German context and the cultures experienced through American, British, and postcolonial or New English literatures (cf. Freitag & Gymnich 2007, Eisenmann et al.: 2010, Hammer et. al.: 2012, Matos 2012: 137–48; see ch. 7.1.2). Learners are motivated to take over perspectives from others and look at their own culture with detachment, to appreciate difference through literature rather than blindly following the dominant sociocultural order of othering, i. e. defining others as deviant from the norm (cf. Decke-Cornill 2007: 240–47, Antor 2006, Fäcke 2006, Nünning 2007, Grimm 2009, Freitag-Hild 2010).

The third place

Advocates of a critical literacy approach maintain that language is socioculturally situated, and that there is no neutral use of language in a society marked by inequality of the distribution of wealth and power (see ch. 3.2.5, cf. Fliethmann 2002: 265–68). *Dominant ideologies*, which define the hierarchical order and differences in a culture, are below the threshold of conscious perception because they form its basic norms, for example, that white skin is 'normal' or that migrants 'belong' elsewhere. *Reflecting on silent preconceptions* is an important part of (critical) intercultural competence. Suppressive ideology is "a falsifying collectively held system of ideas and beliefs that inter-

Culture, power, and critical literacy

pret the world [...] in the interests of those who are in power, covers up contradictions and conflicts in society" (Meyer 2011: 181–82; emphasis deleted)
in order to maintain and legitimize the status quo. For example, a gendered
perspective analyses how heterosexual norms impose constraints on individuals of any sexual orientation. 'Race' is no longer considered to be a scientifi-
cally sound concept backed up by biological evidence but defined as a "significant social and cultural construction, which has been used to classify others
as subordinate and legitimize social, economic and political practices, such as
segregation, exploitation and disenfranchisement" (Meyer 2011: 196; emphasis deleted). In sum, critical approaches have adopted cultural approaches to
race, class, and gender in order to uncover the ideological underpinnings of
literature (cf. Surkamp & Nünning 2009: 237–68, Hammer et al. 2012, Volkmann 2013).

Aesthetic and critical reading

Critical literacy conceives a *resistant reader* instead of a 'neutral' reader,
who is supposed to empathize with others (cf. Delanoy 2002: 58–62). Ideally,
critical readings generate *emancipatory reflections* on the text and the reader's own positioning in ideologies. However, readers should have the opportunity to explore and discuss their personal understanding of the text before
they are encouraged to employ critical concepts, because otherwise their aesthetic response would be narrowed down and the text reduced to an example
for 'wrong' (or 'right') politics (Delanoy 2002: 29, Fliethmann 2002: 269–70,
Felski 2008: 1–9). Most advocates of critical readings would complement aesthetic and critical approaches, and "combine a willingness to suspect with an
eagerness to listen" (Felski 2008: 22).

Culture as text

In a postmodern perspective, which is less concerned about ideology, *culture is textual and texts are cultural.* The concept of culture as text does not
ignore that texts have 'real' conditions and effects, but argues that these are
only understandable in the sense of being culturally significant and readable:
for example, satires can be motivated by strong resentment, provoke real laugh-
ter, deeply felt anger, legal trouble, or violent acts of revenge, all of which are
culturally meaningful and therefore 'texts' in a metaphorical sense (see the violent responses to the cartoons of *Charlie Hebdo* in 2015). People both perceive
and 'read' pictures, body language, fashion, or the taste of wine (e. g., 'a flavor
of peach and lemon with a smooth texture').

Intertextual processes in culture, teaching, and learning

Hallet takes **intertextuality** as the unifying concept of culture, literature,
the individual subject, intersubjective communication, and teaching (2002,
2007b). The individual is both an intersection of discourses and an actant who
constructs meaning in new texts by selecting and combining discourses (Hallet 2002: 60–61). *Learners need the competences of orientation, selection, and
(re)construction of meaning in an intertextual, intermedial, and intercultural
world* (ibid.: 46–48). The teacher should select representative texts (in a wide
sense), which circulate collective issues, symbols, or myths (e. g., British insu-
larity, the 'mother country,' the Statue of Liberty, multiculturalism). *Literature*

184

as an inter-discourse forms intertextual nodes around core symbols and negotiates the values and functions of myths (ibid.: 64–65). The combination of selected texts should motivate students to explore the circulation and interplay of meanings, and to create new webs of significance in dialog with the texts and each other in the classroom as a hybrid third place (ibid.: 39–45, 69–72).

The classroom can be seen as a space of rich intertextual encounters, and students need a good combination of texts and the opportunity to participate as much as possible in the *dialogic negotiation of interpretations*, which includes the weighing of *opposite voices within and between texts and readers*. Some textbook units, such as "American Truths" (Ashford et al. 2009: 148–63), already combine a wide range of non-fictional and fictional texts and images, which form a '*didactic text*' of different perspectives that provoke critical comparisons (cf. Delanoy 2015: 39–42). Intermedial input is the norm in current textbooks, but often, pictures are only used as a stimulus to talk instead of paying close attention to the particular visual quality and experience of pictures before they are read as 'texts.' Besides, in any multimodal text, from a picture book to a comic, a graphic novel, or a website, attention should be paid to the look and meaning of pictures themselves, the combination or sequence of pictures, and the interaction between image and text. In spite of their entertainment, movies can present a big challenge to learners due to their moving image/text combination (see ch. 9.1). For example, the highly intermedial movie *Forrest Gump* would complement the unit on "American Truths" mentioned above. This movie shows an amiable, mentally challenged Southerner living the American Dream in connection with iconic American symbols and events. Due to its clever manipulation of historical news footage, the movie offers numerous options to relate its episodes to the treatment of American values and myths in other media. Last, but not least, a comparison with the novel reveals that the comic and touching combination of the wise fool's success story and a sentimental plot in the movie only covers half the story, which is completely undermined in the novel as it turns out to be the unreliable narrative of a homeless drifter.

The rich input of multiple texts and media will certainly generate communication and is also highly attractive to learners because it is very similar to their private media consumption (see ch. 9.2). However, rich input of media runs the *risk of dispersing the learners' attention* because they may be tempted to merely surf on the sea of texts rather than reflecting on critical issues. A critical evaluation, which is not at the center of Hallet's model, explores, for example, whether the American Dream (1) is hampered by disadvantages regarding race, class, and gender, (2) allows individuals to overcome these barriers, or (3) is used to legitimize discrimination by attributing inequality to individual failure rather than social conditions and power.

The subsequent model takes into account individual, social, and contex-

[margin note:] Rich intermedial input: the 'didactic text'

[margin note:] Rich input and critical literacy

[margin note:] Comprehensive model and practical consequences

tual factors of understanding texts (see fig. 8.3). *Making sense of a literary text at school is a process involving the interaction between reader and text, text and context, among peers, and with the teacher.* The *aesthetic experience* of reading may affect readers in ways they cannot wholly grasp in language because it is a holistic experience inflected by cognition, affect, motivation, and imagination. The text may challenge their schemata and hamper understanding. The *subjective responses* of learners on an emotional and cognitive level may hardly be related to the *answers expected by the teacher.* Instead, the subjective response is influenced by the knowledge of literary genres, cultures, life, languages, reading skills, motivation, attitude, expectations, attention, and memory. These factors, in turn, may be inflected by the reader's race, class, gender, and generation, and the way these are dealt with in the text. The teacher frames texts through generic and contextual information, asking questions and defining objectives of reading, which ask for specific strategies (e. g., skimming or critical read-

Fig. 8.3 |

Dynamic model of reading as experience and interactive information processing in combination with the social negotiation of meaning in an institutional framework (cf. Meyer 2012, adapted from Reichl 2009: 214)

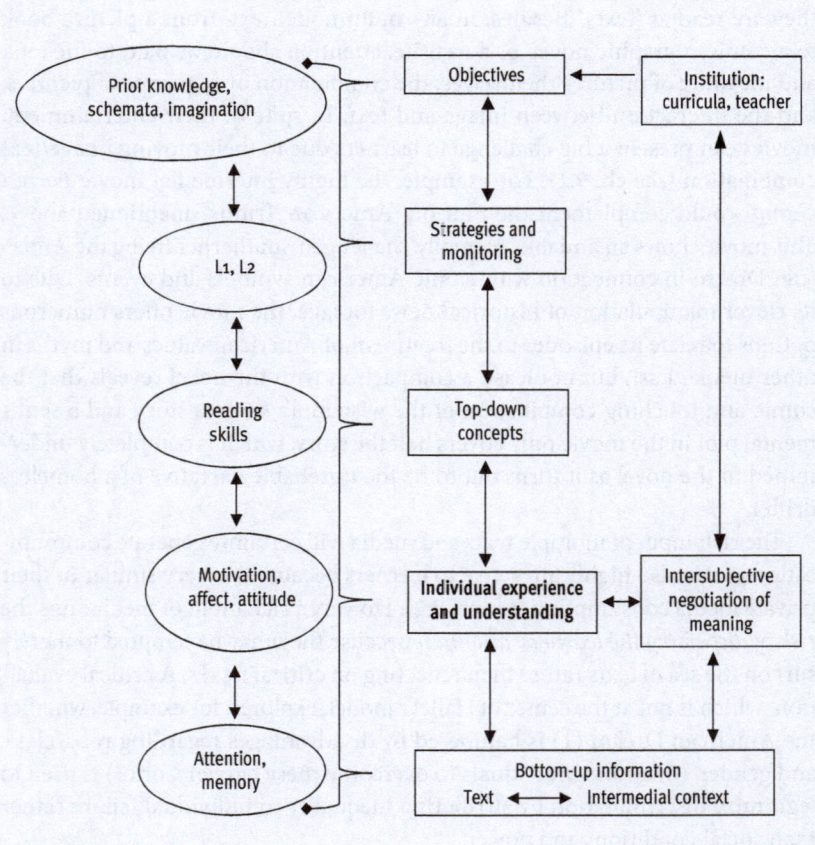

ing) and their monitoring in order to understand particular aspects of the text in question. However, learners respond to the text and to these demands with diverse individual competences and interests, which may interfere with the required purpose, strategy, and concepts (see the double arrows). The objectives will be beyond learners if they cannot employ appropriate reading strategies. In basic terms, learners who do not master scanning will not be able to perform certain tasks in a given time. Talking about the text with the teacher and other learners adds further perspectives. The intersubjective negotiation of meaning ideally expands a learner's understanding, but may also reveal that his/her understanding is incompatible with those of other readers. Of course, all of the factors in the diagram (fig. 8.3) also apply to the teacher as an individual reader in a social and institutional context. *The teacher should try to strike a balance between educational objectives, the individual 'realization' of a text, and the negotiation of meaning among learners* even if it is very difficult to maneuver between pursuing a certain goal and promoting an open process (cf. Delanoy 2007: 113, Hermes 2007: 81).

'Doing' literature: task-based and creative work | 8.2.4

Task-based as well as holistic and action-oriented approaches (*aufgabenorien-*   Phases of teaching
tierter Unterricht, handlungsorientierter Unterricht) have gained ground in   reading
teaching literature as a result of the turn from cognitive, text- and teacher-centered approaches to learner-centered ones (see ch. 4.3). Delanoy (2007: 115) contends that aesthetic reading is complex and needs to be stimulated by *phases of evocation* that precede those of interpretation: teachers need to nudge learners (1) to feel like reading, and (2) to get into the text before they are able (3) to live through the text, and (4) to get out of the text in the sense of being able to realize some preliminary meaning of the experience as a whole. Language problems may interfere both with aesthetic pleasure and interpretation as an attempt to come to grips with the reading experience, activate presuppositions, and arrive at a reflected understanding in follow-up communication. Therefore, Delanoy continues, *phases of interpretation* need to build up gradually from (5) reviewing one's experience and preliminary grasp (*Bestandsaufnahme*) to (6) modifying and expanding one's understanding through the comments of others and refocusing on selected aspects of the text in more depth through the lens of literary and cultural concepts (2007: 116–18). Delanoy's steps 1 and 2 roughly correspond to pre-reading, 3 and 4 to reading, and 5 and 6 to post-reading in a task-based scenario (see ch. 6.1.2).

    The following task sequence can be aligned with reading strategies (cf. Hesse   Smart reading
2009: 89, Nünning & Surkamp 2006: 71–80, Thaler 2008: 51–52):

Fig. 8.4 |

Pre-reading, read-
ing, and post-reading
phases

Pre-reading strategies to trigger motivation, activate schemata, and facilitate language input
▶ Activating knowledge about genre, structure, and (inter-)cultural schemata ▶ Predicting the topic and development on the basis of the title, cover picture, blurb, movie trailer
Reading strategies to enhance involvement and intermittent reflection
▶ Reflecting on (inter-)cultural schemata and noticing deviations ▶ Visualization of characters, setting, events, and action (imagination and externalization: sketch, diagram, journal, blog) ▶ Filling the gaps and predicting conflicts and solutions ▶ Skimming for global and scanning for detailed understanding (e. g., doing preliminary summaries and close readings) ▶ Inferring word meanings and textual meanings
Post-reading strategies to reflect on various meanings
▶ Reviewing the major topic, plot, and development (*what*) ▶ Analyzing the relationship between narrative voice, perspective, characters as social agents, representatives of opinions and values, the kinds of problems and solutions (*how*), and visualizing results ▶ Interpreting and evaluating the text concerning its subjective, social, cultural significance, for example, from the position of race, class, and gender (*why*)

The use of tasks and strategies varies with learning objectives, genres, and readers. If learners read a short story or a poem straight through, they may analyze a central image *after* reading, whereas more proficient readers of a novel may pause to reflect in depth on an image or a moral dilemma *while* reading, or in a segmented approach, *after* reading a certain part of the book.

The *post-reading phase* provides space for creative activities, which center on the interests, knowledge, and competences of learners and motivate them to work individually or with others on palpable products. *Creative tasks encourage the aesthetic transformation of subjective responses via considerable reflection and problem solving into verbal, visual, and performative expressions.*

Playing with language

Creative writing is a close relative of aesthetic reading because the ambiguity and gaps of literary texts give rise to the imagination and creation of learner texts. Given some guidance or scaffolding concerning discourse and structure, learners rewrite beginnings and endings, rewrite the story from another character's perspective, in another setting, or in another genre (e. g., parody), spell out the concealed thoughts and feelings of characters in an interior monolog, a diary, or a personal letter. Learner texts have many *functions* (cf. Hellwig 2005: 7–8, Kimes-Link 2013: 41–48, Legutke 2009: 204–10, Nünning & Surkamp 2006: 232–44, Surkamp 2007: 94–101, Thaler 2008: 110, Thaler 2009):

▶ *Motivation* through identification, individual expression, and autonomy
▶ *Recognition* of the perspectives of others, supporting empathy and tolerance
▶ *Meaningful communication* addressed to peers (and the teacher)
▶ Challenging but playful *experiment with language and culture*
▶ Object of mutual *reflection* and trigger of linguistic and cultural awareness

188

▶ *Holistic learning* that combines affect, cognitive insight, and imagination
▶ Opportunity for both teachers and learners to give *feedback*
▶ Opportunity for *appreciation, assessment, and evaluation* according to transparent criteria

More or less the same functions apply to *visualization* and *performance* (acting out, *darstellendes Spiel*). Learners can visualize characters, events, actions, settings, or imagery in sketches or collages, build stage settings, create a comic or a short animated movie online (see ch. 9.5; cf. Elsner et al. 2013, Elsner & Ludwig 2014).

Role-playing assumes the willingness to give voice to and embody characters in experiential and social learning, reading selected scenes in separate roles, trying to express the character's emotions and relationships, freeze-frames, short sketches based on role cards, answering questions as a character in an interview on the hot seat, simulating a talk show, psychotherapy, a trial, etc. (cf. Hesse 2009: 94–5, 104; Nünning & Surkamp 2006: 174–93). Peer tutoring, in which learners take on the role of the teacher, involves learners in planning, implementing, and reflecting on both the dialogic reading of literature and the learning process in the classroom (cf. Meyer 1997, Blau 2003: 2–5, Delanoy 2015: 31). `Performance`

The multiple opportunities to learn and the pleasure of creative work for both the teacher and the learners come at a cost: it is quite time-consuming to plan, implement, and reflect on the tasks as well as to assess and evaluate the processes and products (cf. Surkamp 2007: 103; Kimes-Link 2013: 365, 378–80). In addition, creative tasks have come under fire because they may give rise to arbitrary, superficial, and subjective responses without reference to the text, without any progress in language or critical reflection on the product and its discursive or ideological problems (cf. Kimes-Link 2013: 48–50). However, this critique is rendered void if the creative learner products are, in turn, used as a means of taking a second, analytical and critical look at the 'original' (cf. Surkamp 2007: 101–02). `Discussion`

In order to combine the strengths of the diverse approaches to teaching literature and counter-balance their weaknesses, it is recommendable to *com-* `Finding the right balance`

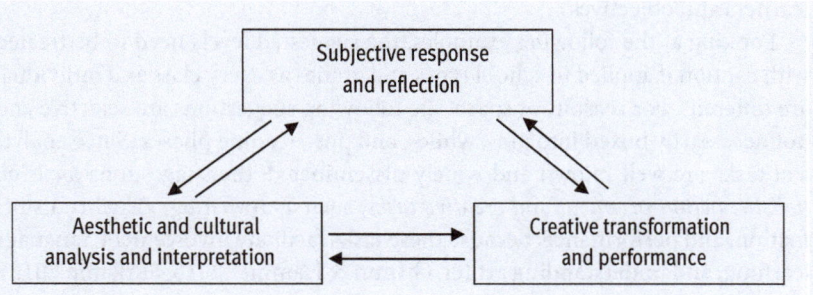

Fig. 8.5

Interaction of complementary approaches to teaching literature

bine and alternate phases of (1) subjective response and reflection, (2) aesthetic and cultural (intermedial and critical) analysis, interpretation, and evaluation, as well as (3) creative transformation and performance (see fig. 8.5; cf. Nünning & Surkamp 2006: 62–70, Delanoy 2015: 21–24). The subjective response usually comes first (unless the cultural context is introduced to facilitate comprehension), analysis second, and creative transformation last, but both analysis and creative transformation can lead back to reflect on the subjective response and on each other.

8.3 | Literature for all levels

Teacher knowledge and criteria of selection

There has been an extensive – and inconclusive – debate about the usefulness of a literary canon, whether of traditional or more recent primary texts (cf. Nünning & Surkamp 2006: 39–44, Thaler 2008: 18–22). Instead of adhering to a prescriptive canon, it is more important to follow some basic principles of selecting literary texts. Teachers need to read and appreciate literature themselves, have an overview of relevant texts from different genres with respect to their (inter-)cultural significance and to their appeal to young and adolescent readers. Last, but not least, teachers need to know and combine various approaches to studying and teaching literature. They may consider the following *principles when selecting literature for learners* (cf. Bredella & Burwitz-Melzer 2004: 140–41, Nünning & Surkamp 2006: 45–50, Hermes 2007: 76, Hesse 2009: 12–15, Schubert 2013: 66–70, Matz & Stieger 2015: 130–32):

We shouldn't teach great books; we should teach a love of reading. Knowing the contents of a few works of literature is a trivial achievement. Being inclined to go on reading is a great achievement. –
B. F. Skinner

- ▶ Texts should be manageable (length, difficulty of vocabulary, topic, structure: available editions with vocabulary aids and study questions)
- ▶ Texts should be interesting and engaging
- ▶ Texts should offer insights into other cultures
- ▶ Texts should be comparable to learners' lives and cultures
- ▶ Text should motivate active and creative work

Many teachers search for texts with ready-to-use teaching material. This criterion should not eclipse the ones mentioned above. What is more, available teaching material should not be blindly adopted but *adapted* to particular learners and objectives.

Looking at the following examples, the suggested levels need to be treated with caution if applied to school types and grades as every class and individual are different. For reasons of space, the following suggestions are selective and not necessarily boxed into pre-, while-, and post-reading phases. Since analytical tasks are well-known and widely disseminated, the suggestions *focus on holistic, action-oriented, and creative tasks*, such as rewriting, visual transformation, and performance, because these tasks facilitate involvement, language learning, and understanding art (cf. Grimm & Hammer 2015, Surkamp 2015).

Beginners at primary school take pleasure in rhythm, rhyming, harmony, nonsense, physical activity, and singing, which is catered to in *Total Physical Response* (TPR, see ch. 4.1). *Playful repetition* in texts and teaching rituals fosters the acquisition of pronunciation, intonation, and vocabulary, while creating a positive attitude toward English (cf. Regitz 2012: 154–62, Bland 2015: 85–89). Besides learning nursery rhymes and singing classical children's songs, teachers can easily build on the popularity of English *pop songs* among children, who can – quite often – sing along and perform some of the choreography. The 'cool' teacher becomes a learner, too, and can ask for the most popular English songs in class, and decide with the learners which of these to study upon the basis of appropriate content and language. An up-to-date version of TPR would make children watch a music video on YouTube or Vimeo as a source of learning both the lyrics and some of the moves and let gifted learners help teach these to their peers. For instance, *Dumb Ways to Die* is a children's favorite and comes along with a funny animated movie (on YouTube or as an app) as ready-made EFL material.

Beginners: playing with language

Vivid story-telling with the help of *Big Books* (or projected scans) relates to the reading of picture books many children are familiar with and aims at children's *holistic response, lexical, narrative, and visual understanding* (cf. Thaler 2008: 96–98). Since the foreign language skills of learners at this level are behind their interpretive skills, pictures help scaffold comprehension (cf. Hempel 2015: 4–5). However, pictures are not self-evident. Therefore the individual pictures, their sequence, and their interaction with the verbal text require close attention. *Rise and Shine* (Allen et al. 2007) shows the morning routines of various characters on Sesame Street in simple, alliterative language and funny pictures that reveal some cultural differences in architecture, clothes, and food. Using a *hand puppet* of Elmo as the narrator of his own story may motivate some children to tell him their morning routines before the children draw a cartoon or talk to each other about the similarities and differences of their morning routines (see fig. 8.6). Learners could also pantomime some of their daily activities and let their peers guess what they are doing.

Holistic story-telling with multimodal texts

| Fig. 8.6

The picture book *Very Short Scary Tales* (Hoberman & Emberley 2011) in the series *You Read to Me, I Read to You* caters to playfully teaching reading skills to beginners in connection with **cultural learning** about Halloween (see fig. 8.7). The stories in rhythmic, rhymed lines are divided into couplets alternatingly read by the teacher and the learner, or later two learners. The funny illustrations play with children's fears and their desire for conquering them. The readings can stimulate learners to perform little sketches or draw and write little booklets about their own monsters (cf. Dunn 2014: 220–25).

'Monstrous' readings

| Fig. 8.7

> Search for 'classical' fairy tales in English and discuss which of these would be of particular interest to beginners.

Intermediate
learners: boys and
girls

Intermediate learners will be truly entertained by "A Relationship in 8 Pages" (Hoover 2007), which helps to raise awareness of *face-to-face inter-action* in real life and *narrative communication in comics* because it highlights the gap between revealed and concealed emotions and thoughts in opposition to expressive body language. In this comic, a shy boy, who has a crush on a girl in his class, finally manages to ask her out, but their relationship is nipped in the bud by her peers. The panels superbly capture the characters' inner lives in drawings which highlight their expressive body language in contrast to the characters' loss for words and the strategic silence of the dominant girls. The following subjective, analytical, intermedial, and creative tasks can promote *communicative competence and media literacy* (receptive/productive).

Pre-reading:

▸ What's in a title and in a picture? Discuss what your understanding of a rela-tionship is, and predict how it may be depicted on just eight pages. Imitate the pose of the boy in the picture and spell out what he feels and is think-ing about.

Reading/viewing:

▸ Spell out what the characters feel and think in thought bubbles, observing their body language and their verbal communication. Write neatly and leg-ibly so that your version can be read by others when posted on the walls. (Half of the class gets the comic with erased speech bubbles and fills in the words on the basis of their visual interpretation.)

Post-reading:

▸ Compare the combination of body language, verbal communication, and the inferred inner feelings and thoughts in different versions. Choose the best ideas and collate one story from several versions (in class or as homework).
▸ Discuss how the comic mirrors real-life body language and verbal inter-action. Discuss whether you find gender-specific attitudes and patterns of communication in friendships and relationships.
▸ View and listen to Stefanie Scott's "Girl I Used to Know" (2011) and com-pare her lyrics and her drawings to the comic.
▸ Complement the work on the comic by reading and subsequently perform-ing Draper's sketch "Friends and Lovers" (2013), in which a boy ends a rela-tionship with a girl and it turns out that her best girlfriend is his new lover.

Global issues and
awareness

The educational goals of promoting an awareness of *social values, ethics, and the environment* are often combined with teaching critical literacy and global issues to upper intermediate learners (see ch. 7.2.1). Volkmann notices the "greening of the EFL classroom" (2012: 397) and the controversy whether *eco-critical literature* should initiate an open discussion of culture and nature or serve as a tool to raise ecological awareness in a more directive way to change the learners' attitude and practical behavior (cf. Gerhardt 2006, Küchler 2011, Volkmann 2012, Lütge 2015). Moderate ecocritics warn that the complexity of environmental global issues as well as basic epistemological and political problems raise questions such as: who can claim to have 'the truth' about nature? Who controls which discourses about nature and the environment (politics, multinational corporations, science, the media)? How could ecological insight translate into social and political action? (cf. Hollm & Uebel 2006: 182–83).

Ecologically committed pedagogues see the chance to easily connect life, language, and literature through eco-utopian or -dystopian writing. The speculation about the future as a reflective reader of *eco-utopian or -dystopian literature* and a responsible citizen may result in questions about what the individual can do to make the world a better place (cf. Hollm & Uebel 2006: 179–80, 185; Grimm 2011, Matz 2015). David Macaulay's short graphic novel: *BAAA* (1985) ideally complements textbook sections on environmental issues. The highly entertaining, dystopian, and satiric animal fable shows a country after the rather sudden demise of human beings (about which readers can speculate, and get one version in the course of the book). Surviving sheep leave their pastures and enter urban space, gradually adopt human culture, and re-live modern human history in a fast-forward mode until they ruin the world and disappear from the face of it. In playful, ironic, and highly symbolic drawings with dry comments, Macaulay addresses ethical, social, ecological, and political problems: mass society and identity, greed and consumerism, mobility and congestion, manipulative politics and the media, need and crime, overpopulation, economic boom and bust cycles, and ecological decline. The novel makes readers take a fresh look at the world and possible developments through the eyes of ignorant sheep. The novel invites numerous analytical and creative tasks:

> Graphic novel: visual and critical literacy

- ▶ Consider where people behave more like sheep rather than rational beings.
- ▶ Complement the panels with snippings from various media and compare the topics with current ecological, social, and political debates.
- ▶ Discuss whether the fictional version is an appropriate warning, including the question of what people would need to do in order to avoid environmental decline.
- ▶ Analyze the relationship between the perspective and style of the drawings and the brief narrative comments within and between panels.
- ▶ Redraw or retell the story to develop alternative turns for each stage of the story.

The novel *The House on Mango Street* (1984) by Sandra Cisneros presents coming-of-age in the *contact zone between Mexican and American culture* from the marginalized perspective of a Chicana girl. The narrator and protagonist, Esperanza, feels bound to her family but suffers from poverty and the male

> Intercultural communicative competence

constraints put on women. She is drawn to the American Dream of independence and a home of her own. The novel consists of many short sketches and stories, which are written in the first person in very simple but vivid English and a few understandable Spanish words and phrases. With less advanced classes or under time pressure, teachers can select individual stories with great potential for intercultural learning. The stories easily lend themselves to visualization (the present home and the desired one, portraits of women at windows, girls dressing up in their mother's clothes), role play, and the creative inversion of scenes from the perspective of a 'white' American boy who happens to fall in love with the girl and encounters her culture (cf. Fliethmann 2002: 165–80, 295–303).

> Search the Internet for prizes for young adult literature, and discuss which of the award-winning texts from last year would be suited for intermediate learners (major booksellers offer the first few pages online as a preview).

Advanced: intercultural poetry slam

Advanced learners should be able to cope with – and enjoy – literature from young adult fiction to selected classics. The *Bronx Masquerade* (2002) by Nikki Grimes is a fascinating novel about school, the power of poetry as self-expression, and the *American Dream in the multicultural or postethnic US* (cf. Hollinger 2006). The short novel presents a series of narrative self-portraits of adolescents of different ethnic backgrounds and the poems they write about their concerns for 'open mike Friday' in class. Most of these teenagers are not interested in school, but in their poems they share their problems with looks, bodies, peers, and families, as well as their need for respect, love, and a future. The first-person narratives offer insights into similarities that suggest a post-ethnic nation, but also differences in the impact of race, class, and gender on teenage selves and careers. The intense stories about the gap between personal and social identity as well as reality and dreams call for identification. The poems raise awareness of the significance of language and can inspire creative expression. The book lends itself to numerous receptive and productive, analytical and creative activities, which can be implemented in a sequence or offered for choice:

- ▶ Closely watch and critically discuss the visual and verbal narrative of the American Dream in Madonna's "American Life" (2003; cf. Freese 2015: 203). This task can serve as a lead-in to the topics of class-based, gendered, and (post)ethnic identity, dreams, and opportunities.
- ▶ Pick your favorite character and interpret his/her choice of a voice (*how*) and a self-image in relationship to the images others have of them (*what*): how does the story help you to understand the poem and the poem to understand the story?
- ▶ Read, respond to, and critically discuss one of the poems "I, Too, Sing Amer-

ica" (1925) and "Theme for English B" (1949) by the African American Langston Hughes. Compare one of his poems to one of your choice from the novel. Can you understand differences in voice, mood, topic, or language in relation to the sociocultural context? Do research on segregation and Harlem in the 1920s and on ethnic issues in the Bronx in recent years.

▶ Girls watch Kiri Davis' *A Girl Like Me* (2012) and discuss its racial and gendered significance concerning a black girl from the novel; boys watch Byron Hurt's "Barak & Curtis: Manhood, Power & Respect" (2008) and its significance concerning a black boy from the novel. A girl and a boy each compare and discuss the impact of gender and race on identity.

▶ Take a selfie and write a short poem about a topic that concerns you. Organize open-mike meetings in class or a poetry slam in school.

Vikas Swarup's fast-paced novel *Slumdog Millionaire* (2008) and its colorful movie adaptation appeal to boys and girls because of the suspenseful and sensational, but also tragicomic and sentimental plot. The Indian underdog Ram Mohammed Thomas struggles for survival, but ultimately manages to win the heart of a beautiful girl and the show *Who Wants to Be a Millionaire*. The multifaceted novel and movie provoke discussions of *inter-, trans-, and intracultural similarities and differences* (see ch. 7.1.3–7.2.2), Indians and international tourists, Hindus and Muslims, class and gender, crime and justice, as well as reality and the media. The international show offers an excellent stimulus for pre-reading discussions of the media in Germany as a point of comparison to media in India. The episodic structure of the novel and the movie facilitates the selection of relevant chapters for discussion. Last, but not least, the novel relates to the topical issues of global capital and the asymmetric distribution of wealth and opportunity.

Intercultural competence & critical literacy

Many learners accept or even appreciate dealing with Shakespeare as a cultural icon, but they often struggle with his language (cf. Schmidt 2004). Suggestions of teaching Shakespeare often propose reading the original before its modern adaptations in various media, but starting with an adaptation can be more motivating. *Hamlet* can be attractive to adolescents due to its young and idealistic protagonist with high principles, who is troubled by the corruption he senses around him. Facing uncertainty and complexity, he feels the urge to arrive at a decision and to act upon it. He feels he can no longer trust anybody, not even himself at times, and worries about his future, but finally decides to stand up and fight. The play is rather long, but starting with discussing the highly symbolic Manga adaptation and a few selected scenes of the original, producing an animated movie online (cf. Sexton & Pantoja 2008, Grimm 2014), or working with the significantly shortened, animated *Hamlet* (1992) is closer to learners' capacity and interests, and addresses visual as well as media literacy.

To read, or not to read, that is the question …

In the animated *Hamlet,* a narrator introduces the play and gives spectators orientation. The highly expressive audiovisual quality of the movie draws the

195

spectator into the plot. For example, the symbolic use of little light and a lot of darkness symbolizes that Hamlet is in a dark mood and left in the dark about the secrets and machinations of his uncle. The characters are drawn in a highly suggestive style, and their superb voices express a large range of emotions from sadness and despair to joy and desire. The claustrophobic architecture with its long, dark halls and winding staircases adds to the oppressive atmosphere. The 'camera work,' or rather, the chosen perspectives, which repeatedly move in circles, make the spectator share Hamlet's confusion. Drawing attention to the impressive use of light, color, voice, sound, and architecture supports the understanding of the characters and the action. Selected key scenes can be compared to the passages from the original. Current parodies are fun and prove the play's popularity (cf. Grimm 2014: 197).

> Inform yourself about mandatory texts in the curriculum of your state, and compare these to the literary texts which you have read so far and find suitable for use in the EFL classroom. Check which of your favorite movies are book adaptions and discuss which of these would be attractive to students. What would be your teaching goals and preferred activities with the texts and movies of your choice?

Recommended reading

Delanoy, Werner; Maria Eisenmann & Frauke Matz, eds. (2015). *Learning with Literature in the EFL Classroom*. Frankfurt a. M. et al.: Lang.

Hallet, Wolfgang & Ansgar Nünning, eds. (2007). *Neue Ansätze und Konzepte der Literatur- und Kulturdidaktik*. Trier: WVT.

Nünning, Ansgar & Carola Surkamp (2006). *Englische Literatur unterrichten: Grundlagen und Methoden*. Seelze-Velber: Klett/Kallmeyer.

Surkamp, Carola & Ansgar Nünning (2009). *Englische Literatur unterrichten: Unterrichtsmodelle und Materialien*. Seelze-Velber: Klett/Kallmeyer.

Thaler, Engelbert (2008). *Teaching English Literature*. Paderborn et al.: Schöningh.

Media: a balanced approach

Contents

A wide range of media has always been instrumental in Teaching English as a Foreign Language (TEFL). Recently, digital technologies have been heralded as a major driving force in school innovation. This chapter favors a balanced use of media across the entire range of the media repertoire available in schools. It will first focus on the importance of media education and the general potential of media in educational settings. It will then outline the ever-expanding media repertoire available for English as a Foreign Language (EFL), including the potential of information and communications technology (ICT). Selected examples of utilizing media in EFL will round off this chapter.

Abstract

Have a look at the cartoon and discuss the following questions: (1) What experiences (good and bad) have you had with the use of media in school and in the EFL classroom in particular? (2) How can media ('old' and 'new') be utilized in the EFL classroom? (3) What is your opinion regarding current trends involving the 'digitalization' of schools (e. g., using learning platforms such as Moodle, laptop classes, Blended and Mobile Learning, digital textbooks)?

9.1 | Media pedagogy and media literacy

Media pedagogy = education, didactics, studies, research

Media pedagogy (*Medienpädagogik*) and positions on media education (*Medienerziehung*) in schools have gone through different phases. There is no space here to elaborate on this in greater detail. It must suffice to say that after the predominance of approaches to media studies (*Medienkunde*) and media didactics (*Mediendidaktik*) informed by *ideological and socio-cultural criticism* between the 1960s and 1980s, media pedagogy and TEFL now support a more *practical and action-oriented* approach (cf. Grünewald 2010b: 210, Moser 2010: 281–84, Spanhel 2011: 228–31). Media pedagogy consists of *four focal areas* (see fig. 9.1):

Media pedagogy	**Media education** is concerned with ways of using media *sensibly*. It centers around enabling individuals to *reflect critically* on their use of media.
	Media didactics is concerned with the functions, effects, and forms of utilizing media in teaching and learning scenarios. It aims at *improving and optimizing* teaching and learning processes and the facilitation of *self-directed acquisition of knowledge and competences*.
	Media studies imparts knowledge about all media across the media repertoire and basic *technological competences*. Foci include historical developments relating to media, legal issues (e.g., data protection), media monopolies, the power of the media, etc.
	Media research entails the *analysis and exploration* of issues pertinent to media education as well as to media sozialization across all age groups. Foci include media use in everyday life, the impact of different media, reception habits, media and gender, etc.

Fig. 9.1

Focal areas of media pedagogy (based on Hug 2002: 8–9)

Media literacy (*Medienkompetenz*) is considered both of paramount importance and in high demand in light of the breakneck speed of developments in ICT and the impact this has on society and global communication. In 2012, the *Kultusministerkonferenz* (KMK) issued the document *Medienbildung in der Schule*. It provides a *national framework* – albeit not a binding curriculum – for media education in Germany. The document features media education as part of the *educational mandate of schools* and media literacy as a *Kulturtechnik* equal in importance to reading, arithmetic, and writing (cf. Kultusministerkonferenz 2012: 9).

While the potential of (digital) media will be discussed throughout this chapter, it is necessary to first take a closer look at the *risks* involved (cf. Volkmann 2005, 2008a, 2008b; Grimm 2012; Frees & Busemann 2012):

▶ The stimulation of various senses through media may lead to *over-stimulation resulting in attention deficits*. Media use for mere stimulation may result in *a disinterest in the actual media contents*. The media landscape with the various forms of media stimuli it offers may *overtax the human mind*.

Which risks do media pose?

▶ Media use may lead to *anxieties, delusive perceptions of reality, and to a problematic set of norms and values as well as problematic behavior*. These may have a negative impact on the intellectual development of individuals as well as their social relationships, especially in case of a person's withdrawal from the *real into an illusory world, or the consumption of violence and pornography*.

▶ The *access to media still varies* on grounds of social and economic disadvantages, which, in turn, may lead to *social exclusion*.

▶ Media can be used for *manipulative and propagandistic purposes*. Pertinent issues include public will and opinion formation, data protection and security, the protection of minors and consumers, as well as the safeguarding of personal rights and intellectual property.

Multiliteracies

Against this background, the facilitation of media literacy must be seen as an important part of a *'pedagogy of multiliteracies'* (cf. Cazden et al. 1996, The New London Group 2000, Blell & Kupetz 2005: 13–15), which greatly expands the understanding of literacy and the objectives of literacy teaching:

> First, we want to expand the idea and scope of literacy pedagogy to account for the context of our culturally and linguistically diverse and increasingly globalized societies, for the multifarious cultures that interrelate and the plurality of texts that circulate. Second, we argue that literacy pedagogy now must account for the burgeoning variety of text forms associated with information and multimedia technologies. This includes understanding and competent control of representational forms that are becoming increasingly significant in the overall communications environment [...]. (Cazden et al. 1996: 61)

Today we are beginning to notice that the new media are not just mechanical gimmicks for creating worlds of illusion, but new languages with new and unique powers of expression. – Marshall McLuhan

The *multiliteracies model* illustrates the elements of different modes of meaning that need to be taken into consideration in multiliteracies pedagogy (see fig. 9.2):

Fig. 9.2 |
Multiliteracies model
(Cazden et al. 1996: 83)

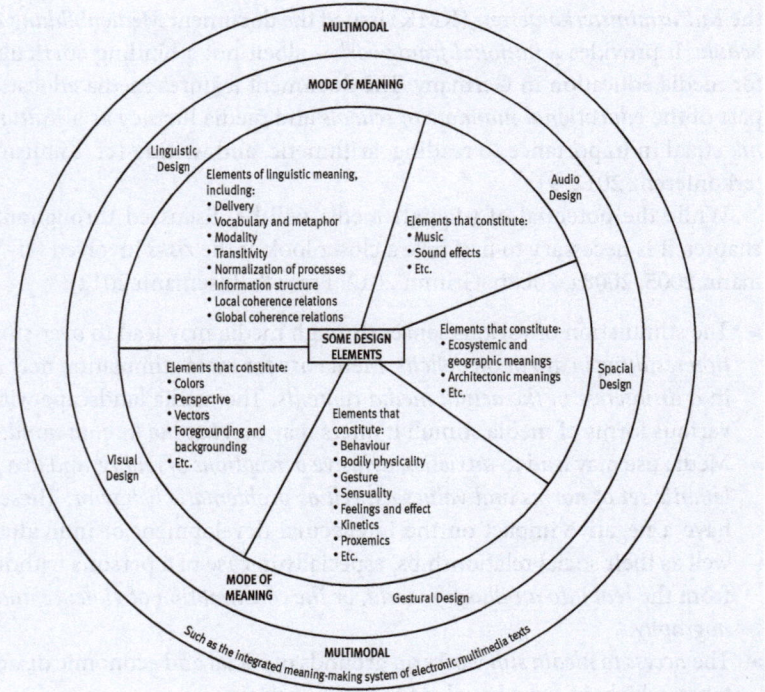

200

Media literacy has been defined by many scholars in the field of media studies, for example by Baacke (1997), Tulodziecki (1997), and Groeben (2002, for an overview of the concepts see Rosebrock & Zitzelsberger 2002: 149–56). The model by Wermke (1997: 145, see fig. 9.3) follows a *subject-specific approach* in terms of teaching and learning objectives: Media literacy

Dimension	Media literacy	Integrative characteristics		
Processes	**General**	**Aesthetics**	**Creativity**	**Reflection**
Emotion, motivation	Enjoyment, distancing	In association with various qualities involving functions, genres, style, etc.	Expression, experiment	Sensual perception, psychological mobility
Perception, recognition	Analysis, critique		Complexity, transmission speed	Contextual knowledge, power of judgment
Conduct, action	Usage, production		Modification, design	Negotiation and construction of meaning

| Fig. 9.3
Media literacy –
objectives (our trans.,
adapted)

As an example, a movie poster is perceived sensually on a rather emotional basis since it is meant to advertise a movie and invite a large audience. In the EFL classroom, students may speculate about the content of the movie on the basis of a variety of available movie posters and elaborate on whether or not they like the poster(s) (*emotion, motivation*). As to *perception and recognition*, students should be introduced to the defining features of movie posters (e. g., title, director, actors, tagline, attention-grabbing illustration), discuss how (well) these work to advertise the movie at hand, and reflect on manipulative functions (e. g., gender, race). Finally, as to *conduct and action*, students could design their own movie posters (e. g., with Glogster; see ch. 11.3), showcase them, provide peer feedback, and vote for a winner and runner-up.

The *semiotic framework of intertextuality or intermediality* frequently tends to subject multimodal texts to the paradigm of reading rather than recognizing the specific visual quality and experience of pictures (cf. Rymarczyk 2007; Ludwig & Pointner 2013; Meyer 2013, 2015; Uhlig 2014; Hecke & Surkamp 2015). However, on the basis of shapes on the page or the canvas, *the text needs to be 'realized' by the reader as the picture by the spectator*. The phenomenological experience partly precedes and partly interacts with the understanding of pictures, guided by general cultural codes of recognition and visual or 'graphic codes' (Jewitt & Oyama 2001, Wolf 2006: 20, Moebius 2009: 316–19): Visual literacy

► Picture frame and caption
► Size and format (landscape- or portrait-format)
► Composition (line, shape, color, texture, rhythm, contrast, salience)
► Genre and motif

- ▶ Point of view/perspective, angle, horizon, and space (visible – invisible, seen – unseen)
- ▶ Position and size of subject on the page

A 'strange picture' can affect someone through its peculiar quality of shapes, color, or contrast that catches the observer's attention and motivates a *subjective response* before he or she may recognize what it is and understands what it means by employing *pictorial and cultural codes*. One can have a feeling of being looked at before one notices that there is a portrait, which can be fascinating before one understands why through reflecting on one's subjective experience and the particular use of visual or cultural codes. After all, viewing and understanding pictures is an interactive process between bottom-up phenomenological experience and top-down cultural concepts (see chs. 3.2.3; 8.2.3, fig. 8.3). Teachers need to raise awareness to the making of pictures, thus facilitating *visual literacy*. In addition, learners should be alerted to the contexts in which pictures are embedded:

> [T]here are no purely visual images; images never appear without words, music, or other sounds. Even in art galleries images appear with labels, and their assumed significance is deeply grounded in art history texts and columns of written critique. The multimodal nature of imagery is even more evident when considering the forms in which imagery mostly occurs today, on television, at the movies, in print, and on computer screens. Words, music, and sound effects anchor the meaning of images. (Duncum 2010: 10)

Therefore, dealing with pictures in the classroom should find a balance between the subjective experience and reflection of pictures, the aesthetic and cognitive analysis of how pictures work, and the (inter-)cultural and critical reflection on the functions of visual media (cf. Meyer 2013: 160–62).

The educational objectives of media studies

Media studies curricula cover a *broad spectrum of educational objectives* to be integrated across all school subjects (Thüringer Ministerium für Bildung, Wissenschaft und Kultur 2010: 5–26, adapted extracts):

- ▶ *Information*: students can describe the historical development of different media (e. g., from smoke signals to the Internet). Students can obtain information through appropriate search engines (e. g., search strategies). Students can apply criteria regarding the trustworthiness of sources (e. g., operator, source citation, quality of content). Students can differentiate between the 'real' world and the world constructed by the media.
- ▶ *Communication and cooperation*: students can define the term 'communication' and are aware of different ways and models of communication. Students can describe their own media use and the overall media landscape. Students can apply synchronous and asynchronous ways of communication to share information and cooperate (e. g., email vs. chat). Students can describe and apply rules of communication (e. g., netiquette).

202

▶ *Production and presentation*: students can create media products. Students can describe options of publishing media products. Students can select a mode of presentation based on general criteria (e.g., text, visuals, logical structure). Students can present information (e.g., wall newspaper, computer-supported presentation). Students can give/request feedback (e.g., peer feedback, constructive feedback culture).

▶ *Analysis and evaluation*: students can identify potentials and limits of media (e.g., topicality, availability, costs). Students can analyze media design (e.g., from a political, ideological, historical, religious, and cultural angle). Students can fathom the dangers of an uncritical use of media (e.g., addictiveness, social isolation, loss of a sense of reality, violence). Students can perceive of media as agents of socialization (e.g., social networking, norms and values).

▶ *Reflection on media society*: students can outline the formative influence of media in different areas of life (e.g., the socio-cultural impact of technology, commercialization, agenda setting). Students can reflect on the power and influence of the media on politics and society (e.g., media monopolies, manipulation, media as 'fourth power,' 'transparent citizens'). Students can evaluate the impact of information technologies on the world of work (e.g., globalization, acceleration of workflow, professional qualifications for new jobs).

▶ *Legal issues, data protection, and protection of minors*: students can outline the basics of the copyright law as well as of personality rights (e.g., downloads, sources, citation, licensing, data protection, legal basics pertaining to the freedom of speech). Students can detect potential risks related to the use of digital media (e.g., false identities, scripting of cookies, the unintentional signing of contracts online).

Cross-curricular approaches to media education and the integration of media literacy components in subject-specific curricula are indicative of a growing interest in media education. However, *there is still work to do in the following fields*: (1) long-term implementation of media education topics in the curricula and exams of all school forms and subjects, including the definition of age-specific standards of media education, (2) integration of media education in extra-curricular activities, cooperation with media institutes, the press, TV stations, etc., (3) advancement of media education among educationally disadvantaged people, (4) improvement of media infrastructure and regular funding of media resources and infrastructure, (5) mandatory training of pre-service and in-service teachers in media education, training of regional media experts, and (6) more research on media education, especially in terms of practical implementations in schools and their evaluation (cf. Medienanstalt Hamburg/Schleswig Holstein 2010; Keine Bildung ohne Medien! 2011, 2014; Bos et al 2014; Wetterich et al. 2014).

There is room for improvement!

Why should (English) teachers care about media?

Considering the many *demands and challenges* teachers in general and especially EFL teachers face (see ch. 2), why should the use of and reflection upon media be yet another issue to be added to their concerns? *There are three interrelated reasons for this*: (1) Media have always had an established place in TEFL. They should be understood in their *three-layered function* as teaching and learning aids, as communicative tools, *and* as subjects of reflection. The EFL classroom in particular plays an important role in showing students how to make sensible use of media. While today's student generation has grown up with digital media, *using media does not equal using it competently* (cf. Schulmeister 2009: 124, Klimsa et al. 2011). One salient example worth mentioning here is the social network Facebook – many social networkers neglect security settings and are often unaware of the range and durability of the information they share (cf. Frees & Busemann 2012). (2) Facilitating media literacy is an *interdisciplinary endeavor*. Media education is already integrated into the curricula, but its scope and foci vary and are often inconsistent. In this context, teachers must act as *agents of change and innovation*. (3) The sensible use of media is required of *competent EFL teachers* (see ch. 2.1.4). Teachers are called upon to use media based upon a sound didactic reflection on:

► how the choice of a medium contributes to the *learning objectives* they are aiming at
► which *method as well as activities and tasks* they want to use
► which *learning environment and media infrastructure* they have at their hands
► which *prior knowledge on the part of students* they can work with

In other words, media should never be used for their own sake or for anticipated student motivation only, *but must always be part of a well-structured didactic concept.*

> Collect and discuss tasks, activities, projects that could be carried out in the EFL classroom to facilitate media literacy and address the teaching objectives outlined above.

9.2 | Potential

Potential for students

Media can *bridge the gap between students' everyday and school life* (e. g., a contemporary pop song discussed in EFL, employing readily available apps on the smartphone for learning). Media can be used *productively as well as creatively*, with students designing their own media (e. g., a themed YouTube video in English). Different forms of media offer diverse perspectives and thus cater to a *negotiation of meaning*, the broadening of the students' minds, and a critical reception of media (e. g., divergent coverage of a current event in newspapers, on TV, in blogs, forums, or social networks). Negotiating multiple perspectives on relevant issues teaches learners to keep an *open and critical mind*. Media offers opportunities for *collaboration as well as for self-directed and autonomous learning* (e. g., intercultural exchanges via email or chat).

Media can bring *greater variety* to the classroom. They can also help *bridge the gap between teachers and students* in that they foster a more informal learning environment (e. g., teachers inviting media suggestions and contributions from students, teachers as helpful 'guides on the side' in Blended Learning scenarios, teachers as learners employing the technical expertise of students). Reflections on a variety of media resources, involving a negotiation of meaning, can facilitate an *open and tolerant learning atmosphere that is characterized by mutual respect*. Thus, media support the development of *social competences*.

Potential for teachers

Media can induce *critical reflection and discussion between teachers* (e. g., on the use of media in general, on the school's infrastructure, and on school innovation). They can enrich school life, management, resources, etc., and lead to an 'opening-up' of schools in terms of collaborating with external partners. The Internet especially offers new opportunities for *global communication* on pressing topics and problems relating to the present and the future (e. g., the "Going Green"-project initiated by the US embassy: www.goinggreen2014.org). New ways of communicating also offer *new opportunities for action* (e. g., global school partnerships, Erasmus+ and Comenius projects, eTwinning). Media projects can also invite more *interest and initiative by parents and the larger public* by communicating individual as well as socially relevant content to the larger public (e. g., documenting and presenting the results of a school project or class trip, showcasing expressive learner products; cf. Volkmann 2008a: 122–24, 2008b: 176–78; Tulodziecki et al. 2010: 16–17; Spanhel 2011: 267–68).

Potential for schools

Media repertoire

| 9.3

Media can be described "*as those sociotechnical systems and cultural practices of the dissemination and storage of information which serve for the design of communication and interaction*" (Banse & Metzner-Szigeth 2012: 235, emphasis added; cf. Tulodziecki et al. 2010: 28–31). Media can be grouped into different categories: primary, secondary, tertiary, and quaternary (Banse & Metzner-Szigeth 2012: 235, emphasis added; cf. Faulstich 2000: 21, 2004; Voigts-Virchow 2005: 20–22):

Categorizing media

> An important differentiation in the connection of media and technology is that between **primary media** for the functioning of which the use of technology is not necessary (e. g., theatre), **secondary media** for the functioning of which the use of technology is necessary as far as production is concerned, but not for reception (e. g., daily newspaper), **tertiary media** for the functioning of which the use of technology is necessary for both sides, i.e., for both production and recep-

tion (e.g., record). In addition, there are **quaternary media** for the functioning of which besides technical support of production and reception, the technical mediation of the distribution is indispensable (online media, which are suitable for dissolving the conventional receiver/sender relationship).

A brief history of media use in schools

In the history of employing media in teaching and learning scenarios, the *picture* – next to *language as the dominant medium and content of learning* – is considered the oldest medium (cf. Reinfried 1992, Grünewald 2010a: 207). Its use in education dates back to the 17th century when Comenius (see ch. 1.1) published his textbook *Orbis sensualium pictus* (*Visible World in Pictures*, see fig. 9.4). *Orbis pictus* also features the picture of a *chalkboard*, proving it to be a long-established medium used in schools.

Fig. 9.4 |
Comenius' Orbis
sensualium pictus

Schola.

Die Schul.

While the textbook with its media package (see. ch. 10) can still be considered as the *key medium* across most school subjects, *the educational media repertoire has expanded dramatically in the last decades.* The use of ICT is now instrumental in **Computer-assisted Language Learning** (CALL) and **Mobile-assisted Language Learning** (MALL). These are forms of **E-Learning** that allow for **Blended Learning** scenarios – *the combination of face-to-face with computer- or mobile device-mediated teaching and learning* (see fig. 9.5; cf. Warschauer 2000, Albers et al. 2011, Heim & Ritter 2012, Würffel 2014). These teaching scenarios allow for learning beyond school, across multiple contexts, as well as through social interactions. For example, mobile devices enable

[T]hese days, most of us carry a fully functional multimedia studio around in our smartphones. – Austin Kleon

> users to create and distribute a wide variety of digital content (such as images, sound, and video) on the spot, opening up new opportunities for the development and implementation of brand-new mobile services, as well as new patterns of interaction between users, mobile devices, and mobile services. In the case of educational contexts, learners can easily produce different kinds of digital contents (e.g., with their mobile phones, iPods, handheld consoles, etc.), which they can rapidly edit and share with learners and/or teachers through the Internet. (Díaz Vera 2012: xiv)

A balanced approach:
'old' *and* 'new' media

However, "the impact of these transformations on the ways students learn at schools and universities *is so far definitely lower than initially expected*" (ibid., emphasis added). Too often, the disadvantages (e.g., restricted access, data security, technological constraints) outweigh the advantages (cf. Albers et al. 2011: 10–11, Díaz Vera 2012: xii-xv). This calls for a **balanced approach** to

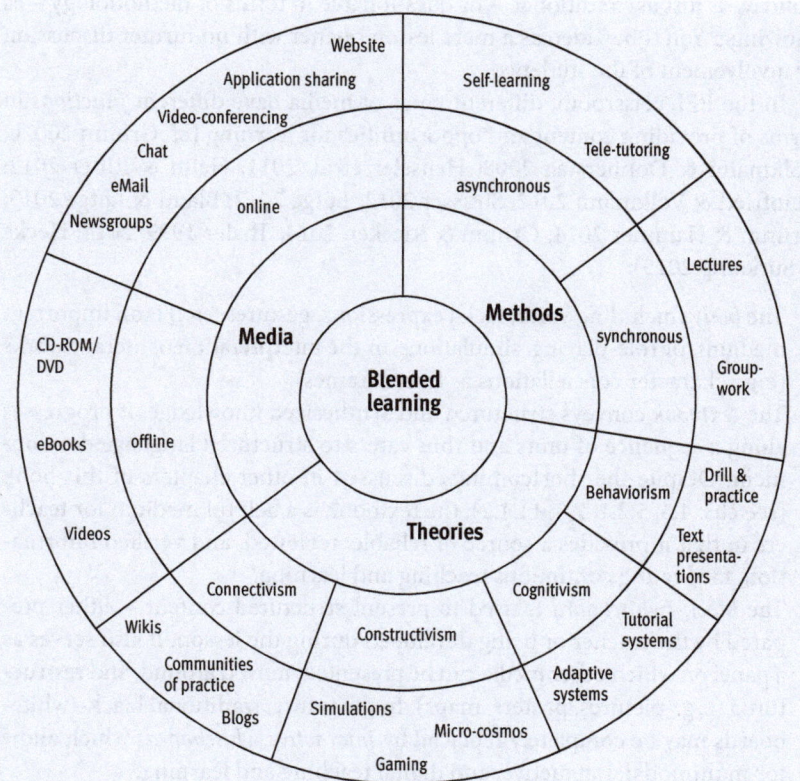

Fig. 9.5
Blended learning:
media, methods, and
theories (Wiepcke et
al. 2008: 30, adapted)

media use in education. While it has become quite commonplace to create a dichotomy between 'old' and 'new' media, *often insinuating a preference for the latter*, teachers should always keep the following in mind:

▶ "*[I]t is not media but the uses made of them* that can be characterised as traditional or modern." (Evans 2012: 217, emphasis added)
▶ "*[F]undamental continuities and interdependencies* between new media and 'old' media (such as television) [...] exist at the level of form and content, as well as in terms of economics." (Buckingham 2008: 14, emphasis added)
▶ "[T]he advent of a new technology may change the functions or uses of old technologies, *but it rarely completely displaces* them." (ibid., emphasis added)
▶ "*[L]earning is influenced more by the content and instructional strategy in a medium* than by the type of medium." (Clark 1994: 21, emphasis added)

In other words, teachers should refrain from selecting a medium merely for its own sake. *They must reflect soundly on the educational 'surplus value' of the medium.* As an example, using films for entertainment purposes before the holidays is just as 'traditional' – or questionable in terms of methodology – as showing a YouTube video as a mere lesson opener with no further discussion or involvement of the students.

In the EFL classroom, different types of media have different *functions* in terms of providing content and opportunities for learning (cf. Grimm 2007b; Volkmann & Donnerstag 2008; Henseler et al. 2011; Heim & Ritter 2012; Reinfried & Volkmann 2012; Strasser 2012; Lütge 2012; Bland & Lütge 2013; Grimm & Hammer 2014; Grimm & Riecken 2014; Thaler 1999, 2014; Hecke & Surkamp 2015):

Functions along media types

▶ The *body* (including voice, facial expressions, gestures, etc.) is an important medium for role-playing, simulations, or the interpretation of literary works (e. g., character constellations as freeze frames).

▶ The *textbook* conveys structured and synthesized knowledge. It progresses along a sequence of units and thus caters to structured language development. Despite the shortcomings discussed in other chapters of this book (see chs. 4.5, 5.2.1, 7.3, 11.1.2), the textbook is a helpful medium for teachers in that it provides a source of reliable, reviewed, and verified information, facilitating continuous teaching and learning.

▶ The *black-/whiteboard* is used to present structured content – either prepared by the teacher or being developed during the lesson. It also serves as a panel on which other media can be presented, moved around, and restructured (e. g., pictures, posters, maps). In the future, traditional black-/whiteboards may be completely replaced by *interactive whiteboards* which allow for multimodal, interactive, and digital teaching and learning.

▶ The *overhead projector* (OHP) can be used to present, gradually reveal, or to develop teaching content. Textbook and magazine publishers usually offer transparencies to be used in addition to their printed material.

▶ *Pictures* help contextualize vocabulary items, explain grammatical structures, illustrate stories, and provide impulses for communication. They also have a potential for intercultural learning: informative and striking pictures of landscapes, famous persons, sights, objects, etc. convey impressions of the target culture(s) and stimulate reflection – as do *cartoons* with their often funny, thought-provoking, and hyperbolic take on current issues. *Posters* can be created in the EFL classroom to visualize learning results that remain in the classroom so that one can always fall back on the information published on them. Professionally created *wall charts and maps* are not only decorative, but also provide geographical information, language structures, etc.

▶ *Non-fictional and fictional texts* (e. g., political speeches, pamphlets, stories) offer insights into social-political, cultural, and emotional situations. They facilitate reading and analytical as well as social and intercultural competences (see chs. 7, 8).

▶ *Audiovisual files* provide access to topical and authentic radio or TV coverage of important events. Audiovisual files gleaned from the Internet (e.g., *podcasts, vodcasts*) can be used for listening practice and serve as impulses for classroom discussions – the same goes for *songs and music video clips*. *Audio books* can be employed together with reading a literary work (print version or ebook). *Movies* offer authentic language input on a wide range of topics and in various formats. *Documentaries* convey socio-political, historical, economic, or ecological processes and events. *Film adaptations of literary works* serve, for example, to compare and contrast the film version with the literary work and also cater to lessons on literature that are rich in methodological variety. *Feature films* on a variety of student-related topics can often speak to students on an emotional basis and invite them to respond to problems presented in them. *Film analyses* should always be added to the focus on content in order to understand how movies are made to have a particular impact on the audience

▶ The *multimedia projector (Beamer)* with multimedia presentations (e.g., via PowerPoint) helps to create coherent, reusable, and adaptable teacher and student presentations. If planned and structured properly (avoiding the overuse of distractive features), multimedia presentations, including a sophisticated use of text, visuals, audio, and audio-visual files, add variety to traditional presentation formats.

▶ *CD-ROMs* come in the form of learning software, dictionaries, encyclopedias, etc. They are often part of the textbook media package with additional information, exercises, etc. CD-ROMs can also be learning products created by students.

▶ *Smartphones* can be employed in multiple ways: as a research tool (e.g., online dictionaries), for recording presentations, recitals, etc. (thus making them accessible for reviewing and archiving), taking pictures, recording role plays, creating short films, and also for MALL.

▶ The *computer* is a flexible multimedia tool for word processing, editing, archiving, using learning software, educational games, etc. The *Internet* can be used for target-oriented research. It also supports communication, creating and sharing learning products, as well as Blended Learning. *Digital applications and tools* allow for blogging, cloud computing, virtual learning, creating media products, etc.

Regarding the media repertoire at hand, how can these media be utilized efficiently and sensibly to facilitate activities, tasks, and competences? Discuss the advantages and disadvantages of using different types of media.

9.4 | Digital technologies: new horizons, new challenges

Digital media: friend or foe?

In the discussion about digital technologies and their use in education, positions deviate between (1) *euphoric proposals* promoting digital media in teaching (cf. Abfalter 2007, Richardson 2010, Poore 2013, Wampfler 2013), (2) *pessimistic stances* on how digital media have caused a 'dumbing-down' of society (cf. Keen 2008, Spitzer 2012), and (3) opinions which stress that the *risks of digital media need to be addressed, but generally opt for an integrative and reflected use* (cf. Blell & Kupetz 2005; Volkmann 2005, 2008a, 2008b; Albers et al. 2011; Reinfried & Volkmann 2012; Grimm 2012). This debate about the educational function of digital media relates to the 'hype' about the 'net generation' that allegedly thinks and acts differently than any generation before and therefore needs to be educated in different ways. Ever since Prensky (2001a, 2001b) coined the terms *'digital natives'* (those who have grown up with digital media) and *'digital immigrants'* (those born before the advent of digital media) and suggested that "Digital Immigrant instructors, who speak an outdated language (that of the pre-digital age), are struggling to teach a population that speaks an entirely new language" (Prensky 2001a: 2), an extensive body of publications on the defining characteristics of the net generation has been disseminated (cf. Schulmeister 2009 for an overview).

The 'net generation' – beware of generalizations!

However, the alleged rift between these two generations has now been relativized. First, because of "inept generalizations [...] which simplify and override the diversity of today's student and teacher generation" (Grimm 2012: 231). Second, because the call for a revolution in teaching ignores "the fact that media use, competencies and motivation not only differ according to individual preferences, lifestyles etc., but that these may be influenced or restricted by variables stemming from social status, ethnicity, and gender" (Schulmeister 2010: 52; cf. Mikos 2012, Kübler 2012). Third, because the statistics paint a diverse picture. According to *15 Jahre JIM-Studie: Jugend, Information, (Multi-)Media*, a survey of the results of a longitudinal study that was initiated in 1998, the picture is this (Medienpädagogischer Forschungsverbund Südwest 2013a: 8–28): first of all, *'the book is not dead.'* 40 % of the young people that were included in the survey read books daily or several times a week – the percentage has remained steady since 1998. It is however a worrying process that "the percentage of male non-readers has increased over the past years" (Medienpädagogischer Forschungsverbund Südwest 2014: 62). When it comes to the question of *credibility*, teenagers favor daily newspapers (40 %) over TV (26 %), the radio (17 %), and the Internet (14 %, ibid.: 15). As to the use of other media among the youth (Medienpädagogischer Forschungsverbund Südwest 2013a: 8–28), 79 % listen to the radio, and 88 % watch TV daily or several times a week. 80 % of the young people own a computer/laptop, 88 % have access to the Internet, and 89 % use the Internet. Access to the Internet via mobile devices has skyrocketed: 73 % access the Internet via smartphones, as compared to only 5 %

in 2006. Young people use the Internet for communication (45 %, 80 % are on Facebook), entertainment (24 %), games (17 %), and finding information (13 %). In their concluding remarks, the authors of *15 Jahre JIM-Studie* stress two points in particular (2013a: 33): (1) *traditional media are by no means being replaced by digital media.* The media repertoire is being continually complemented and expanded. (2) *Media education and the facilitation of media literacy – especially among young people – are essential in order to enable this generation and generations to come to behave sensibly in the ever-changing media landscape.* This is a clear mandate for teachers and calls for school innovation (cf. Schnoor 1998, Röll 2010, Eickelmann 2010, Grell et al. 2010, Albers et al. 2011, Grimm 2012).

While the media infrastructure in schools has improved considerably, the actual pedagogical use of this technical equipment by teachers is lagging behind. This is also true for EFL (Initiative D21 2006: 11–12). *Students, on the other hand, are eager to use media productively in school. They also want teachers to advise them on the safe use of media and acknowledge their media use. Students expect their teachers to be competent users of media themselves* (cf. Keine Bildung ohne Medien! 2010). Consider these statements by learners (ibid.: 1–5, our trans.):

What students expect of their teachers

> In my opinion, one should learn more about cyber-bullying because that is one of the worst things in chatrooms. Data protection is another important issue! Which kind of information is one allowed to share and publish?! These topics should be addressed more at school.

> A lot of students know more about the use of media than most teachers. [...] It is a real shame that our so-called media teacher is not able to play a video because he does not know how to open the media player.

> Teachers could learn more about what young people think and how they reflect on media such as computer games.

> Reflect on the student statements above. Assess your technology-related instructional competences (see ch. 2.1.4) and discuss how these could be improved.

In response to the mediocre results for Germany concerning the media literacy of students as well as the competences of teachers, revealed by the *International Computer and Information Literacy Study* (ICILS 2013, cf. Bos et al. 2014), the initiative *"Keine Bildung ohne Medien!"* (2014) has renewed the urgent call for *mandatory basic media-pedagogical training especially in the first phase of teacher education.*

While there is a fundamental body of research on the learning effects of using digital media in teaching and learning scenarios, it should be mentioned here that the empirical findings are rather shaky in terms of methodology and

The impact of digital technology on learning

applicability (cf. Tulodziecki et al. 2010: 77–78, Schulmeister 2010). One often cited study is *SITES-M2* (1999–2002), whose results point to changes *in the roles of teachers and learners with more cooperative and self-directed learning taking place* (Schulz-Zander 2003: n.p.; cf. Albers et al. 2011, Magenheim & Meister 2011, Herzig & Grafe 2011):

▶ Digital media are often used in problem-oriented learning scenarios as well as in project-oriented and open teaching and learning scenarios.
▶ In these learning scenarios, students adopt increasingly active roles: more self-regulated learning takes place in autonomous information research, the presentation of results, and the creation of products as well as their dissemination.
▶ Students assume more responsibility for the learning process and the learning outcome when results are being published online or when cooperating with external partners.
▶ Digital media foster peer-tutoring as well as cooperation within and across classes and with external partners (e.g., classes in other countries, authors, media experts).

Pachler et al. (2014: 146) also stress the "collaborative and communicative potential" of digital technologies and add the following characteristics of digital technologies which allow for new learning scenarios (ibid., adapted):

▶ *Access to authentic/contextualized/situated materials, interaction, tasks, and settings*
▶ *Multifunctionality and convergence*, i.e. the availability of multiple tools in one device linked to online services, networks, and repositories
▶ *Portability, ubiquity, personal ownership*
▶ *User-generated* content and contexts
▶ *Interactivity and non-linearity*; particularly relevant in terms of active learner engagement and the provision of feedback
▶ *Distributed knowledge construction*, allowing learners who are not co-located to work together in real or delayed time on the production of digital artefacts
▶ *Multimodal knowledge representation*, i.e. the combination of the written and the spoken word with still and moving images

To tap the full potential of digital technologies, teachers need to structure the learning process coherently. They have to provide structure, support, advice, guidance, and monitoring. They also need to draw on their *technological pedagogical content knowledge* to make digital learning scenarios work (see ch. 2.1.4).

Have a look at these recommended websites and discuss how helpful they are for teaching and learning purposes:

▶ *Pictures, visuals, cartoons, comics:* commons.wikimedia.org, pixabay. com, search.getty.edu, openclipart.org, www.copyrightfreephotos.com, nieonline.com/aaec, www.gocomics.com
▶ *Audio and video files:* learnenglish.britishcouncil.org, www.history.com, www.pbs.org, www.open.edu, www.teachertube.com, www.youtube.com/ education, www.englishlistening.com, ed.ted.com, explore.org
▶ *Games:* learnenglish.britishcouncil.org/en/games, gamestolearnenglish. com, www.teachingenglish.org.uk/language-assistant/games
▶ *Learning platforms:* www.lo-net2.de, moodle.de, www.edmodo.com
▶ *Apps:* learningapps.org, www.helblinglanguages.com/mindtheapp
▶ *Comenius, Erasmus+, eTwinning:* www.kmk-pad.org/programme/alle-programme.html, www.epals.com
▶ *Portals:* www.zum.de, www.lehrer-online.de, www.teachingenglish.org. uk, www.educatorstechnology.com, sester-online.de, www.bildungs server.de

Four examples of media use

| 9.5

The following four examples of media use in the EFL classroom have been *tried and tested in EFL classrooms*. Most of them have also been published in book and magazine editions, where one can find more detailed information on the respective classroom activities and projects.

Writing and illustrating a picture book

| 9.5.1

Picture books are multimodal texts combining narrative and visuals. Aimed at young children, they are both entertaining and educational. They aim at children's holistic response as well as lexical, narrative, and visual understanding (see ch. 8.3). Writing and illustrating a two- or three-page picture book as in the example in figure 9.6 addresses learners' interests and facilitates an early understanding how certain combinations of visual aspects and text layout create different effects (cf. Stafford 2011: 26–53).

Beginners

Grade, duration	▶ 3–5, ca. 90 minutes
Equip-ment	▶ *Mungo and the Dinosaur Island* (Knapman & Stower 2008), a selection of picture books, computer word-processing software

| Fig. 9.6
Writing and illus-trating a picture book (Stafford 2011: 48–49, adapted)

Procedure	▸ *Activity 1 (pre)*: T reads *Mungo and the Dinosaur Island!* (2008) to S. T and S discuss the features which make the picture book different from a prose text (e. g., the 'WANTED' poster on p. 4, the film cell comic on p. 6, the panels on p. 8, the onomatopoeia and the curving sentences on pp. 13 and 14). T asks S why the author and artist have included these things (T encourages S to view the visual flourishes as deliberate and adding to the feel of the story for the reader). ▸ *Activity 2 (pre)*: T asks S to think about one of their favorite picture books and imagine entering its pages. T tells S that they are going to write and illustrate a two- or three-page picture book showing what happened when they jumped into their favorite picture book. ▸ *Activity 3 (pre)*: on the board, T suggests different ways in which S might make their pages visually interesting. ▸ *Activity 4 (during)*: S draw pictures, color them, and then decide where the text needs to go. They could type out their text on the computer and print it off so that they are able to cut it up into individual words and play with the shape of the sentences on their illustrated pages. This also makes the finished work look more like a page from a book. T encourages S to make the finished pages visually interesting but not overly complex and to play with the layout and text in different ways (even if the book they are jumping into has a regular sentence format). ▸ *Activity 5 (post)*: S show their pages to the rest of the class. T comments on the visual aspects of the work and questions S as to why they have made the decisions they have in the design. ▸ *Activity 6 (post)*: The work can be displayed on the board or made into individual picture books to give S a sense of authorship.
Objectives	▸ Using an existing narrative as a model for a new and original story ▸ Combining pictures and words to tell a story ▸ Considering the effects of the visual aspects and layout of a text on its audience ▸ Selecting appropriate and interesting words and pictures to tell a story ▸ Using word-processing software to create stories

9.5.2 | Weather reports with fun

Intermediate learners

Games are still underrepresented in the EFL classroom, although they carry enormous potential: they can motivate students, create playful as well as competitive learning scenarios, and provide intrinsic impulses for communication as illustrated by the example in figure 9.7 (cf. Grimm & Riecken 2014).

Fig. 9.7 |
Weather reports
with fun (Grimm
& Riecken 2014,
adapted)

Grade, duration	▸ 7–8, ca. 45 minutes
Equipment	▸ Weather maps, rules of the game on OHP transparency or slide, cardboards, felt-tipped pens
Procedure	▸ *Activity 1 (pre)*: S receive a worksheet with a word cloud containing weather vocabulary. S are asked to categorize the vocabulary items into a table with columns reading 'hot words,' 'cold words,' 'wet words,' 'other words,' 'collocations,' and 'phrases/sentences.' ▸ *Activity 2 (pre)*: T explains the game and provides the necessary material. S form 5 teams and choose their weatherman, who studies the weather map and is prepared to deliver a short weather report (2.5 min). The teams prepare sets of cards (3 cards with weather-related words/collocations, 1 card with a random/unrelated word).

214

> ▶ *Activity 3 (during)*: the game starts with the weatherman from team 1, followed by teams 2 through 5. The weatherman delivers a short weather report. At the same time, the members of the four opposing teams present him/her with one card each so that at any given time there will be a total of four cards visible. The challenge is to meaningfully incorporate as many words as possible into the weather report. As soon as a word is incorporated (successfully or not), this card disappears from sight and a new card appears. The weatherman's team receives 1 point for each word that was incorporated successfully.
> ▶ *Activity 4 (post)*: T announces the winner and awards a small prize. T and S evaluate the game during a short feedback phase. Depending on the feedback, T adapts the game.

Objec-tives	▶ Revising and consolidating weather-related vocabulary ▶ Improving speaking skills ▶ Facilitating social competences through teamwork ▶ Giving and receiving feedback

Telling stories in pictures

9.5.3

Movies have a well-established place in the EFL classroom, yet teachers often *do not* tap their full potential in terms of linguistic input, information about target cultures, and film analysis. The example provided in figure 9.8 is meant to facilitate *visual literacy* and could be used as an activity prior to more complex film analyses (cf. Grimm 2007a, 2007b, Henseler et al. 2011, Lütge 2012, Thaler 2014).

Upper-intermediate learners

Grade, duration	▶ 9–10, ca. 90 minutes
Equip-ment	▶ Smartphones, laptops
Procedure	▶ *Activity 1 (pre)*: short introduction to mise-en-scène and camera work (e. g., settings, composition, lighting, focus, distance, perspective, angles). ▶ *Activity 2 (during)*: in groups, S agree upon a topic and tell a story in three pictures only (no text!). They are asked to exploit the options of mise-en-scène and the camera on the school grounds. ▶ *Activity 3 (during)*: one member of each group shows the sequence of three pictures (on the smartphone or a laptop) to peers that walk from group to group. The peers narrate the stories suggested by the pictures. ▶ *Activity 4 (post)*: S discuss the results with a focus on camera work, visual, and verbal narrative.
Objec-tives	▶ Learning about camera/film techniques and technical vocabulary in a conceptual and creative way ▶ Applying this knowledge by having a go at camera work and creating a story in pictures ▶ Telling stories on the basis of picture sequences ▶ Assessing and discussing results of visual and verbal interaction

Fig. 9.8

Telling stories in 'cinematographic' pictures (project: M. Meyer)

Platform-based literature project

Advanced learners   Learning platforms carry great potential for Blended Learning scenarios. The example suggested in figure 9.9 combines the traditional analysis of a literary work with an online classroom on the learning platform Edmodo, which has specifically been created for school purposes "to bridge the gap between how students live their lives and how they learn in school" (www.edmodo.com/about). *Plus, Edmodo has the 'look and feel' of Facebook.*

Fig. 9.9 |
Platform-based liter-
ature project (Klemm
& Grimm 2013,
adapted)

Grade, duration	► 11–13, project (10 to 16 45-minute lessons)
Equipment	► Computers, Internet, an online classroom on Edmodo (www.edmodo.com) with tasks, worksheets, and handouts
Procedure	► *Activity 1 (during)*: While reading the novel *A Long Way Down* (2005) by Nick Hornby, student groups are given the main task to choose one of the four protagonists in the novel and to study and describe his/her development throughout the novel. S post their results (e. g., character sketches) on Edmodo at regular intervals (T sets deadlines). The other student groups are invited to comment on the posts, provide feedback, and suggest improvements in terms of language and content. In class, these products serve as a basis for further literary analysis and discussion. ► *Activity 2 (during/post)*: S choose either a focus on multiperspectivity or intertextuality/intermediality in the novel. (1) Multiperspectivity: as an alternative to writing a journal entry from the point of view of a fictional character, student groups are asked to become psychological experts and write a medical report (based on the suicide intent scale: http://ebookbrowsee.net/suicidalrisk-assessment-becks-suicide-intentscale-doc-d356 722 235) about their character. Since the novel alternates between the four characters' perspectives, students are provided with detailed insights into the characters' minds. S publish their medical reports on Edmodo for them to be commented on and also present their expert opinion in class. S compare and reflect on the difference between literary and psychological discourses. (2) Musical references: the protagonists mention certain songs throughout the novel. These songs describe the situations the characters are in as well as their emotional state. S do research on these intertextual/intermedial references, post their results on Edmodo for commenting, and report back to the class. ► *Activity 3 (post)*: S are invited to share on Edmodo songs they tend to listen to when they feel in emotional turmoil. All S are advised to provide thoughtful feedback, avoiding insensitive and insulting comments.
Objectives	► Researching background information ► Analyzing stylistic aspects of a novel ► Writing formal and creative texts ► Commenting and giving feedback
Sample project	► By Uwe Klemm, teacher at Angergymnasium Jena: toppersjump.wordpress.com (the blog version on WordPress with project results; Edmodo classrooms are not available to the public)

Recommended reading

Albers, Carsten; Johannes Magenheim & Dorothee M. Meister (2011). Der Einsatz digitaler Medien als Herausforderung von Schule: Eine Annäherung. In: Carsten Albers; Johannes Magenheim & Dorothee M. Meister, eds. *Schule in der digitalen Welt: Medienpädagogische Ansätze und Schulforschungsperspektiven*. Wiesbaden: VS, 7–16.

Grimm, Nancy (2012). Digital Media: Promise for or Threat to Education? In: Maria Eisenmann & Theresa Summer, eds. *Basic Issues in EFL Teaching and Learning*. Heidelberg: Winter, 229–40.

Groeben, Norbert (2002). Dimensionen der Medienkompetenz: Deskriptive und normative Aspekte. In: Norbert Groeben & Bettina Hurrelmann, eds. *Medienkompetenz: Voraussetzungen, Dimensionen, Funktionen*. Weinheim et al.: Juventa, 160–97.

Medienanstalt Hamburg/Schleswig Holstein (2010). *Medienbildung – (k)ein Unterrichtsfach? Eine Expertise zum Stellenwert der Medienkompetenzförderung in Schulen*. Hamburg: Universität Hamburg.

Reinfried, Marcus & Laurenz Volkmann, eds. (2012). *Medien im neokommunikativen Fremdsprachenunterricht: Einsatzformen, Inhalte, Lernerkompetenzen*. Frankfurt a. M. et al.: Lang.

Voigts-Virchow, Eckhart (2005). *Introduction to Media Studies*. Stuttgart et al.: Klett.

Volkmann, Laurenz (2005). 'Demokratisierung des Lernens' oder 'Medienverwahrlosung'? Überlegungen zum didaktischen Umgang mit dem Internet. In: Gabriele Blell & Rita Kupetz, eds. *Fremdsprachenlernen zwischen Medienverwahrlosung und Medienkompetenz: Beiträge zu einer kritisch-reflektierenden Mediendidaktik*. Frankfurt a. M. et al.: Lang, 43–66.

Lesson planning and classroom management

All lessons are about learning. Good lessons can create what is called a rewarding 'learning experience.' Can such a positive and hopefully lasting experience be pre-planned? Are there certain elements or characteristics which are germane to a good and effective English as a Foreign Language (EFL) lesson? Some seem to be quite obvious, as good lessons are supposed to have a certain structure, composition, and aim. While textbooks can offer guidelines, teachers should use them wisely and in combination with other material. Other elements of good lessons need to be practiced time and again by teachers, such as classroom interaction. This chapter provides a survey of how to plan effective lessons, suggesting that teachers work flexibly with lesson plans.

Abstract

Look at the cartoon. Does a good lesson need exact pre-planning? What do teachers need to consider when planning a lesson? What would be a generic structure of a good lesson?

10.1 | Lesson frameworks

Think about the metaphors for a lesson (see fig. 10.1) and discuss which of them seem closest to your vision of an ideal lesson. Then compare with the concepts presented below.

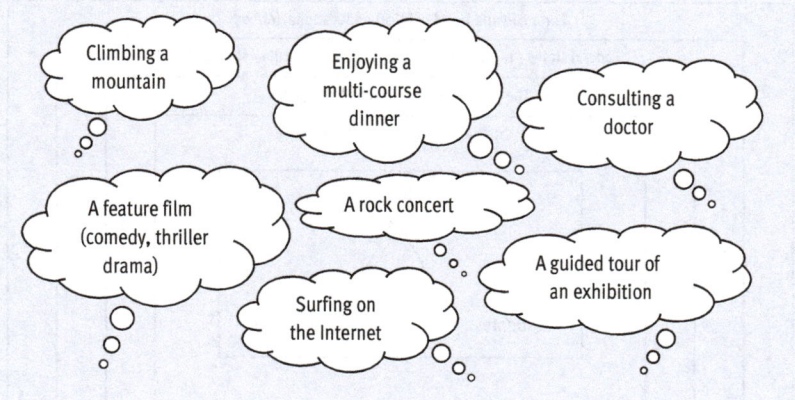

| Fig. 10.1

Metaphors for a lesson (based on Ur 1996: 213)

As the metaphors above indicate, there is *never only one possible concept of a lesson*. Rather, depending on one's preferences and expectations, an EFL lesson may have elements of

Functions of a lesson

- an *exchange*, something is transferred such as knowledge and skills
- an *interaction*, where some social interaction with lasting impressions or effects occurs
- a *goal-oriented effort*, where an effort takes place and something lasting is achieved
- a satisfying, *enjoyable experience*, where pleasure and fun are created
- a role-based and *ritualized construct*, where all participants must act according to their pre-determined roles and the whole event is somehow structured
- a *series of free choices*, where participants can pick and choose as far as the structure or progression of the event is concerned (cf. Ur 1996: 214).

John Lennon once quipped about life: "Life is what happens while you are making plans." This can also be applied to lessons: lessons happen while teachers are using plans. Even meticulously pre-planned lessons can turn out to be an utter disappointment and failure. Consequently, *good lessons 'happen'* on the basis of a sound *balance* of pre-planning and improvisation, of a pre-given structure and impromptu modifications.

Before directing attention to individual EFL lessons, one should take a sensible step back and look at the *larger picture* of what constitutes the broader and very intricate framework of a single lesson (see fig. 10.2). Below is a visualization of the major spatial, temporal, personal, and *socio-political factors* forming and shaping each lesson. At the center there is, of course, the so-called *pedagogic-didactic triangle* of teacher-students-topic (cf. Finkbeiner 2007: 39–40, Weskamp 2003: 46–54, Thaler 2012: 13–18, Volkmann 2012: 480–81; for a critique see Jank & Meyer 2002: 55):

External factors

Fig. 10.2 |

Factors forming and
shaping lessons

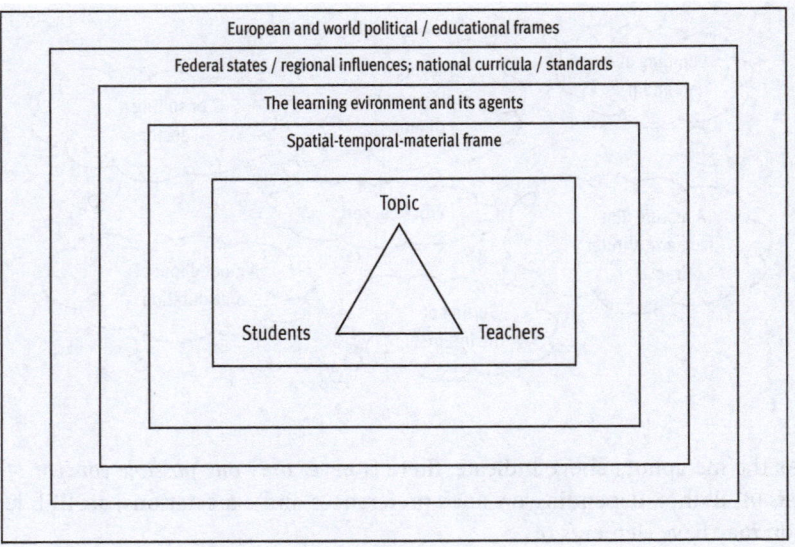

Regarding planning, conceptualizing, and implementing EFL lessons, these *interrelated factors* can be further described as follows, beginning with the more concrete elements and extending to the broader framework:

Spatio-temporal and material frame: EFL lessons usually take place in a *highly regulated* spatio-temporal framework. Short time slots are allotted for a couple of days a week in an artificial classroom environment. English lessons are squeezed in between other subject lessons. They are often hampered by non-communicative seating arrangements and a lack of opportunities to include a variety of media or to reach out beyond the classroom. Additionally, teaching and learning English depends on factors such as the dynamics of the classroom, the personalities involved, the availability of resources as well as the expectations and motivations of learners (cf. Islam & Mares 2003: 88).

The learning environment and its agents: teachers and students are part of a *socio-cultural network* of teaching and learning, which is subject to the forces of a competitive society as well as to individual and social needs and demands (cf. Finkbeiner 2007: 26). The goal of acquiring practical language skills is embedded in the *overall educational objective* of providing opportunities for personal growth and equipping students for life in a society where they are social beings as well as competitive agents. The school administration (headmaster), the representatives of EFL teachers at a school (*Englischfachschaft*), colleagues, mentors, parents, as well as politicians influence individual teaching decisions. A school with a focus on the natural sciences adheres to a different educational agenda than one focusing on foreign languages. Some schools may have a long tradition of English drama groups performing a whole play every year; other schools may have a well-established yearly exchange with a native-speaker school. As Thaler points out, individual teachers can make a difference and start *effective initiatives*: "If, as a teacher, I start a school exchange with Scotland or found a drama group or get a monthly movie night going, I can enlarge opportunities of young people of my circle of influence to get in touch with the foreign language and culture." (2012: 18, our trans.)

Regional curricula: in Germany, education policy (*Bildungspolitik*) – including school forms, resource allocation, exam frameworks, the order of foreign languages to be taught, and the approval of *textbooks* – is determined by each federal state. The principle of federalism has created a diversity of school and learning traditions, with the sixteen federal states competing among each other concerning the most effective and successful education system. The drive toward standardization and compatibility has been reflected in the implementation of standardized state exams and national standards of education (*Bildungsstandards*). For English teachers of any given federal state, the curriculum (*Lehrplan, Bildungsplan, Rahmenplan*) is the standard document of reference (cf. www.bildungsserver.de). While they will differ from state to state, curricula leave enough space for *individual lesson planning*, providing guidelines for competence development, grammatical and communicative sequencing as well as topics and themes to be dealt with. While some state curricula have always been quite open with regard to issues and texts to be dealt with for advanced learners, others, such as those of Baden-Wuerttemberg or North Rhine-Westphalia, tend to prescribe certain topics and even texts which need to be dealt with in grades 11 or 12 – e.g., the 'asterisked topics' (*Sternchenthemen*) of Baden-Wuerttemberg. For example, for many years Shakespeare's *Macbeth* was a mandatory text for advanced students in many states. Recently, state curricula have been thoroughly revised or are *still undergoing revision* with some of them now resembling a rather general framework requiring of schools and teachers to conceptualize their own school- and subject-specific curricula (*schulinterne Lehr- und Lernplanung*). Since textbooks need to be approved of by the federal states, all textbooks by major publishers, such as Klett, Cornelsen, or Diesterweg, reflect the regional curricula and are frequently used as a '*secret curriculum*' (*geheimer Lehrplan*), often making curricula appear rather superfluous for everyday teaching practice. Yet, a comparison of curricula and textbooks can show clearly that teachers do not need to follow textbooks obediently, but should rather use the curriculum as their guideline for planning lessons (see ch. 11.1.1).

National curricula and standards: notwithstanding the fact that the federal education system in Germany does not allow for much centralized influence, the introduction and implementation of national standards of education have marked a gradual if only partial shift from a seemingly incompatible and incommensurable field of education to a more comparable education system. It was in the wake of the 'PISA shock' of 2000 that the *Standing Conference of the Ministers of Education and Cultural Affairs of the Länder in the Federal Repub-*

Federalism vs. standardization

National guidelines

lic of Germany (Kultusministerkonferenz, KMK) decreed in 2003 and 2004 that all federal states are to implement *Bildungsstandards für den Primarbereich, für den Hauptschulabschluss bzw. den Mittleren Schulabschluss.* More drives toward a more unified, comparable, and testable system have followed (e. g., *Zentralabitur, länderübergreifendes Abitur*). All standardization aims to improve the quality of teaching and learning, mainly by shifting the focus from input- toward output-orientation. As some critics state, this has meant a shift from a focus on (meaningful) content to one of measurable output in terms of FL skills (see ch. 1.2.2).

International guidelines

European and world political / educational frames: concepts of **global education** and **transcultural competence** as well as, for instance, concepts of **inclusion** (see chs. 6, 8), constitute a wide socio-cultural, ecological, and value-oriented framework for institutionalized FL learning. Key issues such as global governance, peace keeping, international understanding (*Völkerverständigung*), and sustainable development (*nachhaltiger Umweltschutz*) are reflected in documents such as the 1995 OECD-manifestos *The Curriculum Redefined: Schooling for the 21st Century* and *Environmental Learning for the 21st Century.* For FL learning, the seminal document is the *Common European Framework of Reference for Languages* (CEF) from 2001, which was initially designed to further FL learning and plurilingualism (every European should learn two or more foreign languages) by describing competence levels and by making output comparable. While it originally aimed at fostering *curriculum and syllabus development* along the lines of output- and competence-orientation (see ch. 11.1), the overall pragmatic and 'communication-before-content' approach of the CEF has had far-reaching repercussions 'down' the levels of national, regional, and local FL teaching and learning (cf. Hallet & Müller-Hartmann 2006, Decke-Cornill & Küster 2014: 143–61).

Dilemmas

The various influences of the above-mentioned forces can confuse and sometimes frustrate teachers, who will have to find individual solutions to *dilemmas* such as the following:

▸ As an avid fan of Shakespeare, can a teacher still use a complete play, maybe even a complex one like *Hamlet* with advanced classes? Most regional curricula no longer explicitly refer to Shakespeare or suggest a different author of a non-British area.

Teachers open the door. You enter by yourself. – Chinese proverb

▸ Given the fact that textbooks apparently seem to spoon-feed students all the input they need, do teachers still need to consult the curriculum or use teaching material other than the textbook?

▸ Given the dominant standardization and output-orientation, how do teachers deal with physically or mentally handicapped students in inclusive classes who will not achieve the same level of proficiency?

▸ How do teachers foster life-long and autonomous learning, as propagated by all the political documents on FL teaching, if they are pressed to 'teach to the test'? Due to the infamous 'backwash effect' created by output-orientation, only what is tested or testable will be taught and learned.

According to a model provided by Thaler (2012: 24), teachers need to find a *sound balance* between the current focus on testable, optimizable language training (*Ausbildung*) and the overarching objectives of education (*Bildung*) (see fig. 10.3; see chs. 1.2, 3.1, 8.1.2):

Education (*Bildung*) – training (*Ausbildung*)

English language education	
Education (*Bildung*)	Language training (*Ausbildung*)
▸ Character formation ▸ Critical & reflective competences ▸ Inter- & transcultural competences ▸ Literary & aesthetic competences ▸ Language awareness	▸ Comprehensibility ▸ Fluency ▸ Accuracy
▸ Knowledge: language and culture(s) ▸ Skills: action- and situation-oriented, transferable ▸ Attitudes: openness and willingness to engage further with foreign language(s) and culture(s)	

Fig. 10.3

English language education

Using the textbook and other material

10.2

As will be discussed in chapter 11, teachers may be tempted to rely solely on the textbook by the publisher used at their schools. However, adaptations, additional sources as well as authentic and up-to-date material are just as important in the classroom because of the following questions, which teachers should think about *before* planning a lesson. In other words, do the textbook and/ or the materials meet the following criteria, and if not, what other materials should be used (Islam & Mares 2003: 88–89, adapted)?

Criteria for material use

▸ *Methods:* are the activities and exercises too mechanical, too inauthentic, too vague in meaning, too simple or too complicated, or too difficult to access or engage in? Do they create a dependency on teacher guidance or provide opportunities for learner autonomy?
▸ *Language and content:* is the emphasis on grammar too monotonous, too difficult, or too simple? Is new vocabulary presented in context and in a memorizable manner?
▸ *Appeal to learners:* do the materials cater to different learning styles/learner types?
▸ *Balance of skills:* what skills should be taught in this lesson? Are the materials appropriate for this lesson or is there, for example, too much emphasis on writing as a skill?
▸ *Progression and grading:* does the order of language items fit the curriculum and is it in accordance with the *Processability Hierarchy* (see ch. 5.1.2)? Does the staging need to be steeper or shallower? Do the activities provide challenging input (also encouraging higher-level cognitive skills)?

225

▶ *Cultural content:* are the cultural references appropriate and fair to the target culture(s)? Can additional and up-to-date cultural content be added?

▶ *Visuals:* are the textbook or the materials used in the lesson of high quality regarding layout and visuals (e. g., is the layout or visual material functional or decorative, too much or too little)?

Media package
(Lehrwerk)

The *authenticity* of language, cultural representations, and media is often the *crucial criterion* for choosing and using material in the EFL classroom. Textbooks, especially for beginners, often include scripted texts and altered images specifically produced for language learners. To maximize the value of a textbook, teachers can use the media package (*Lehrwerk*) that is provided by all publishers and includes supplementary tailor-made material. In addition, teachers can find numerous materials of similar content for EFL purposes on the Internet, both by individual co-teachers and by commercial or non-commercial organizations. The media package, which is available with the textbook, can be used selectively and together with additional material, as suggested in figure 10.4 (cf. Kieweg 1998: 28, updated). Any material can be adapted to learners' needs by reducing, adding, omitting, modifying, and supplementing (see ch. 11.2). This is, of course, done to make it *more suitable* for a particular group of learners. However, on principle, such changes should only be made if deemed absolutely necessary and rather in the language acquisition phase –

Materials for classroom use

adaptations can *deskill learners*, create a lack of motivation, or lead to '*reality shock*' when learners are exposed to authentic language use.

Fig. 10.4 |
Supplementing the media package with other material

Media package ◀──────▶ Other material	
Supplement	
▶ Students' book as key medium (also called textbook, course book, *Lehrbuch, Schülerbuch*)	▶ Realia: real objects, especially for (inter-)cultural learning and vocabulary work (from coins to tram tickets to larger objects)
▶ Workbook for students	▶ Texts: newspapers, journals, cartoons, comics, literature (including 'graded readers')
▶ Audio file(s) (online/offline) / CDs	▶ Visual material: signs, pictures, maps
▶ Online / offline material (CD) for grammar and vocabulary training, intercultural learning, games	▶ Audio files: speeches, conversations, announcements at airports, radio plays, audiobooks
▶ Online / offline videos and pictures	▶ Multimedia: movies, games, Internet, mobile devices
▶ (Virtual) vocabulary indexes, grammar aids, self-instructed learning	
▶ (Virtual) tasks and self-evaluation tests (also only for teachers)	
▶ Teacher's manual	
▶ Additional material for teachers only (tests)	
▶ Material for group work	
▶ Virtual platform for teachers and students	

In general, the material used in class should meet the following two objectives: (1) It should be *personalized and individualized* so as to fit the preferences and needs of teachers and learners. (2) It should be *localized and modernized* so as not to appear as a one-size-fits-all solution to language learning, which would lessen motivation (cf. Islam & Mares 2003: 89).

> Consult the homepages of textbook publishers (e. g., www.klett.de, www. cornelsen.de, www.diesterweg.de). Look for supplementary material to the EFL textbooks offered by theses publishers. Consider the following questions: (1) Is the material provided appealing and comprehensive? (2) How much is free of charge? (3) How is it related to the textbook? (4) How motivating and useful do you consider the material?

For both novice teachers and experienced teachers, the 'lure' of the *teacher's manual* (*Lehrerhandreichung*) as a step-by-step method guide to planning a lesson should not be underestimated. While for young teachers such manuals offer a conceptually sound introduction to planning each individual lesson on the basis of the textbook and the material provided by the publishing house, experienced teachers may simply appreciate the time-saving amenities of such a guide. However, manuals accompanying the students' textbooks pose the serious danger of *deskilling teachers* by leaving little room for own thoughts and creativity. They could create dependency on the seemingly facile task of following phase-by-phase instructions (see ch. 11.1.2).

The teacher's manual: pros & cons

Planning a lesson

| 10.3

> Discuss the statement below and rephrase it so that it reflects your own attitudes:
> "Good teachers plan their classes minutely so that everything they do is prearranged. Once they are in the classroom, they follow their plan without deviation, always watching out for irrelevances which the students may bring up and which would disrupt the plan." (Harmer 2000: 138)

Advance reflection

| 10.3.1

The choice of the teaching method is only one element within a sequence of interrelated curriculum development activities. With the preponderance of method guides available for teachers there is a tendency to foreground methods and activities (e. g., a task-based WebQuest or direct instruction or the Presentation-Practice-Production pattern, PPP). Instead, the question of which method to use should take the mid-position in a sequentialized *reflection process* (see fig. 10.5, based on Richards & Rodgers 1986: 159):

Needs and goals *before* methods

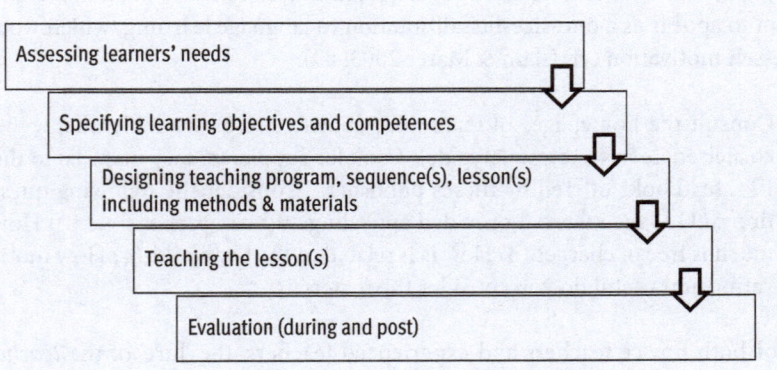

Fig. 10.5 |
The reflection process

General and specific
learning objectives

The first two steps are interrelated: initially, there is the question of what *learners need to learn* in order to make progress (according to a syllabus, a curriculum, a program for their group; depending on age, stage of learning, etc.). This needs to be related to the next step, which consists of defining the *learning objectives (Lernziele)* and competences in accordance with a taxonomy that starts with general objectives *(Groblernziele)* and specific objectives *(Feinlernziele)* and *competences,* which could be of general educational value and of specific value for the EFL classroom. It is only then that the methods and the material to be used should be defined with regard to the learning objectives and the needs of students: *which method(s) do I use to develop the defined objectives, goals, and competences of this specific learner group?* Adjustments need to be made while teaching. In a post-teaching phase, lessons can be evaluated by teachers themselves, colleagues (peer evaluation), and students.

Richards and Rodgers (1986: 156) provide a typical example to illustrate the need to put the issue of which method(s) to use into the framework displayed above:

> Choice of teaching approach or method, materials, and learning activities is usually made within the context of language program design and development. When the director of a language school or institution announces to the staff that an incoming client group will consist of forty-five Japanese businessmen requiring a six-week intensive course in spoken English, the teachers will not leap to their feet and exclaim 'Let's use Silent Way!' or 'Let's use Total Physical Response!' Questions of immediate concern will focus on who the learners are, what their current level of language proficiency is, what sort of communicative needs they have, the circumstances in which they will be using English in the future, and so on. Answers to such questions must be made before program objectives can be established and before choice of syllabus, method, or teaching materials can be made. Such information provides the basis for language curriculum devel-

228

opment. Curriculum development requires analysis, development of goals and objectives, selection of teaching and learning activities, and evaluation of the outcomes of the language program.

Since individual school teachers have only a minor say in the development of EFL curricula, it is crucial to pay particular attention to the first stages of lesson preparation: the analysis of the *learners' needs* and their *levels of proficiency* followed by the question of what competences or learning objectives should be reached at the end of this lesson as well as at the end of a teaching program (a sequence, a unit, a school year). Essentially, as Magnan states, the focus must be on the learners: "Who are our learners? What are they learning? What do they wish to learn? Where and how are they learning? What is our role in the learning process?" (qtd. in Weskamp 2007: 153)

Focus on learners

Structuring a lesson

| 10.3.2

"No [lesson] plan is written on tablets of stone" (Harmer 2000: 121). Lesson planning is quite an *art*: every lesson has a number of components or phases. The art of lesson planning consists of combining these components and adapting them flexibly while teaching. As to working with *components of a lesson plan*, it is advisable to follow these steps:

▶ Take *notes* with the overall structure to class. It seems advisable to note time slots in advance. Planning should include shortening phases and/or prolonging phases and/or adding an extra phase (such as a useful, short 'Let's look at the new vocabulary again' phase). Such notes should not be exposed overtly to students.

Combining components of a lesson plan

▶ It is of great importance to think in advance of what one wants to achieve with the planned activities. *What can go wrong?* Can a switch to another activity or another method or another medium be done easily? *Time management* is of utmost importance. Usually, activities take longer than planned (especially when planned by novice teachers).

▶ Novice teachers are advised to write down *key questions and instructions* and think about possible student answers.

▶ A good lesson has a certain *composition* with – especially for beginners – ritualized, though not monotonous, components. It should have a positive, focused beginning and end on a positive note (e. g., with a ritual at the beginning such as singing an English song) and a 'pulling together' of the class (the class focuses on the fact that their English lesson starts at a certain time and that their English learning ends at a certain time).

▶ A good lesson should be *clearly structured with smooth transitions*. Teachers consider how activities fit together (usually oral activities should come before written activities). Thought should be given to transition activities such as 'rounding off' one phase by simultaneously tying over to the next, especially if the topics or activities differ (such as moving from writing activities to interactive activities).

▶ There is a *variation* of tempo, active and quiet activities; harder tasks are 'couched' in easier ones.

▶ Students leave the lesson with a *sense of achievement*, which could be experienced especially if at the end of the lesson there is a recapitulation or a phase where students notice that something new has been learned, something they can use in real life. Goals have been achieved, which creates a "self-energizing effect if they are appropriately challenging for the student" (Hattie 2009: 164).

▶ Lessons should neither be predictable nor always the same: "the need for variety in classroom activities and teacher behaviour [is] an antidote to student (and teacher) boredom" (Harmer 2000: 125; cf. Ur 1996: 216–17).

Principles of lesson planning

Keeping the students and their needs in mind, teachers should plan the lesson with regard to the following principles (see ch. 4.7):

▶ *Using different methods*: choosing methods best suited for students gaining the defined competences and reaching the pre-set learning goals

▶ *Using different social forms*: a variety of forms which depend on the skills to be furthered (including a variety of open forms)

▶ *Considering individual learners*: catering to different learner types and heterogeneous groups through different types of tasks, material, etc.

▶ *Scaffolding*: anticipating where students will need extra help, more input, more explanations

▶ *Material and media*: chosen according to the learning objectives, competences, and activities in focus, and with the aim of motivating students

▶ *Output- and competence-orientation*: keeping the question in mind what students will actually have learned after a class. This includes testing as part of a lesson sequence, but also phases of summarizing and assessing what has been learned (*consolidating knowledge, Ergebnissicherung*).

Integrating single lessons

Since a lesson is part of a *teaching sequence* (*Unterrichtseinheit*), it has to be considered how it fits into the overall composition of such a sequence stretching, for example, over a week or a month. Just as a lesson needs some kind of *inner coherence*, a lesson sequence should have a coherent pattern with overall objectives. Ideally, a sequence has threads running through it which are based on a topic or topics and covers various skills; it follows a certain logic and offers a range of various activities (Harmer 2000: 125–26.). For example, if a teaching sequence is built 'around' a short story, teachers must plan how to stretch the structure of (1) pre-encounter (pre-reading), (2) encounter (reading), and (3) **Pre – during – post** post-encounter (post-reading) not just over one lesson, but over a stretch of several lessons, keeping their students engaged in various activities (e. g., from intensive reading to responding to the text to using the text as a trigger for discussion and creative activities).

Models for lesson planning | 10.3.3

Pre-, while- (during), post-activities: the above-mentioned phases of (1) pre-encounter, (2) encounter, and (3) post-encounter have become well-established phases of dealing with texts of all sorts (see ch. 4.3.2). Similar descriptions of four or five phases which can be found in the literature must actually be seen as variations of this pattern, modifying one phase or the other. For example, Weskamp (2001: 124) suggests a four-part TQLR-method for listening activities: Tune in (activate pre-knowledge) – Question (speculate about what will be listened to) – Listen (actively, comparing with expectations) – Review (reflecting on what has been listened to). Obviously, the phases of Tune in and Question could be subsumed under the heading 'pre-listening.'

Presentation-Practice-Production (PPP): the much-used PPP method is   PPP
sometimes modified, as in the Ziegésar-model (*Acquisition-based Model*) on introducing new grammar items (see ch. 5.2.2.3). Basically, the PPP model can stretch over several lessons, particularly with complex grammatical phenomena. The Presentation Phase tends to be teacher-centered, with the teacher presenting the context and situation for the new item to be learned (e. g., grammar, vocabulary). Meaning and form of the new item are 'demonstrated' by means of meaningful, student-oriented scenarios (e. g., with the help of recordings, images, texts). The ensuing Practice Phase follows a pattern from more rigid and simple responses (students merely respond to cues or present short answers) to more complex ones, generally from oral to written activities. Ideally, there is a smooth transition from practicing a new item to integrating it into the communicative system of the learners, with the use of the new language item becoming increasingly 'habitualized.' This Production Phase should be seen as a long continuum which would include *implicit revisions* (*immanente Wiederholungen*) to ascertain that the new item has really been fully integrated. The acquisition of a new item usually takes much longer than this approach suggests and "far more experience of the item in communication is necessary for any lasting learning to take place" (Tomlinson 2003: xii). The PPP model is usually seen as being very effective for *teaching simple language structures at lower levels* (Harmer 2000: 31); it is very systematic and takes into consideration the learners step-by-step integration of the new item. Controversial issues related to the PPP-method in EFL classroom instruction remain with regard to when or whether to make grammar rules explicit and whether or not to use mother-tongue expressions when doing so (see ch. 5.2.1). Also, the PPP method tends to be teacher-centered, and as a structured presentation could bore or deskill more advanced learners.

Engage-Study-Activate (ESA): Harmer suggests an alternative to the PPP   ESA
model. It follows a straight line: first, the teacher gets the students' attention (*Engage*), then the students become active and do something (*Study*), and lastly, they try to apply their newly learned skills (*Activate*). Harmer (2000: 27) uses

the following *illustrative example* for teaching the grammatical items 'can' and 'can't':

1. *Engage:* students and teacher look at a picture or video of modern robots. They say what the robots are doing. They say why they like or don't like robots.
2. *Study:* the teacher shows students (the picture of) a particular robot. Students are introduced to 'can' and 'can't' (how they are pronounced and constructed) and say things like 'It can do maths' and 'It can't play the piano.' The teacher tries to make sure the sentences are pronounced correctly and that the students use accurate grammar.
3. *Activate:* students work in groups and design their own robot. They make a presentation to the class saying what their robot can and can't do.

Not unlike other 'phase models,' the ESA-structure tends to work well at lower levels for vocabulary and grammar acquisition. However, as Harmer concedes, it does not take into account the students' own *learning styles* and may not be appropriate for learning complex issues. Here, teachers should plan a "mixture of procedures and mini-procedures" (ibid.). Harmer's model integrates a certain focus on activities and tasks rather than on form, which in essence can be defined as the core principle of the more student-centered *task-based approach* (TBLL; cf. Willis 2000, see ch. 4.3.2).

10.3.4 | Generic structure of a lesson plan

Generic lesson plan   As to lesson plans for the EFL classroom, an overall structure could follow the principles of good teaching as outlined by Meyer (2004, 2006; see ch. 2.1.3). In the following, a lesson plan consisting of generic components is presented. This plan was developed in international EFL circles in the 1970s and has been modified over the decades (see fig. 10.6). The following table outlines this generic lesson plan in the first three columns. The fourth includes references concerning German EFL practices. In the fifth column, remarks can be added as to how the consecutive phases could be modified or specified (lesson plan based on Farrell 2002: 33; the German terminology follows Benecke 2007: 36–37).

> Look at the following lesson plan. (1) Where would you find the phases of the PPP and ESA models? (2) Consider a typical EFL lesson for beginners, introducing new vocabulary, or for advanced learners, tackling a cultural issue. How would you modify the plan below?

Lesson phase	Role of teacher	Role of students	German EFL practice	Modifications needed
1. Perspective (opening)	Asks what students have learned in previous lesson; previews new lesson	Tell what they've learned previously; respond to preview	Wiederholung; Sicherung des Erlernten: Konsolidierung des Kenntnisstandes; Anknüpfung an die vergangene Stunde (Kontrolle der Hausaufgabe)	
2. Stimulation	Prepares students for new activity; presents attention grabber	Relate activity to their lives; respond to attention grabber	Motivationsphase; (Vorbereitung der) erste(n) Begegnung mit neuem Item, Text, Inhalt	
3. Instruction / participation	Presents activity; checks for understanding; encourages involvement	Do activity; show understanding; interact with others	Präsentation des Neuen / Einführung im Anwendungskontext; Aneignung (sukzessive Vertiefung); Interaktion; Anwendung	
4. Closure	Asks what students have learned; previews future lesson	Tell what they have learned; give input on future lessons	Lernerfolgskontrolle; Evaluation; Feedback; Hausaufgabe	
5. Follow-up	Presents other activities to reinforce some concepts; presents opportunities for interaction	Do new activities; interact with others	In most German models this is not included; instead there is the option of a transition to the next lesson	

Fig. 10.6

Generic lesson plan

Again, it must be stated that teachers can and must use *variations of this generic model*. For instance, timing, social forms of activity, and media can be included in additional columns in such plans. It has been stressed that, as time passes and both teachers and students gain competence, learners "can gradually take on a larger role in choosing the content and even in the structure of the lessons themselves" (Shrum & Glisan in Farrell 2002: 34). *Just how important is it to follow a pre-arranged lesson plan?* One needs to take into account whether the chosen method and process lead to the objectives or need to be modified. Of course, being flexible is of great importance when the lesson is in progress.

Variations

Consider the following scenario and discuss how teachers should respond to it:

"[T]he teacher has planned that the students should prepare a dialogue and then act it out, after which there is a reading test and some exercises for them to get through. The teacher has allowed twenty minutes for dialogue preparation and acting out. But when the students start working on the activity, it is obvious they need more time. The teacher then discovers that they would like to spend at least half the lesson on just the acting-out phase which they find helpful and enjoyable. At that moment, he or she has to decide whether to abandon the original plan and go along with the students' wishes or whether it is better to press ahead regardless." (Harmer 2000: 5)

10.3.5 | Assessing and evaluating lessons

Evaluating good teaching

Lesson plans and subsequent lessons should always be assessed and evaluated in some form. Teachers can reflect on their teaching while in class, after class, together with their students or in peer-evaluation scenarios, asking their peers to sit in and give feedback later. Teachers are also evaluated throughout most of their career by the school administration and the Ministry of Education, which includes regular visitations (*Unterrichtsbesuche*). In Germany, every federal state has a list of how teachers should be evaluated, and, surprisingly, the actual teaching practices (meaning good teaching skills) are only a small part of it, with administrative and organizational skills being featured most. What constitutes 'good teaching' is defined by Horster (2004), for example, through his list of 78 *criteria*, which has been eclipsed by lists of more than 100 criteria that have been introduced by some federal states! A short list of criteria of a good and effective lesson could look like the following (cf. Farrell 2002: 35, Ur 1996: 219, Weskamp 2003: 142, 145; Thaler 2012: 31, Hattie 2009: 244; see chs. 2, 4):

Criteria

▶ Were the learners attentive and active? All the time? Did the teacher make a (successful) effort to engage all students? If not, what was the reason for their inactivity? What about discipline?

▶ Did the teacher respond to students individually? Did the learners seem to enjoy the lesson; were they challenged, motivated? Did they experience a sense of achievement?

▶ What did the students actually learn? Can 'output' or 'outcome' be clearly assessed?

▶ Was there a phase of consolidating knowledge?

▶ Was English used communicatively throughout?

▶ What tasks were most successful? Least successful? Why?

▶ Did the lesson follow a certain trajectory? Was it finished on time?

▶ What changes (if any) will have to be made in the future in one's teaching and why?

Put the criteria in an order of priority. Put the most important first, the least important last.

The lesson in progress

| 10.4

Teacher talk and student talk

| 10.4.1

It is one of the *truisms* of foreign language teaching that student motivation, learning, and at best, proficiency depend to a great degree on how teachers *interact* with their students (cf. Hattie 2009). A first part of this truism is that there is great room for improvement, given the artificial time- and space-restricted scenario of institutionalized learning. It is a second part of this truism that (verbal) exchanges in class need to be more authentic and truer to *real-life communicative situations*. Just how can this be achieved? Of course, teachers can follow the guidelines sketched out below. Yet, as always, the proof is in the pudding: what is the use of planning to use certain meaningful principles to have more real-life classroom communication if teachers do not put them into practice? It is certainly worth monitoring oneself as a teacher or having oneself monitored by one's peers (cf. Helmke & Leske 2013) with regard to one's communicative style and *idiosyncrasies* (such as the typical overuse of 'fillers' like 'err,' 'you know,' 'well'). It seems helpful to first look at the characteristics of verbal interaction as it usually takes place in everyday talk and then contrast them with classroom habits. Here are some of the basic characteristics of ordinary communication (cf. Maybin 2002: 5–12).

Classroom communication and interaction

▶ While people use the structural resources of English to *express ideas*, they are also simultaneously using language to express and pursue relationships.
▶ What is said draws meaning from a vast amount that is left unsaid because of the way language is embedded in social activities and relationships; *a lot of things are implied* or are taken for granted in a certain social context.
▶ Talk is used to bind people together and to enable them to *negotiate* shared understandings about the world.
▶ Talk is *dialogic*. In other words, people constantly refer implicitly to what previous speakers have said, anticipate what they might say next, and assume a large amount of shared experience.
▶ Especially small talk aims to establish an *interactional framework* for encounters between people. This happens through *face work*; for example, through showing that one appreciates the persona and status of the other person (positive face work: using laudatory remarks; negative face work: avoiding threats and impositions).

Elements of authentic communication

▶ Conversations are frequently highly *repetitive*, marked by turn-taking and rituals such as greetings; they are also marked by hesitant, ambiguous utterances, half-finished sentences, and interruptions.

▶ *Intonation and body language* significantly convey and inflect meaning.

> Compare each characteristic of verbal interaction in everyday conversation with how language is used in the classroom. Why is language in the classroom different? Could it use the characteristics above as a benchmark?

Inauthentic classroom communication

There are numerous studies on how *classroom interaction* appears deficient and artificial when compared with the characteristics of everyday talk. Hüllen explains how this depends to a large degree on the communicative framework established at schools:

> The partners in the conversation are usually a teacher and a whole class; the role of the teacher dominates the role of the learners for reasons of the teacher's professionalism, his/her age and advanced knowledge; beginning and end of a conversation are defined by the lesson plan; the proxemics between communication partners are pre-given through certain conventions, such as the seating arrangement, etc. (1987: 195, our trans.)

Summing up research by Hüllen and other researchers (cf. Rowe 1986, Lindner 2011 for a useful survey), the following *deficiencies* of classroom interaction can be singled out:

▶ A "strong asymmetry between communication partners" (Hüllen 1987: 224, our trans.)

▶ A "preoccupation with linguistic correctness" (ibid., our trans.)

▶ Generally not enough student talk time (STT), especially when it comes to long utterances

▶ Too much teacher talk time (TTT); teachers especially do not wait long enough for students' answers and ask too many 'teacher questions'

▶ The artificial, monotonous, and asymmetrical pattern of Instruction by teacher – Response by student – Evaluation by teacher (IRE)

10.4.2 | Optimizing classroom interaction

The classroom as a place of communication and action

How then can a *change* for better, more meaningful, student-centered and closer to real-life conversation be practiced in class? *How do teachers involve the students?* Legutke (2007, 2009; cf. Decke-Cornill & Küster 2014: 123–24) suggests the following guidelines for creating what he calls *"the classroom as a place of learning"* (Lernwelt Klassenzimmer) or as *"a place of action"* (Handlungsraum Klassenzimmer):

▶ *Authentic texts and situations* take away the artificiality of progression patterns and the reductive approach of grammatical spoon-feeding; email projects, for example, create a more real-to-life situation in the classroom.

▶ Classes need to be more *task-oriented with clear goals* of what students need to achieve.

▶ Students increasingly produce their own utterances and texts in an interactive process involving *active student participation*.

▶ Students use a great variety and number of *learning resources* apart from the textbook; they themselves integrate these resources into class.

▶ Evaluation and feedback are more *student-centered*, with students regularly taking stock of how they learn, what they learn, and what progress they are making.

▶ Teaching is cooperative and participatory, with students habitually taking on the role of teachers themselves (*students teach students*).

"A person teaching and a person learning," he said, "should have the same end in view: the improvement of the latter." – Seneca

In addition to creating this student-centered, *cooperative atmosphere* in the classroom, teachers need to become aware of and optimize their skills regarding the following concrete elements, which influence classroom interaction:

▶ Their physical presence in class
▶ Seating arrangement and student groupings
▶ Knowing the problems of 'teacherese' and teacher talk
▶ Dealing with uncooperative students

Physical presence in class: the way in which teachers use their physical presence and their voice in class is *one of the most crucial skills of teachers* (cf. Harmer 2000: 15). Apart from 'coming across' as a proficient and understandable, yet not artificial language user, teachers – to a large degree – create interaction through their physical presence: the way they dress, the way they use gestures, expressions, mime, and the way they move in the classroom and interact with students. Teachers should pay attention to (1) *proximity and closeness:* how close teachers should be physically to their students, how they should make contact, and how close this contact should be is a complicated issue teachers need to be aware of and consider carefully (especially with regard to age, gender, ethnicity); (2) *appropriacy:* do teachers want to appear more formal or informal (e.g., through the way they dress, speak, or sit)? Teachers need to consider what effects their physical behavior may have on their students; (3) *movement:* this involves the question of where teachers position themselves. Do they move around the classroom or do they prefer to stay in one place?

Optimizing teaching skills

When regarding the teacher's physical presence in class, one would also need to consider how this affects different learner groups – with regard to age, gender, ethnicity, cultural background, group set-up, etc. How, for example, would a teacher's physical presence and interaction with students differ when (1) she or he is teaching grammar in grade 6 to (2) her or him teaching Shakespeare in grade 12?

As to the very *instrument of interaction*, the teacher's *voice*, attention needs to be paid to audibility, variety, and taking care of 'vocal hygiene.' This entails controlling one's volume to be audible even to students in the back of the classroom without shouting, varying the quality of one's voice depending on the type of lesson and the type of activity, practicing to breathe and speak from the diaphragm ('projecting') in order not to strain the larynx (cf. ibid.: 17).

Seating arrangement and student groupings: the frequently used seating arrangement of orderly rows with students sitting at desks behind each other and the teacher standing or sitting in front of them appears as absolutely counter-productive to any close-to-life interaction. Just consider: do interactants in a conversation ever have to turn their heads around to talk to each other, then swivel their heads back to talk to the person who initiated the exchange? It is therefore of paramount importance that seating arrangements are changed, if necessary, to a more communicatively conducive arrangement: alternative arrangements include, for example, (1) students sitting in a large circle along the walls of the classroom, (2) seating arrangements resembling a horseshoe shape with students almost sitting around the teacher, or (3) arranging separate tables as work stations in different parts of the room (cf. ibid.: 18). Obviously, the preferred seating arrangement depends on the different student groupings teachers can use, from whole class discussion to group work and pair work (a useful survey is provided in Wiechmann 1996 and at methodenpool.uni-koeln.de/uebersicht.html, covering such groupings and social forms as 'group puzzle' and 'learning at stations').

Knowing the problems of teacherese and teacher talk: the term 'teacherese' denotes a type of speaking which uses *language appropriate for the target learner group*, with just a little bit of challenge so learners feel encouraged to make an effort to deduce the meaning of unknown words or grammatical items (*comprehensible input*). In other words, teachers use different language patterns in beginner and more advanced classes; and they are used to speaking clearly, with repetitions, and the use of *set phrases* such as 'Open your books at / to page x' (not *'on page x') and 'Let's look at the examples on pages 7 and 8' (not *'page 7 and 8'). Such teacherese, however, potentially deskills students, not preparing them for authentic language, and it can be *simply boring*.

IRE pattern   Another *must* is that teachers become aware of the restrictions of the usual pattern of much of classroom talk, which follows a certain sequence consist-

238

ing of three acts (see fig. 10.7): "an act initiated by the teacher (usually a question), a response act by one of the students (usually the answer to a question),
and an act of evaluation by the teacher (on the quality of the response, very
often focussing on the form and not on the meaning of a message)" (Müller-
Hartmann & Schocker-v. Ditfurth 2009: 29). A typical example of this IRE-
pattern is the following exchange (cf. Decke-Cornill & Küster 2014: 116 for a
more elaborate example):

> T: What is the capital of Great Britain?
> S: London.
> T: Very good.

Variations here would include exchanges like the following:

▶ If student A fails to respond immediately, another student is asked until the
  right answer is elicited, possibly with a little help by the teacher (e. g., 'It is
  by the river Thames,' 'It starts with an L').
▶ If student A fails to give the correct answer, another student is asked, with
  the teacher signaling verbally or non-verbally that student A answered
  incorrectly.
▶ Often there is a chain of such 'teacher questions.'

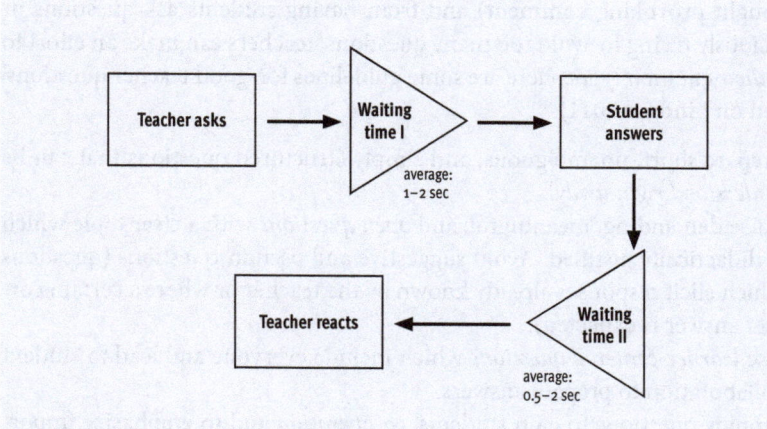

| Fig. 10.7
The IRE pattern (cf.
Lindner 2011: 40,
based on Rowe 1986)

Müller-Hartmann and Schocker-v. Ditfurth (2009: 29) describe the detrimental
effects of the IRE-pattern if it is established and maintained in the classroom:

> This interactive pattern both impedes the quality of language input (which lan-
> guage acquisition research has identified to be one factor to contribute to suc-
> cessful language acquisition) and restricts learners' opportunities for language
> production and conversational interaction which again play an important part
> for second language acquisition.

Look at figure 10.7, and consider the following statistics (Lindner 2011: 49):

▶ A teacher asks a question every 37 seconds.
▶ A class of students asks the teacher 2.2 questions a lesson.
▶ A student asks a question every 3 days.
▶ A teacher asks more than 800 questions in the course of three days.

Suggest ways to improve communication in EFL classes.

Tackling the IRE problem

There are two ways of *tackling the problem of IRE monotony*: (1) Generally, teachers should make a deliberate effort to speak less, wait longer for answers, and avoid sessions where their voice drones on and on and the students have little student talk time. *Students need the practice, not the teacher*: if students are not allowed to speak, they do not learn to speak (cf. Harmer 2000: 4, Thaler 2012: 42). (2) Teachers should become more aware of which questions to ask and which impulses to give. For example, teachers could use verbal stimuli instead of questions: an utterance like 'I have heard that some students did some extra research on the topic' can be seen as a teacher's impulse, a request for more information within a certain (classroom) situation. Apart from substituting questions by pictorial or verbal stimuli (showing a caricature or using a thought-provoking comment) and from having students ask questions or consciously trying to avoid too many questions, teachers can make an effort to *vary their question types*. Here are some guidelines for 'good teacher questions' (based on Lindner 2011):

Good teacher questions

▶ Prepare short, unambiguous, and simply structured questions that can be *understood right away*.
▶ Raise demanding, meaningful, and *open questions* with a clear topic which is didactically justified. Avoid suggestive and pseudo-questions (questions which elicit responses already known by the teacher or where a certain correct answer is expected).
▶ Use *learner-centered questions* which include everyone and lead to student collaboration to prepare answers.
▶ Employ questions to gain students' *co-operation* and to emphasize important learning goals or organizational aspects.
▶ Use alternatives to questions such as *impulses* and non-verbal communication.
▶ Allow *enough time* to prepare the answers (cf. Rowe 1986) and do not repeat students' answers (*Lehrerecho*). If students fail to answer, do not give the answer yourself; instead, give small hints.

In spite of aiming at overall more student talk time, *teacher talk* should not be seen as inherently detrimental to good communication and good learning (cf. Hattie 2009: 22: "what teachers *do* matters"). Good *teacher talk time* can have its benefits if teachers, at appropriate moments or in the appropriate phases of a lesson, provide well-tuned input in a relaxed and unthreatening manner: for example, telling a story which includes new vocabulary and using mime and gestures to make it more understandable, or summing up a discussion or several answers to a problem. Teachers should also be aware of the importance of giving clear and unambiguous *instructions*, especially when they are given in the foreign language (cf. Hattie 2009: 125–26 on the importance of 'teacher clarity'). A number of set phrases need to be clarified from the onset: "The best activity in the world is a waste of time if the students don't understand what it is they are supposed to do." (Harmer 2000: 4) Instructions should follow these guidelines (ibid.):

▶ Convey only *important information* and clear instructions.
▶ Consider what students *need to know* to tackle and complete an activity successfully.
▶ Clearly communicate the *steps* of an activity.
▶ Provide a *time frame*.
▶ Check whether students *understood* the instructions, for example by asking students to explain the activity again after the teacher has given the instruction.

Dealing with uncooperative students: another important aspect of *classroom management* is dealing with the behavior of uncooperative students. It is important for teachers to have at their fingertips a number of responses to problematic behavior of individual students, mainly for distractive or disruptive behavior (e. g., constant chattering in class), for students who do not take part in assigned activities or bluntly refuse to engage in classroom activities, and for rude und undisciplined behavior (e. g., foul remarks, not doing one's homework; cf. Lewis 2002: 42–43). How to best manage a particular type of behavior depends on a number of factors, including overall effective classroom management (cf. ibid., Thaler 2012: 45). Problematic behavior can be avoided or – better – nipped in the bud right away ('prevention is the best medicine'):

▶ Teachers convey the impression that they are on top of the teaching scenario and group dynamics. They appear 'to have eyes in the back of their heads' (or at least are capable of *peripheral vision*), and their instructions are precise, assertive, and brief.
▶ Teachers are able to '*multitask*': they can do several tasks simultaneously in class (e. g., speaking while writing on the board while checking if student X is paying attention). Teachers maintain eye contact while continuing to speak.

▶ The session proceeds fluently and smoothly and at an *appropriate pace* so that students do not get bored or lose touch with what is being taught or learned.

▶ The *whole class stays involved*, with the teacher giving every student the impression that he or she is taking part. Teachers talk with students about problematic behavior after class. In doing so, teachers avoid threats and do not take problems personally.

If a student exhibits *disruptive behavior* it is worth considering whether this was a single occurrence, whether this is specific to more students, and whether this is noticed by other teachers as well: "teachers should not have to suffer on their own! They should talk to colleagues and, if possible, get a friend to come and observe the class to see if they notice things that the teacher himself or herself is not aware of." (Harmer 2000: 131)

Finally, here is a list of ten *Do's and Don'ts* for teachers and the way they should perform in class. It is based on suggestions originally devised for Berlitz schools (cf. Richards & Rodgers 1986: 10):

Ten rules for classroom performance

1. Avoid translating where you can demonstrate.
2. Avoid explaining where you can act.
3. Avoid making a speech when you can ask questions.
4. Avoid speaking too much when you can make your students speak.
5. Avoid using your textbook solely when you can use other sources or react to your students' responses.
6. Avoid jumping around and appearing unstructured; follow your plan but leave space for improvisation.
7. Avoid going too fast or too slow; keep the pace of your students.
8. Avoid speaking too slowly or too quickly; speak normally and naturally.
9. Avoid gearing your lessons toward just a few students; try to include as many as possible.
10. Try not to be impatient; 'take it easy.'

Recommended reading

Benecke, Ingrid (2007). Zur Grobstruktur von Englischunterricht: Eine Planungshilfe. In: *Praxis Fremdsprachenunterricht* 4.6, 35–38.

Farrell, Thomas S. C. (2002). Lesson Planning. In: Jack C. Richards & Willy A. Renandya, eds. *Methodology in Language Teaching: An Anthology of Current Practice*. Cambridge et al.: Cambridge University Press, 30–39.

Finkbeiner, Claudia (2007). Lehrplan – Lehrwerk – Stoffverteilungsplan – Unterricht. In: Johannes-P. Timm, ed. *Englisch lernen und lehren: Didaktik des Englischunterrichts*. Berlin: Cornelsen, 36–44.

Harmer, Jeremy (2000). *How to Teach English: An Introduction to the Practice of English Language Teaching*. Harlow: Longman.

Lindner, Michael (2011). *Gute Frage! Lehrerfragen als pädagogische Schlüsselkompetenz.* Marburg: Tectum.

Meyer, Hilbert (2006). *Criteria of Good Instruction: Empirical Findings and Didactic Advice.* Trans. Dave Kloss. http://www.member.uni-oldenburg.de/hilbert.meyer/download/Criteria_of_Good_Instruction.pdf (10 September 2014).

Materials design

Contents

In light of the pragmatic approach to language teaching and learning adopted in the *Common European Framework of Reference for Languages* (CEF) as well as the introduction of educational standards in Germany, new curricula with a focus on communicative competences have been implemented. While the new generation of textbooks mirror this change, they "remain […] fundamentally language learning oriented, i. e., based on the view that the kind of authenticity most required for foreign language learning should relate first and foremost to the learner as a current interim acquirer rather than as a potential future user of the language" (Waters 2011: 315). This chapter focuses on strategies of curriculum and syllabus design as necessary background information for materials designers as well as on essential features of self-designed materials and tasks. It also provides examples of digitally designed materials.

Abstract

Have a look at the cartoon. Reflect on the status as well as the advantages and disadvantages (for teachers, students, lessons) of using the textbook, comparing this to the use of self-designed materials.

11.1 | Curricula and textbooks

11.1.1 | Curriculum design

Before any materials and task designing begins, teachers need to be well informed of the *educational and instructional framework* they are working with. This includes (1) the educational standards they have to address, the subject-specific curriculum they have at their hands, and the in-school syllabus (*schulinterner Lehr-/Lernplan*) outlined by the representatives of Englisch as a Foreign Language (EFL) teachers at a school (*Englischfachschaft*); (2) their position vis-à-vis the textbook; and (3) the needs of their students (see chs. 1.2, 10.1, 10.3.1).

Richards (2013) has introduced *three different approaches to curriculum and syllabus design* (forward, central, backward). These approaches differ fundamentally in their emphasis on compulsory content (*input*), methodological considerations (*process*), and learning objectives (*outcome*).

Forward design: input first   *Forward design* adheres to the *principle of linearity*. The content, defined by the curriculum, forms the starting point of any teaching considerations. Since

246

forward design does not enlighten teachers as to the methods they should employ, this decision is left to the individual teacher. Forward design was popular with the *Audiolingual and Audiovisual Methods,* since the process of learning could be more or less neglected in the hope that the input provided would – via drill exercises – result directly in an output of correct language patterns (see chs. 3.2.1, 4.2.3).

Central design is, first and foremost, interested in *methodological considerations and the facilitation of learner-centered processes* involving problem-solving activities that require students to investigate, come to decisions, and engage in critical thinking. Content and materials are chosen on the basis of how they can contribute to this *constructivist approach* to learning. Central design pays less attention to curriculum specifications of compulsory input and predetermined learning outcomes. It is central to *communicative approaches* to teaching and learning a foreign language (FL) such as *Task-based Language Teaching* (TBLT; see chs. 4.3.2, 5.2.2.2, 10.3.3).

Central design: process first

Backward design is prominent in the CEF. It departs from a *detailed outline of desired learning outcomes,* delineated in the form of 'can do'-descriptors (see chs. 1.2.1, 6.1.1). Methods and content are selected on the basis of how well they cater to reaching the desired learning outcomes. *Competency-based Instruction* (CpBI) is a methodological approach that adheres to the principles of backward design. An overview of the three approaches and their implications regarding syllabus design, methodological decisions, as well as the role of teachers and learners in the learning process are summarized in figure 11.1:

Backward design: output first

	Forward design	Central design	Backward design
Syllabus	▸ Language-centered ▸ Content divided into its key elements ▸ Sequenced from simple to complex ▸ Pre-determined prior to a course	▸ Activity-based ▸ Content negotiated with learners ▸ Sequence may be determined by the learners ▸ Evolves during course ▸ Reflects the process of learning	▸ Ends-means approach ▸ Objectives- or competence-based ▸ Sequenced from part-skills to whole ▸ Pre-determined prior to course
Methodology	▸ Transmissive and teacher-directed ▸ Practice and control of elements ▸ Imitation of language models ▸ Explicit presentation of rules ▸ Emphasis on accuracy	▸ Learner-centered ▸ Experiential learning ▸ Active engagement in communication and the negotiation of meaning ▸ Meaning prioritized over accuracy	▸ Practice of part-skills ▸ Practice of real-life situations ▸ Emphasis on appropriacy

Fig. 11.1

Characteristics of forward, central, and backward design (Richards 2013: 30, adapted)

Role of teacher	▶ Instructor, model of language performance, explainer ▶ Transmitter of knowledge ▶ Reinforcer of correct language	▶ Facilitator of learning process ▶ Negotiator of content and process ▶ Encourager of learner self-expression and autonomy	▶ Organizer and planner of learning experiences ▶ Model of language performance
Role of learner	▶ Accurate mastery of language forms ▶ Application of learned material to new contexts ▶ Understanding of language rules	▶ Negotiator of learning content and modes of learning ▶ Development of learning strategies ▶ Responsibility for learning	▶ Awareness and mastery of situationally appropriate language usage ▶ Development of fluency

Dilemma Many teachers have settled on forward design because the competence-based output defined in the CEF seems too opaque to help with the day-to-day decisions of *what* and *how* to teach. The German EFL curricula mirror the backward design of the CEF with pages full of descriptions of language achievements along the line of the CEF competence levels. However, these curricula usually *do not* promote methodological suggestions for long-term achievements in FL acquisition. As a result, central design *tends to be neglected* due to the amount of time that would need to be spent on carefully planning learning processes and then choosing learner-centered content as well as designing appropriate learning materials.

Variety is the spice of life. While one could go on criticizing the obsession with *output and testing* (see chs. 1.2.2, 8.1.2, 12.1), it might be more fruitful to point to the *advantages* such circumstances bring with them. In other words, the power of the curriculum ends when it comes to individual approaches to FL teaching and learning. In turn, teachers are given the opportunity to develop *their full potential as educators* and can make *their own informed decisions* about the learning processes they want to employ to facilitate excellent learning outcomes and the positive development of each individual learner. Therefore, central design should not be rejected as utopian, but rather inform *every teacher's reflections* on current educational standards, curricula, and textbooks.

Study the EFL curriculum in the area you are studying or teaching in. Which design elements can you identify in the curriculum? With fellow students or colleagues, discuss how well the curriculum supports the planning of lessons.

248

The textbook: friend or foe?

The textbook and the wide range of supplementary materials offered by publishers, *present a resource of materials, content, teaching ideas, learning support, and reference* (cf. Cunningsworth 1995: 7, see ch. 10.2). While textbooks "continue to constitute the guiding principle of many foreign language courses throughout the world" (Sercu 2000: 626), the quantity of the use of textbooks by teachers depends on a *variety of factors*: their *academic background and educational principles*, their *teaching experience*, as well as their *personal commitment as reflective practitioners and life-long learners* (see chs. 2.1.1, 1.3.1, 12.3.3.). One can usually observe *three different types of teachers* (see fig. 11.2; cf. Sercu 2000: 627, Nold 2007: 128):

Status of the textbook

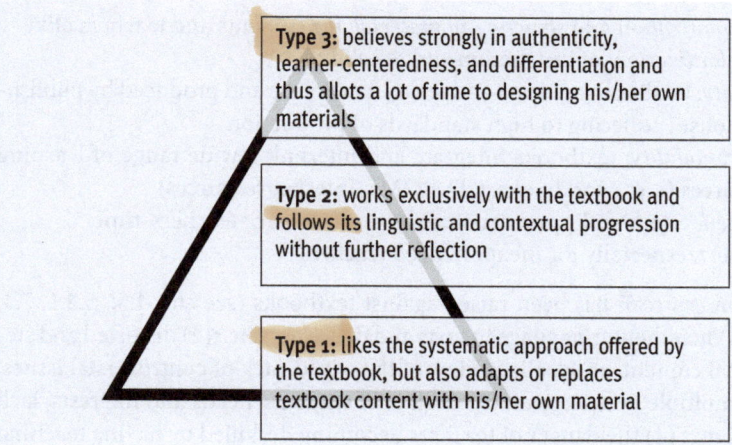

Type 3: believes strongly in authenticity, learner-centeredness, and differentiation and thus allots a lot of time to designing his/her own materials

Type 2: works exclusively with the textbook and follows its linguistic and contextual progression without further reflection

Type 1: likes the systematic approach offered by the textbook, but also adapts or replaces textbook content with his/her own material

| Fig. 11.2
Teacher types along textbook use

Most teachers (type 1) certainly do not use textbooks uncritically, but try to add their own materials whenever it seems apt for reasons of topicality, authenticity, motivation, etc. These teachers may also choose to modify textbook content and tasks (cf. Saraceni 2013: 50–59, Tomlinson 2013c: 141–53). However, there is also a large number of teachers (type 2) that use the textbook almost exclusively – not only because they do not want to invest time in materials design, but probably also because the alluring '*all-inclusiveness*' of the textbook presents the safest choice to them. Often deemed the classroom's '*secret syllabus*,' the textbook directly follows and implements educational standards as well as the grammatical and lexical progression proposed in curricula (cf. Volkmann 2010: 236). A minority of teachers (type 3) invests a large amount of time in designing their own teaching and learning materials. To them, the textbook serves "only as a resource for developing their own innovative plans" (Sercu 2000: 627).

While this chapter is exclusively dedicated to materials design, it nevertheless promotes a *middle ground* between using the textbook and designing

Feasibility

one's own materials. This decision is based on three reasons: (1) teacher type 2 will soon realize that a *'page-turning approach'* with the textbook as the only source of materials will make his/her lessons unbearably monotonous. It will also *deskill* him/her gradually (cf. Masuhara 2011: 245–49). (2) Teacher type 3 should be honored, but will probably soon reach a limit when his/her investment in self-designing materials will run into conflict with *his/her personal resources*. (3) Textbooks *have changed considerably* and offer peer-reviewed, high-quality, and multimodal educational materials (cf. Volkmann 2010: 238, Tomlinson 2013a: 10–11).

Pros   The *moderate and well-reflected* use of textbooks can be seen in a positive light, especially with regard to the following reasons (cf. Sercu 2000: 627, Richards 2007: 254–55):

▶ *Systematization and structure of material*: for students and teachers alike
▶ *Standardization*: of instruction and testability
▶ *Quality*: textbooks are tried and tested in advance and produced by publishing houses adhering to high standards of production
▶ *Multimodality*: textbooks integrate and interlink a wide range of learning resources (e.g., workbooks, CD-ROMs, Internet resources)
▶ *Efficiency*: textbooks pre-structure lessons and save teachers' time
▶ *Support*: especially for inexperienced teachers

Cons   However, *criticism* has been raised against textbooks (see chs. 4.5., 5.2.1, 7.3, 10.2): (1) inauthentic language in texts and dialogues, etc.; (2) distorted and stereotypical content, an idealized view of the world, lack of controversial issues, lack of multiple perspectives; (3) neglect of students' needs and interests, lack of creativity; (4) the danger of teachers becoming deskilled by having teaching styles imposed onto them; and (5) the substantial amount of money needed for supplementary materials (cf. Sercu 2000: 627, Richards 2007: 255–56, Volkmann 2010: 235–37, Tomlinson 2013a: 11–12).

> Study a current EFL textbook. Which of the aforementioned advantages and disadvantages do you find in the textbook? How would you counteract the disadvantages?

11.2 | Designing effective materials

If you want a thing done well, do it yourself. – Napoleon Bonaparte

For reasons of *topicality, authenticity, motivation, differentiation, and variation*, it is of great importance that teachers choose to add their own materials to complement the use of the textbook. Richards (2007: 252–53, adapted) foregrounds the following *advantages* of self-designed materials:

▶ They can have a positive effect on *learner motivation*. There is a huge supply of interesting materials for language learning in the media and on the

Internet (cf. Mishan 2005: 132–281). These often relate more closely to the needs and interests of learners.

▶ They can provide *authentic cultural information* about the target culture. Materials can be selected to illustrate many aspects of the target culture, including culturally based practices and beliefs and both linguistic and non-linguistic behavior (cf. Pulverness & Tomlinson 2013).

▶ They can provide exposure to *real language* rather than the artificial texts found in textbooks, which have been specially written to illustrate particular grammatical rules or discourse types (cf. Bao 2013, Hill & Tomlinson 2013, Hyland 2013, Masuhara 2013, Nation 2013, Stranks 2013).

▶ They can support a more *creative approach to teaching.* Teachers can develop their full potential as teachers by designing materials that better match their teaching styles and the learning styles of their students (cf. Emery 2013, Tomlinson 2013d, Tomlinson & Masuhara 2013).

While these advantages are indeed rather convincing, one should not for-get about possible *disadvantages* of self-designed materials. These drawbacks include questions of inferior quality, copyright infringement, linguistic diffi-culty or mistakes, lack of structure, limited time, and the financial burden for teachers who choose to design and copy a large amount of specially designed materials for use in their classrooms. Schools and teachers should be aware of these downsides and – whenever possible – *counteract* them by, for example, forming and training materials design teams, asking colleagues for evaluations of materials, sharing and collecting materials on databases, and making use of materials distributed online on quality websites for teachers (e. g., www.lehrer-online.de, www.teachingenglish.org.uk).

Cons

Materials and tasks

11.2.1

The table below presents a *checklist* for individual teachers or a group of col-leagues who want to design and evaluate their own materials (see fig. 11.3; cf. Tomlinson 2011: 8–23, Jolly & Bolitho 2011: 111–30, Tomlinson 2013b: 28–43):

Evaluation of materials

Check	For example	Rank
Contextualization	▶ Curriculum objectives ▶ Prior knowledge and learning experience of students ▶ Topics and themes meaningful and relevant for learners	
Stimulation of interaction	▶ Real-life topics ▶ Sufficient scope of challenges ▶ Language progress	

Fig. 11.3

Materials design checklist (based on Howard & Major 2005: 104–07)

Facilitation of learner autonomy	► Learning strategies essential for lifelong learning ► Language learning opportunities outside the class-room
Focus on form and function	► Closer look at how language works from a linguistic point of view
Integrated language use	► Integration of all language skills ► Coverage of extra-linguistic factors (e. g., non-verbal aspects)
Authenticity	► Wide range of texts and media representing a variety of English(es) in use ► Tasks appropriate for facilitating authentic language use
Appropriate instructions	► Complexity of instructions appropriate for target learners (e. g., age, grade, level of language proficiency)
Progression	► Coherent materials which are interlinked, have clear underlying learning objectives, and facilitate language acquisition
Visual appeal	► Appropriate density of text ► Type size ► Spacing ► Layout ► Durability ► Copiability
Flexibility	► Teaching approach ► Methodology ► Language level ► Logistics ► Technology ► Evaluation ► Outcomes

With fellow students or colleagues, discuss which of the above guidelines are more/less important. If possible, try to agree on a ranking.

Tasks Tasks lie at the heart of FL learning materials for the communicative classroom. Therefore, sketching out and sequencing tasks should be considered of great importance (see chs. 6.1.5, 6.3.1, 12.4.3). Consideration should be given to (1) the *complexity* of the tasks (the number and level of cognitive processes they require), (2) matching the complexity of tasks with learner proficiency (*grading*), and (3) the *sequence* in which tasks are delivered (cf. García Mayo 2007; Robinson 2007, 2011). General guidelines are provided by the *Kultusminis-terkonferenz* (KMK, see fig. 11.4) in the form of a graded list of language performance requirements (*Anforderungsbereiche*) and associated *Operatoren*:

Language performance requirements I		
Operatoren	**Definition**	**Example**
Summarize	Give a concise account of the main points	*Summarize* the information given in the text about the hazards of cloning.
Present	(Re-)structure and write down	*Present* the situation of the characters.

Language performance requirements II		
Operatoren	**Definition**	**Example**
Characterize	Describe the character of someone or something	*Characterize* the heroine.
Contrast	Emphasize the differences between two or more things	*Contrast* the author's idea of human aggression with the theories of aggression you have read about.

Language performance requirements III		
Operatoren	**Definition**	**Example**
Discuss	Investigate or examine by argument, give reasons for and against	*Discuss* the implications of globalization as presented in the text.
Justify	Show adequate grounds for decisions	You are the principal of a school. *Justify* your decision to forbid smoking on the school premises.

Fig. 11.4

Language performance requirements (Kultusministerkonferenz 2012: 1–2, adapted extracts)

While the complete list issued by the KMK certainly helps with the evaluation of task complexity, grading tasks should also be informed by the following factors (Nunan 2000: 102–03, adapted):

Learner factors

▶ *Confidence*: Does the learner have the necessary level of confidence to carry out the task?
▶ *Motivation*: How motivating is the task?
▶ *Prior learning experience*: Does the learner have the necessary learning skills to carry out the task?
▶ *Learning pace*: Can the learner handle the materials?
▶ *Observed ability in language skills*: What overall level of performance can reasonably be expected on the basis of the learner's skills?
▶ *Cultural knowledge/awareness*: Does the learner master the cultural or topical knowledge assumed by the task?
▶ *Linguistic knowledge*: Does the learner master the linguistic knowledge assumed by the task?

These guiding questions do not explicitly address the issue of **heterogeneity**. If teachers want to provide comprehensible input for all learners in any given class, they first need to *diagnose* the different learner types and competence levels. If the outcome of this diagnosis shows that there is indeed a great variety, then teachers might want to consider creating two or three different ver-

Differentiated materials

sions of the original materials with different requirements (see chs. 2.1.3, 6.2., 6.3, 10.3.2).

If teachers have kept all of the above in mind and have drafted their materials, they should *take a step back and review them* (and/or have colleagues look at them). In addition, if teachers have designed a set of consecutive materials for a multi-lesson teaching sequence, they should go over this set of materials again and check for *coherence and continuity*.

> Have a look at two or three pages from a current textbook. Evaluate the complexity of the tasks, if and how they are graded, and if the task sequence seems coherent.

11.2.2 | Basic tips for designing worksheets

Teachers need to have a clear view of the *learner group* (e. g., concerning age, ability, motivation) and the *purpose(s)* of the worksheet. Is it meant to be (1) a source of information (e. g., a fact sheet), (2) an illustration (e. g., a cartoon), (3) a sheet accompanying different phases of a lesson and to be filled with learning content during the lesson (e. g., a grid accompanying presentations or supporting learning at different work stations), (4) an exercise sheet, or (5) a test? In the following, *basic tips* for designing worksheets are briefly delineated and illustrated (see fig. 11.5; cf. Neumann 2012, Egle 2013).

Header, footer
For teachers and learners to be able to *keep track of their worksheets*, the header should contain the following information: subject, grade, topic, date, and a blank space for the learners' names. The space in the footer can be used for page numbers and a short code that helps the teacher to find his/her materials in files.

Margins
Worksheets are to be filed in a folder. Therefore, the left margin should be 3 to 4 centimeters in width. If students are required to write down notes, comments, or annotations, the right margin should leave *enough space* for them to do so (3 centimeters in width).

Line spacing
Depending on the *purpose* of the worksheet, teachers need to adjust the space between text lines accordingly. For a fact sheet, a single-spaced line pitch would do. However, if students are required to skim or scan a text for information and highlight or underline it in the text, a one-and-a-half times or double-space line pitch is recommended.

Font, font size
Considering the enormous amount of fonts one can choose from in text processing programs, there is a danger of getting carried away, using too many fonts on a single worksheet or choosing awkward font types. As a rule of thumb, *no more than two or three font types should be used.* In view of perception psychology findings, serif font types (e. g., Times New Roman, Century Schoolbook) should be favored over sans-serif typefaces (e. g., Arial, Verdana). A 12pt font size is sufficient for continuous text. Headlines should be 14pt.

Highlighting
To draw attention to specific parts of or words in a text, teachers may use bold or italic print or they may choose to underline certain passages. However, it is *not advisable* to clutter worksheets with highlighting features.

Layout
Worksheets need to have a *clear structure.* Therefore, paying attention to the layout is very important. Teachers should use spacing, headings and subheadings, consecutive numbering, paragraphs and text columns, as well as frames to structure their worksheets. Generally, full justification is recommended for continuous text (use automatic hyphenation to avoid large gaps in the text). Ragged left or centered alignment can be used for poems, in the task section, or for annotations. Of course, pictures, graphs, and charts also help to 'break up the gray.'

Annotations
A list of annotations for providing background information or definitions of difficult vocabulary items may help students to work *more efficiently* with the worksheet. However, teachers should avoid handing everything to students on a silver platter or overloading worksheets with annotations.

Visuals
Sometimes, visuals (e. g., pictures, cartoons, illustrations, graphs) *can say more than words.* Of course, teachers have to comply with the copyright law when reproducing pictures on their worksheets. Pictures must not be reproduced without permission from the author. Exceptions apply to pictures whose copyright has expired and to royalty-free pictures provided by image databases such as Pixelio (www.pixelio.de), Wikimedia Commons (commons.wikimedia.org), or TiBS (www.bilder.tibs.at). In any case, the sources of visual materials should be mentioned on the worksheet.

Sources
Teachers should lead by example. Therefore, all sources used to compile a worksheet should be cited at the bottom of the worksheet.

Copying

Since it is simply impossible to provide students with sufficient color copies of worksheets on a regular basis, teachers should design their materials *in black and white or grayscale*. When doing so, they need to check the quality and size of pictures and, most importantly, whether or not information is lost when printing or copying a colored original in black and white or grayscale.

Fig. 11.5 |

Sample worksheet

English, grade 11, Shakespeare's Life and Work, 22 October 2014

The Original Globe Theatre

1. Beginnings

During the first years of Elizabeth's reign, the English playing companies used inns, inn yards, college halls and 5 private houses for their performances. It was not until 1576 that the actor-manager James Burbage built the Theatre in Shoreditch, the first purpose-built playhouse in London. 10 Shakespeare joined the resident troupe at the Theatre in the 1580s and the company (later known as the Chamberlain's and then the King's Men) flourished[1] there for 20 years.

2. Dispute and Heydays

15 In 1596 a dispute arose over the renewal of the lease and negotiations[2] were begun to acquire a disused hall in the precincts of the old Blackfriars 20 priory[3] to use as an indoor theatre. James Burbage died in February 1597; in April the lease expired, but the dispute continued for two years, during which time the company per-25 formed at the nearby Curtain play-house. In Christmas 1598 the company sought a drastic solution: they leased a plot[4] near the Rose, a rival theatre in Southwark, demolished the 30 Theatre and carried its timbers over the river. To cover the cost of the new playhouse, James Burbage's sons Cuthbert and Richard, offered some members of the company shares in

35 the building. Shakespeare was one of four actors who bought a share in the Globe. By early 1599 the theatre was up and running and for 14 years it thrived[5], presenting many of Shake-40 speare's greatest plays.

3. Fire and Demolition

In 1613, during a performance of Henry VIII, wadding[6] from a stage cannon ignited the thatched roof and 45 the theatre burned to the ground 'all in less than two hours, the people having enough to do to save themselves'. The theatre was quickly rebuilt, this time with a tiled roof. 50 Shakespeare may have acted in the second Globe, but he probably never wrote for it. It remained the home for Shakespeare's old company until the closure of all the theatres under Eng-55 land's Puritan administration in 1642. No longer of use, it was demolished to make room for tenements in 1644.

Tasks

1. Choose six vocabulary items from the text and paraphrase their meaning.
2. Select one piece of information from the text that you find interesting and explain your choice to the class.
3. Find out more about 'Shakespeare's Globe,' the reconstruction of the Globe Theatre at http://en.wikipedia.org/wiki/Shakespeare's_Globe.

Sources

- http://www.shakespearesglobe.com/about-us/history-of-the-globe/original-globe
- http://en.wikipedia.org/wiki/Globe_Theatre#mediaviewer/File:Hollar_Long_View_detail.png

---

[1] to flourish: to grow and succeed
[2] negotiations: talks
[3] priory: religious community

[4] plot: area
[5] to thrive: to flourish
[6] wadding: insulation

1

Digitally designed materials

Technological advances have helped to make the design of educational mate-rials more *effective and less time-consuming*. Next to functions provided by text processing programs, *digital technologies and applications* may also help to make materials more appealing or to design and work on motivating tasks online (cf. Kervin & Derewianka 2011; Strasser 2012; Heckmann & Strasser 2012; Kiddle 2013; Grimm & Hammer 2014a, 2014b; Fritze 2014; Schnit-ter 2014; Heckmann & Baus 2014; Strasser 2014; Pachler et al 2014: 140–43, 149–60):

Digital technology

> Web 2.0 allows many more people to be creative with digital technologies. [...]
> This puts the possibilities of the adaptation and creation of a broad range of lan-
> guage-learning materials directly into the hands of the teacher, but also into the
> hands of the learners. [...] Teachers like to be able to adapt materials [...], as
> do learners. Teachers need to do this to meet localised learning needs. Mate-
> rials do need mediation and with Web 2.0 this is increasingly possible. (Mot-
> teram 2011: 304)

The following pages present a few examples of digitally designed materials. For reasons of limited space, these cannot cover the full range of potential uses for beginners as well as for intermediate and advanced learners. Readers can get a more complete picture by visiting the websites mentioned below. Additionally, Strasser's *Mind the App! Inspiring Internet Tools and Activities to Engage Your Students* (2012) provides a useful introduction to the digital tools introduced below and many more.

Popplet

Popplet (www.popplet.com) is an *online mind-mapping and presentation tool* that can be used in many ways: to collect thoughts, explore ideas, collaborate, and present. Popplet can help with materials design in a variety of ways: on the simplest level, teachers may use it as an easy tool to create pre-structured mind maps that students work with on print handouts. On a medium level, teachers set a task, create a Popplet for it and have students work on the task online – either individually or collaboratively, in and out of class. Teachers may also opt for using Popplet to create instant digital mind maps from student input on any given topic (e. g., in connection with an initial brainstorming of ideas), which they can then save and use as a basis for discussion. On the most advanced level, teachers and students can use a Popplet, such as the one in figure 11.6, with Popplet's integrated presentation mode. Popplet also offers add-ons, such as uploading visual as well as audio and video files (clarifications concerning copyright infringement are recommended). Potential uses include (cf. http:// blog.popplet.com/category/popplets-in-education):

Organizing and presenting ideas

▶ *Beginners*: family tree, structuring vocabulary, picture dictionaries, mini-presentations on a variety of beginners' topics (hobbies, food, pets)
▶ *Intermediate learners*: timelines, galleries, mapping out the structure of an essay
▶ *Advanced learners*: multimedia presentations on more elaborate topics (e. g., global warming, population growth), visualizing character constellations in a literary work

Fig. 11.6 |
Sample popplet

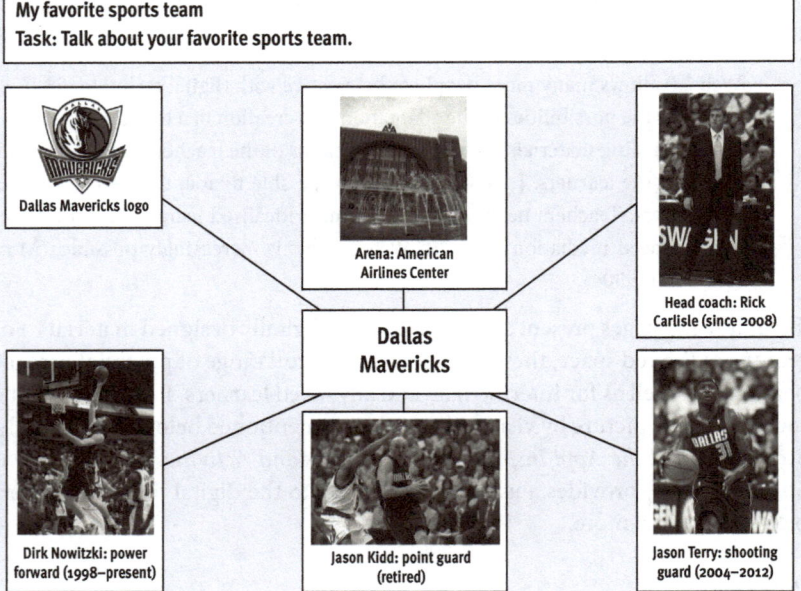

My favorite sports team
Task: Talk about your favorite sports team.

Dallas Mavericks logo

Arena: American Airlines Center

Head coach: Rick Carlisle (since 2008)

Dallas Mavericks

Dirk Nowitzki: power forward (1998–present)

Jason Kidd: point guard (retired)

Jason Terry: shooting guard (2004–2012)

Word clouds with style

Tagxedo

Tagxedo (www.tagxedo.com) is a *word cloud creator*. The word clouds come in different shapes and with a visually appealing choice of themes, colors, and fonts. Once created, they can be saved as high-resolution images. What is particularly interesting about Tagxedo is that it enlarges words that appear more frequently in the source text that is pasted or typed into the text box. This function makes Tagxedo an optimal tool for the analysis and discussion of literary and non-literary texts (e. g., register, repetition, rhyme). On a more basic level, Tagxedo can be used to provide vocabulary or keywords as a basis for further activities. As with Popplet, Tagxedo also lends itself perfectly for collecting and instantly visualizing student ideas on any given topic in the form of a word cloud – again, ideas mentioned more often are given greater prominence. For example, a brainstorming on German learners' perceptions of US-American culture might result in a word cloud as in figure 11.7. Potential uses include (cf. http://blog.tagxedo.com/101-ways-to-use-tagxedo-completed):

| Fig. 11.7

Sample word cloud

- ▶ *Beginners*: guessing a topic, categorizing vocabulary, finding simple colloca-tions, gap-fill exercises, creating invitation cards
- ▶ *Intermediate learners*: guessing (e.g., a topic, famous person, historical event), summarizing a presentation, checking one's own essays (e.g., regis-ter, repetitions), creating book covers
- ▶ *Advanced learners*: turning a logo into a word cloud, creating a portrait of a famous person, keeping track of current events

Glogster

Glogster (edu.glogster.com) is a helpful *source of and tool for creating interac-tive multimedia learning materials*. Glogster helps to create interactive post-ers (glogs: short for graphic blog) that can be used for simple to more complex topics and assignments. For example, the header of a teacher-cre-ated poster could simply consist of the task to create an interactive poster on 'Your favorite movie' with a structure and some keywords or guidelines as to what students should include (see fig. 11.8). This way, the guidelines on the interactive poster help learners to accomplish the task, while still being free to use their own creativity. As with Popplet and Tagxedo, the products can be archived and shared. Possible uses include (cf. edu.glogster.com/glogpe-dia):

Interactive working space

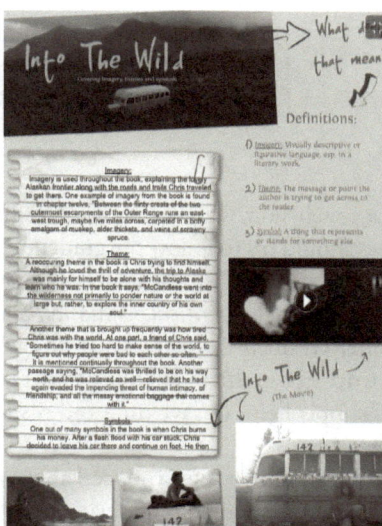

| Fig. 11.8

Sample glog

▶ *Beginners*: vocabulary posters (e. g., days of the week, the weather, the alphabet), classroom phrases, presenting different meanings of a word, festivities, basic facts about a region or a country

▶ *Intermediate learners*: grammar posters, favorite singer or band, biographies, book reports

▶ *Advanced Learners*: literary genres, politics, history, current events

LearningApps

Small interactive teaching modules

LearningApps (learningapps.org) is an *ever-growing online materials pool* that promotes itself as "support[ing] learning and teaching processes with small interactive modules. Those modules can be used directly in learning materials, but also for self studying [sic]. The aim is to collect reusable building blocks and make them available to everyone." (learningapps.org/about.php) While teachers are free to use the activities created and shared by other teachers, LearningApps also helps teachers to efficiently create their own materials. Learning Apps offers teachers a rich pool of educational materials that come in a wide range of activity formats for different subjects (e. g., word grid, quiz, crossword, millionaire game; see fig. 11.9). The activities are especially useful for beginners and intermediate learners. Advanced learners could create their own little app (e. g., a quiz for their classmates).

Fig. 11.9
Activity formats on LearningApps

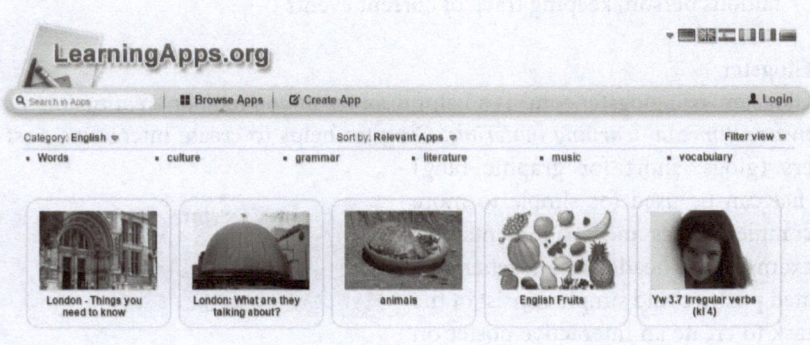

Materials archive

In conclusion, whether for print or digitally designed learning materials, teachers should try to follow the guidelines of materials and task design presented in this chapter. If they use materials created by others, the same applies, especially with regard to a *critical evaluation* of these materials. It is also recommended to *carefully archive and label* self-designed materials. Teachers will find that well-structured archiving in filing folders and data files will pay off in the long run – it simply helps to save time and *easily access and adapt* materials.

> Try out the tools introduced above and create a mind map or an interactive poster about materials design as introduced in this chapter.

Recommended reading

García Mayo, María del Pilar, ed. (2007). *Investigating Tasks in Formal Language Learning*. Clevedon: Multilingual Matters.

Mishan, Freda (2005). *Designing Authenticity into Language Learning Materials*. Bristol: Intellect.

Motteram, Gary (2011). Developing Language-Learning Materials with Technology. In: Brian Tomlinson, ed. *Materials Development in Language Teaching*. 2nd ed. Cambridge et al.: Cambridge University Press, 303–27.

Richards, Jack C. (2007). *Curriculum Development in Language Teaching*. Cambridge et al.: Cambridge University Press.

Tomlinson, Brian, ed. (2011). *Materials Development in Language Teaching*. 2nd ed. Cambridge et al.: Cambridge University Press.

Tomlinson, Brian, ed. (2013). *Developing Materials for Language Teaching*. 2nd ed. London et al.: Bloomsbury.

Assessment and evaluation

This chapter discusses the diagnostic, informational, social, and educational functions of testing achievement against the background of the current standardization and output-orientation paradigm. It surveys criteria for testing related to teaching goals, test and task types, as well as grading schemes. It makes suggestions for alternative testing formats and effective testing. Grading skills can be tested with authentic examples provided at the end of the chapter.

Abstract

The cartoon suggests several functions of assessment and evaluation. Write down possible functions and compare them with those discussed in this chapter.

Achievement as social parameter

Testing, assessment, and *evaluation* (*Leistungsüberprüfung, Leistungsmessung, Leistungsbeurteilung*) are terms which are frequently used interchangeably and with reference to each other (cf. Finkbeiner 2012: 386). On a general level, they comprise "a judgment of the quality, worth, importance, or value of something and someone" (ibid.: 387). With regard to education and school this entails "the process of finding out who the students are, what their abilities are, what they need to know, and how they perceive the learning will affect them" (Peñaflorida 2002: 346). In the EFL classroom, teachers assess their learners' skills and competences with regard to language and communication, but also in the fields of culture, literature, and the media. In this chapter, for reasons of clarity, the term 'assessment' is used in the sense of providing information about how *learning and teaching processes can be diagnosed and improved*; 'evaluation' measures what has been learned and how this can be *graded* (cf. Angelo & Cross 1993: 427).

> *The difference between school and life? In school, you're taught a lesson and then given a test. In life, you're given a test that teaches you a lesson. –*
> *Tom Bodett*

Against the background of the current output- and competence paradigm (see ch. 1.2),

Standardization & 'testmania'

> there has been an unbelievable increase in the development of high-stakes testing and assessment modelling as well as in the creation of test and assessment centers around the world. This goes hand in hand with a growing job market for a rather new profession of so-called testing and assessment experts. The focus of standardization in classrooms across the globe can be seen as an effect caused through insights we seem to have gained from results of studies such as TIMMS, PISA, PIRLS and DESI […]. (Finkbeiner 2012: 385)

The underlying belief is that *educational standards* ensure quality and innovation on all levels of *competition*: from the international and national level to that of federal states, and to the interpersonal level of single students.

However, such prioritizing of output and assessment is in danger of creating lopsided beliefs – that students will be better performers if only their output is measured regularly. Schneider uses the following comparison to point toward the downsides of the current '*standardization and evaluation mania*':

Fallacy

> To use an example from industry, it is not just the control at the end of the conveyor belt that enhances the quality of the product, but the quality of the production process at the preceding work stations – and, of course, the quality of the material used. End control can always only result in a quality judgment, but it cannot generate quality itself. (2010: 79–80, our trans.)

The *booming test industry* and the persistent focus on testing in the EFL classroom as a result of the shift toward competence, output, and standardization frequently aims at *testing what can be tested*. Skills and competences are tested without questioning or at least discussing or considering some of the most pressing social issues involved in practices of assessing and evaluating achievement.

Performance & competition

Testing, assessment, and evaluation are clearly related to concepts of the *performance principle* (*Leistungsprinzip*), which in its social and economic sense is inherently based on *competition*. Etymologically, performance and achievement are related to 'following,' 'persevering,' 'fulfilling expectations,' and 'putting something into practice.' In the 18th century, Benjamin Franklin formulated – and lived up to – the quintessence of *maximizing individual performance* in a mobile capitalist society: 'time is money.' In the 19th century, new criteria, such as 'efficiency,' 'effectiveness,' 'high-performance,' and 'performance-capability' (*Leistungsfähigkeit*) were introduced to measure an individual's performance. Consequently, being able to perform or to achieve was defined as being able to live up to what is expected by one's peers, by one's superiors or by society concerning a certain skill or set of skills (cf. Schneider 2010: 96–97). Certainly, the *performance principle* and its impact on the modern world and modern states can and should not be called into question here. As a foundational principle of modern societies, it is supposed to serve three basic social functions (cf. ibid.: 98):

► It ensures distribution: performance and achievement are coupled with a reward (primarily with monetary gain and a higher social status).
► It fosters the productivity and prosperity of societies.
► It regulates the distribution and allocation of professional and social positions according to the principle of competition (*Konkurrenzprinzip*).

Competitive vs. pedagogical principles

However, there are differing and partly *contradictory concepts* of what achievement and performance are. The *economic, competition-oriented, and non-cooperative* performance principle is different from the **pedagogical performance principle** (*pädagogischer Leistungsbegriff*).

> As to the *competition-oriented performance or achievement principle*, consider and discuss the following critique expressed by pedagogues (our trans.). Sum up the critique in three points.

In reality, coveted positions in our society are not at all solely bequeathed according to the performance an individual exhibits. Instead, the performance principle is only one among the principles of distribution of life chances [such as being liked or having the right social connections]. (Jürgens 2000: 16, our trans.)

The principle of performance as give and take and its direct linkage with competition-driven relations between individuals is negative; it hampers and obstructs solidarity. Indeed, it supports processes of social fragmentation and the destruction of solidarity (*Ent-solidarisierung*). (ibid.: 18, our trans.)

The performance society equals stress, rivalry, and the struggle for self-identity. (ibid.)

Until now, assessment has mostly served to allot students their place in the academic hierarchy of their class. This process has resulted in numerous disadvantages. According to estimates, about one fourth to one third of all students perceive school as a constant source of failure and frustration. (Rampillon 1999: 34, slightly adapted)

Pedagogues such as Jürgens (2000, 2010; cf. Jürgens & Sacher 2008) or Bohl (2009) have criticized current practices of assessment as socially corrosive processes of "competition, product-orientation, and social screening (*Auslese*)" (Jürgens 2000: 18, our trans.; cf. Schneider 2010: 96–100, Tillmann & Vollstädt 2000, Winter 2010). Instead, they argue in favor of a less competitive and more integrative and socially oriented *pedagogical concept*: "At the center of a pedagogical concept of performance and assessment is the right of the student for individual care and support, being considered as a whole person and with regard to his or her learning as part of a group or community." (Jürgens & Sacher 2008: 28, our trans.) The basic parameters of this concept encompass the following *five principles* (cf. Jürgens 2000, Jürgens & Sacher 2008; also cf. Rampillon 1999: 34, Schneider 2010: 98–99):

▶ Achievement and assessment are "*constructs*" (Bohl 2009: 6) and as such need to be related to cultural norms and standards. They need to be subject to rational reflection about testing as such, especially with regard to the general educational goals of schools (*Allgemeinbildung*). Performance should not only be subject to outside definitions, but also to the individual learner's own decisions.

Pedagogical performance concepts

▶ Performance must be interpreted as subject to the influences both of *nature* (genes) and *nurture* (environment): performance can be the result of life-long learning, but can also be impeded by circumstances.

▶ Performance is both *product and process-oriented*: although product-oriented performance is more easily testable, the assessment of performance should entail process-oriented forms.

▶ Performance can be the result of both *individual and cooperative achievement*: the competitive principle, stressing individualism and self-reliance, should be complemented by elements of cooperative learning and by fostering social competences.

▶ Performance should be interpreted in a more *holistic manner*, leaving space for creativity, personal growth, emancipation, and the developing of *critical and reflective thinking skills* as well as the fostering of aesthetic-literary skills.

In practice, this means developing an *assessment culture* which encourages students "to become more autonomous learners and take on more responsibility for their own learning processes" (Rampillon 1999: 34, our trans.), teaching them learning strategies which, in turn, should be reflected in the test formats implemented by teachers.

'Testable' skills

The current **standardization and output paradigm** is in danger of fostering the ills of '*teaching to the test*' and the '*backwash-effect*' of bolstering up 'testable skills.' Teaching and testing happens at the expense of less 'optimizable' competences such as literary, aesthetic, and social ones. Adhering merely to competitive concepts of performance appears to reinforce the counter-productive and detrimental effects of assessment: "assessment seems to 'drive' teaching by forcing teachers to teach what is going to be assessed" (Cameron in Müller-Hartmann & Schocker-von Ditfurth 2009: 144). Instead, a more pedagogically informed concept of assessment would, in a nutshell, aim at an "[a]ssessment [which] places the needs of the students at the center of the teacher's planning" (Peñaflorida 2002: 346).

12.2 | Functions of assessment and evaluation

Assessment, as described so far, involves coming to and formulating an evaluation and analysis of a student (e.g., his/her writing skills) on the basis of a norm of reference set by the teacher. Teachers need to consider and reflect on the various *functions of testing* (cf. Weskamp 2001: 166, Jürgens & Sacher 2008: 20–28, Thaler 2012: 298):

Functions: diagnosis, information, selection, education

▶ *Diagnosis* has primarily *bureaucratic functions* when "teachers provide information on the attainment standards achieved by individual students as these are specified in a particular curriculum, so that students may be screened and placed" (Müller-Hartmann & Schocker-von Ditfurth 2009: 145). In a more positive vein, diagnosis can be defined as detecting a student's *strengths* (which should be furthered) and *weaknesses* (which call for support and help) with regard to, for example, understanding a literary text.
▶ *Information*: diagnosis provides information. Diagnosis can be the basis for informing the student or parents and for *suggesting as well as supporting development*. Based on the information gleaned, teachers can *monitor* student progress with regard to the learning goals set by the curriculum, the achievement and proficiency of individual students, as well as learner groups. *Feedback* about strengths and weaknesses of individual students as well as groups of students can then be provided to learners, parents, and colleagues teaching the same student(s).
▶ *Differentiation and selection*: assessment is used for differentiation, ranking and rating, for placement, report cards, and for allocating special training. Finally, *certificates of education* are based on test results, which in turn allow access to institutions of further, tertiary education – school, after all, allocates chances for future professional careers; it is a "Lebens-Chancen-Verteilungsinstanz" (Thaler 2012: 298).
▶ *Education*: it may be counterproductive to mention only the negative aspects of grading – its 'extrinsic' function as an instrument to discipline learners

('*Disziplinierungsinstrument*'). Crucially, regular and systematic testing, if transparent and related to *feasible teaching objectives*, can foster learning motivation and lead to a sense of achievement. Finally, students have a right to experience different kinds of assessment and evaluation at school as a *necessary preparation for a competitive society*.

> Reflect on memorable tests of your school career. Which of the four functions mentioned above did they serve? What will be the functions of the tests you will have to pass yet?

Assessment and testing | 12.3

Parameters and criteria | 12.3.1

There are *three reference frames* which can determine parameters for testing: **norm referencing**, **group referencing**, and **individual referencing** (cf. Jürgens & Sacher 2008: 72–73):

▶ *Norm referencing or criterion referencing* (*sachliche/kriteriale Bezugsnorm*): Referencing
the teacher sets a test and pre-designs an answer key and a model solution (*Erwartungshorizont*) and a rating scale (*Bewertungsmaßstab*, including a checklist) *before* the test is administered. Grading and assessment are done with reference to *pre-set norms*. Rating scales and grading parameters are set *before* the test is given.
▶ *Group referencing* (*soziale Bezugsnorm*): individual achievement is assessed with regard to a social group norm (e. g., a learner group or a class). Traditionally, grades are distributed according to how the overall distribution corresponds to the '*bell curve*' (*Gaußsche Normalverteilung*, see fig. 12.1). The rating scales and grading parameters are set *after* the test is finished.

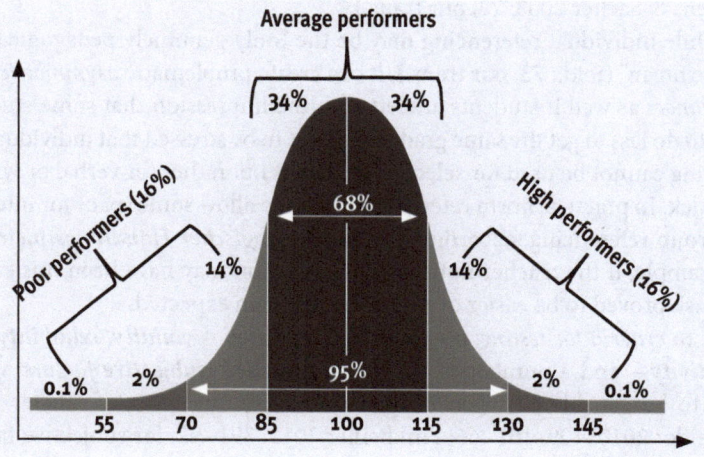

| Fig. 12.1
The bell curve
(example)

▶ *Individual referencing or self-referencing (individuelle Bezugsnorm)*: the individual learner's progress is assessed with a focus on how the level of competence in the field tested corresponds to previous test results of the learner. Individual feedback is provided.

Assessment
challenges

The three forms of referencing have their respective merits and downsides.

> Consider the following assessment problems:
>
> 1. Why do some class tests have (overall) extremely bad results, and others extremely good results?
> 2. Why does an average student get better grades in one class than in another?
> 3. Why do some students feel that they can never get a good grade in a particular class?
> 4. If a student makes progress in a dictation test and has 'only' 35 mistakes instead of his usual 45–50, should he still get a 'no pass/fail' (grade 6) or possibly – according to the concept of individual referencing – a better grade? How can this be justified vis-à-vis his or her classmates?

As the examples above indicate, norm referencing appears to be fair and just, as an overall good or bad performance of a class does not have to be bent toward 'bell curve' results. However, a certain *degree of flexibility* must be allowed for as the teacher may not have formulated clear instructions or used tasks whose problems only become apparent retrospectively (e. g., a certain text passage was too obscure for all the students). Group referencing can be unjust and create *problematic forms of competition* (cases 2 and 3): "To get good marks, you need to be better than the others. If all are good, all performances are measured with reference to a higher average, which in turn means that marking gets stricter." (Jürgens & Sacher 2008: 72, our trans.)

Integrating forms of
referencing

While individual referencing may be the "only genuinely pedagogical reference norm" (ibid.: 73, our trans.), it can create problematic *asymmetries and imbalances* as well if students are left with the impression that some students need to do less to get the same grades. It needs to be stressed that individual referencing cannot be used for selective decisions but rather for verbal or written feedback. In practice, norm referencing needs to allow some space for integrating group referencing, according to the *pädagogischer Handlungsspielraum*, for example, if the teacher notices that a question may have been misleading or a task proved to be easier or more difficult than expected.

The 'big three':
validity, reliability,
objectivity

As to *criteria for testing*, there are the 'big three' – *validity, reliability*, and *objectivity* – and a number of what may be called '*subjective factors*' which need to be considered when designing and grading tests (cf. Thaler 2008; Schneider 2010: 109, 161–66; Finkbeiner 2012: 391–92; for subjective factors cf. Jürgens & Sacher 2008: 54–71). Crucially, the three factors, *validity, reliability, and objectivity,* need to be considered for any test design.

▶ *Validity* (*Gültigkeit/Validität*): does the test measure *what it is supposed* to measure? "An instrument is deemed to be *trustworthy* if it has *credibility* (i. e., truth-value) and *auditability* (i. e., consistency). In other words, does it measure what it is supposed to measure and would the instrument give the same results if replicated?" (Huerta-Macías 2002: 340) A salient problem, for example, is that reading comprehension tests are often not just designed to test reading skills but also text composition when students are required to write a response to the text (cf. Finkbeiner 2012: 391). Listening comprehension tests, to use another example, do not just test listening skills, but often also oral or writing skills.

▶ *Reliability* (*Zuverlässigkeit/Reliabilität*): is the test *consistent* in its measurement? This means that two teachers should come to the same assessment of a student performance independent of the learning context. However, teachers tend to have different priorities: for example, even if a performance is graded on the basis of an error index (*Fehlerindex*), two teachers might still grade the student performance differently due to their *different assessment of mistakes*. Closed test formats (see below) tend to produce more reliable results than open tasks (see fig. 12.8). Clear criteria should be set in advance and both criteria and raters should be *monitored periodically* to ensure consistent manners of testing (cf. Huerta-Macías 2002: 340).

▶ *Objectivity* (*Objektivität*): is the test *unbiased*? This seems to be the most important and strictest criterion as it suggests that assessment should be *independent of subjective factors*. Objectivity and reliability seem to be obtainable if several independent or different tests yield the same result (cf. Finkbeiner 2012: 391). Macht surmises that objective tasks can be graded according to the criteria of 'right' or 'wrong,' meaning the end result provides "a numerically clear evaluation of the student performance which is tested" (2007: 373, our trans.). Strictly speaking, only the following **test types** would fit into this rubric:
  ▶ *True/false tasks*: e. g., about orthography, grammatical items
  ▶ *Multiple-choice tasks*: typically with four options, of which only one is completely right, others are used as distractors; they can test knowledge and skills of different complexities
  ▶ *Matching tasks*: items or utterances from two groups, presented in tables, need to be matched
  ▶ *Construction tasks*: language segments need to be put together, as with a jumbled sentence task
  ▶ *Completion tasks*: a word is left out in an utterance and the word to be filled in is clearly marked as correct, as in cloze-tests (words have been removed from a text and need to be replaced)

As understandable as the goal of having valid, reliable, and objective forms of testing in foreign language education may appear, there are a number of *peda-gogical caveats*. Especially, *the idea of language proficiency as the sum of skills which can be tested in isolation of each other has been seriously questioned under the new paradigm of communicative competence.*

> Since the yardstick of communicative competence is the 'real world out there', consider and discuss which competences cannot be tested with regard to validity, reliability, and objectivity. Also, what other factors might come into play when teachers grade student performances?

12.3.2 | Subjective factors

To err is human! Apart from issues of validity, reliability, and objectivity, a number of more 'sub-jective factors', all related to the 'human factor', need to be considered when it comes to testing foreign language skills (cf. Finkbeiner 2012: 391, Jürgens & Sacher 2008: 61–62). Language skills are, after all, *interpersonal skills*; language teaching and learning do not take place in a laboratory. As will become obvious, these factors are more distinctly felt when it comes to testing aural-oral skills and when complex and open forms of tests are used (e.g., essays, creative writing).

- ▶ *Feasibility*: in testing, the *time factor* is of crucial importance. Teachers only have a limited amount of time to assess both written and oral tests. Consequently, there are limits to the type and amount of categories and criteria they can handle simultaneously.
- ▶ *The issue of how teaching and test results are interrelated*: are good test results a product of *good teaching*? Conversely, are bad test results an outcome of *poor teaching*? Just as there is a tendency among students to blame teachers for bad results, there seems to be a tendency among teachers to attribute good results to their own teaching performance and bad results to 'lazy' or 'stupid' students.
- ▶ *Personality and culture of students*: only recently have teachers been reminded of ethical issues of testing stemming from how "[v]ariations in cultural, ethnic and national characteristics within and among individual students affect classroom dynamics" (Finkbeiner 2012: 392) and the culture-specific ways tests are designed. The issue of *equity (Gleichbehandlung, Fairness)* in evaluating learners from diverse linguistic, ethnic, and cultural backgrounds needs to be taken into consideration when designing tests. Standardized tests such as the *Cambridge Certificate of Proficiency* are often based on processes of "norming on a population unlike the one being tested and [may include] cultural and language biases" (Huerta-Macías 2002: 338).

▶ *The influence of prior knowledge and additional knowledge on the teacher*: all teaching and testing is influenced by what teachers know about their students and how stereotypes or prejudices influence them (cf. Hattie 2009: 124–25). They may be influenced in their judgment by factors such as (1) the student being the *child of a colleague*, (2) the student being from a certain *social background* (e.g., poor vs. influential family, ethnic minority background), (3) *gender*, (4) the *school history* of a student (e.g., students who had to repeat a grade level), (5) *personal sentiments*, possibly simply influenced by a student's friendliness or unfriendliness, (6) other *psychological effects* such as the effect of the learner's name, the halo-effect (e.g., a student who is good orally is seen as being good in written tests, a student who is attractive is considered to be a better performer), a teacher's *personal tendency* and conviction to be generally more lenient (*Milde-Effekt*), more strict (*Strenge-Effekt*), or to avoid grades indicating extremely good or bad student performances (*Tendenz zur Mitte*), (7) the form of answers (e.g., bad handwriting).

▶ *Test formats and testing situation*: poor performances in tests can also sometimes be attributed to *a lack of test-taking skills*. For example, a student may lack knowledge and practice concerning the format and language of a test rather than knowledge and skills in the field to be tested. Therefore, a seemingly 'objective' test, such as a multiple-choice test, needs to be practiced in class so that students can *develop specific test-taking skills*. In addition, the testing situation itself often produces anxieties within students up to the point that they feel unable to think clearly. Teachers need to help students to cope with difficulties preparing for a test and taking the test (e.g., time management during a written test, coping with stress and exam anxiety).

▶ *Effects of grading itself*: this includes deficiencies concerning how tasks are set, how tests are composed, how they are put into practice, how they are corrected (including grading repetitive mistakes or marking correct English expressions as wrong, simple scaling or calculating of mistakes, mistakes arising from correction fatigue, etc.); series effects (*Reihenfolgeeffekt*) such as assessing all tests with reference to the first or the best test answer(s).

▶ *Extenuating circumstances*: personal problems or illness at the time of the test can hamper the performance of students; if teachers are affected by them, this can also have an impact on how they set, do, correct, and grade tests.

Taking all these problematic factors into consideration, it may come as no surprise that studies perennially come up with *alarming findings* concerning the subjectivity of assessing and grading in tests. One such survey was conducted by Arendt (2006): twenty-six teachers from twenty-two different schools were asked to *assess the speaking skills* of students taking an English exam. The students' oral exams had been recorded on video, showing two students taking a

Subjectivity: examining the examiners

joint exam consisting of two parts. First, they had to reproduce the information given in a short text; then they were asked to have a conversation about the topics mentioned in the text. When the teachers were asked to grade the video-taped performance, this resulted in an astonishing range of grades given for the same performance. As Arendt sums up, the majority of teachers, almost 70 %, more or less lacked the appropriate objectivity in their assessment. The most striking example of *misjudgment* became apparent with the case of 'Dan,' one of the students on tape, who was a native speaker and whose performance included all the important information and showed hardly any grammar or vocabulary mistakes. While his high level of proficiency and thorough reproduction of the information in the text would raise expectations that he should get a top grade (e. g., grade 1 in accordance with the German 1 to 6-scale), only two teachers decided that his performance was indeed 'excellent.' Most other teachers graded it as 'good' to 'mediocre,' with one teacher even giving a 'not pass' assessment.

The testing dilemma What, then, is the bottom line in all these *difficulties* of fair and correct assessing? All in all, while "[t]here are still many educators who take test results at face value" (Finkbeiner 2012: 398), it seems of paramount importance to consider the practical *dilemma* teachers are faced with (Haß et al. 2008: 270): the individual teacher

- ▶ defines what will be tested, graded, and assessed, as well as how this is done (*Lernziele, Lernzielkontrolle*)
- ▶ administers the test
- ▶ assesses and evaluates the test results
- ▶ corrects or adjusts the test results according to his/her criteria
- ▶ assesses the overall and the individual outcome of the test

How the student performance which is tested comes about can be partly attributed to what and how the teacher teaches. The lesson to be learned from the above must surely be what Jürgens and Sacher put as a leading question: "Who really wants to claim that they can assess correctly and without a mistake?" (2008: 61, our trans.)

12.3.3 | Toward a fair assessment culture

The following *guidelines* of good and successful testing can alleviate some of the problems outlined above (cf. Jürgens & Sacher 2008: 84–85, Schneider 2010: 109–10):

Guidelines ▶ *Becoming systematic*: teachers need to be aware of testing as a *complex process*. They need to prepare students for test formats and let them know in advance what will be tested and how this will be tested. Furthermore, *systematic testing* involves the following processes: (1) finding an adequate test format, considering skills, competences, and how they can be assessed best according to the criteria of validity, reliability, and objectivity; (2) organizing the test, including giving clear instructions; (3) grading and returning the test within a short period after the test; (4) discussing the test, providing answer keys, model solutions; (5) discussing good answers; and (6) helping students correct incorrect or bad answers in effective ways.

▶ *Developing self-reflexivity*: in testing, teachers again should follow the ideal of the *'reflective practitioner'* (see ch. 2.1.1). They need to be and stay aware of how the factors outlined above influence their judgment and remain open to revising their pre-conceived notions about the elements involved in testing (e. g., concerning the 'halo-effect'). This requires them to stay *lifelong learners* themselves with the aim of optimizing their assessment and evaluation skills.

▶ *Nonjudgmental observation first*: it is one of the *déformations professionnelle* of educators to always be in the *'judgmental mode.'* However, teachers need to be and stay aware of the difference between objective observation and the evaluation of performance. A prolonged period of systematic observation should precede assessment and evaluation. In plain English, one should not jump to conclusions but allow for multiple perspectives and a variety of practicing and testing scenarios before coming to a judgment about a student's skills and competences.

▶ *Focus on elements of performance before overall impression*: rather than relying on the overall impression of a student's skills, individual aspects of performance should be considered first to come to a more *nuanced test result*.

▶ *Avoiding stereotyping*: teachers should make an effort to become aware of and eclipse prior knowledge such as that from a student's report card or staff-room talk about a student.

▶ *'Blind assessment'*: written assessments should be done 'blind,' thus *avoiding subjective corrections* resulting from having a student's name at the back of one's mind. Parts of a test should be graded and corrected separately; credits should be added up in the end to come to a *more objective result*.

▶ *Asking for assistance*: in problematic cases, if, for instance, a student's future school career depends on one test, colleagues should be asked for *assistance* (e. g., for additional or comparative grading). All in all, the more assessors involved, the better – especially with oral exams, even students can be asked to participate in the assessment process according to pre-set criteria.

▶ *Presenting more than just a grade*: a written class exam with red ink all over the student's writing, correction marks in the margins, a few caustic remarks, and just a grade at the end – this prevalent format of grading appears as emblematic of concepts expressing authority and control. Instead, assessing is to be regarded as a *'service to the learner'* (a *Dienstleistung*) (cf. Schneider 2010: 110). It should go without saying that exam papers should be annotated with short remarks in the margins on what could be improved (*Verbalurteile*, e. g., short references to typical mistakes and howlers). Good passages should not remain without *laudatory remarks*, indicating how the process of language production is appreciated. By the same token, grades should always be accompanied by remarks on language, content, and style. In doing so, teachers should *avoid cynical comments* and instead encourage students to improve their performance the next time. In oral evaluations, it seems recommendable to follow the 'British model': feedback should start with positive remarks ('Your performance was remarkable …') and go on to more critical comments ('but, …'). Similar is the *sandwich feedback technique*: critical comments as constructive feedback are 'sandwiched' between nice remarks or words of appraisal as distinctly positive feedback (see fig. 12.2):

Fig. 12.2 |
The sandwich feed-
back technique

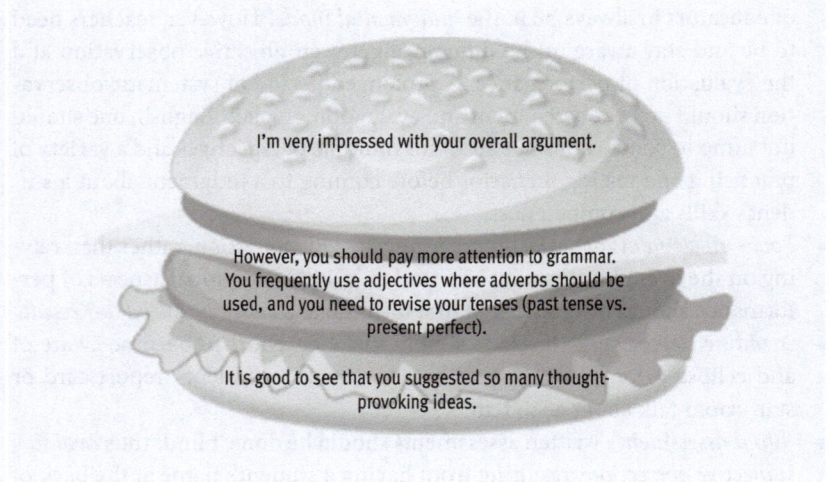

I'm very impressed with your overall argument.

However, you should pay more attention to grammar. You frequently use adjectives where adverbs should be used, and you need to revise your tenses (past tense vs. present perfect).

It is good to see that you suggested so many thought-provoking ideas.

12.4 | What are we testing and how?

12.4.1 | The process of testing

Phases of testing

The process of testing consists of *five steps* (see fig. 12.3): when *preparing* the test, the teacher identifies the learning goals to be taught during a certain sequence. The course is taught in accordance with these goals. There is time for individual assistance and revisions, if needed. Students become familiar with test formats and test content. The teacher pre-plans time and setting of the actual testing scenario (*design*, then accordingly *administration/Durchführung*). After the *assessment* phase, there is a *follow-up* phase (*Nachbereitung*, debriefing, feedback): after discussing the test results with the students, the teacher may use the assessment results to revise goals or teaching methods for future tests.

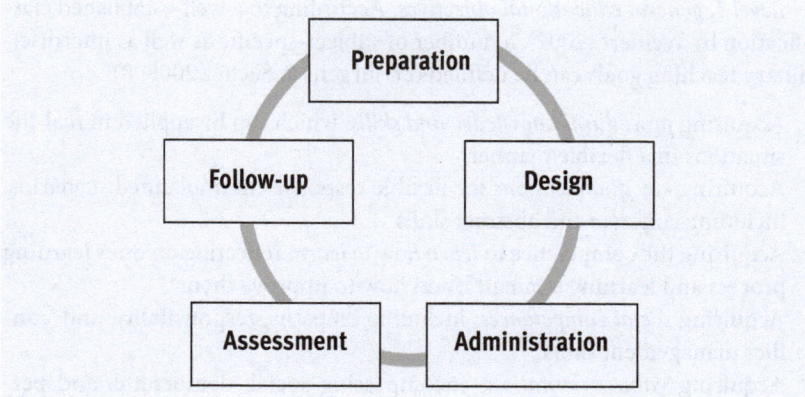

Fig. 12.3
The process of testing

Teaching objectives

12.4.2

Teaching objectives
on three levels

Before setting a test design, teachers should consider what is to be tested. What are the teaching goals or competences that form the basis of the test design and the assessment? Objectives on three interrelated levels need to be taken into consideration (see fig. 12.4): (1) the level of *general educational objectives* or interdisciplinary goals and competences (*allgemeine Bildungsziele, fächerüber-greifende Bildungsziele/Kompetenzen*), (2) the *macro-level of communicative competences*, and (3) the *micro-level of skills*.

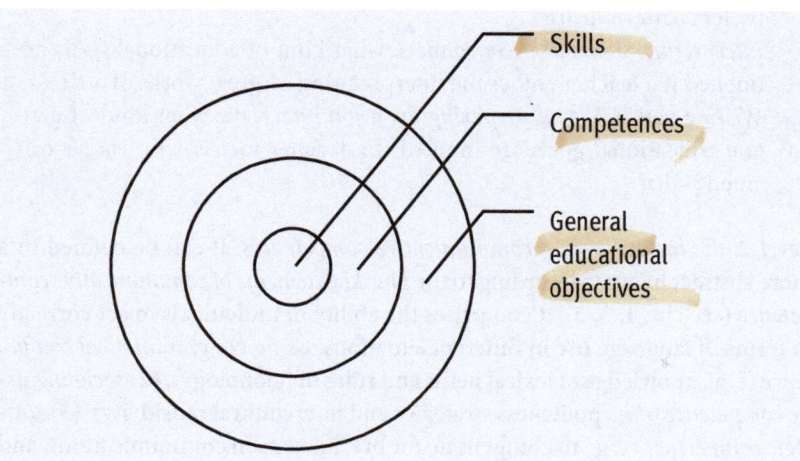

Fig. 12.4
Teaching objectives
on three interrelated
levels

As to the issue of *testability*, it seems obvious that the more specific such a test objective is defined, the easier and more efficient it can be tested. It goes without saying that general educational goals are subject to long and complex learning processes, while, for instance, testing whether a student has command of ten irregular verb forms presents a facile test challenge.

General objectives

Level 1: general educational objectives. According to a well-established classification by Weinert (2002), a number of subject-specific as well as interdisciplinary teaching goals can be defined (cf. Jürgens & Sacher 2008: 8):

- Acquiring *procedural knowledge and skills*, which can be applied in real-life situations in a flexible manner
- Acquiring *key qualifications* for flexible responses in unplanned scenarios, including concrete and abstract skills
- Acquiring the competence to *learn how to learn*: reflecting on one's learning process and learning strategies, and how to improve them
- Acquiring *social competences*: including empathy, responsibility, and 'conflict management skills'
- Acquiring *value orientation*: encompassing social, democratic, and personal values

These general educational goals are, of course, broad enough to include competences currently under debate, such as **media competence** or **intercultural competence** (see chs. 7, 9). General educational objectives are related to the macro- and micro-level competences and skills, as should become clear by considering the following questions:

> How are the following test formats related to general educational goals:
>
> - *Pattern drills:* what kind of student personality is fostered if a teacher prefers pattern drills?
> - *Interpreting Shakespearean sonnets:* what kind of educational goals are implied if a teacher enjoys the interpretation of 'great works of art'?
> - *Writing your CV and preparing for a job interview:* what kind of general educational goals are implied if a teacher focusses on career-oriented skills?

Competences

Level 2: the macro-level of communicative competences. It can be defined in a more abstract manner according to the *four key elements of communicative competence* (see chs. 1, 3, 5): it comprises the ability of individuals to act correctly in terms of language use in different situations, using (1) *grammatical competence* (e. g., knowledge of lexical items and rules of phonology), (2) *sociolinguistic competence* (e. g., politeness strategies and intercultural sensitivity), (3) *strategic competence* (e. g., to compensate for breakdowns in communication), and (4) *discourse competence* (e. g., cohesion in form and coherence in meaning).

Skills and sub-skills

Level 3: the micro-level of skills. In the context of assessing skills in the EFL classroom, the *Common European Framework of Reference for Languages* (CEF) lists and elaborates the *five basic skills* of listening, reading, speaking, writing, and mediation (Council of Europe 2001: 43–100, see ch. 6.1). The five skills above can be further subcategorized and defined in terms of **sub-skills**. For example, speaking skills can be defined according to the *twelve categories* mentioned and explained in the CEF (ibid.: 193, see fig. 12.5):

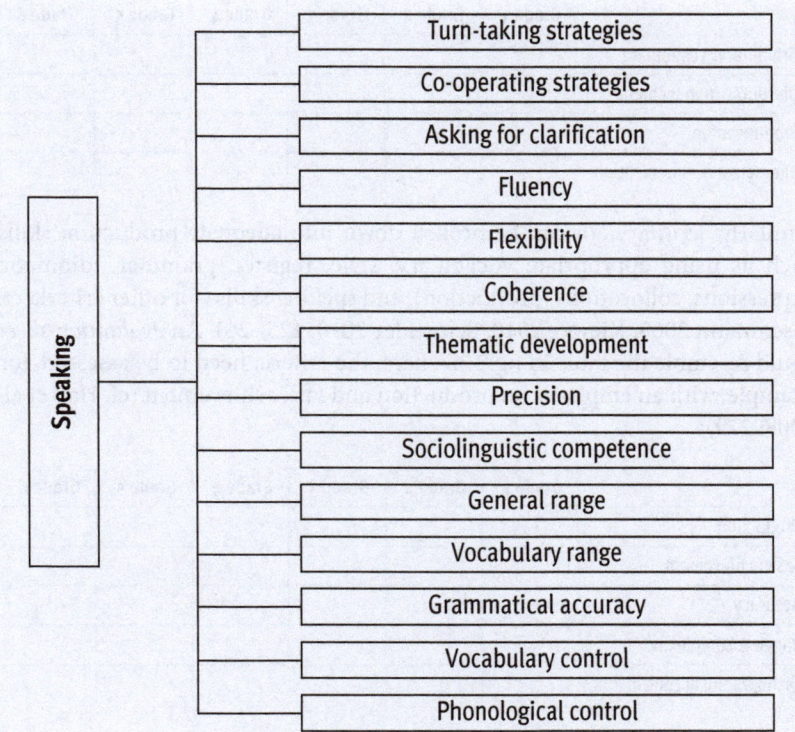

| Fig. 12.5
The sub-skills of speaking

It is very unlikely – and would indeed be a superhuman skill – that teachers are able to consider all aspects at the same time without major gaps or deficiencies in their assessment. According to the CEF, *four to five criteria* seem to be feasible in practical testing, while seven must be regarded as the cognitive upper level where the human brain starts to make mistakes (cf. ibid.: 193). For testing oral skills, to use one model, the list of criteria defined for the Preliminary English Test (PET) could provide a guideline, which differentiates four categories defined by three aspects each. Teachers should use these key words to assess the single categories and only then arrive at an overall evaluation as a sum of the grades given in every category (cf. Zydatiß 2006: 10, an elaborate list of test criteria is offered in Eisenmann & Summer 2012: 424):

Feasibility

▶ *Grammar and vocabulary*: range, accuracy, appropriacy
▶ *Discourse management*: relevance, coherence, extent
▶ *Pronunciation*: stress and rhythm, intonation, individual sounds
▶ *Interactive communication*: initiating and responding, hesitation, turn-taking

Oral skills

279

An *evaluation sheet*, also called 'impression grading scheme' (cf. Haß et al. 2008: 278), for oral performance could resemble the one in fig. 12.6:

	Grade 1	Grade 2	Grade 3	Grade 4	Grade 5	Grade 6
Grammar & vocabulary						
Discourse management						
Pronunciation						
Interactive communication						

Writing skills

Similarly, *writing skills* can be broken down into adequate production skills such as using appropriate vocabulary, style, register, grammar, idiomatic expressions, collocations (production), and spelling skills (for other criteria cf. Eisenmann 2008, Kieweg 2010, Schneider 2010: 125–26). An *evaluation sheet* could resemble the table in fig. 12.7: here, the criteria need to be assessed, for example, with an emphasis on production and task achievement (cf. Haß et al. 2008: 279):

	Grade 1	Grade 2	Grade 3	Grade 4	Grade 5	Grade 6
Production						
Task achievement						
Accuracy						
Range & complexity						
Orthographical control						

For the purpose of setting *written tests (Klassenarbeiten, Klausuren)*, Weskamp (2001: 174, with additions) suggests the following concept:

Preparing and designing tests

▶ *Determining the purpose of the test*: placement, feedback, achievement, proficiency, or diagnosis
▶ *Defining the type of learner(s)* to be tested (age, social background, proficiency level(s))
▶ *Defining the types of skills or competences* to be tested as well as the general educational goals
▶ Which *language functions* are to be tested (e. g., expressing pleasure, expressing dislike, advising someone)?
▶ Which *text types* are included in or elicited by the test type? Teachers need to consider length, difficulty, and genre/media type of the sources used.
▶ Which *type* or combination of tasks are to be used (closed, semi-open, open tasks – see fig. 12.8)?
▶ Taking care of *correct and understandable instructions* and possible (vocabulary) aids and explanations

▶ Considering how the single parts of a test are evaluated and how the *overall grade* is to be computed

▶ Considering *how errors and mistakes will be evaluated* and how form and content will be regarded respectively

Typology of tests and tasks

| 12.4.3

In general, there has been a shift from *discrete point testing* (DPT, e. g., multiple choice test), which was popular in the 1960s, to *open and communicative testing*. DPT focused on discrete, isolated items and thus resulted in insufficient knowledge and feedback about a learner's 'real' communicative competence. *Semi-open or open formats* were frequently used in the 1970s, assessing one or more proficiency levels (e. g., guided interviews). Open or communicative forms of testing came into focus in the 1980s, with an emphasis on "communicative, integrated 'real life' tasks" (Müller-Hartmann & Schocker-von Ditfurth 2009: 147). Having defined competences to be tested, teachers are advised to consider if and how the three types defined and illustrated in fig. 12.8 should be used individually or in combination (cf. Macht 2007: 374, 376; Kieweg 1999a, b; Weskamp 2001: 174–79; Eisenmann 2008):

Tests & tasks: closed – semi-closed – open

Task type	Definition	Examples
Closed tasks	Tasks with little room for individual solutions or reactions	▶ Multiple-choice ▶ Matching/sequencing ▶ Crossword/true-false statements ▶ Fill-in (simple)/cloze
Semi-open tasks	Tasks with some or more room for individual solutions or reactions	▶ Gap-filling (more elaborate, several options)/guided dialog ▶ Summing up texts ▶ Writing according to certain formats (e. g., description of pictures) ▶ Mediation
Open tasks	Tasks with much room for individual solutions or reactions, simulation of real communication	▶ Comment, essay, statement, explanation, description, response to text, creative writing ▶ Oral presentation, role play, debate ▶ Project work

| Fig. 12.8
Task types

Advantages and *disadvantages* of test types containing certain tasks are presented here:

	Test types	Advantages	Disadvantages
Fig. 12.9 Advantages and dis- advantages of task types	**Discrete point testing** (e. g., multiple choice questions)	▶ Setting, correcting, and marking are simple ▶ Validity and reliability ▶ Effective and objective information on skill(s) tested	▶ Isolated skills ▶ No or little context ▶ Relevance with regard to communicative competence problematic
	Integrative / prag-matic testing (e. g., text compo-sition)	▶ Testing several skills and competences ▶ Detailed feedback regarding learner's individual skills and competences	▶ More time-consuming ▶ More difficult to assess (validity? reliability?) ▶ Real-world relevance?
	Communicative testing (e. g., real-world tasks)	▶ Imitates real communicative situations ▶ Complex tasks and performance (receptive, productive, creative, inter-active, etc.)	▶ Time-consuming ▶ More subjective factors come into play (objectivity?)

Oral tasks/tests

To specify this *typology of tasks*, the list of task types for *oral tests* (see fig. 12.10) can show both how students can practice speaking and how their speaking skills can be examined (Eisenmann & Summer 2012: 425–26) – they involve *transactional speech* (without interaction), *interactional speech*, and a mixture of both (see ch. 6.1.3):

Fig. 12.10
Task types for oral tests

Presentation	Students prepare a speech on a selected topic, followed by question-ing or critique.
Free discussion	Students exchange opinions while following rules.
Mini-debate	Students conduct a topic-based conversation while adopting conflict-ing views according to a specific role and proposing them in a group.
Role play	Students conduct a 'closed' or 'open' interaction – with or without a structured de-briefing component.
Improvisation	Students perform something (e. g., a sketch or role play) without any preparation.
Interview	Students conduct interviews either with experts (e. g., other teachers) or with their classmates.
Expert groups	Students form small groups. Each group collects information about a specific topic. They then split up and form new groups (now being 'experts') in class and inform their group about their specific topic.
Illustrated talks	Students prepare and present posters, illustrations, or leaflets.
Storytelling	Students choose a story or invent one, then tell as enthusiastically as possible.
Formal speeches	Students practice rhetoric, intonation, visual contact, etc.
Describing pictures	Students interpret visual elements. They may speculate about the atmosphere, what happened before/after, etc.
Closing information gaps	Students have to find information on their own to solve a problem.
Interpreting	Students mediate a conversation into the target language or vice versa.

Consider the advantages and disadvantages of the following task types.

Example 1: closed task (Kieweg 1999b: 18)
[Tick the right answer]

Frank: Do you know Mrs Miller? – Peter: Of course, I do.

- ▶ We know each other for almost two years.
- ▶ We're knowing each other for almost two years.
- ▶ We've been knowing each other for almost two years.
- ▶ We've known each other for almost two years.

Here, the teaching goal is receptive grammar knowledge, specifically the correct use of the present perfect continuous.

Example 2: semi-open task (TMBWK 2010: 2, adapted)
[Response to a text]

Do the following tasks, using your own words as far as appropriate.

- ▶ Write a text in which you contrast the decline and fall of traditional bookshops with the new trends and their advantages in the publishing, printing, and selling of books.
- ▶ Analyze the author's view about recent developments in the book industry and the language he employs.
- ▶ *"If you are a lover of well-stocked bookshops, then you should enjoy them while you can."* Discuss the pros and cons of traditional bookshops. Write at least 350 words and count your words.

Here, the tasks set are a guided response to a text, where the restriction of "at least 350 words" provides a clear limitation of a 'semi-open' task.

Example 3: open tasks

- ▶ Write an essay on 'Beauty.'
- ▶ Write a letter to the editor of a newspaper, responding to an article on the death penalty.
- ▶ Critically discuss the elements of the American Dream (e. g., with reference to the tragedy *Death of a Salesman*).
- ▶ Conduct an interview at an international company, asking international employees about their jobs. Present your findings in class.

12.5 | Grading

12.5.1 | Grading scales

Error index

The *error index* (grading according to mistakes, cf. Macht 2007: 375) is still frequently used to assess foreign language skills. Written mistakes are counted – as half or full mistakes – and set into relation to the amount of words used. The calculated coefficient is then set in relation to a point or marking scale (cf. Haß et al. 2008: 277). As objective as this procedure appears, it is marred by two *serious downsides* : (1) different assessors weigh mistakes differently, and (2) if communicative competence is the aim of foreign language learning (see ch. 4.3.1), the number of mistakes cannot be the (sole) yardstick to be used for assessment. As the principle of communicative competence is often associated with the idea that *fluency should be favored over accuracy* and *meaning over form*, other factors need to be considered. Assessors, especially of tests for advanced learners, tend to assess according to the *criteria of language, content*, and *style/expression(s)*. The *categories* are weighted against each other, for instance language counting as 50 %, content as 40 %, and style as 10 %. Then marks are given according to scales, where there are three options: linear, nonlinear, and partially linear scales (cf. Jürgens & Sacher 2008: 74–76). Here are examples of such scales (see fig. 12.12):

Fig. 12.11 |
Spot the mistake!

Scales	Grades – points
Linear scale	1: 35–30, 2: 29–24, 3: 23–18, 4: 17–12 (lowest competence level, 'just passed'), 5: 11–6, 6: 5–0
Non-linear scale	the distribution appears random and therefore unjust: 1: 35–34, 2: 33–28, 3: 27–20, 4: 19–12 ('just passed'), 5: 11–4, 6: 3–0
Partially linear scale	'bell curve,' frequently applied, distributing the levels below and above the lowest competence level evenly. 1: 48–43, 2: 42–37, 3: 36–31, 4: 30–25 ('just passed'), 5: 24–0

Fig. 12.12 |
Grading scales

Below are two typical grading grids (see fig. 12.13 and 12.14) for the German A-level / high school diploma exam (TMBWK 2010: 2–4, adapted):

Qualität von Informationsgewinnung und -verarbeitung	10 BE
aufgabengemäß, inhaltlich richtig, vollständig, präzis	10 BE
aufgabengemäß, inhaltlich richtig, nahezu vollständig, weitestgehend genau	9–8 BE
aufgabengemäß, im Wesentlichen inhaltlich richtig, im Wesentlichen vollständig	7–6 BE
im Wesentlichen aufgabengemäß, inhaltlich teilweise lückenhaft bzw. fehlerhaft	5–4 BE
in Ansätzen aufgabengemäß, inhaltlich unvollständig	3–2 BE
kaum noch oder nicht aufgabengemäß, inhaltlich bruchstückhaft bzw. falsch	1–0 BE

Fig. 12.13 |
Assessing content
(BE: *Bewertungseinheit*)

Qualität von Informationstransfer	6 BE
aufgabengemäß, textsortengerecht, differenziert, prägnant, überzeugend, ggf. kreativ	6 BE
aufgabengemäß, textsortengerecht, differenziert	5–4 BE
in Ansätzen aufgabengemäß, in Ansätzen differenziert	3–2 BE
kaum noch oder nicht aufgabengemäß, nicht differenziert	1–0 BE
Qualität der Darstellung	**3 BE**
intentionsgerechte, logische, übersichtliche, im Schriftbild saubere Darstellung	3 BE
im Wesentlichen intentionsgerechte, logische, übersichtliche sowie im Schriftbild weitgehend klare und saubere Darstellung	2 BE
kaum noch intentionsgerechte, logische, übersichtliche Darstellung sowie Mängel in der Klarheit und Sauberkeit des Schriftbilds	1 BE
nicht intentionsgerechte, unlogische und unübersichtliche Darstellung sowie erhebliche Mängel im Schriftbild	0 BE

Verständlichkeit und sprachliche Korrektheit	12 BE
nahezu korrekter Sprachgebrauch	12–11 BE
überwiegend geringfügige Normverstöße, die die Verständlichkeit nicht beeinträchtigen	10–9 BE
überwiegend geringfügige Normverstöße, die die Verständlichkeit nicht wesentlich beeinträchtigen	8–7 BE
Häufung geringfügiger Normverstöße, die die Verständlichkeit durch ihre Vielzahl insgesamt beeinträchtigen, und/oder grobe Normverstöße, die die Verständlichkeit beeinträchtigen	6–5 BE
überwiegend grobe Normverstöße, die die Verständlichkeit stark einschränken	4–2 BE
gravierende Normverstöße, die die Verständlichkeit verhindern	1–0 BE
Ausdrucksvermögen	**9 BE**
Variabilität des sprachlichen Ausdrucks, oberstufengemäßer Wortschatz, Komplexität und Variabilität des Satzbaus bzw. treffende Wortgruppen/Stichworte, textsortengerecht	9–8 BE
Bemühen um Variabilität des sprachlichen Ausdrucks, oberstufengemäßer Wortschatz, weitestgehend klarer Satzbau bzw. meist treffende Wortgruppen/Stichworte, textsortengerecht	7–6 BE
wenig Variabilität des sprachlichen Ausdrucks, begrenzter Wortschatz, Ungeschicklichkeiten im Satzbau bzw. in der Formulierung von Wortgruppen/Stichworten, im Wesentlichen textsortengerecht	5–4 BE
Stark eingeschränkter sprachlicher Ausdruck, sehr begrenzter Wortschatz, auffällige Verstöße gegen den Satzbau bzw. gravierende Unsicherheiten bei der Formulierung von Wortgruppen/Stichworten, in Ansätzen textsortengerecht	3–2 BE
gravierende sprachlich-stilistische Mängel, unzureichender Wortschatz, grobe Fehler im Satzbau bzw. bei der Formulierung von Wortgruppen/Stichworten	1–0 BE

Fig. 12.14
Assessing language

Discuss which criteria should be considered as having more importance, which less. How clear is the difference between the level of points?

12.5.2 | Alternative assessment formats

Alternative testing formats

With the goal of *intercultural communicative competence* (see ch. 7.1.3) and the need to facilitate more learner and teacher awareness of language learning as a *lifelong process*, new and alternative testing procedures have been promoted. A number of *alternative formats* of testing have come into focus.

Focus on interaction and real-life tasks: there is an increasing demand to capture cultural and social as well as communicative dimensions of exchanges (cf. Müller-Hartmann & Schocker-von Ditfurth 2009: 150). A typical task for *a task-based approach* could be the following (Bebermeier 1999: 49, adapted):

> You are on holiday in XY and the place and hotel are extremely disappointing. Your friend from Great Britain will join you one week later. Write an email (about 250 words) to your friend and tell him/her about the accommodation and entertainment. Suggest that he/she changes to a different place and/or hotel.

The teaching and testing of interactional skills would be one step in the direction of testing interactive skills. Another would be the evaluation of cooperation in *group work or when displaying media skills* (e. g., PowerPoint presentations, if followed by a question and answer session). Less developed yet and *problematic to categorize* would be the testing of intercultural competence (cf Byram 1997, see ch. 7.2.2)

Portfolio

Self- and peer-assessment: these "nontraditional or alternative forms of classroom-based writing" (Peñaflorida 2002: 347, cf. Jürgens 2005) include the assessment of learning logs, dialog journals (including a dialog between teacher and student over the course of the year), as well as a portfolio which can be assessed. They present an overview of the performance of a learner over a longer period of time (such as the *European Language Portfolio*). A *portfolio* can be a traditional folder in which the students file their work or a notebook with special sections with parts for work in progress or final drafts. If students are allowed to actively participate in the selection and discussion of their work or have fellow students peer-review their work, they may "gain a true sense of ownership, which results in personal satisfaction and feelings of self-worth" (Peñaflorida 2002: 334). Students should be helped with the *definition of evaluation criteria*, which could include a focus on content, language, presentation, creativity, involvement, pace of work, amount of work produced, difficulties and coping strategies, flexibility and range, communication, size, etc. (cf. Bebermeier 1999: 51).

All in all, assessment procedures need to incorporate a greater focus on *learning as a process*, allowing for reflections both of teachers and learners on individual progress and agency. Teachers should be encouraged to focus on what is good and how it can be improved further, and assist students in increasing their own *effectiveness* in avoiding mistakes.

Correcting mistakes

What we call mistakes are deviations from language norms. As *errors*, they mean a gap in the learner's knowledge, as *mistakes* an (occasional) lapse in performance. Errors are *part of the learning process*, part of the developing **Interlanguage** of a learner and can provide information about a learner's progress or level of proficiency (see chs. 3.2.3, 5.1.2). They can have different causes, such as interference, overgeneralization, or simplification. Errors can be seen as *hypothesis-building* and thus as a testing out of language skills (Kleppin 2009: 60). *Errors are unavoidable.* Researchers in the field of error analysis have stressed the importance of the following issues (Kleppin 2009):

► Teachers need to be *sensitive* to how and when errors and mistakes need to be corrected so as not to discourage or hamper language use.
► Teachers need to set their *priorities* when it comes to correcting errors and mistakes: high priority should be given to those that interfere with comprehension (e.g., problematic intonation, pronunciation) and to those that were practiced frequently. High priority should also be given to intercultural mistakes (e.g., lack of politeness, offensive language). Low priority should be given to slips or rare constructions.
► In *pre-writing activities*, teachers can sensitize students to the fact that certain text types create certain grammatical challenges (e.g., a narrative in the past usually does not use the present perfect, unless there is a direct link to the present).
► Teachers can practice *editing techniques* with their students, with learners getting used to reviewing, revising, and editing their texts and being alert to typical mistakes.
► Learners could be asked to regularly *peer-review* their texts, discussing typical mistakes or the reasons for them.
► Both teachers and students *keep track of typical mistakes* of individual students. With the help of the teacher, students could keep notes of grammatical, lexical, or stylistic 'challenges.'

Reflect on and discuss the following statement: "A paper which is excessively marked and scribbled over by the teacher is no longer the student's property. It becomes the teacher's." (Peñaflorida 2002: 345)

As to the *correction of oral mistakes*, clearly, there must be a difference between *presentation and practice phases* as well as the *production and communication phase*. In the presentation and practice phases, students learn, for example,

Sidebar

| 12.6
Errors and mistakes as 'learning chances'

| Fig. 12.15
Error or mistake?

Mistakes are the portals of discovery. – James Joyce

how a new word is pronounced or spelled; and if there is no correction, mistakes can fossilize. Students need to use the new items correctly. In the production phase, or in the 'free conversation' or communicative phase, the focus should, of course, be on *content and meaning, not on form and accuracy*. Mistakes should only be corrected if they lead to semantic or intercultural misunderstandings. Teachers have the following choices:

Ways of correcting oral mistakes

▶ *Explicit corrections should be avoided.* Especially, repetition of an error should generally be avoided – this could create the opposite effect: the mind tends to memorize exactly what it should not memorize.

▶ *Recasts*, if necessary, can be used to elicit correct English if the meaning was unclear or an utterance interculturally problematic (e.g., rude).

▶ A *clarification request* can be used, where the teacher signals that an utterance could not be understood, possibly for acoustic reasons (this can be done verbally and nonverbally).

▶ *Elicitation* can be used, a technique where teachers – not unlike the famous Greek philosopher Socrates – clarify meaning through further meaningful questions.

▶ Teachers can, *at the end of a session*, discuss linguistic difficulties which occurred during the lesson and help students to avoid certain mistakes in the future. This can be done without reference to individual learners.

Teachers should try to discontinue the following (mal-)practices and use alternatives (based on Peñaflorida 2002: 344–45, 352; Jürgens & Sacher 2008: 70):

▶ Assessment, evaluation, and grading are imprecise and unsystematic or not transparent to students.

▶ Teachers give no written feedback; their feedback is only negative, not really constructive, not encouraging, or confusing. Teachers should avoid comments like 'improve,' 'vague,' 'obscure,' 'too broad,' or just 'specify.' Instead, they should provide *helpful comments* closely related to the task and the student utterance.

▶ Teachers take too much time to grade and hand back tests or assignments. Instead, teacher feedback should be *as soon as possible*.

Positive feedback

▶ "Teacher corrects all errors, 'bleeds' students' papers to death, figuratively and literally. Red penciling all over the paper reveals that form, rather than substance, is given more attention. By concentrating on form, students tend to turn in papers which are almost flawless in grammar but lacking in substance." (Peñaflorida 2002: 345) Instead, teachers and students shouldn't 'sweat the small stuff,' but rather *focus on real howlers* and how to avoid them.

▶ To end on a positive note, errors and mistakes are 'learning chances.' Students should learn to detect their own mistakes and become aware of the complexity of language themselves.

Practical examples

| 12.7

Example 1: Student from grade 7
The following test consists of three parts and can be considered 'very traditional' (see fig. 12.16).

> Define the three parts: are they closed, semi-closed, or open? What is being tested and how is the overall grade computed? How could test design and grading be improved?

| Fig. 12.16
Sample test 1

Example 2: Student from grade 7

The following test is a response to a literary text (see fig. 12.17).

> Consider the grading and how it could be done differently. Which grade would you have given, considering content, language, and form? What kinds of comments would have been more helpful than just the question mark in the margin and the wriggle under words?

Fig. 12.17 |
Sample test 2

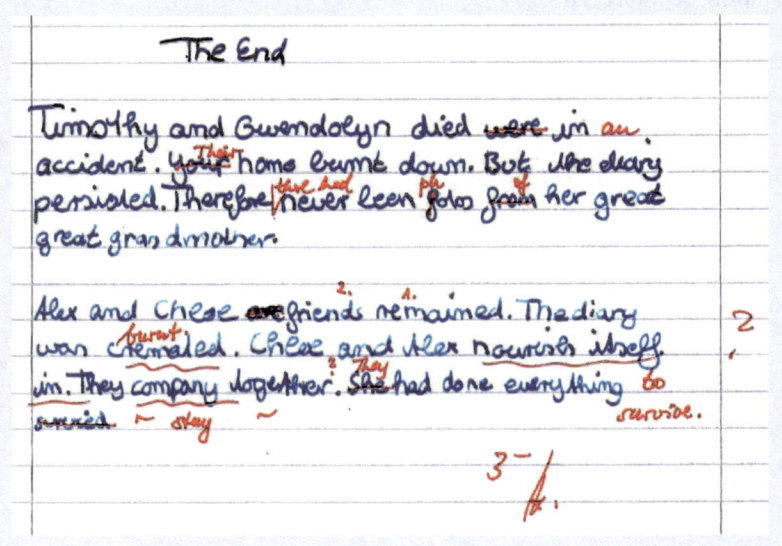

Example 3: Student from grade 10

The following shows a grade 10 student's answer in a test (see fig. 12.18). The task was to write a personal letter of application for a job as an assistant receptionist at a hotel in London (ca. 70 to 90 words). The answer was based on a short information sheet detailing how the applicant is suited for the job.

> In this case, assess the teacher's grading. How do you consider the mistakes in the answer (graded and not graded)? How would your grading differ if the CV had been practised extensively before the test?

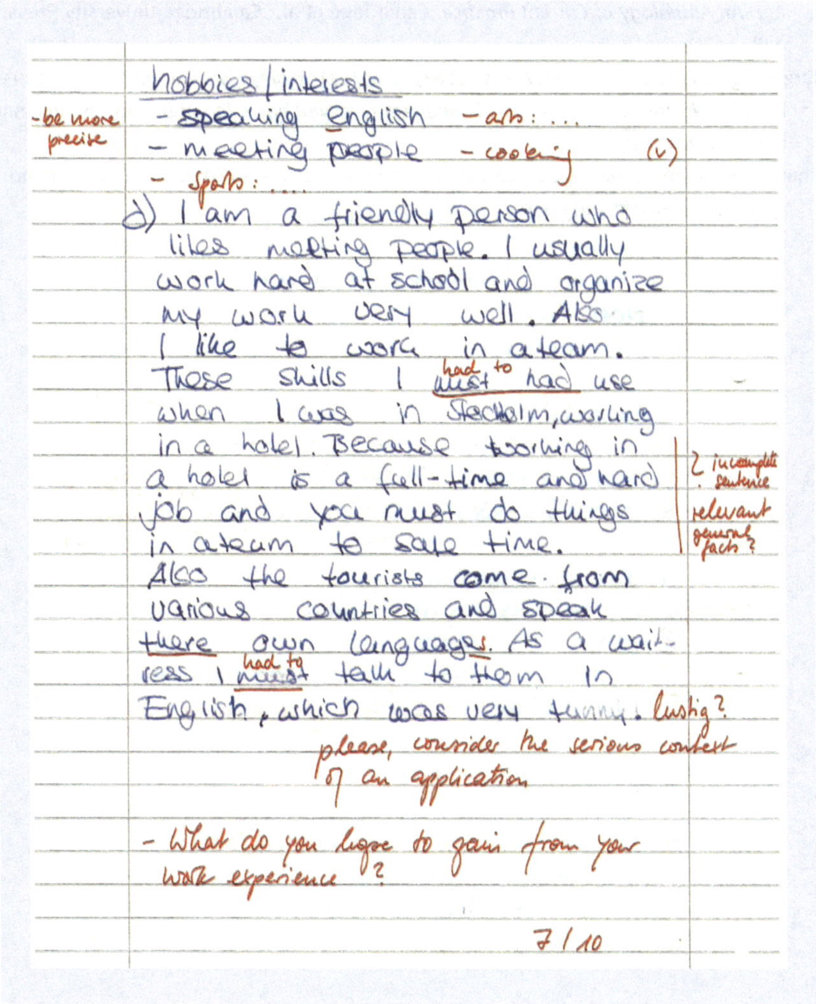

Fig. 12.18
Sample test 3

hobbies / interests

- be more precise   - speaking english   - ask: ...

- meeting people   - cooking   (✓)

- sports: ....

d) I am a friendly person who likes meeting people. I usually work hard at school and organize my work very well. Also I like to work in a team. These skills I ~~must~~ *had to* had use when I was in Stockholm, working in a hotel. Because working in a hotel is a full-time and hard   *| incomplete sentence* job and you must do things   *relevant* in a team to save time.   *general fach?* Also the tourists come from various countries and speak there own languages. As a waitress I ~~must~~ *had to* talk to them in English, which was very funny. *lustig?*

       please, consider the serious context of an application

- What do you hope to gain from your work experience?

                7 / 10

Recommended reading

Arendt, Manfred (2006). Beurteilung mündlicher Leistungen. Eine Untersuchung. In: *Praxis Fremdsprachenunterricht*; Part 1: 3.3, 3–10; Part 2: 3.4, 3–8.

Bebermeier, Hans (1999). Neue Formen der Leistungsfeststellung. In: *Der Fremdsprachliche Unterricht Englisch* 37, 46–51.

Eisenmann, Maria (2008). Formen mündlicher Leistungsmessung im Fach Englisch. In: *Praxis Fremdsprachenunterricht* 5.4, 26–30.

Huerta-Macías, Ana (2002). Alternative Assessment: Responses to Commonly Asked Questions. In: Jack C. Richards & Willy A. Renandya, eds. *Methodology in Language Teach-*

ing: An Anthology of Current Practice. Cambridge et al.: Cambridge University Press, 338–43.

Jürgens, Eiko (2000). Brauchen wir ein pädagogisches Leistungsverständnis? In: Silvia-Iris Beutel & Witlof Vollstädt, eds. *Leistung ermitteln und bewerten.* Hamburg: Bergmann und Helbig, 15–25.

Thaler, Engelbert (2008). Klassenarbeiten – eine Prozessperspektive. In: *Praxis Fremdsprachenunterricht* 5.4, 6–10.

References

References unit 1

Bach, Gerhard & Stephan Breidbach (2013). Fremdsprachenkompetenz in der mehrsprachigen Wissensgesellschaft. In: Gerhard Bach & Johannes-P. Timm, eds. *Englischunterricht: Grundlagen und Methoden einer handlungsorientierten Unterrichtspraxis*. Tuebingen: Francke, 280–303.

Bausch, Karl-Richard; Herbert Christ; Frank G. Königs & Hans-Jürgen Krumm, eds. (2003). *Der Gemeinsame europäische Referenzrahmen für Sprachen in der Diskussion*. Tuebingen: Narr.

Beer, Rudolf (2007). *Bildungsstandards: Einstellungen von Lehrerinnen und Lehrern*. Vienna et al.: LIT.

Bredella, Lothar (2006). Bildungsstandards und ihre Umsetzung. In: Johannes-P. Timm, ed. *Fremdsprachenlernen und Fremdsprachenforschung: Kompetenzen, Standards, Lernformen, Evaluation*. Tuebingen: Narr, 105–20.

Brutt-Griffler, Janina (2008). 'Who Do You Think You Are, Where Do You Think You Are?': Language Policy and the Political Economy of English in South Africa. In: Claus Gnutzmann & Frauke Intemann, eds. *The Globalisation of English and the English Language Classroom*. 2nd ed. Tuebingen: Narr, 27–40.

Bryman, Alan (2004). *The Disneyization of Society*. London et al.: SAGE.

Byram, Michael (1997). *Teaching and Assessing Intercultural Communicative Competence*. Clevedon et al.: Multilingual Matters.

Christ, Herbert (2010). Geschichte der Fremdsprachendidaktik. In: Wolfgang Hallet & Frank G. Königs, eds. *Handbuch Fremdsprachendidaktik*. Seelze-Velber: Klett/Kallmeyer, 17–22.

Council of Europe (2001). *Common European Framework of Reference for Languages: Learning, Teaching, Assessment*. Cambridge: Cambridge University Press.

Council of Europe (2011). *European Language Portfolio*. http://www.coe.int/t/dg4/education/elp/elp-reg/Registered_ELP_EN.asp (15 August 2014).

Decke-Cornill, Helene & Lutz Küster (2014). *Fremdsprachendidaktik: Eine Einführung*. 2nd ed. Tuebingen: Narr.

Der Deutsche Anglistenverband e. V. & die Deutsche Gesellschaft für Amerikastudien e. V. (2012). *Inhaltliche Anforderungen für Fachwissenschaft und Fachdidaktik in der Lehrerinnen- und Lehrerbildung, Studienfach Englisch*. Trier: WVT.

Gnutzmann, Claus (2008). 'Standard English' and 'World Standard English': Linguistic and Pedagogical Considerations. In: Claus Gnutzmann & Frauke Intemann, eds. *The Globalisation of English and the English Language Classroom*. 2nd ed. Tuebingen: Narr, 107–18.

Hallet, Wolfgang & Frank G. Königs (2010). Lehrpläne und Curricula. In: Wolfgang Hallet & Frank G. Königs, eds. *Handbuch Fremdsprachendidaktik*. Seelze-Velber: Klett/ Kallmeyer, 54–58.

Harmer, Jeremy (2007). *The Practice of English Language Teaching*. 4th ed. Harlow: Pearson/Longman.

Harsch, Claudia (2006). *Der Gemeinsame europäische Referenzrahmen: Leistung und Grenzen. Die Bedeutung des Referenzrahmens im Kontext der Beurteilung von Sprachvermögen am Beispiel des semikreativen Schreibens im DESI-Projekt*. Inaugural Dissertation. http://www.opus-bayern.de/uni-augsburg/volltexte/2006/368/ (15 July 2014).

Hüllen, Werner (2005). *Kleine Geschichte des Fremdsprachenlernens*. Berlin: Schmidt.

James, Allan (2008). The Challenges of the Lingua Franca: English in the World and Types of Variety. In: Claus Gnutzmann & Frauke Intemann, eds. *The Globalisation of English and the English Language Classroom*. 2nd ed. Tuebingen: Narr, 133–44.

Jenkins, Jennifer (2008). Teaching Pronunciation for English as a Lingua Franca: A Sociopolitical Perspective. In: Claus Gnutzmann & Frauke Intemann, eds. *The Globalisation of English and the English Language Classroom*. 2nd ed. Tuebingen: Narr, 145–58.

Kachru, Braj (1996). Norms, Models, and Identities. In: *The Language Teacher* 20.10. http:// jalt-publications.org/old_tlt/files/96/oct/englishes.html (10 November 2014).

Kelly, Michael; Michael Grenfell; Rebecca Allan; Christine Kriza & William McEvoy (2004). *European Profile for Language Teacher Education – A Frame of Reference: Final Report*. http://edz.bib.uni-mannheim.de/daten/edz-b/gdbk/04/spr/European_profile_frame_ en.pdf (15 August 2014).

Klieme, Eckard et al. (2007). *Zur Entwicklung nationaler Bildungsstandards: Expertise*. Berlin: Bundesministerium für Bildung und Forschung. http://www.bmbf.de/pub/zur_ entwicklung_nationaler_bildungsstandards.pdf (15 July 2014).

Kultusministerkonferenz (2003). *Bildungsstandards für die erste Fremdsprache (Englisch/ Französisch) für den Mittleren Abschluss*. http://www.iqb.hu-berlin.de/bista/subject (15 July 2014).

Kultusministerkonferenz (2004). *Bildungsstandards für die erste Fremdsprache (Englisch/ Französisch) für den Hauptschulabschluss*. http://www.kmk.org/fileadmin/veroeffent lichungen_beschluesse/2004/2004_10_15-Bildungsstandards-ersteFS-Haupt.pdf (15 July 2014).

Kultusministerkonferenz (2008/2014). *Ländergemeinsame inhaltliche Anforderung für die Fachwissenschaften und Fachdidaktiken in der Lehrerbildung*. http://www.akkreditie rungsrat.de/fileadmin/Seiteninhalte/KMK/Vorgaben/KMK_Lehrerbildung_inhaltliche_ Anforderungen_aktuell.pdf (15 July 2014).

Kultusministerkonferenz (2012a). *Bildungsstandards für die fortgeführte Fremdsprache (Englisch/Französisch) für die Allgemeine Hochschulreife*. http://www.kmk.org/file admin/veroeffentlichungen_beschluesse/2012/2012_10_18-Bildungsstandards-Fort gef-FS-Abi.pdf (15 July 2014).

Kultusministerkonferenz (2012b). *Ländergemeinsame Anforderungen für die Ausgestaltung des Vorbereitungsdienstes und die abschließende Staatsprüfung*. http://www.kmk.org/

fileadmin/veroeffentlichungen_beschluesse/2012/2012_12_06-Vorbereitungsdienst. pdf (15 July 2014).

Locke, John (1693). *Some Thoughts Concerning Education*. London: Churchill.

Lütge, Christiane (2012). Was sind und zu welchem Ende diskutiert man Kompetenzstandards für Fremdsprachenlehrerinnen und -lehrer? In: Gabriele Blell & Christiane Lütge, eds. *Fremdsprachendidaktik und Lehrerbildung: Konzepte, Impulse, Perspektiven*. Muenster et al.: LIT, 185–204.

Mair, Christian (2003). Linguistics, Literature and the Postcolonial Englishes: An Introduction. In: Christian Mair, ed. *The Politics of English as a World Language: New Horizons in Postcolonial Cultural Studies*. Amsterdam et al.: Rodopi, ix-xxi.

Musumeci, Diane (2011). History of Language Teaching. In: Michael H. Long & Catherine J. Doughty, eds. *The Handbook of Language Teaching*. Malden, MA et al.: Wiley-Blackwell, 42–62.

Nold, Günter; Eckhard Klieme & Konrad Schröder (2006). Messung von Schülerkompetenzen: Der Beitrag der DESI-Studie zur Diskussion um Bildungsstandards und Referenzrahmen. In: Johannes-P. Timm, ed. *Fremdsprachenlernen und Fremdsprachenforschung: Kompetenzen, Standards, Lernformen, Evaluation*. Tuebingen: Narr, 85–104.

Organization for Economic Co-operation and Development (2010). *PISA 2009 at a Glance*. OECD Publishing. http://dx.doi.org/10.1787/9789264095298-en (15 July 2014).

Phillipson, Robert (1992). *Linguistic Imperialism*. Oxford: Oxford University Press.

Phillipson, Robert (2010). *Linguistic Imperialism Continued*. New York: Routledge.

Phillipson, Robert & Tove Skutnabb-Kangas (2011). The Politics and Policies of Language and Language Teaching. In: Michael H. Long & Catherine J. Doughty, eds. *The Handbook of Language Teaching*. Malden, MA et al.: Wiley-Blackwell, 26–41.

Quetz, Jürgen & Karin Vogt (2009). Bildungsstandards für die Erste Fremdsprache: Sprachenpolitik auf unsicherer Basis. In: *Zeitschrift für Fremdsprachenforschung* 20.1, 63–89.

Ritzer, George (2011). *The McDonaldization of Society*. 6th ed. Thousand Oaks, CA et al.: Pine Forge.

Schneider, Edgar W. (2011). *English Around the World: An Introduction*. Cambridge et al.: Cambridge University Press.

Timm, Johannes-P., ed. (2006). *Fremdsprachenlernen und Fremdsprachenforschung: Kompetenzen, Standards, Lernformen, Evaluation*. Tuebingen: Narr.

Verma, Mahendra K. (2008). English as an Economic Investment: Who will Earn the Dividends? In: Claus Gnutzmann & Frauke Intemann, eds. *The Globalisation of English and the English Language Classroom*. 2nd ed. Tuebingen: Narr, 41–54.

Viëtor (1882/1905). *Der Sprachunterricht muss umkehren. Ein Beitrag zur Überbürdungsfrage von Quosque Tandem*. Ed. Konrad Schröder (1984). Munich: Hueber.

Vogt, Karin (2012). Assessment: Washback of the Common European Framework and PISA. In: *Anglistik* 23.1, 87–95.

Volkmann, Laurenz (2012). The Theory and Politics of English Language Teaching. In: Martin Middeke; Timo Müller; Christina Wald & Hubert Zapf, eds. *English and American Studies: Theory and Practice*. Stuttgart et al.: Metzler, 473–79.

Zydatiß, Wolfgang (2005). *Bildungsstandards und Kompetenzniveaus im Englischunterricht: Konzepte, Empirie, Kritik und Konsequenzen*. Frankfurt a. M.: Lang.

References unit 2

Bailey, Kathleen M. (2011). Issues in Language Teacher Evaluation. In: Michael H. Long & Catherine H. Doughty, eds. *The Handbook of Language Teaching*. Malden, MA et al.: Wiley-Blackwell, 706–25.

Bauer, Karl-Oswald (2006). Das professionelle Selbst (mit einem Exkurs über die glückliche Lehrkraft). In: Barbara Mergner; Dieter Schoof-Wetzig & Edwin Stiller, eds. *Lehrerfortbildung als Personalentwicklung: Persönliches Lernen begleiten*. Bad Berka: ThILLM, 15–25.

Baumert, Jürgen & Mareike Kunter (2011). Das Kompetenzmodell von COACTIV. In: Mareike Kunter; Jürgen Baumert; Werner Blum; Uta Klusmann; Stefan Krauss & Michael Neubrand, eds. *Professionelle Kompetenz von Lehrkräften: Ergebnisse des Forschungsprogramms COACTIV*. Muenster et al.: Waxmann, 29–53.

Bell, Beverly & John Gilbert (1996). *Teacher Development: A Model from Science Education*. London et al.: Falmer Press.

Burns, Anne (2000). Action Research. In: Michael Byram, ed. *Routledge Encyclopedia of Language Teaching and Learning*. London et al.: Routledge, 7–12.

Burns, Anne (2005). Action Research: An Evolving Paradigm? In: *Language Teaching* 38.2, 57–74.

Ditton, Hartmut (2000). Qualitätskontrolle und Qualitätssicherung in Schule und Unterricht. Ein Überblick zum Stand der empirischen Forschung. In: Andreas Helmke; Walter Hornstein & Ewald Terhart, eds. *Qualität und Qualitätssicherung im Bildungsbereich: Schule, Sozialpädagogik, Hochschule*. Weinheim et al.: Beltz, 73–92.

Foord, Duncan (2009). *The Developing Teacher: Practical Activities for Professional Development*. Surrey: Delta Publishing.

Hallet, Wolfgang (2010). Didaktische Kompetenzen von Fremdsprachenlehrern. In: Wolfgang Hallet & Frank G. Königs, eds. *Handbuch Fremdsprachendidaktik*. Seelze-Velber: Klett/Kallmeyer, 350–53.

Heuer, Helmut & Friederike Klippel (1987). Individualität des Englischlehrers. In: Helmut Heuer & Friederike Klippel, eds. *Englischmethodik: Problemfelder, Unterrichtswirklichkeit und Handlungsempfehlungen*. Berlin: Cornelsen, 15–37.

Hattie, John (2003). *Teachers Make a Difference: What Is the Research Evidence?* https://cdn.auckland.ac.nz/assets/education/hattie/docs/teachers-make-a-difference-ACER-(2003).pdf (10 September 2014).

Hattie, John (2009). *Visible Learning: A Synthesis of over 800 Meta-Analyses Relating to Achievement*. London et al.: Routledge.

Hattie, John (2011). *Visible Learning for Teachers: Maximizing Impact on Learning*. London et al.: Routledge.

Helmke, Andreas (2006). Was wissen wir über guten Unterricht? Über die Notwendigkeit einer Rückbesinnung auf den Unterricht als dem "Kerngeschäft" der Schule. In: *Pädagogik* 58.2, 42–45.

Helmke, Andreas; Tuyet Helmke; Gerlinde Lenske; Giang Pham; Anna-Katharina Praetorius; Friedrich-Wilhelm Schrader & Manuel Ade-Thurow (2014). *EMU: Evidenzbasierte Methoden der Unterrichtsdiagnostik und -entwicklung.* http://www.unterrichtsdiag nostik.info/media/files/Broschuere%20Version%204.2_22.01.14.pdf (12 April 2014).

Helmke, Andreas & Gerlinde Lenske (2013). Unterrichtsdiagnostik als Voraussetzung für Unterrichtsentwicklung. In: *Beiträge zur Lehrerbildung* 31.2, 214–33.

Jantowski, Andreas (2011). Lehreraus- und -fortbildung: Ziele, Aufgaben, Konzepte. In: Andreas Jantowski, ed. *Schule beginnt: Handbuch zur Berufseingangsphase im Lehrerberuf.* Bad Berka: ThILLM, 43–60.

Jantowski, Andreas & Claudia Hartleib (2013). Lehrerbelastung und Lehrergesundheit. In: Andreas Jantowski, ed. *Aspekte moderner Lehrerbildung.* Bad Berka: ThILLM, 47–68.

Jourdenais, Renée (2011). Language Teacher Education. In: Michael H. Long & Catherine H. Doughty, eds. *The Handbook of Language Teaching.* Malden, MA et al.: Wiley-Blackwell, 647–58.

Kemmis, Stephen & Robin McTaggart, eds. (1988). *The Action Research Planner.* 3rd ed. Victoria: Deakin University.

Koehler, Matthew J. & Punya Mishra (2009). What Is Technological Pedagogical Content Knowledge? In: *Contemporary Issues in Technology and Teacher Education* 9.1, 60–70.

Kramsch, Claire (1994). *Context and Culture in Language Teaching.* Oxford et al.: Oxford University Press.

Kunter, Mareike; Jürgen Baumert; Werner Blum; Uta Klusmann; Stefan Krauss & Michael Neubrand, eds. (2011). *Professionelle Kompetenz von Lehrkräften: Ergebnisse des Forschungsprogramms COACTIV.* Muenster et al.: Waxmann.

Kultusministerkonferenz (2004). *Standards für die Lehrerbildung: Bildungswissenschaften.* http://www.kmk.org/fileadmin/veroeffentlichungen_beschluesse/2004/2004_12_16-Standards-Lehrerbildung.pdf (12 April 2014).

Langer, Georgea M.; Amy B. Colton & Loretta S. Goff (2003). *Collaborative Analysis of Student Work: Improving Teaching and Learning.* Alexandria, VA: ASCD.

Lipowsky, Frank (2006). Auf den Lehrer kommt es an: Empirische Evidenzen für Zusammenhänge zwischen Lehrerkompetenzen, Lehrerhandeln und dem Lernen der Schüler. In: Cristina Allemann-Ghionda & Ewald Terhart, eds. *Kompetenzen und Kompetenzentwicklung von Lehrerinnen und Lehrern: Ausbildung und Beruf.* Weinheim et al.: Beltz, 47–70.

Maier, Uwe (2012). *Lehr- und Lernprozesse in der Schule: Studium – Allgemeindidaktische Kategorien für die Analyse und Gestaltung von Unterricht.* Bad Heilbrunn: Klinkhardt.

Mansell, Warwick (2009). *Research Reveals Teaching's Holy Grail.* http://www.tes.co.uk/ article.aspx?storycode=6 005 393 (10 September 2014).

Meyer, Hilbert (2006). *Criteria of Good Instruction: Empirical Findings and Didactic Advice.* Trans. Dave Kloss. http://www.member.uni-oldenburg.de/hilbert.meyer/download/ Criteria_of_Good_Instruction.pdf (10 September 2014).

Meyer, Hilbert (2014). *Was ist guter Unterricht?* 10th ed. Berlin: Cornelsen.

Möllers, Rigobert (2011). Berufsbild Lehrer – Lehrerleitbild – Richtschnur für das eigene pädagogische Handeln? In: Andreas Jantowski, ed. *Schule beginnt: Handbuch zur Berufseingangsphase im Lehrerberuf*. Bad Berka: ThILLM, 15–36.

Richards, Jack C. & Thomas S. C. Farrell (2005). *Professional Development for Language Teachers: Strategies for Teacher Learning*. Cambridge et al.: Cambridge University Press.

Schocker-von Ditfurth, Marita (2008). Auf den (Hochschul-)Lehrer kommt es an: Überlegungen zur Entwicklung von Lehrkompetenz. In: Michael K. Legutke, ed. *Kommunikative Kompetenz als fremdsprachendidaktische Vision*. Tuebingen: Narr, 130–49.

Shulman, Lee S. (1986). Those Who Understand: Knowledge Growth in Teaching. In: *Educational Researcher* 15.2, 4–14.

Shulman, Lee S. (1987). Knowledge and Teaching: Foundations of the New Reform. In: *Harvard Educational Review* 57.1, 1–22.

Shulman, Lee S. (1998). Theory, Practice, and the Education of Professionals. In: *The Elementary School Journal* 98.5, 511–26.

Shulman, Lee S. & Judith H. Shulman (2004). How and What Teachers Learn: A Shifting Perspective. In: *Journal of Curriculum Studies* 36.2, 257–71.

Stiller, Edwin (2006). Biografisches Lernen in der Lehrerbildung. In: Barbara Mergner; Dieter Schoof-Wetzig & Edwin Stiller, eds. *Lehrerfortbildung als Personalentwicklung: Persönliches Lernen begleiten*. Bad Berka: ThILLM, 2006, 33–56.

Terhart, Ewald (2011). Has John Hattie Really Found the Holy Grail of Research on Teaching? An Extended Review of *Visible Learning*. In: *Journal of Curriculum Studies* 43.3, 425–38.

The New London Group (2000). A Pedagogy of Multiliteracies: Designing Social Futures. In: Bill Cope & Mary Kalantzis, eds. *Multiliteracies: Literacy Learning and the Design of Social Futures*. London et al.: Routledge, 9–37.

Thompson, Julia G. (2009). *The First-Year Teacher's Checklist: A Quick Reference for Classroom Success*. San Francisco, CA: Jossey-Bass.

Trilling, Bernie & Charles Fadel (2009). *21st Century Skills: Learning for Life in Our Times*. San Francisco, CA: Jossey-Bass.

Van den Branden, Kris (2011). Diffusion and Implementation of Innovations. In: Michael H. Long & Catherine H. Doughty, eds. *The Handbook of Language Teaching*. Malden, MA et al.: Wiley-Blackwell, 659–72.

Wallace, Michael J. (1991). *Training Foreign Language Teachers: A Reflective Approach*. Cambridge et al.: Cambridge University Press.

References unit 3

Adey, Philip & Michael Shayer (2013). Piagetian Approaches. In: John Hattie & Eric M. Anderman, eds. *International Guide to Student Achievement*. New York: Routledge, 28–30.

Barcroft, Joe & Wynne Wong (2013). Input, Input Processing and Focus on Form. In: Julia Rogers Herschensohn & Martha Young-Scholten, eds. *The Cambridge Handbook of Second Language Acquisition*. Cambridge et al.: Cambridge University Press, 627–47.

Bieri, Peter (2012). Wie wäre es, gebildet zu sein? In: Heiner Hastedt, ed.: *Was ist Bildung? Eine Textanthologie*. Stuttgart: Reclam, 228–40.

Bleyhl, Werner (2013). Sprachlernen: Psycholinguistische Grunderkenntnisse. In: Gerhard Bach & Johannes-P. Timm, eds. *Englischunterricht: Grundlagen und Methoden einer handlungsorientierten Unterrichtspraxis*. 5th ed. Tuebingen: Francke, 23–42.

Decke-Cornill, Helene & Lutz Küster (2014). *Fremdsprachendidaktik: Eine Einführung*. 2nd ed. Tuebingen: Narr.

DeKeyser, Robert M. (2011). Cognitive Psychological Processes in Second Language Learning. In: Michael H. Long & Catherine J. Doughty, eds. *The Handbook of Language Teaching*. Malden, MA et al.: Wiley-Blackwell, 119–38.

Ellis, Nick C. (2008). Usage-based and Form-focused Language Acquisition: The Associative Learning of Constructions, Learned-attention, and the Limited L2 Endstate. In: Peter Robinson & Nick C. Ellis, eds. *Handbook of Cognitive Linguistics and Second Language Acquisition*. New York et al.: Routledge, 372–405.

Guskey, Thomas R. (2013). Defining Student Achievement. In: John Hattie & Eric M. Anderman, eds. *International Guide to Student Achievement*. New York et al.: Routledge, 3–6.

Hallet, Wolfgang (2006). *Didaktische Kompetenzen: Lehr- und Lernprozesse erfolgreich gestalten*. Stuttgart: Klett.

Hattie, John (2009). *Visible Learning: A Synthesis of over 800 Meta-Analyses Relating to Achievement*. London et al.: Routledge.

Hentig, Hartmut von (1996). *Bildung: Ein Essay*. Muenchen et al.: Hanser.

Holme, Randal (2013). Emergentism, Connectionism and Complexity. In: Julia Rogers Herschensohn & Martha Young-Scholten, eds. *The Cambridge Handbook of Second Language Acquisition*. Cambridge et al.: Cambridge University Press, 605–26.

Jank, Werner & Hilbert Meyer (2009). *Didaktische Modelle*. 9th ed. Berlin: Cornelsen Scriptor.

Lantolf, James P. (2012). Sociocultural Theory: A Dialectical Approach to L2 Research. In: Susan M. Gass & Alison Mackey, eds. *The Routledge Handbook of Second Language Acquisition*. London et al.: Routledge, 57–72.

Lieven, Elena & Michael Tomasello (2008). Children's First Language Acquisition from a Usage-based Perspective. In: Peter Robinson & Nick C. Ellis, eds. *Handbook of Cognitive Linguistics and Second Language Acquisition*. New York et al.: Routledge, 168–96.

Lightbown, Patsy M. & Nina Spada (2006). *How Languages Are Learned*. 3rd ed. Oxford et al.: Oxford University Press.

Long, Michael H. (2011). Methodological Principles for Language Teaching. In: Michael H. Long & Catherine J. Doughty, eds. *The Handbook of Language Teaching*. Malden, MA et al.: Wiley-Blackwell, 373–94.

Mayo, María del Pilar García & Eva Alcón Soler (2013). Negotiated Input and Output/Interaction. In: Julia Rogers Herschensohn & Martha Young-Scholten, eds. *The Cambridge Handbook of Second Language Acquisition*. Cambridge et al.: Cambridge University Press, 209–29.

Myles, Florence (2013). Theoretical Approaches. In: Julia Rogers Herschensohn & Martha

Young-Scholten, eds. *The Cambridge Handbook of Second Language Acquisition*. Cambridge et al.: Cambridge University Press, 46–70.

Ohta, Amy Snyder (2013). Sociocultural Theory and the Zone of Proximal Development. In: Julia Rogers Herschensohn & Martha Young-Scholten, eds. *The Cambridge Handbook of Second Language Acquisition*. Cambridge et al.: Cambridge University Press, 648–69.

Ortega, Lourdes (2011). Sequences and Processes in Language Learning. In: Michael H. Long & Catherine J. Doughty, eds. *The Handbook of Language Teaching*. Malden, MA et al.: Wiley-Blackwell, 81–105.

Overmann, Manfred (2002). Konstruktivistische Prinzipien und ihre didaktischen Implikationen. In: Gerhard Bach & Britta Viebrock, eds. *Die Aneignung fremder Sprachen: Perspektiven – Konzepte – Forschungsprogramm*. Frankfurt a. M. et al.: Lang, 65–98.

Piaget, Jean (1977). *The Essential Piaget*. Howard E. Gruber & J. Jacques. Vonèche, eds. New York: Basic Books.

Pienemann, Manfred & Jörg-U. Keßler (2012). Processability Theory. In: Susan M. Gass & Alison Mackey, eds. *The Routledge Handbook of Second Language Acquisition*. London et al.: Routledge, 228–46.

Prisching, Manfred (2012). *Flüchtige Bildung – Lernen in der Spätmoderne*. Koblenz: University of Koblenz-Landau.

Reinfried, Marcus (2002). Der radikale Konstruktivismus: Eine sinnvolle Basistheorie für die Fremdsprachendidaktik? In: Gerhard Bach & Britta Viebrock, eds. *Die Aneignung fremder Sprachen: Perspektiven – Konzepte – Forschungsprogramm*. Frankfurt a. M. et al.: Lang, 29–50.

Robinson, Peter & Nick C. Ellis (2008). Conclusion: Cognitive Linguistics, Second Language Acquisition and L2 Instruction – Issues for Research. In: Peter Robinson & Nick C. Ellis, eds. *Handbook of Cognitive Linguistics and Second Language Acquisition*. New York et al.: Routledge, 489–546.

Roche, Jörg (2013). *Fremdsprachenerwerb – Fremdsprachendidaktik*. 3rd ed. Tuebingen et al.: Francke.

Segalowitz, Norman & Pavel Trofimovich (2012). Second Language Processing. In: Susan M. Gass & Alison Mackey, eds. *The Routledge Handbook of Second Language Acquisition*. London et al.: Routledge, 179–92.

Spaemann, Robert (2012). Wer ist ein gebildeter Mensch? In: Heiner Hastedt, ed. *Was ist Bildung? Eine Textanthologie*. Stuttgart: Reclam, 223–27.

Spiro, Jane (2013). *Changing Methodologies for TESOL*. Edinburgh: Edinburgh University Press.

Straumanis, Joan (2012). What We're Learning about Learning (And What We Need to Forget). In: *Planning for Higher Education* 40.4, 6–11.

Stroud, Christopher & Kathleen Heugh (2011). Language in Education. In: Rajend Mesthrie, ed. *The Cambridge Handbook of Sociolinguistics*. Cambridge et al.: Cambridge University Press, 413–29.

Timm, Johannes-P. (2013). Lernorientierter Fremdsprachenunterricht: Förderung konstruktiver Lernprozesse. In: Gerhard Bach & Johannes-P. Timm, eds. *Englischunter-*

richt: Grundlagen und Methoden einer handlungsorientierten Unterrichtspraxis. 5th ed. Tuebingen: Francke, 43–60.

Tyler, Andrea (2008). Cognitive Linguistics and Second Language Instruction. In: Peter Robinson & Nick C. Ellis, eds. *Handbook of Cognitive Linguistics and Second Language Acquisition*. New York et al.: Routledge, 456–88.

VanPatten, Bill (2012). Input Processing. In: Susan M. Gass & Alison Mackey, eds. *The Routledge Handbook of Second Language Acquisition*. London et al.: Routledge, 268–81.

Von Glasersfeld, Ernst (1995). *Radical Constructivism: A Way of Knowing and Learning*. London et al.: Falmer Press.

Wendt, Michael (2002). 15 Thesen zum erkenntnistheoretischen Konstruktivismus. In: Gerhard Bach & Britta Viebrock, eds. *Die Aneignung fremder Sprachen: Perspektiven – Konzepte – Forschungsprogramm*. Frankfurt a. M. et al.: Lang, 25–28.

Whong, Melinda (2011). *Language Teaching: Linguistic Theory in Practice*. Edinburgh: Edinburgh University Press.

Wolff, Dieter (2002). Instruktivismus vs. Konstruktivismus: 20 Thesen zur Lernbarkeit und Lehrbarkeit von Sprachen. In: Gerhard Bach & Britta Viebrock, eds. *Die Aneignung fremder Sprachen: Perspektiven – Konzepte – Forschungsprogramm*. Frankfurt a. M. et al.: Lang, 19–24.

References unit 4

Arnold, Jane (2011). Attention to Affect in Language Learning. In: *Anglistik* 22.1, 11–22.

Bach, Gerhard & Johannes-P. Timm (2013). Handlungsorientierung als Ziel und Methode. In: Gerhard Bach & Johannes-P. Timm, eds. *Englischunterricht: Grundlagen und Methoden einer handlungsorientierten Unterrichtspraxis*. 5th ed. Tuebingen: Francke, 1–22.

Bejarano, Yael (1994). An Integrated Groupwork Model for the Second-Language Classroom. In: Shlomo Sharan, ed. *Handbook of Cooperative Learning Methods*. Westport, CT et al.: Greenwood, 193–208.

Böttger, Heiner, ed. (2012). *Englisch: Didaktik für die Grundschule*. Berlin: Cornelsen.

Burmeister, Petra (2006). Immersion und Sprachunterricht im Vergleich. In: Manfred Pienemann; Jörg-U. Keßler & Eckhard Roos, eds. *Englischerwerb in der Grundschule: Ein Studien- und Arbeitsbuch*. Paderborn: Schöningh, 197–216.

Butzkamm, Wolfgang (2012). *Lust zum Lehren, Lust zum Lernen: Eine neue Methodik für den Fremdsprachenunterricht*. 3rd ed. Tuebingen: Francke.

Canale, Michael (2013). From Communicative Competence to Communicative Language Pedagogy. In: Jack C. Richards & Richard W. Schmidt, eds. *Language and Communication*. 7th ed. London et al: Routledge, 2–27.

Canale, Michael & Merrill Swain (1980). Theoretical Bases of Communicative Approaches to Second Language Teaching and Testing. In: *Applied Linguistics* 1.1, 1–47.

Christiani, Reinhold & Gabriele Cwik, eds. (2008). *Englisch unterrichten in Klasse 1 und 2: Didaktische Grundlagen, methodische Konzepte, Beispiele und Hilfen*. Berlin: Cornelsen Scriptor.

Crookes, Graham (2011). Radical Language Teaching. In: Michael H. Long & Catherine J.

Doughty, eds. *The Handbook of Language Teaching*. Malden, MA: Wiley-Blackwell, 595–609.

Council of Europe (2001). *Common European Framework of Reference for Languages: Learning, Teaching, Assessment*. Cambridge: Cambridge University Press.

Dausend, Henriette (2013). Bilingual Modules 'My House – Our Town'. In: Daniela Elsner & Jörg-U. Keßler, eds. *Bilingual Education in Primary School: Aspects of Immersion, CLIL, and Bilingual Modules*. Tuebingen: Narr, 131–46.

Dewaele, Jean-Marc (2011). Reflections on the Emotional and Psychological Aspects of Foreign Language Learning and Use. In: *Anglistik* 22.1, 23–42.

Dörnyei, Zoltán (2004). Motivation. In Michael Byram, ed. *Routledge Encyclopedia of Language Teaching and Learning*. London: Routledge, 425–32.

Dörnyei, Zoltán (2010). The Relationship between Language Aptitude and Language Learning Motivation: Individual Differences from a Dynamic Systems Perspective. In: Ernesto Macaro, ed. *Continuum Companion to Second Language Acquisition*. London: Continuum, 247–67.

Dörnyei, Zoltán & Peter Skehan (2003). Individual Differences in Second Language Learning. In: Catherine J. Doughty & Michael H. Long, eds. *The Handbook of Second Language Acquisition*. Malden, MA: Blackwell, 589–630.

Edelenbos, Peter; Richard Johnstone & Angelika Kubanek (2006). *Languages for the Children of Europe: Published Research, Good Practice & Main Principles*. http://ec.europa.eu/languages/policy/language-policy/documents/young_en.pdf (7 December 2014).

Ellis, Rod (2003). *Task-based Language Learning and Teaching*. Oxford et al.: Oxford University Press.

Ellis, Rod (2012). *Language Teaching Research and Language Pedagogy*. Malden, MA: Wiley-Blackwell.

Elsner, Daniela & Jörg-U. Keßler (2013). Bilingual Approaches to Foreign Language Education in Primary School. In: Daniela Elsner & Jörg-U. Keßler, eds. *Bilingual Education in Primary School: Aspects of Immersion, CLIL, and Bilingual Modules*. Tuebingen: Narr, 16–27.

Genetsch, Martin; Wolfgang Hallet; Carola Surkamp & Harald Weisshaar (2012). *Cheap Children*: Individualisierung und Differenzierung mit einer Kompetenzaufgabe für Klasse 7 zu Kinderarbeit und Kinderrechten. In: Wolfgang Hallet & Ulrich Krämer, eds. *Kompetenzaufgaben im Englischunterricht: Grundlagen und Unterrichtsbeispiele*. Seelze-Velber: Klett/Kallmeyer, 98–112.

Grotjahn, Rüdiger & Torsten Schlak (2010). Lernalter. In: Wolfang Hallet & Frank G. Königs, eds. *Handbuch Fremdsprachendidaktik*. Seelze-Velber: Klett/Kallmeyer, 253–57.

Hallet, Wolfgang (2012). Die komplexe Kompetenzaufgabe: Fremdsprachliche Diskursfähigkeit als kulturelle Teilhabe und Unterrichtspraxis. In: Wolfgang Hallet & Ulrich Krämer, eds. *Kompetenzaufgaben im Englischunterricht: Grundlagen und Unterrichtsbeispiele*. Seelze-Velber: Klett/Kallmeyer, 8–19.

Harmer, Jeremy (2011). *The Practice of English Language Teaching*. 4th ed. Harlow: Pearson/Longman.

Haß, Frank (2008). *Red Line 3: Schülerbuch*. Stuttgart & Leipzig: Klett.

Hattie, John (2009). *Visible Learning: A Synthesis of over 800 Meta-Analyses Relating to Achievement*. London et al.: Routledge.

Hattie, John (2012). *Visible Learning for Teachers: Maximizing Impact on Learning*. London et al.: Routledge.

Hedge, Tricia (2007). *Teaching and Learning in the Language Classroom*. Oxford: Oxford University Press.

Heine, Lena (2010). Fremdsprache und konzeptuelle Repräsentation: Bilingualer Unterricht aus kognitiver Perspektive. In: Sabine Doff, ed. *Bilingualer Sachfachunterricht in der Sekundarstufe: Eine Einführung*. Tuebingen: Narr, 199–212.

Jäger, Astrid (2012). Basics: Grundsätze beachten. In: Heiner Böttger, ed. *Englisch: Didaktik für die Grundschule*. Berlin: Cornelsen, 198–208.

Janks, Hilary (2010). Critical Approaches to Teaching Language, Reading and Writing. In: Dominic Wyse; Richard Andrews & James V. Hoffman, eds. *The Routledge International Handbook of English Language and Literacy Teaching*. London: Routledge, 267–81.

Johnson, David W. & Roger T. Johnson (1994). Structuring Academic Controversy. In: Shlomo Sharan, ed. *Handbook of Cooperative Learning Methods*. Westport, CT: Greenwood, 66–79.

Keller, Stefan D. (2013). *Kompetenzorientierter Englischunterricht*. Berlin: Cornelsen Scriptor.

Keßler, Jörg-U. (2006a). *Englischerwerb im Anfangsunterricht diagnostizieren: Linguistische Profilanalysen am Übergang von der Primarstufe in die Sekundarstufe I*. Tuebingen: Narr.

Keßler, Jörg-U. (2006b). Englischerwerb im Anfangsunterricht der Primar- und der Sekundarstufe: Plädoyer für ein empirisch fundiertes Übergangsprofil. In: Manfred Pienemann; Jörg-U. Keßler & Eckhard Roos, eds. *Englischerwerb in der Grundschule: Ein Studien- und Arbeitsbuch*. Paderborn: Schöningh, 159–84.

Keßler, Jörg-U. & Gérald Schlemminger (2013). Babylonisches Sprachengewirr: Wie benennen wir unseren Untersuchungsgegenstand? In: Jan Hollm; Armin Hüttermann; Jörg-U. Keßler; Gérald Schlemminger & Benjamin Ade-Thurow, eds. (2013). *Bilinguales Lehren und Lernen in der Sekundarstufe I: Sprache, Sachfach und Schulorganisation*. Landau: Verlag Empirische Pädagogik, 15–26.

Kumaravadivelu, Balasubramanian (2006). *Understanding Language Teaching: From Method to Postmethod*. London: Lawrence Erlbaum Associates.

Lamsfuß-Schenk, Stefanie (2010). Inhalt und Sprache: Vom Einfluss des Fremdsprachengebrauchs auf das Lernen im Sachfach. In: Sabine Doff, ed. *Bilingualer Sachfachunterricht in der Sekundarstufe: Eine Einführung*. Tuebingen: Narr, 213–27.

Larsen-Freeman, Diane & Marti Anderson (2011). *Techniques & Principles in Language Teaching*. 3rd ed. Oxford et al.: Oxford University Press.

Legutke, Michael K. (2013). Lernwelt Klassenzimmer: Szenarien für einen handlungsorientierten Fremdsprachenunterricht. In: Gerhard Bach & Johannes-P. Timm, eds. *Englischunterricht: Grundlagen und Methoden einer handlungsorientierten Unterrichtspraxis*. 5th ed. Tuebingen: Francke, 91–120.

Lightbown, Patsy & Nina Spada (2006). *How Languages Are Learned.* 3rd ed. Oxford et al.: Oxford University Press.

Long, Michael H. (2011). Methodological Principles for Language Teaching. In: Michael H. Long & Catherine J. Doughty, eds. *The Handbook of Language Teaching.* Malden, MA et al.: Wiley-Blackwell, 373–94.

Mandler, George (1985). *Cognitive Psychology: An Essay in Cognitive Science.* Hillsdale: Lawrence Erlbaum.

Mayer, Nikola (2013). Wo Fremdsprachenlernen beginnt: Grundlagen und Arbeitsformen des Englischunterrichts in der Primarstufe. In: Gerhard Bach & Johannes-P. Timm, eds. *Englischunterricht: Grundlagen und Methoden einer handlungsorientierten Unterrichtspraxis.* 5th ed. Tuebingen: Francke, 61–90.

Mehisto, Peeter; David Marsh & María Jesús Frigols (2008). *Uncovering CLIL: Content and Language Integrated Learning in Bilingual and Multilingual Education.* Oxford: Macmillan.

Meyer, Hilbert (2014). *Was ist guter Unterricht?* 10th ed. Berlin: Cornelsen.

Mindt, Dieter & Gudrun Wagner (2009). *Innovativer Englischunterricht für die Klassen 1 und 2.* Braunschweig: Westermann.

Montijano Cabrera, Ma del Pilar (2012). Materials and Resources for CLIL Classrooms. In: Juan de Dios Martinez Agudo, ed. *Teaching and Learning English through Bilingual Education.* Newcastle upon Tyne: Cambridge Scholars, 111–48.

Müller-Hartmann, Andreas & Marita Schocker-von Ditfurth (2011). *Teaching English: Task-Supported Language Learning.* Paderborn: Schöningh.

Niemeier, Susanne (2005). Bilingualismus und 'bilinguale' Bildungsgänge aus kognitiv-linguistischer Sicht. In: Gerhard Bach & Susanne Niemeier, eds. *Bilingualer Unterricht: Grundlagen, Methoden, Praxis, Perspektiven.* 3rd ed. Frankfurt a. M.: Lang, 23–46.

Poarch, Gregory (2013). Some Thoughts on Bilingualism. In: Daniela Elsner & Jörg-U. Keßler, eds. *Bilingual Education in Primary School: Aspects of Immersion, CLIL, and Bilingual Modules.* Tuebingen: Narr, 7–15.

Reinfried, Marcus (2004). Audio-visual Language Teaching. In: Michael Byram, ed. *Routledge Encyclopedia of Language Teaching and Learning.* London et al.: Routledge, 61–64.

Riemer, Claudia (2010). Motivation. In: Wolfang Hallet & Frank G. Königs, eds. *Handbuch Fremdsprachendidaktik.* Seelze-Velber: Klett/Kallmeyer, 168–73.

Schlak, Torsten (2010). Sprachlerneignung. In: Wolfang Hallet & Frank G. Königs, eds. *Handbuch Fremdsprachendidaktik.* Seelze-Velber: Klett/Kallmeyer, 257–61.

Schmid-Schönbein, Gisela (2008). *Didaktik und Methodik für den Englischunterricht. Kompakter Überblick: Ziele – Inhalte – Verfahren für die Klassen 1 bis 4.* Berlin: Cornelsen Scriptor.

Schwarz, Hellmut, ed. (2006). *English G21, A1: Handreichungen für den Unterricht mit Kopiervorlagen.* Berlin: Cornelsen.

Spada, Nina (2007). Communicative Language Teaching: Current Status and Future Prospects. In: Jim Cummins & Chris Davison, eds. *International Handbook of English Language Teaching.* New York: Springer, 271–88.

Spiro, Jane (2013). *Changing Methodologies for TESOL*. Edinburgh: Edinburgh University Press.

Summer, Theresa (2012). From Method to Postmethod. In: Maria Eisenmann & Theresa Summer, eds. *Basic Issues in EFL Teaching and Learning*. Heidelberg: Winter, 1–15.

Ushioda, Ema & Szu-An Chen (2011). Researching Motivation and Possible Selves among Learners of English: The Need to Integrate Qualitative Inquiry. In: *Anglistik* 22.1, 43–61.

Wagner, Ute (2009). *Übergang Englisch: Fallanalysen zum Wechsel von der Grundschule zur weiterführenden Schule*. Tuebingen: Narr.

Widdowson, Henry G. (2012). Closing the Gap, Changing the Subject. In: Julia Hüttner; Barbara Mehlmauer-Larcher; Susanne Reichl & Barbara Schiftner, eds. *Theory and Practice in EFL Teacher Education: Bridging the Gap*. Bristol et al.: Multilingual Matters, 3–15.

Zydatiß, Wolfgang (2010). Die Überprüfung fächerübergreifender transferfähiger Diskurskompetenzen im bilingualen Sachfachunterricht. In Sabine Doff, ed. *Bilingualer Sachfachunterricht in der Sekundarstufe: Eine Einführung*. Tuebingen: Narr, 258–72.

References unit 5

Bleyhl, Werner & Johannes-P. Timm (2007). Wortschatz und Grammatik im Kontext. In: Johannes-P. Timm, ed. *Englisch lernen und lehren: Didaktik des Englischunterrichts*. Berlin: Cornelsen, 259–71.

Brandl, Klaus (2008). *Communicative Language Teaching in Action: Putting Principles to Work*. Upper Saddle River, NJ: Prentice Hall.

Browne, Charles; Brent Culligan & Joe Phillips (2013). *A New General Service List*. http://www.newgeneralservicelist.org (26 August 2014).

Cherrington, Ruth (2000). Interlanguage. In: Michael Byram, ed. *Routledge Encyclopedia of Language Teaching and Learning*. London et al.: Routledge, 307–09.

Council of Europe (2001). *Common European Framework of Reference for Languages: Learning, Teaching, Assessment*. Cambridge: Cambridge University Press.

Coxhead, Averil (2010). *Academic Word List*. http://www.victoria.ac.nz/lals/resources/academicwordlist (26 August 2014).

De Bot, Kees (2000). Mental Lexicon. In: Michael Byram, ed. *Routledge Encyclopedia of Language Teaching and Learning*. London et al.: Routledge, 407–10.

Doughty, Catherine J. & Jessica Williams (1998). Issues and Terminology. In: Catherine J. Doughty & Jessica Williams, eds. *Focus on Form in Classroom Second Language Acquisition*. Cambridge et al.: Cambridge University Press, 1–11.

Doughty, Catherine J. & Michael H. Long (2003). Optimal Psycholinguistic Environments for Distance Foreign Language Learning. In: *Language Learning & Technology* 7.3, 50–80.

Doyé, Peter (1985). *Systematische Wortschatzvermittlung im Englischunterricht*. 7th ed. Hanover: Schroedel et al.

Ellis, Nick C. (2007). The Weak-Interface, Consciousness, and Form-focused Instruction: Mind the Doors. In: Sandra Fotos & Hossein Nassaji, eds. *Form-focused Instruction and Teacher Education: Studies in Honour of Rod Ellis*. Oxford et al.: Oxford University Press, 17–33.

Ellis, Rod (2002). The Place of Grammar Instruction in the Second/Foreign Language Curriculum. In: Eli Hinkel & Sandra Fotos, eds. *New Perspectives on Grammar Teaching in Second Language Classrooms*. Mahwah, NJ et al.: Lawrence Erlbaum, 17–34.

Ellis, Rod (2006). Current Issues in the Teaching of Grammar: An SLA Perspective. In: *TESOL Quarterly* 40.1, 83–107.

Gass, Susan M. (2013). *Second Language Acquisition: An Introductory Course*. 4th ed. New York et al.: Routledge.

Grimm, Nancy & Olesya Riecken (2014). What's the Weather Like? Oder: Weather Reports With Fun. In: *Praxis Schule 5–10* 6, 21–27.

Haß, Frank; Werner Kieweg; Margitta Kutty; Andreas Müller-Hartmann & Harald Weisshaar (2008). *Fachdidaktik Englisch: Tradition, Innovation, Praxis*. Stuttgart: Klett.

Hutz, Matthias (2012). Storing Words in the Mind: The Mental Lexicon and Vocabulary Learning. In: Maria Eisenmann & Theresa Summer, eds. *Basic Issues in EFL Teaching and Learning*. Heidelberg: Winter, 105–17.

Jentges, Sabine (2009). Sprachlernspiele: Mit Spielen Sprachen lernen. In: Udo O. H. Jung, ed. *Praktische Handreichung für Fremdsprachenlehrer*. 5th ed. Frankfurt a. M. et al.: Lang, 94–99.

Keßler, Jörg-U. (2006). *Englischerwerb im Anfangsunterricht diagnostizieren: Linguistische Profilanalysen am Übergang von der Primarstufe in die Sekundarstufe I*. Tuebingen: Narr, 2006.

Keßler, Jörg-U. & Mathias Liebner (2011). Diagnosing L2 Development: Rapid Profile. In: Manfred Pienemann & Jörg-U. Keßler, eds. *Studying Processability Theory: An Introductory Textbook*. Amsterdam: John Benjamins, 133–47.

Keßler, Jörg-U. & Anja Plesser (2011). *Teaching Grammar*. Paderborn: Schöningh.

Kilp, Elóide (2010). *Spiele für den Fremdsprachenunterricht: Aspekte einer Spielandragogik*. 2nd ed. Tuebingen: Stauffenburg.

Larsen-Freeman, Diane (2011). Teaching and Testing Grammar. In: Michael H. Long & Catherine J. Doughty, eds. *The Handbook of Language Teaching*. Malden, MA et al.: Wiley-Blackwell, 518–42.

Laufer, Batia & Zahava Goldstein (2004). Testing Vocabulary Knowledge: Size, Strength, and Computer Adaptiveness. In: *Language Learning* 54.3, 399–436.

Lenzing, Anke (2008). Teachability and Learnability: An Analysis of Primary School Textbooks. In: Jörg-U. Keßler, ed. *Processabilty Approaches to Second Language Development and Second Language Learning*. Newcastle upon Tyne: Cambridge Scholars, 221–41.

Levelt, Willem J. M. (1994). The Skill of Speaking. In: Paul Bertelson, Paul Eelen & Géry D'Ydewalle, eds. *International Perspectives on Psychological Science*. Vol. 1. Hove: Lawrence Erlbaum, 89–104.

Lightbown, Patsy & Nina Spada (2006). *How Languages Are Learned*. 3rd ed. Oxford: Oxford University Press.

Long, Michael H. (1991). Focus on Form: A Design Feature in Language Teaching Methodology. In: Kees De Bot; Ralph B. Ginsberg & Claire Kramsch, eds. *Foreign Language Research in Cross-Cultural Perspective*. Amsterdam et al.: Benjamins, 39–54.

Long, Michael H., ed. (2005). *Second Language Needs Analysis*. Cambridge et al.: Cambridge University Press.

Nation, Paul (1990). *Teaching and Learning Vocabulary*. New York: Newbury House.

Nation, Paul (2008). *Teaching Vocabulary: Strategies and Techniques*. Boston, MA et al.: Heinle.

Nation, Paul (2012). Introduction: Teaching Vocabulary. In: Maria Eisenmann & Theresa Summer, eds. *Basic Issues in EFL Teaching and Learning*. Heidelberg: Winter, 93–104.

Nation, Paul & Teresa Chung (2011). Teaching and Testing Vocabulary. In: Michael H. Long & Catherine J. Doughty, eds. *The Handbook of Language Teaching*. Malden, MA et al.: Wiley-Blackwell, 543–59.

Neveling, Christiane (2010). Wortschatz und Wortschatzvermittlung. In: Carola Surkamp, ed. *Metzler Lexikon Fremdsprachendidaktik*. Stuttgart et al.: Metzler, 331–35.

Parkes, Geoff (2003). *The Mistakes Clinic for German-speaking Learners of English: Error Correction Exercises and Detailed Error Analysis for German-speaking Students and Teachers of English*. Southampton: England Books.

Pienemann, Manfred (1998). *Language Processing and Second Language Development: Processability Theory*. Amsterdam et al.: Benjamins.

Pienemann, Manfred, (2005). An Introduction to Processability Theory. In: Manfred Pienemann, ed. *Cross-Linguistic Aspects of Processablity Theory*. Amsterdam et al.: Benjamins.

Pienemann, Manfred (2008). A Brief Introduction to Processability Theory. In: Jörg-U. Keßler, ed. *Processability Approaches to Second Language Development and Second Language Learning*. Newcastle upon Tyne: Cambridge Scholars, 9–29.

Piepho, Hans-Eberhard (1974). *Kommunikative Kompetenz als übergeordnetes Lernziel im Englischunterricht*. Dornburg-Frickhofen: Frankonius.

Quetz, Jürgen (2007). Der systematische Aufbau eines "mentalen Lexikons". In: Johannes-P. Timm, ed. *Englisch lernen und lehren: Didaktik des Englischunterrichts*. Berlin: Cornelsen, 272–90.

Reinisch, Katrin (2013). Wortschatzarbeit im Englischunterricht. In: Senatsverwaltung für Bildung, Jugend und Wissenschaft, ed. *Sprachsensibler Fachunterricht: Handreichung zur Wortschatzarbeit in den Jahrgangsstufen 5–10 unter besonderer Berücksichtigung der Fachsprache*. Ludwigsfelde-Struveshof: LISUM, 96–122.

Rodríguez-Bonces, Mónica & Jeisson Rodríguez-Bonces (2010). Task-Based Language Learning: Old Approach, New Style. A New Lesson to Learn. In: *Profile Issues in Teachers' Professional Development* 12.2, 165–78.

Savignon, Sandra J. (2002). Communicative Language Teaching: Linguistic Theory and Classroom Practice. In: Sandra J. Savignon, ed. *Interpreting Communicative Language Teaching: Contexts and Concerns in Teacher Education*. New Haven, CT et al.: Yale University Press, 1–27.

Schwarz, Hellmut, ed. (2013). *English G 21: A1 – für Gymnasien*. Berlin: Cornelsen.

Selinker, Larry (1972). Interlanguage. In: *International Review of Applied Linguistics in Language Teaching* 10.3, 209–32.

Stork, Antje (2003). *Vokabellernen: Eine Untersuchung zur Effizienz von Vokabellernstrategien.* Tuebingen: Narr.

Swan, Michael & Bernard Smith, eds. (2013). *Learner English: A Teacher's Guide to Interference and Other Problems.* 2nd ed. Cambridge et al.: Cambridge University Press.

Thornbury, Scott (2002). *How to Teach Vocabulary.* Harlow: Longman.

Timmis, Ivor (2012). Introduction: Teaching Grammar. In: Maria Eisenmann & Theresa Summer, eds. *Basic Issues in EFL Teaching and Learning.* Heidelberg: Winter, 119–30.

Tonks, Robert (2011). *It Is Not All English What Shines: English Makes German Werbung Funny!* Borsdorf: Winterwork.

Tonks, Robert (2012). *Denglisch in Pool Position: English Makes German Werbung Funny!* 2. Borsdorf: Winterwork.

Tonks, Robert (2013). *The Denglisch Doosh Reader: 4 the Bad & Worse.* Borsdorf: Winterwork.

Turton, Nigel J. & John B. Heaton (2004). *Longman Dictionary of Common Errors.* 2nd ed. Harlow et al.: Longman.

Van den Branden, Kris (2006). Introduction: Task-Based Language Teaching in a Nutshell. In: Kris Van den Branden, ed. *Task-Based Language Education: From Theory to Practice.* Cambridge et al.: Cambridge University Press, 1–16.

West, Michael, ed. (1953). *A General Service List of English Words.* London et al.: Longman.

Ziegésar, Detlef von & Margaret von Ziegésar (2007). Die systematische Einführung von Grammatik. In: Johannes-P. Timm, ed. *Englisch lernen und lehren: Didaktik des Englischunterrichts.* Berlin: Cornelsen, 291–98.

Ziegésar, Detlef von & Margaret von Ziegésar (2009). *Einführung von Grammatik im Englischunterricht: Materialien und Modelle.* 2nd ed. Munich: Oldenbourg.

References unit 6

Arendt, Manfred (1999). Entrümpelung des Methodenrepertoires. In: *Fremdsprachenunterricht* 43.52, 401–08.

Argyle, Michael (1975). *Bodily Communication.* New York: International Universities Press.

Banton Smith, Nila (2002). *American Reading Instruction.* Newark: International Reading Association.

Bartosch, Roman & Andreas Rohde, eds. (2014). *Im Dialog der Disziplinen: Englischdidaktik – Förderdidaktik – Inklusion.* Trier: WVT.

Bland, Janice (2012). Within and between Texts – Indeterminacy and Empowerment. In: Marcus Reinfried & Laurenz Volkmann, eds. *Medien im neokommunikativen Fremdsprachenunterricht. Einsatzformen, Inhalte, Lernerkompetenzen.* Frankfurt a. M.: Peter Lang, 141–54.

Börner, Otfried; Christoph Edelhoff & Christa Lohmann, eds. (2010). *Individualisierung und Differenzierung im kommunikativen Englischunterricht.* Braunschweig: Diesterweg.

Borras, Laurence; Maria Boucherie; Sylvia Mohr; Tania Lecomte; Nader Perroud & Philippe Huguelet (2009). Increasing Self-esteem: Efficacy of a Group Intervention for Individuals with Severe Mental Disorders. In: *European Psychiatry* 24.5, 307–16.

Bowler, Bill & Sue Parminter (2002). Mixed-level Teaching: Tiered Tasks and Biased Tasks. In: Jack C. Richards & Willy A. Renandya, eds. *Methodology in Language Teaching: An Anthology of Current Practice*. Cambridge: Cambridge University Press, 59–64.

Booth, Tony & Mel Ainscow (2002). *Index for Inclusion: Developing Learning and Participation in School*. Bristol: CSIE.

Bundesministerium für Arbeit und Soziales (2011). *Unser Weg in eine inklusive Gesellschaft: Der nationale Aktionsplan der Bundesregierung zur Umsetzung der UN-Behindertenrechtskonvention*. http://www.bmas.de/DE/Service/Publikationen/a740-aktionsplan-bundesregierung.html (20 December 2014).

Bygate, Martin (2011). Teaching and Testing Speaking. In: Michael H. Long & Catherine J. Doughty, eds. *The Handbook of Language Teaching*. Malden, MA: Wiley-Blackwell, 412–40.

Byram, Michael (1997). *Teaching and Assessing Intercultural Communicative Competence*. Clevedon et al.: Multilingual Matters.

Cohen, Andrew D. (1998). *Strategies in Learning and Using a Second Language*. London: Longman.

Council of Europe (2001). *Common European Framework of Reference for Languages: Learning, Teaching, Assessment*. Cambridge: Cambridge University Press.

Dam, Leni (1995). *Learner Autonomy 3: From Theory to Classroom Practice*. Dublin: Authentik.

Dam, Leni & Lienhard Legenhausen (2013). Learner Autonomy – A Possible Answer to Inclusion. In: Maria Eisenmann & Margit Hempel, eds. *Medien und Interkulturalität im Fremdsprachenunterricht: Zwischen Autonomie, Kollaboration und Konstruktion*. Duisburg: Universitätsverlag Rhein-Ruhr, 115–32.

Eisenmann, Maria (2012). Introduction: Heterogeneity and Differentiation. In: Maria Eisenmann & Theresa Summer, eds. *Basic Issues in EFL Teaching and Learning*. Heidelberg: Winter, 297–311.

Felder, Richard M. & Eunice R. Henriques (1995). Learning and Teaching Styles in Foreign and Second Language Education. In: *Foreign Language Annals* 28.1, 21–31.

Field, John (2002). The Changing Face of Listening. In: Jack C. Richards & Willy A. Renandya, eds. *Methodology in Language Teaching: An Anthology of Current Practice*. Cambridge et al.: Cambridge University Press, 242–47.

Friedrich, Helmut F. & Heinz Mandl (1992). Lern- und Denkstrategien: Ein Problemaufriss. In: Heinz Mandl & Helmut F. Friedrich, eds. *Lern- und Denkstrategien: Analyse und Intervention*. Goettingen et al.: Hogreve, 3–54.

Grabe, William (2011). Teaching and Testing Reading. In: Michael H. Long & Catherine J. Doughty, eds. *The Handbook of Language Teaching*. Malden, MA: Wiley-Blackwell, 441–62.

Hallet, Wolfgang & Andreas Müller-Hartmann (2006). For better or for worse? Bildungsstandards Englisch im Überblick. In: *Der fremdsprachliche Unterricht Englisch* 40.81, 2–11.

Haß, Frank (2008). Keiner wie der andere: Im differenzierenden Unterricht Lernprozesse individualisieren. In: *Der fremdsprachliche Unterricht Englisch* 42.94, 2–9.

Hattie, John (2009). *Visible Learning: A Synthesis of over 800 Meta-Analyses Relating to Achievement.* London et al.: Routledge.

Haudeck, Helga (2007). Lernstrategien und Lerntechniken für Schüler. In: Johannes-P. Timm, ed. *Englisch lernen und lehren: Didaktik des Englischunterrichts.* Berlin: Cornelsen, 342–51.

Henseler, Roswitha & Carola Surkamp (2007). Leselust statt Lesefrust: Lesemotivation in der Fremdsprache Englisch fördern. In: *Der fremdsprachliche Unterricht Englisch* 89, 2–10.

Hermes, Liesel (2007). Leseverstehen. In: Johannes-P. Timm, ed. *Englisch lernen und lehren: Didaktik des Englischunterrichts.* Berlin: Cornelsen, 229–36.

Kielhöfer, Bernd (1994). Wörter lernen, behalten und erinnern. In: *Neusprachliche Mitteilungen aus Wissenschaft und Praxis* 47.4, 211–20.

Klippert, Heinz (2010). *Heterogenität im Klassenzimmer: Wie Lehrkräfte effektiv und zeitsparend damit umgehen können.* Weinheim et al.: Beltz.

Küster, Lutz (2014). Zur Einführung in den Themenschwerpunkt. In: *Fremdsprachen Lehren und Lernen* 43.2, 3–11.

Müller, Frank (2012). *Differenzierung in heterogenen Lernergruppen: Praxisband für die Sekundarstufe I.* Schwalbach: Debus Pädagogik.

Nunan, David (2002). Listening in Language Learning. In: Jack C. Richards & Willy A. Renandya, eds. *Methodology in Language Teaching: An Anthology of Current Practice.* Cambridge et al.: Cambridge University Press, 238–41.

O'Malley, J. Michael & Anna Uhl Chamot (1996). *Learning Strategies in Second Language Acquisition.* Cambridge et al.: Cambridge University Press.

Oomen-Welke, Ingelore (2004). Körpersprachen und Extrasprachliches verschiedener Kulturen in Welt, Schule und Unterricht. In: Heinz S. Rosenbusch & Otto Schober, eds. *Körpersprache und Pädagogik: Das Handbuch.* Baltmannsweiler: Schneider Verlag Hohengehren, 68–98.

Osel, Johann (2012). Revolution fürs Klassenzimmer. http://www.sueddeutsche.de/bildung/behinderte-im-regelunterricht-revolution-fuers-klassenzimmer-1.1543889 (29 December 2014).

Oxford, Rebecca L. (1990). *Language Learning Strategies: What Every Teacher Should Know.* Boston, MA: Heinle & Heinle.

Oxford, Rebecca L. (2002). Language Learning Strategies in a Nutshell: Update and ESL Suggestions. In: Jack C. Richards & Willy A. Renandya, eds. *Methodology in Language Teaching: An Anthology of Current Practice.* Cambridge et al.: Cambridge University Press, 124–32.

Polio, Charlene & Jessica Williams (2011). Teaching and Testing Writing. In: Michael H. Long & Catherine J. Doughty, eds. *The Handbook of Language Teaching.* Malden, MA: Wiley-Blackwell, 486–517.

Rampillon, Ute (2007). Lerntechniken. In: Karl-Richard Bausch; Herbert Christ & Hans-Jürgen Krumm, eds. *Handbuch Fremdsprachenunterricht* 5th ed. Tuebingen: Francke, 340–44.

Rampillon, Ute (1991). Fremdsprachenlernen – gewusst wie. In: *Der fremdsprachliche Unterricht Englisch* 25.2, 2–9.

Reid, Joy M. (1998). *Understanding Learning Styles in the Second Language Classroom.* Upper Saddle River, NJ: Prentice Hall.

Rivers, Wilga M. (1981). *Teaching Foreign-Language Skills.* 2nd ed. Chicago: Chicago University Press.

Rosenberg, Marjorie (2013). *Spotlight on Learning Styles: Teacher Strategies for Learner Success.* Peaslake: Delta Publishing.

Schubert, Christoph (2006). Politeness Rules: Pragmatic Approaches to Intercultural Competence in the EFL Classroom. In: Werner Delanoy & Laurenz Volkmann, eds. *Cultural Studies in the EFL Classroom.* Heidelberg: Winter, 195–209.

Seow, Anthony (2002). The Writing Process and Process Writing. In: Jack C. Richards & Willy A. Renandya, eds. *Methodology in Language Teaching: An Anthology of Current Practice.* Cambridge et al.: Cambridge University Press, 315–20.

Shumin, Kang (2002). Factors to Consider: Developing EFL Students' Speaking Abilities. In: Jack C. Richards & Willy A. Renandya, eds. *Methodology in Language Teaching: An Anthology of Current Practice.* Cambridge et al.: Cambridge University Press, 204–11.

The Examination Office for TELC – The European Language Certificates (2002). *The ABC of the Common European Reference for Languages (CEFR): A Brief Introduction for Teachers and Learners.* DVD.

Tillmann, Klaus-Jürgen (2007). Kann man in heterogenen Lerngruppen alle Schülerinnen und Schüler fördern? Der Blick der Bildungsforschung in das Regelschulsystem. http://bildungsserver.berlin-brandenburg.de/fileadmin/bbb/schulqualitaet/lehren_und_lernen/schulanfang/tillmann07heterogenitaet_selektion_auch_GSOR071230__1_.pdf (20 December 2014).

UNESCO (2005). *Guidelines for Inclusion: Ensuring Access to Education for All.* Paris: UNESCO.

Vandergrift, Larry & Christine Goh (2011). Teaching and Testing Listening Comprehension. In: Michael H. Long & Catherine J. Doughty, eds. *The Handbook of Language Teaching.* Malden, MA: Wiley-Blackwell, 395–411.

Viebrock, Britta (2010). Lernertypen. In: Carola Surkamp, ed. *Metzler Lexikon Fremdsprachendidaktik. Ansätze – Methoden – Grundbegriffe.* Stuttgart: Metzler, 186–88.

Weskamp, Ralf (2001). *Fachdidaktik: Grundlagen & Konzepte.* Berlin: Cornelsen.

References unit 7

Anderson, Benedict (1983). *Imagined Communities: Reflections on the Origin and Spread of Nationalism.* London et al.: Verso.

Assmann, Aleida (2006). *Einführung in die Kulturwissenschaft: Grundbegriffe, Themen, Fragestellungen.* Berlin: Erich Schmidt Verlag.

Blell, Gabriele & Sabine Doff (2014). It Takes More than Two for This Tango: Moving Beyond the Self/Other-Binary in Teaching about Culture in the Global EFL-Classroom. In: *Zeitschrift für Interkulturellen Fremdsprachenunterricht* 19.1, 77–96.

Bredella, Lothar (2010). *Das Verstehen des Anderen: Kulturwissenschaftliche und literatur-didaktische Studien*. Tuebingen: Narr.

Byram, Michael (1997). *Teaching and Assessing Intercultural Communicative Competence*. Clevedon et al.: Multilingual Matters.

Byram, Michael (2000). Learning English without a Culture? The Case of English as a Lingua Franca. In: Lothar Bredella; Franz-Joseph Meißner; Ansgar Nünning & Dietmar Rösler, eds. *Wie ist Fremdverstehen lehr- und lernbar?* Tuebingen: Narr, 1–17.

Cates, Kip A. (2002). Teaching for a Better World: Global Issues and Language Education. In: *Human Rights Education in Asian Schools* 1. http://www.hurights.or.jp/archives/human_rights_education_in_asian_schools/section2/2002/03/teaching-for-a-better-world-global-issues-and-language-education.html (25 January 2015).

Coperías-Aguilar, Maria José (2007). Dealing with Intercultural Communicative Competence in the Foreign Language Classroom. In: Eva Alcón Soler & Maria Pilar Safont Jorda, eds. *Intercultural Language Learning and Language Use*. Dordrecht: Springer, 58–78.

Delanoy, Werner (2005). A Dialogic Model for Literature Teaching. In: *ABAC Journal* 25.1, 53–66.

Delanony, Werner (2015). Literature Teaching and Learning. Theory and Practice. In: Werner Delanoy; Maria Eisenmann & Frauke Matz, eds. *Learning with Literature in the EFL Classroom*. Heidelberg: Winter, 19–48.

Delanoy, Werner & Laurenz Volkmann, eds. (2006). *Cultural Studies in the EFL Classroom*. Heidelberg: Winter.

Eisenmann, Maria; Nancy Grimm & Laurenz Volkmann, eds. (2010). *Teaching the New English Cultures and Literatures*. Heidelberg: Winter.

Freese, Peter (2002). The Chances and Limits of 'Intercultural Understanding' in the Advanced EFL-Classroom. In: *Teaching 'America': Selected Essays*. Munich: Langenscheidt-Longman, 11–30.

Gibson, Robert (1994). The Intercultural Dimension: Hidden Differences between British Culture and Other Cultures. In: *Fremdsprachenunterricht* 38.2, 127–129.

Gibson, Robert (2000). *Intercultural Business Communication: Fachsprache Englisch*. Berlin: Cornelsen.

Hallet, Wolfgang (2002). *Fremdsprachenunterricht als Spiel der Texte und Kulturen: Intertextualität als Paradigma einer kulturwissenschaftlichen Didaktik*. Trier: WVT.

Hammer, Julia (2012). *Die Auswirkungen der Globalisierung auf den modernen Fremdsprachenunterricht: Globale Herausforderungen als Lernziele und Inhalte des fortgeschrittenen Englischunterrichts – Are We Facing the Future?* Heidelberg: Winter.

Harris, Philip R. & Robert T. Moran (1993). *Managing Cultural Differences*. 3rd ed. Houston, TX: Gulf Publishing.

Jandt, Fred E. (1998). *Intercultural Communication: An Introduction*. 2nd ed. Thousand Oaks, CA et al.: Sage.

Kramsch, Claire (1998). *Language and Culture*. Oxford et al.: Oxford University Press.

Lippmann, Walter (1922). *Public Opinion*. New York: Harcourt, Brace.

Mayer, Sylvia & Graham Wilson, eds. (2006). *Ecodidactic Perspectives on English Language, Literatures and Cultures*. Trier: WVT.

Nünning, Vera & Ansgar Nünning (2000). British Cultural Studies konkret: 10 Leitkonzepte für einen innovativen Kulturunterricht. In: *Der fremdsprachliche Unterricht Englisch* 43.1, 4–9.

Outsourced (2006). Dir. John Jeffcoat. ShadowCatcher Entertainment.

Straub, Jürgen; Steffi Nothnagel & Arne Weidemann (2010). Interkulturelle Kompetenz lehren: Begriffe und theoretische Voraussetzungen. In: Arne Weidemann; Jürgen Straub & Steffi Nothnagel, eds. *Wie lehrt man interkulturelle Kompetenz? Theorien, Methoden und Praxis in der Hochschulausbildung. Ein Handbuch*. Bielefeld: Transcript, 15–27.

Teske, Doris (2006). Cultural Studies: Key Issues and Approaches. In: Werner Delanoy & Laurenz Volkmann, eds. *Cultural Studies in the EFL Classroom*. Heidelberg: Winter, 23–33.

The New London Group (2000). A Pedagogy of Multiliteracies: Designing Social Futures. In: Bill Cope & Mary Kalantzis, eds. *Multiliteracies: Literacy Learning and the Design of Social Futures*. London et al.: Routledge, 9–37.

Thomas, Alexander (2005). *Grundlagen der interkulturellen Psychologie*. Nordhausen: Bautz.

Volkmann, Laurenz (2010). *Fachdidaktik Englisch: Kultur und Sprache*. Tuebingen: Narr.

Volkmann, Laurenz (2011a). The 'Transcultural Moment' in English as a Foreign Language. In: Sabine Doff & Frank Schulze-Engler, eds. *Beyond 'Other Cultures': Transcultural Perspectives on Teaching the New Literatures in English*. Trier: WVT, 113–28.

Volkmann, Laurenz (2011b). Intercultural Learning and Postcolonial Studies: 'Never the Twain Shall Meet'? In: Maria Eisenmann & Theresa Summer, eds. *Basic Issues in EFL Teaching and Learning*. Heidelberg: Winter, 191–204.

Volkmann, Laurenz (2012). Ecodidactics als Antwort auf die planetare Bedrohung? Zum Einsatz von *ecopoetry* im Englischunterricht. In: Rüdiger Ahrens; Maria Eisenmann & Julia Hammer, eds. *Literatur im Interkulturellen Kontext – Zukunftsperspektiven für den Englischunterricht*. Heidelberg: Winter, 393–408.

Volkmann, Laurenz (2014). Die Abkehr vom Differenzdenken: Transkulturelles Lernen und *global education*. In: Frauke Matz; Michael Rogge & Philipp Siepmann, eds. *Transkulturelles Lernen im Fremdsprachenunterricht: Theorie und Praxis*. Frankfurt a. M.: Lang, 7–51.

Volkmann, Laurenz; Klaus Stierstorfer & Wolfgang Gehring, eds. (2002). *Interkulturelle Kompetenz. Konzepte und Praxis des Unterrichts*. Tuebingen: Narr.

Volkmann, Laurenz; Nancy Grimm; Katrin Lorenz & Ines Detmers, eds. (2010). *Local Natures, Global Responsibilities: Ecocritical Perspectives on the New English Literatures*. Amsterdam: Rodopi.

Welsch, Wolfgang (1999). Transculturality: The Puzzling Form of Cultures Today. In: Mike Featherstone & Scott Lash, eds. *Spaces of Culture: City, Nation, World*. London et al.: Sage, 194–213.

References unit 8

Ahrens, Rüdiger (2013). Introduction: Teaching Literature. In: Maria Eisenmann & Theresa Summer, eds. *Basic Issues in EFL Teaching and Learning*. 2nd ed. Heidelberg: Winter, 181–90.

Albers, Carsten (2015). Poetry in the Intermediate EFL Classroom. In: Werner Delanoy; Maria Eisenmann & Frauke Matz, eds. *Learning with Literature in the EFL Classroom*. Frankfurt a. M.: Lang, 103–20.

Allen, Constance & David Prebenna (2007). *Rise and Shine!* Franklin, TN: Dalmatian.

Antor, Heinz, ed. (2006). *Inter- und transkulturelle Studien: Theoretische Grundlagen und interdisziplinäre Praxis*. Heidelberg: Winter.

Ashford, Stephanie et al. (2009). American Truths. In: Stephanie Ashford et al. *Green Line; Oberstufe Rheinland-Pfalz, Saarland*. Stuttgart et al.: Klett, 148–63.

Bieri, Peter (2012). Wie wäre es, gebildet zu sein? In: Heiner Hastedt, ed. *Was ist Bildung? Eine Textanthologie*. Stuttgart: Reclam, 228–40.

Bland, Janice (2015). Performing Poems in the Primary School. In: Werner Delanoy; Maria Eisenmann & Frauke Matz, eds. *Learning with Literature in the EFL Classroom*. Frankfurt a. M.: Lang, 85–102.

Blau, Sheridan D. (2003). *The Literature Workshop: Teaching Texts and Their Readers*. Portsmouth, NH: Heinemann.

Bredella, Lothar (2004a). Unterschiedliche Verstehensformen bei der Rezeption literarischer Texte. In: Lothar Bredella & Eva Burwitz-Melzer, eds. *Rezeptionsästhetische Literaturdidaktik: Mit Beispielen aus dem Fremdsprachenunterricht Englisch*. Tuebingen: Narr, 81–138.

Bredella, Lothar (2004b). Interkulturelles Verstehen mit multikulturellen Bildungsromanen. In: Lothar Bredella & Eva Burwitz-Melzer, eds. *Rezeptionsästhetische Literaturdidaktik: Mit Beispielen aus dem Fremdsprachenunterricht Englisch*. Tuebingen: Narr, 139–200.

Bredella, Lothar (2004c). Literaturdidaktik im Dialog mit Literaturunterricht und Literaturwissenschaft. In: Lothar Bredella; Werner Delanoy & Carola Surkamp, eds. *Literaturdidaktik im Dialog*. Tuebingen: Narr, 21–64.

Bredella, Lothar (2007). Bildung als Interaktion zwischen literarischen Texten und Leser/innen: Zur Begründung der rezeptionsästhetischen Literaturdidaktik. In: Wolfgang Hallet & Ansgar Nünning, eds. *Neue Ansätze und Konzepte der Literatur- und Kulturdidaktik*. Trier: WVT, 49–68.

Bredella, Lothar (2010). *Das Verstehen des Anderen: Kulturwissenschaftliche und literaturdidaktische Studien*. Tuebingen: Narr.

Bredella, Lothar & Eva Burwitz-Melzer, eds. (2004). *Rezeptionsästhetische Literaturdidaktik: Mit Beispielen aus dem Fremdsprachenunterricht Englisch*. Tuebingen: Narr.

Bredella, Lothar & Wolfgang Hallet, eds. (2007). *Literaturunterricht, Kompetenzen und Bildung*. Trier: WVT.

Brosch, Renate (2007). *Short Story: Textsorte und Leseerfahrung*. Trier: WVT.

Burwitz-Melzer, Eva (2003). *Allmähliche Annäherungen: Fiktionale Texte im interkulturellen Fremdsprachenunterricht der Sekundarstufe I*. Tuebingen: Narr.

314

Burwitz-Melzer, Eva (2007). Ein Lesekompetenzmodell für den fremdsprachlichen Literatur-unterricht. In: Lothar Bredella & Wolfgang Hallet, eds. *Literaturunterricht, Kompetenzen und Bildung*. Trier: WVT, 127–57.

Carle, Eric (1969/1994). *The Very Hungry Caterpillar*. New York: Philomel Books.

Cisneros, Sandra (1984/2013). *The House on Mango Street*. New York: Vintage.

Davis, Kiri (2012) *A Girl Like Me*. https://www.youtube.com/watch?v=EivX77ORIls (15 January 2015).

Decke-Cornill, Helene (2007). Literaturdidaktik in einer 'Pädagogik der Anerkennung': *Gender* and Other Suspects. In: Wolfgang Hallet & Ansgar Nünning, eds. *Neue Ansätze und Konzepte der Literatur- und Kulturdidaktik*. Trier: WVT, 239–58.

Delanoy, Werner (2002). *Fremdsprachlicher Literaturunterricht: Theorie und Praxis als Dialog*. Tuebingen: Narr.

Delanoy, Werner (2007). Literaturdidaktik als Zusammenspiel von Rezeptionsästhetik und *Task-Based Learning*. In: Wolfgang Hallet & Ansgar Nünning, eds. *Neue Ansätze und Konzepte der Literatur- und Kulturdidaktik*. Trier: WVT, 107–21.

Delanoy, Werner (2015). Literature Teaching and Learning: Theory and Practice. In: Werner Delanoy; Maria Eisenmann & Frauke Matz, eds. *Learning with Literature in the EFL Class-room*. Frankfurt a. M.: Lang, 19–48.

Donnerstag, Jürgen & Martina Wolff (2007). Literarische Texte und Emotionen im Fremd-sprachenunterricht. In: Wolfgang Hallet & Ansgar Nünning, eds. *Neue Ansätze und Konzepte der Literatur- und Kulturdidaktik*. Trier: WVT, 143–64.

Draper, Dave (2013). *Eight Plays for Teenagers*. Stuttgart: Klett.

Dunn, Opal (2014). *Introducing English to Young Children: Reading and Writing*. London: Collins.

Eisenmann, Maria; Nancy Grimm & Laurenz Volkmann, eds. (2010). *Teaching the New English Cultures & Literatures*. Heidelberg: Winter.

Eisenmann, Maria & Theresa Summer, eds. (2013). *Basic Issues in EFL Teaching and Learning*. 2nd ed. Heidelberg: Winter.

Eisenmann, Maria (2015): Crossovers: Postcolonial Literature and Transcultural Learning. In: Werner Delanoy; Maria Eisenmann & Frauke Matz, eds. *Learning with Literature in the EFL Classroom*. Frankfurt a. M.: Lang, 217–36.

Elsner, Daniela; Sissy Helff & Britta Viebrock, eds. (2013). *Films, Graphic Novels & Visuals: Developing Multiliteracies in Foreign Language Education – An Interdisciplinary Approach*. Vienna et al.: LIT.

Elsner, Daniela & Christian Ludwig (2014). Comics selbst gestalten: Websites zur Erstellung von Webcomics. In: *Praxis Fremdsprachenunterricht Englisch* 11.3, 16–17.

Estes, Eleanor (2005). The Hundred Dresses. In: Jack Zipes; Lissa Paul; Lynne Vallone; Peter Hunt & Gillian Avery, eds. *The Norton Anthology of Children's Literature: The Traditions in English*. New York et al.: Norton, 1906–19.

Fäcke, Christiane (2006). *Transkulturalität und fremdsprachliche Literatur: Eine empirische Studie zu mentalen Prozessen von primär mono- oder bikulturell sozialisierten Jugendlichen*. Frankfurt a. M. et al.: Lang.

Felski, Rita (2008). *Uses of Literature*. Malden, MA et al.: Blackwell.

315

Fliethmann, Reinhild (2002). *Weibliche Bildungsromane: Genderbewusste Literaturdidaktik im Englischunterricht*. Tuebingen: Narr.

Forrest Gump (1994). Dir. Robert Zemeckis. Writ. Winston Groom, Eric Roth. DVD. Paramount, 2001.

Freese, Peter (2015). Teaching Narrative Competence: American Short Stories in the EFL Classroom. In: Werner Delanoy; Maria Eisenmann & Frauke Matz, eds. *Learning with Literature in the EFL Classroom*. Frankfurt a. M.: Lang, 159–80.

Freitag, Britta & Marion Gymnich (2007). *New English and Postcolonial Literatures* im Fremdsprachenunterricht. In: Wolfgang Hallet & Ansgar Nünning, eds. *Neue Ansätze und Konzepte der Literatur- und Kulturdidaktik*. Trier: WVT, 259–76.

Freitag-Hild, Britta (2010). *Theorie, Aufgabentypologie und Unterrichtspraxis inter- und transkultureller Literaturdidaktik: 'British Fictions of Migration' im Fremdsprachenunterricht*. Trier: WVT.

Gardner, Graham (2007). *Inventing Elliot*. Ernst Kemmer, ed. Stuttgart: Reclam.

Gerhardt, Christine (2006). Literature, Nature, and the Crux of Consciousness-Raising. In: Sylvia Mayer & Graham Wilson, eds. *Ecodidactic Perspectives on English Language, Literatures and Cultures*. Trier: WVT, 223–33.

Grimes, Nikki (2009). *Bronx Masquerade*. New York: Speak.

Grimm, Nancy (2009). *Beyond the "Imaginary Indian": Zur Aushandlung von Stereotypen, kultureller Identität & Perspektiven in/mit indigener Gegenwartsliteratur*. Heidelberg: Winter.

Grimm, Nancy (2011). *Utopia & Dystopia: Bright Future or Impending Doom?* Resource Book. Viewfinder. Munich: Langenscheidt/Klett.

Grimm, Nancy (2014): *Hamlet* Goes Manga: Texts, Topics, Teaching. In: Maria Eisenmann & Christiane Lütge, eds. *Shakespeare in the EFL Classroom*. Heidelberg: Winter, 183–200.

Grimm, Nancy & Julia Hammer (2015). Performative Approaches and Innovative Methods. In: Werner Delanoy; Maria Eisenmann & Frauke Matz, eds. *Learning with Literature in the EFL Classroom*. Frankfurt a. M.: Lang, 321–40.

Groom, Winston (1996). *Forrest Gump*. Dieter Hamblock, ed. Stuttgart: Reclam.

Hallet, Wolfgang (2002). *Fremdsprachenunterricht als Spiel der Texte und Kulturen: Intertextualität als Paradigma einer kulturwissenschaftlichen Didaktik*. Trier: WVT.

Hallet, Wolfgang (2007a). Literatur, Kognition und Kompetenz: Die Literarizität kulturellen Handelns. In: Lothar Bredella & Wolfgang Hallet, eds. *Literaturunterricht, Kompetenzen und Bildung*. Trier: WVT, 31–64.

Hallet, Wolfgang (2007b). Literatur und Kultur im Unterricht: Ein kulturwissenschaftlicher didaktischer Ansatz. In: Wolfgang Hallet & Ansgar Nünning, eds. *Neue Ansätze und Konzepte der Literatur- und Kulturdidaktik*. Trier: WVT, 31–47.

Hallet, Wolfgang; Carola Surkamp & Ulrich Krämer, eds. (2014). *Literaturkompetenzen Englisch: Modellierung – Curriculum – Unterrichtsvorschläge*. Seelze-Velber: Klett/Kallmeyer.

Hammer, Julia; Maria Eisenmann & Rüdiger Ahrens, eds. (2012). *Anglophone Literaturdidaktik: Zukunftsperspektiven für den Englischunterricht*. Heidelberg: Winter.

Hellwig, Karlheinz (2005). *Bildung durch Literatur: Individuelles Sinnverstehen fremdsprachiger Texte – Eine literaturdidaktische Tour d'Horizon*. Frankfurt a. M. et al.: Lang.

Hellwig, Karlheinz (2007). Prozessorientierte Literatur- und Kulturdidaktik: Genese und Kontur eines Konzepts. In: Wolfgang Hallet & Ansgar Nünning, eds. *Neue Ansätze und Konzepte der Literatur- und Kulturdidaktik*. Trier: WVT, 295–309.

Hempel, Margit (2015). A Picture (Book) is Worth a Thousand Words: Picture Books in the EFL Primary Classroom. In: Werner Delanoy; Maria Eisenmann & Frauke Matz, eds. *Learning with Literature in the EFL Classroom*. Frankfurt a. M.: Lang, 69–84.

Hentig, Hartmut von (1996). *Bildung: Ein Essay*. Munich et al.: Hanser.

Hermes, Liesel (2007). Literaturdidaktik in der Lehrerbildung. In: Wolfgang Hallet & Ansgar Nünning, eds. *Neue Ansätze und Konzepte der Literatur- und Kulturdidaktik*. Trier: WVT, 69–85.

Hermes, Liesel (2009). "Reading Can Be Fun If …": Lektüren in der Sekundarstufe I. In: Jan Hollm, ed. *Literaturdidaktik und Literaturvermittlung im Englischunterricht der Sekundarstufe I*. Trier: WVT, 7–22.

Hesse, Mechthild (2009). *Teenage Fiction in the Active English Classroom*. Stuttgart: Klett.

Hoberman, Mary Ann & Michael Emberley (2011). *You Read to Me, I'll Read to You: Very Short Scary Tales to Read Together*. Toronto: Scholastic.

Hollinger, David A. (2006). *Postethnic America: Beyond Multiculturalism*. New York: Basic Books.

Hollm, Jan (2009). Curriculare Rahmenbedingungen der Literaturvermittlung im Englischunterricht. In: Jan Hollm, ed. *Literaturdidaktik und Literaturvermittlung im Englischunterricht der Sekundarstufe I*. Trier: WVT, 41–61.

Hollm, Jan & Anke Uebel (2006). Utopias for our Time: Teaching Ecotopian and Ecodystopian Writing. In: Sylvia Mayer & Graham Wilson, eds. *Ecodidactic Perspectives on English Language, Literatures and Cultures*. Trier: WVT, 179–92.

Hoover, Jim (2007). A Relationship in Eight Pages. In: Ariel Schrag, ed. *Stuck in the Middle: Seventeen Comics from an Unpleasant Age*. New York: Viking, 159–67.

Hughes, Langston (1925, 1949). I, Too, Sing America, Theme for English B. In: Henry Louis Gates, Jr. & Nellie Y. McKay (2004). *The Norton Anthology of African American Literature*. 2nd ed. New York et al.: Norton, 1295, 1309–10.

Hurt, Byron (2008). *Barak & Curtis: Manhood, Power & Respect*. https://www.youtube.com/watch?v=H5YoS3bqk5g&x-yt-ts=1421782837&x-yt-cl=84359240 (15 January 2015).

Jewitt, Carey & Rumiko Oyama (2001). Visual Meaning: A Social Semiotic Approach. In: Theo van Leeuwen & Carey Jewitt, eds. *Handbook of Visual Analysis*. Los Angeles et al.: Sage, 134–56.

Kimes-Link, Ann (2013). *Aufgaben, Methoden und Verstehensprozesse im englischen Literaturunterricht der gymnasialen Oberstufe: Eine qualitativ-empirische Studie*. Tuebingen: Narr.

Klemm, Uwe & Nancy Grimm (2013). Go Edmondo: Plattformgestützte Lektüre des Romans *A Long Way Down*. In: *Babylonia* 3, 50–54.

Kramsch, Claire (1998). *Language and Culture*. Oxford et al.: Oxford University Press.

Küchler, Uwe (2011). "Am I Getting Through to Anyone?" Foreign Language Education and the Environment. In: Alexander Brock; Uwe Küchler & Anne Schröder, eds. *Explora-

317

tions and Extrapolations: Applying English and American Studies. Muenster et al.: LIT, 105–35.

Legutke, Michael K. (2009). Lernertexte im handlungsorientierten Fremdsprachenunterricht. In: Dagmar Abendroth-Timmer; Daniela Elsner; Christiane Lütge & Britta Viebrock, eds. *Handlungsorientierung im Fokus: Impulse und Perspektiven für den Fremdsprachenunterricht im 21. Jahrhundert*. Frankfurt a. M. et al.: Lang, 203–17.

Ludwig, Christian & Frank Erik Pointner, eds. (2013). *Teaching Comics in the Foreign Language Classroom*. Trier: WVT.

Lütge, Christiane (2013). Developing "Literary Literacy"? Towards a Progression of Literary Learning. In: Maria Eisenmann & Theresa Summer, eds. *Basic Issues in EFL Teaching and Learning*. 2nd ed. Heidelberg: Winter, 191–202.

Lütge, Christiane, ed. (2015). *Global Education in English Language Teaching*. Muenster: LIT.

Macaulay, David (1985). *BAAA*. Boston, MA: Houghton Mifflin.

Madonna (2003). American Life. *American Life*. Maverick/Warner.

Matos, Ana Gonçalves (2012). *Literary Texts and Intercultural Learning: Exploring New Directions*. Oxford et al.: Lang.

Matz, Frauke (2015). Alternative Worlds – Alternative Texts: Teaching (Young Adult) Dystopian Novels. In: Werner Delanoy; Maria Eisenmann & Frauke Matz, eds. *Learning with Literature in the EFL Classroom*. Frankfurt a. M.: Lang, 263–82.

Matz, Frauke & Anne Stieger (2015). Teaching Young Adult Fiction. In: Werner Delanoy; Maria Eisenmann & Frauke Matz, eds. *Learning with Literature in the EFL Classroom*. Frankfurt a. M.: Lang, 121–40.

Mays, Kelly J. (2013). *The Norton Introduction to Literature*. 11th ed. New York: Norton.

Meyer, Michael (1997). Schüler als Regisseure und Lehrer von *A Midsummer Night's Dream*: Irrungen und Wirrungen? In: *Praxis des neusprachlichen Unterrichts* 44.2, 126–34.

Meyer, Michael (2010). *Bedford Introduction to Literature: Reading, Thinking, Writing*. 10th ed. Boston, MA: Bedford.

Meyer, Michael (2011). *English and American Literatures*. 4th ed. Tuebingen et al.: Francke.

Meyer, Michael (2012). Notes towards a Comprehensive Model of Reading. Unpublished.

Meyer, Michael (2013). Von visueller und multimodaler Kompetenz über Bild/Texte. In Wolfgang Hallet, ed. *Teaching Literature and Culture in Higher Education – Hochschuldidaktik in den Literatur- und Kulturwissenschaften*. Trier: WVT, 155–72.

Meyer, Michael (2015). The Intermedial Framing of Narrative Fiction. In: Gabriele Rippl, ed. *Handbook of Intermediality: Literature – Image – Sound – Music*. Berlin et al.: De Gruyter.

Moebius, Wiliam (2009). Picturebook Codes. In: Janet Maybin & Nicola J. Watson, eds. *Children's Literature: Approaches and Territories*. Basingstoke et al.: Palgrave Macmillan, 311–20.

Naylor, Amanda & Audrey B. Wood (2012). *Teaching Poetry: Reading and Responding to Poetry in the Secondary Classroom*. London et al.: Routledge.

Nünning, Ansgar (2007). Fremdverstehen und Bildung durch neue Weltansichten: Perspektivenvielfalt, Perspektivenwechsel und Perspektivenübernahmen durch Literatur. In:

Wolfgang Hallet & Ansgar Nünning, eds. *Neue Ansätze und Konzepte der Literatur- und Kulturdidaktik*. Trier: WVT, 123–42.

Nünning, Ansgar & Carola Surkamp (2006). *Englische Literatur unterrichten: Grundlagen und Methoden*. Seelze-Velber: Klett/Kallmeyer.

Nünning, Vera & Ansgar Nünning (2014). *An Introduction to the Study of English and American Literature*. Stuttgart: Klett.

Regitz, Barbara (2012). Musikalische Elemente. In: Heiner Böttger, ed. *Englisch: Didaktik für die Grundschule*. Berlin: Cornelsen, 154–62.

Reichl, Susanne (2009). *Cognitive Principles, Critical Practice: Reading Literature at University*. Goettingen et al.: Vandenhoeck & Ruprecht.

Rymarczyk, Jutta (2007). Zum Wechselspiel von Text und Bildender Kunst in einer intermedialen Literatur- und Kulturdidaktik. In: Wolfgang Hallet & Ansgar Nünning, eds. *Neue Ansätze und Konzepte der Literatur- und Kulturdidaktik*. Trier: WVT, 329–50.

Schmidt, Isolde (2004). *Shakespeare im Leistungskurs Englisch: Eine empirische Untersuchung*. Frankfurt a. M. et al.: Lang.

Schneider, Ralf (2013). The Cognitive Theory of Character Reception: An Updated Proposal. In: *Anglistik* 24.2, 117–34.

Schubert, Anke (2013). *Fremdverstehen durch amerikanische Jugendliteratur: Ein Beitrag zu einem authentischen Englischunterricht*. Trier: WVT.

Sendak, Maurice (2013). *Where the Wild Things Are*. New York: HarperCollins.

Sexton, Adam & Tintin Pantoja (2008). *Shakespeare's Hamlet: The Manga Edition*. Hoboken, N. J.: Wiley.

Shakespeare, William (1992). *Hamlet*. Shakespeare for Children (S4C). Dir. Natalia Orlova. Screenplay Leon Garfield. Shakespeare Animated Films: Soyuzmultfilm, Christmas Film, Channel 4 Wales & BBC Wales.

Shakespeare, William (2014). *Hamlet*. Holger Michael Klein, ed. Stuttgart: Reclam.

Spaemann, Robert (2012). Wer ist ein gebildeter Mensch? In: Heiner Hastedt, ed. *Was ist Bildung? Eine Textanthologie*. Stuttgart: Reclam, 223–27.

Steininger, Ivo (2014). *Modellierung literarischer Kompetenz: Eine qualitative Studie im Fremdsprachenunterricht der Sekundarstufe I*. Tuebingen: Narr.

Strasen, Sven (2013). The Return of the Reader: The Disappearance of Literary Reception Theories and Their Revival as a Part of a Cognitive Theory of Culture. In: *Anglistik* 24.2, 31–48.

Surkamp, Carola (2007). Handlungs- und Produktionsorientierung im fremdsprachlichen Literaturunterricht. In: Wolfgang Hallet & Ansgar Nünning, eds. *Neue Ansätze und Konzepte der Literatur- und Kulturdidaktik*. Trier: WVT, 89–106.

Surkamp, Carola (2012). Literarische Texte im kompetenzorientierten Fremdsprachenunterricht. In: Wolfgang Hallet & Ulrich Krämer, eds.: *Kompetenzaufgaben im Englischunterricht: Grundlagen und Unterrichtsbeispiele*. Seelze-Velber: Klett/Kallmeyer, 77–90.

Surkamp, Carola (2015). Playful Learning with Short Plays. In: Werner Delanoy; Maria Eisenmann & Frauke Matz, eds. *Learning with Literature in the EFL Classroom*. Frankfurt a. M.: Lang, 141–58.

Surkamp, Carola & Ansgar Nünning (2009). *Englische Literatur unterrichten: Unterrichtsmodelle und Materialien*. Seelze-Velber: Klett/Kallmeyer.

Swarup, Vikas (2008). *Slumdog Millionaire*. New York et al.: Scribner.

Thaler, Engelbert (2008). *Teaching English Literature*. Paderborn et al.: Schöningh.

Thaler, Engelbert (2009). *Method guide: Kreative Methoden für den Literaturunterricht in den Klassen 7–12*. Paderborn: Schöningh.

Uhlig, Bettina (2014). "Ich sehe was, was Du nicht siehst." Bildsehen und Bildimagination bei der Betrachtung von Bilderbüchern. In: Gabriela Scherer; Steffen Volz; Maja Wiprächtiger-Geppert & Andrea Wetterauer, eds. *Bilderbuch und literar-ästhetische Bildung: Aktuelle Forschungsperspektiven*. Trier: WVT, 9–22.

Volkmann, Laurenz (2009). Trotz Bildungsstandards und Output-Orientierung: Literatur auch und gerade jetzt in der Sekundarstufe I! In: Jan Hollm, ed. *Literaturdidaktik und Literaturvermittlung im Englischunterricht der Sekundarstufe I*. Trier: WVT, 23–40.

Volkmann, Laurenz (2012). *Ecodidactics* als Antwort auf die planetare Bedrohung? Zum Einsatz von *ecopoetry* im Englischunterricht. In: Julia Hammer; Maria Eisenmann & Rüdiger Ahrens, eds. *Anglophone Literaturdidaktik: Zukunftsperspektiven für den Englischunterricht*. Heidelberg: Winter, 393–408.

Volkmann, Laurenz (2013). Intercultural Learning and Postcolonial Studies: "Never the Twain Shall Meet"? In: Maria Eisenmann & Theresa Summer, eds. *Basic Issues in EFL Teaching and Learning*. 2nd ed. Heidelberg: Winter, 169–80.

Volkmann, Laurenz (2015). Learning with Literature in the EFL Classroom. In: Werner Delanoy; Maria Eisenmann & Frauke Matz, eds. *Learning with Literature in the EFL Classroom*. Frankfurt a. M.: Lang. 49–66.

Wolf, Werner (2006). Introduction: Frames, Framings and Framing Borders in Literature and other Media. In: Werner Wolf & Walter Bernhart, eds. *Framing Borders in Literature and Other Media*. Amsterdam et al.: Rodopi, 1–40.

Woolf, Virginia (1944/2007). *Mrs Dalloway's Party: A Short Story Sequence*. Hans-Christian Oeser, ed. Stuttgart: Reclam.

References unit 9

Abfalter, Erwin (2007). *Foren, Wikis, Weblogs und Chats im Unterricht*. Boizenburg: vwh.

Albers, Carsten; Johannes Magenheim & Dorothee M. Meister (2011). Der Einsatz digitaler Medien als Herausforderung von Schule: Eine Annäherung. In: Carsten Albers; Johannes Magenheim & Dorothee M. Meister, eds. *Schule in der digitalen Welt: Medienpädagogische Ansätze und Schulforschungsperspektiven*. Wiesbaden: VS, 7–16.

Baacke, Dieter (1997). *Medienpädagogik*. Tuebingen: Niemeyer.

Banse, Gerhard & Andreas Metzner-Szigeth (2012). Cultural Diversity and New Media – Their Interaction as an Element of European Integration: Elaborating a European Research Network. In: Annely Rothkegel & Sonja Ruda, eds. *Communication on and via Technology*. Berlin et al.: de Gruyter, 217–258.

Bland, Janice & Christiane Lütge, eds. (2013). *Children's Literature in Second Language Education*. London: Bloomsbury Academic.

Blell, Gabriele & Rita Kupetz (2005). Fremdsprachenlernen zwischen 'Medienverwahrlosung' und Medienkompetenz: Ein Beitrag zur kritisch-reflektierenden Mediendidaktik.
In: Gabriele Blell & Rita Kupetz, eds. *Fremdsprachenlernen zwischen Medienverwahrlosung und Medienkompetenz: Beiträge zu einer kritisch-reflektierenden Mediendidaktik*. Frankfurt a. M. et al.: Lang, 9–29.

Bos, Wilfried; Birgit Eickelmann; Julia Gerick; Frank Goldhammer; Heike Schaumburg;
Knut Schwippert; Martin Senkbeil; Renate Schulz-Zander & Heike Wendt, eds. (2014).
*ICILS 2013: Computer- und informationsbezogene Kompetenzen von Schülerinnen und
Schülern in der 8. Jahrgangsstufe im internationalen Vergleich*. http://ifs-dortmund.de/
assets/files/icils2013/ICILS_2013_Berichtsband.pdf (20 December 2014).

Buckingham, David (2008). Introducing Identity. In: David Buckingham, ed. *Youth, Identity,
and Digital Media*. Cambridge, MA et al.: MIT, 1–22.

Cazden, Courtney; Bill Cope; Norman Fairclough & James P. Gee (1996). A Pedagogy of
Multiliteracies: Designing Social Futures. In: *Harvard Educational Review* 66.1,
60–92.

Clark, Richard E. (1994). Media Will Never Influence Learning. In: *Educational Technology:
Research & Development* 42.2, 21–29.

Díaz Vera, Javier E. (2012). Great Expectations: Formalizing and Transforming Mobile-
Assisted Language Learning. In: Javier E. Díaz Vera, ed. *Left to My Own Devices: Learner
Autonomy and Mobile-Assisted Language Learning*. Bingley: Emerald, xi-xix.

Donnerstag, Jürgen & Laurenz Volkmann, eds. (2008). *Media and American Studies in the
EFL-Classroom*. Heidelberg: Winter.

Duncum, Paul (2010). Seven Principles for Visual Culture Education. In: *Art Education* 63.1,
6–10.

Eickelmann, Birgit (2010). *Digitale Medien in Schule und Unterricht erfolgreich implemen-
tieren: Eine empirische Analyse aus Sicht der Schulentwicklungsforschung*. Muenster
et al.: Waxmann.

Evans, Michael (2012). Introduction: Traditional and Modern Media. In: Maria Eisenmann
& Theresa Summer, eds. *Basic Issues in EFL Teaching and Learning*. Heidelberg: Winter, 217–27.

Faulstich, Werner (2000). *Grundwissen Medien*. 4th ed. Munich: Fink.

Faulstich, Werner (2004). *Medienwissenschaft*. Paderborn: Fink.

Frees, Beate & Katrin Busemann (2012). Internet Goes Community: Grundlagen zur Internet-
nutzung von Teenagern. In: Ullrich Dittler & Michael Hoyer, eds. *Aufwachsen in sozia-
len Netzwerken: Chancen und Gefahren von Netzgemeinschaften aus medienpsycholo-
gischer und medienpädagogischer Sicht*. Munich: kopaed, 15–27.

Grell, Petra; Winfried Marotzki & Heidi Schelhowe, eds. (2010). *Neue digitale Kultur- und
Bildungsräume*. Wiesbaden: VS.

Grimm, Nancy (2007a). *Teaching Films: In America, Whale Rider, Bend It Like Beckham*.
Goettingen: Vandenhoeck & Ruprecht.

Grimm, Nancy (2007b). Filme. In: Julia Drumm, ed. *Methodische Elemente des Unterrichts:
Sozialformen, Aktionsformen, Medien*. Goettingen: Vandenhoeck & Ruprecht.

Grimm, Nancy (2012). Digital Media: Promise for or Threat to Education? In: Maria Eisenmann & Theresa Summer, eds. *Basic Issues in EFL Teaching and Learning*. Heidelberg: Winter, 229–40.

Grimm, Nancy & Julia Hammer (2014). Now, Here, and Everywhere: Mit Edu-Apps Blended Learning-Szenarien gestalten und mobil lernen. In: *Der fremdsprachliche Unterricht Englisch* 48.128, 2–7.

Grimm, Nancy & Olesya Riecken (2014). What's the Weather Like? Oder: Weather Reports with Fun. In: *Praxis Schule* 6, 21–27.

Groeben, Norbert (2002). Dimensionen der *Medienkompetenz*: Deskriptive und normative Aspekte. In: Norbert Groeben & Bettina Hurrelmann, eds. *Medienkompetenz: Voraussetzungen, Dimensionen, Funktionen*. Weinheim et al.: Juventa, 160–97.

Grünewald, Andreas (2010a). Medien. In: Carola Surkamp, ed. *Metzler Lexikon Fremdsprachendidaktik: Ansätze – Methoden – Grundbegriffe*. Stuttgart et al.: Metzler, 207–10.

Grünewald, Andreas (2010b). Mediendidaktik. In: Carola Surkamp, ed. *Metzler Lexikon Fremdsprachendidaktik: Ansätze – Methoden – Grundbegriffe*. Stuttgart et al.: Metzler, 210–13.

Hecke, Carola & Carola Surkamp, eds. (2015). *Bilder im Fremdsprachenunterricht: Neue Ansätze, Kompetenzen und Methoden*. 2nd ed. Tuebingen: Narr.

Heim, Katja & Markus Ritter (2012). *Teaching English: Computer-assisted Language Learning*. Paderborn: Schöningh.

Henseler, Roswitha; Stefan Möller & Carola Surkamp (2011). *Filme im Englischunterricht: Grundlagen, Methoden, Genres*. Seelze-Velber: Klett/Kallmeyer.

Herzig, Bardo & Silke Grafe (2011). Wirkung digitaler Medien. In: Carsten Albers; Johannes Magenheim & Dorothee M. Meister, eds. *Schule in der digitalen Welt: Medienpädagogische Ansätze und Schulforschungsperspektiven*. Wiesbaden: VS, 67–95.

Hornby, Nick (2005). *A Long Way Down*. New York: Riverhead.

Hug, Theo (2002). Medienpädagogik: Begriffe, Konzeptionen, Perspektiven. In: Gebhard Rusch, ed. *Einführung in die Medienwissenschaft: Konzeptionen, Theorien, Methoden, Anwendungen*. Wiesbaden: Westdeutscher Verlag, 189–207.

Initiative D21 (2006). *Lehre oder Leere? Computerausstattung und -nutzung an deutschen Schulen*. http://www.tns-infratest.com/presse/pdf/Presse/20060927_TNS_Infratest_eEducation_Prez.pdf (30 October 2014).

Jewitt, Carey & Rumiko Oyama (2001). Visual Meaning: A Social Semiotic Approach. In: Theo van Leeuwen & Carey Jewitt, eds. *Handbook of Visual Analysis*. Los Angeles et al.: Sage, 134–56.

Keine Bildung ohne Medien! (2010). *Schüler fordern: Mehr* mit *und über Medien lernen!* http://www.keine-bildung-ohne-medien.de/presse/svz-auswertung_offene-fragen.pdf (30 October 2014).

Keine Bildung ohne Medien! (2011). *Keine Bildung ohne Medien! Bildungspolitische Forderungen*. http://www.keine-bildung-ohne-medien.de/kongress-dokumentation/keine-bildung-ohne-medien_bildungspolitische-forderungen.pdf (30 October 2014).

Keine Bildung ohne Medien! (2014). *"Keine Bildung ohne Medien!" fordert: Grundbildung Medien für alle pädagogischen Fachkräfte*. http://www.keine-bildung-ohne-medien.

de/wp-content/uploads/2014/06/Position_Grundbildung_KBoM.pdf (30 December 2014).

Keen, Andrew (2008). *The Cult of the Amateur: How Blogs, MySpace, YouTube, and the Rest of Today's User-generated Media are Destroying our Economy, our Culture, and our Values*. New York et al: Doubleday.

Klemm, Uwe & Nancy Grimm (2013). Go Edmodo: Plattformgestützte Lektüre des Romans *A Long Way Down*. In: *Babylonia* 3, 50–54.

Klimsa, Paul; Anja Klimsa; Janine Liebal & Anett Grobe (2011). *Lernstand Medien in Thüringen: Ergebnisse einer digitalen Befragung zur Überprüfung der Medienkompetenz der Thüringer Schüler und Schülerinnen der 7. Klassen sowie zur Bewertung der Eignung von Erhebungssoftware aus der Sicht der Schüler und Lehrer*. Ilmenau: Universitätsverlag Ilmenau.

Knapman, Timothy & Adam Stower (2008). *Mungo and the Dinosaur Island*. London: Puffin.

Kultusministerkonferenz (2012). *Medienbildung in der Schule*. http://www.kmk.org/fileadmin/veroeffentlichungen_beschluesse/2012/2012_03_08_Medienbildung.pdf (30 October 2014).

Kübler, Hans-Dieter (2012). Mediengenerationen – gibt's die? Theoretische und analytische Sondierungen. In: Anja Hartung; Bernd Schorb & Claudia Kuttner, eds. *Generationen und Medienpädagogik: Annäherungen aus Theorie, Forschung und Praxis*. Munich: kopaed, 41–64.

Ludwig, Christian & Frank Erik Pointner, eds. (2013). *Teaching Comics in the Foreign Language Classroom*. Trier: WVT.

Lütge, Christiane (2012). *Mit Filmen Englisch unterrichten*. Berlin: Cornelsen-Scriptor.

Magenheim, Johannes & Dorothee M. Meister (2011). Potenziale von Web 2.0-Technologien für die Schule. In: Carsten Albers; Johannes Magenheim & Dorothee M. Meister, eds. *Schule in der digitalen Welt: Medienpädagogische Ansätze und Schulforschungsperspektiven*. Wiesbaden: VS, 19–42.

Medienanstalt Hamburg/Schleswig Holstein (2010). *Medienbildung – (k)ein Unterrichtsfach? Eine Expertise zum Stellenwert der Medienkompetenzförderung in Schulen*. Hamburg: Universität Hamburg.

Medienpädagogischer Forschungsverbund Südwest (2013a). *15 Jahre JIM-Studie: Jugend, Information, (Multi-)Media – Studienreihe zum Medienumgang 12- bis 19-Jähriger (1998–2013)*. http://www.mpfs.de/fileadmin/JIM15/PDF/15JahreJIMStudie.pdf (30 October 2014).

Medienpädagogischer Forschungsverbund Südwest (2014). *Jim-Studie 2014: Jugend, Information, (Multi-) Media – Basisuntersuchung zum Medienumgang 12-bis 19-Jähriger*. http://www.mpfs.de/fileadmin/JIM-pdf14/JIM-Studie_2014.pdf (30 October 2014).

Meyer, Michael (2013). Von visueller und multimodaler Kompetenz über Bild/Texte. In: Wolfgang Hallet, ed. *Teaching Literature and Culture in Higher Education: Hochschuldidaktik in den Literatur- und Kulturwissenschaften*. Trier: WVT, 155–72.

Meyer, Michael (2015). The Intermedial Framing of Narrative Fiction. In: Gabriele Rippl, ed. *Handbook of Intermediality: Literature – Image – Sound – Music*. Berlin et al.: De Gruyter.

Mikos, Lothar (2012). Mediengenerationen, Mediennutzung, Medienkompetenz. In: Sonja Ganguin & Dorothee Meister, eds. *Digital native oder digital naiv? Medienpädagogik der Generationen*. Munich: kopaed, 41–54.

Moebius, Wiliam (2009). Picturebook Codes. In: Janet Maybin & Nicola J. Watson, eds. *Children's Literature: Approaches and Territories*. Basingstoke et al.: Palgrave Macmillan, 311–20.

Moser, Heinz (2010). *Einführung in die Medienpädagogik: Aufwachsen im Medienzeitalter*. 5th ed. Wiesbaden: VS.

Pachler, Norbert; Michael Evans; Ana Redondo & Linda Fisher (2014). *Learning to Teach Foreign Languages in the Secondary School: A Companion to School Experience*. 4th ed. London et al.: Routledge.

Prensky, Marc (2001a). Digital Natives, Digital Immigrants Part I. In: *On the Horizon* 9.5, 1–6.

Prensky, Marc (2001b). Digital Natives, Digital Immigrants Part II: Do They Really Think Differently? In: *On the Horizon* 9.6, 1–6.

Poore, Megan (2013). *Using Social Media in the Classroom: A Best Practice Guide*. Los Angeles, CA et al.: SAGE.

Reinfried, Marcus (1992). *Das Bild im Fremdsprachenunterricht: Eine Geschichte der visuellen Medien am Beispiel des Französischunterrichts*. Tuebingen: Narr.

Reinfried, Marcus & Laurenz Volkmann, eds. (2012). *Medien im neokommunikativen Fremdsprachenunterricht: Einsatzformen, Inhalte, Lernerkompetenzen*. Frankfurt a. M. et al.: Lang.

Richardson, Will (2010). *Blogs, Wikis, Podcasts, and other Powerful Web Tools for Classrooms*. 3rd ed. Thousand Oaks, CA: Corwin.

Rosebrock, Cornelia & Olga Zitzelsberger (2002). Der Begriff Medienkompetenz als Zielperspektive im Diskurs der Pädagogik und Didaktik. In: Norbert Groeben & Bettina Hurrelmann, eds. *Medienkompetenz: Voraussetzungen, Dimensionen, Funktionen*. Weinheim et al.: Juventa, 148–59.

Röll, Franz Josef (2010). Web 2.0 als pädagogische Herausforderung. In: Bardo Herzig; Dorothee M. Meister; Heinz Moser & Horst Niesyto, eds. *Jahrbuch Medienpädagogik 8: Medienkompetenz und Web 2.0*. Wiesbaden: VS, 201–20.

Rymarczyk, Jutta (2007). Zum Wechselspiel von Text und Bildender Kunst in einer intermedialen Literatur- und Kulturdidaktik. In: Wolfgang Hallet & Ansgar Nünning, eds. *Neue Ansätze und Konzepte der Literatur- und Kulturdidaktik*. Trier: WVT, 329–50.

Schnoor, Detlev (1998). Neue Medien verlangen nach Schulentwicklung. In: *Pädagogische Führung* 9.1, 6–12.

Schulmeister, Rolf (2009). *Gibt es eine 'Net Generation'? Erweiterte Version 3.0*. http://www.zhw.uni-hamburg.de/uploads/schulmeister_net-generation_v3.pdf (30 October 2014).

Schulmeister, Rolf (2010). Deconstructing the Media Use of the Net Generation. In: *Qwerty Interdisciplinary Journal of Technology, Culture and Education* 5.2, 26–60.

Schulz-Zander, Renate (2003). *Nationale Ergebnisse der internationalen IEA-Studie SITES Modul 2, Second Information Technology in Education Study: Zusammenfassung zen-*

traler Ergebnisse. http://ipso.ifs-dortmund.de/pdf/Kurzfassungschlussbericht4.pdf (30 October 2014).

Spanhel, Dieter (2011). *Medienerziehung: Erziehungs- und Bildungsaufgaben in der Medi-engesellschaft*. 2nd ed. Munich: kopaed.

Spitzer, Manfred (2012). *Digitale Demenz: Wie wir uns und unsere Kinder um den Verstand bringen*. Munich: Droemer.

Stafford, Tim (2011). *Teaching Visual Literacy in the Primary Classroom: Comic Books, Film, Television and Picture Narratives*. Abingdon et al.: Routledge.

Strasser, Thomas (2012). *Mind the App! Inspiring Internet Tools and Activities to Engage Your Students*. Innsbruck: Helbling.

Thaler Engelbert (1999). *Musikvideoclips im Englischunterricht: Phänomenologie, Legit-imität, Didaktik und Methodik eines neuen Mediums*. Munich: Langenscheidt-Long-man.

Thaler, Engelbert (2014). *Teaching English With Films*. Paderborn: Schöningh.

The New London Group (2000). A Pedagogy of Multiliteracies: Designing Social Futures. In: Bill Cope & Mary Kalantzis, eds. *Multiliteracies: Literacy Learning and the Design of Social Futures*. London et al.: Routledge, 9–37.

Thüringer Ministerium für Bildung, Wissenschaft und Kultur (2010). *Medienkunde*. http://www.schulportal-thueringen.de/web/guest/media/detail?tspi=1897 (30 October 2014).

Tulodziecki, Gerhard (1997). *Medien in Erziehung und Unterricht: Grundlagen und Beispiele einer handlungs- und entwicklungsorientierten Medienpädagogik*. 3rd ed. Bad Heil-brunn: Klinkhardt.

Tulodziecki, Gerhard; Bardo Herzig & Silke Grafe (2010). *Medienbildung in Schule und Unterricht: Grundlagen und Beispiele*. Bad Heilbrunn: Klinkhardt.

Uhlig, Bettina (2014). "Ich sehe was, was Du nicht siehst." Bildsehen und Bildimagina-tion bei der Betrachtung von Bilderbüchern. In: Gabriela Scherer; Steffen Volz; Maja Wiprächtiger-Geppert & Andrea Wetterauer, eds. *Bilderbuch und literar-ästhetische Bil-dung. Aktuelle Forschungsperspektiven*. Trier: WVT, 9–22.

Voigts-Virchow, Eckhart (2005). *Introduction to Media Studies*. Stuttgart et al.: Klett.

Volkmann, Laurenz (2005). 'Demokratisierung des Lernens' oder 'Medienverwahrlosung'? Überlegungen zum didaktischen Umgang mit dem Internet. In: Gabriele Blell & Rita Kupetz, eds. *Fremdsprachenlernen zwischen Medienverwahrlosung und Medienkom-petenz: Beiträge zu einer kritisch-reflektierenden Mediendidaktik*. Frankfurt a. M. et al.: Lang, 43–66.

Volkmann, Laurenz (2008a). Designing CD-ROMs: A New Approach to Promoting Learner Autonomy. In: Werner Delanoy & Laurenz Volkmann, eds. *Future Perspectives for Eng-lish Language Teaching*. Heidelberg: Winter, 119–38.

Volkmann, Laurenz (2008b). Throw Away Your Textbook – Log In?! Reflections on the Inter-net as a Teaching/Learning Resource. In: Jürgen Donnerstag & Laurenz Volkmann, eds. *Media and American Studies in the EFL-Classroom*. Heidelberg: Winter, 173–92.

Wampfler, Philippe (2013). *Facebook, Blogs und Wikis in der Schule: Ein Social-Media-Leit-faden*. Goettingen: Vandenhoeck & Ruprecht.

Warschauer, Mark (2000). The Death of Cyberspace and the Rebirth of CALL. In: *English Teachers' Journal* 53, 61–67.

Wermke, Jutta (1997). *Integrierte Medienerziehung im Fachunterricht: Schwerpunkt Deutsch*. Munich: kopaed.

Wetterich, Frank; Martin Burghart & Norbert Rave (2014). *Medienbildung an deutschen Schulen: Handlungsempfehlungen für die digitale Gesellschaft*. http://www.initiatived21.de/wp-content/uploads/2014/11/141106_Medienbildung_Onlinefassung_komprimiert.pdf (30 December 2014).

Wiepcke, Claudia; Ewald Mittelstaedt & Andreas Liening (2008). Blended Learning Approaches to Enhance Gender Mainstreaming. In: *Asian Women* 24.4, 21–41.

Wolf, Werner (2006). Introduction: Frames, Framings and Framing Borders in Literature and Other Media. In: Werner Wolf & Walter Bernhart, eds. *Framing Borders in Literature and Other Media*. Amsterdam et al.: Rodopi, 1–40.

Würffel, Nicole (2014). Auf dem Weg zu einer Theorie des Blended Learning: Kritische Einschätzung von Modellen. In: Klaus Rummler, ed. *Lernräume gestalten: Bildungskontexte vielfältig denken*. Muenster et al.: Waxmann, 150–162.

References unit 10

Benecke, Ingrid (2007). Zur Grobstruktur von Englischunterricht: Eine Planungshilfe. In: *Praxis Fremdsprachenunterricht* 4.6, 35–38.

Council of Europe (2001). *Common European Framework of Reference for Languages: Learning, Teaching, Assessment*. Cambridge: Cambridge University Press.

Decke-Cornill, Helene & Lutz Küster (2014). *Fremdsprachendidaktik*. Tuebingen: Narr.

Farrell, Thomas S. C. (2002). Lesson Planning. In: Jack C. Richards & Willy A. Renandya, eds. *Methodology in Language Teaching: An Anthology of Current Practice*. Cambridge et al.: Cambridge University Press, 30–39.

Finkbeiner, Claudia (2007). Lehrplan – Lehrwerk – Stoffverteilungsplan – Unterricht. In Johannes-P. Timm, ed. *Englisch lernen und lehren: Didaktik des Englischunterrichts*. Berlin: Cornelsen, 36–44.

Hallet, Wolfgang & Andreas Müller-Hartmann (2006). For better or for worse? Bildungsstandards Englisch im Überblick. In: *Der fremdsprachliche Unterricht Englisch* 40.81, 2–11.

Hallet, Wolfgang (2011). *Lernen fördern: Englisch – Kompetenzorientierter Unterricht in der Sekundarstufe I*. Seelze-Velber: Klett/Kallmeyer.

Harmer, Jeremy (2000). *How to Teach English: An Introduction to the Practice of English Language Teaching*. Harlow: Longman.

Hattie, John (2009). *Visible Learning: A Synthesis of over 800 Meta-Analyses Relating to Achievement*. London et al.: Routledge.

Head, Katie & Pauline Taylor (1997). *Readings in Teacher Development*. Oxford: Heinemann.

Helmke, Andreas & Gerlinde Lenske (2013). Unterrichtsdiagnostik als Voraussetzung für Unterrichtsentwicklung. In: *Beiträge zur Lehrerbildung* 31.2, 214–33.

Horster, Leonhard (2004). *Unterricht analysieren, beurteilen, planen*. Bönen: Verlag für Schule und Weiterbildung.

Hüllen, Werner (1987). *Englisch als Fremdsprache: Beiträge zur Theorie des Englischunterrichts an deutschen Schulen*. Tuebingen: Francke.

Islam, Carlos & Chris Mares (2003). Adapting Classroom Materials. In: Brian Tomlinson, ed. *Developing Materials for Language Teaching*. London: Continuum, 86–100.

Jank, Werner & Hilbert Meyer (2002). *Didaktische Modelle*. Berlin: Cornelsen.

Kieweg, Werner (1998). Lernprozessorientierte Kriterien zur Evaluierung von Englisch-Lehrwerken. In: *Der Fremdsprachliche Unterricht Englisch* 32.34, 27–38.

Legutke, Michael (2007). Handlungsraum Klassenzimmer and beyond. In: Johannes-P. Timm, ed. *Englisch lernen und lehren: Didaktik des Englischunterrichts*. Berlin: Cornelsen, 93–109.

Legutke, Michael (2009). Lernerwelt Klassenzimmer: Szenarien für einen handlungsorientierten Fremdsprachenunterricht. In: Gerhard Bach & Johannes-P. Timm, eds. *Englischunterricht*. Tuebingen, Basle: Francke, 91–120.

Lewis, Marilyn (2002). Classroom Management. In: Jack C. Richards & Willy A. Renandya, eds. *Methodology in Language Teaching: An Anthology of Current Practice*. Cambridge et al.: Cambridge University Press, 40–48.

Lindner, Michael (2011). *Gute Frage! Lehrerfragen als pädagogische Schlüsselkompetenz*. Marburg: Tectum.

Maybin, Janet (2002). Everyday Talk. In: Janet Maybin & Neil Mercer, eds. *Using English: From Conversation to Canon*. London et al.: Routledge, 5–27.

Meyer, Hilbert (2004). *Was ist guter Unterricht?* Berlin: Cornelsen Scriptor.

Meyer, Hilbert (2006). Criteria of Good Instruction: Empirical Findings and Didactic Advice. Transl. Dave Kloss. http://www.member.uni-oldenburg.de/hilbert.meyer/download/Criteria_of_Good_Instruction.pdf (10 September 2014).

Müller-Hartmann, Andreas & Marita Schocker-von Ditfurth (2009). *Introduction to English Language Teaching*. Stuttgart et al.: Klett.

Richards, Jack C. & Theodore S. Rodgers (1986). *Approaches and Methods in Language Teaching: A Description and Analysis*. Cambridge et al.: Cambridge University Press.

Rowe, Marry Budd (1986). Wait Time: Slowing Down May Be a Way of Speeding Up. *Journal of Teacher Education* 37.1, 43–50.

Thaler, Engelbert (2012). *Englisch unterrichten: Grundlagen – Kompetenzen – Methoden*. Berlin: Cornelsen.

Tomlinson, Brian, ed. (2003). *Developing Materials for Language Teaching*. London: Continuum.

Unterrichtsmethoden im konstruktiven und systemischen Methodenpool: Lehren, Lernen, Methoden für alle Bereiche didaktischen Handelns (n.y.). http://methodenpool.uni-koeln.de/index.html (24 February 2015).

Ur, Penny (1996). *A Course in Language Teaching: Practice and Theory*. Cambridge et al.: Cambridge University Press.

Volkmann, Laurenz (2012). Language Learning. In: Martin Middeke; Timo Müller; Christina Wald & Hubert Zapf, eds. *English and American Studies: Theory and Practice*. Stuttgart et al.: Metzler, 480–87.

Weskamp, Ralf (2001). *Fachdidaktik: Grundlagen und Konzepte*. Berlin: Cornelsen.

Weskamp, Ralf (2003). *Fremdsprachenunterricht entwickeln: Grundschule – Sekundarstufe I – Gymnasiale Oberstufe*. Hanover: Schroedel et al.

Weskamp, Ralf (2007). *Mehrsprachigkeit: Sprachevolution, kognitive Sprachverarbeitung und schulischer Fremdsprachenerwerb*. Braunschweig: Schroedel et al.

Wiechmann, Jürgen, ed. (1996). *Zwölf Unterrichtsmethoden: Vielfalt für die Praxis*. 3rd ed. Weinheim et al.: Beltz.

Willis, Jane (2000). *A Framework for Task-Based Learning*. Harlow et al.: Longman.

References unit 11

Bao, Dat (2013). Developing Materials for Speaking Skills. In: Brian Tomlinson, ed. *Developing Materials for Language Teaching*. London et al.: Bloomsbury, 407–28.

Council of Europe (2001). *Common European Framework of Reference for Languages: Learning, Teaching, Assessment*. Cambridge: Cambridge University Press.

Cunningsworth, Alan (1995). *Choosing Your Coursebook*. Oxford: Heinemann et al.

Egle, Gert (2013). *Arbeitstechniken: Arbeitsblattgestaltung*. http://teachsam.de/arb/ab_gestalt/arb_abgesto.htm (12 February 2015).

Emery, Helen (2013). Working with Student-Teachers to Design Materials for Language Support within the School Curriculum. In: Brian Tomlinson, ed. *Developing Materials for Language Teaching*. London et al.: Bloomsbury, 521–36.

Fritze, Martin (2014). I Wanna Be a Rock Star: Eine Bewerbung mit Padlet schreiben. In: *Der fremdsprachliche Unterricht Englisch* 48.128, 12–17.

García Mayo, María del Pilar, ed. (2007). *Investigating Tasks in Formal Language Learning*. Clevedon: Multilingual Matters.

Grimm, Nancy & Julia Hammer (2014a). Now, Here, and Everywhere: Mit Edu-Apps Blended Learning-Szenarien gestalten und mobil lernen. In: *Der fremdsprachliche Unterricht Englisch* 48.128, 2–7.

Grimm, Nancy & Julia Hammer (2014b). Einen Wikipedia-Eintrag mit Apps analysieren und selbst formulieren. *Der fremdsprachliche Unterricht Englisch* 48.128, 10–11.

Heckmann, Verena & Thomas Strasser (2012). Von der technischen Komplexität hin zur didaktischen Vielseitigkeit: "3-Clicks-Edu-Apps" zur Steigerung der Sprechkompetenz im fremdsprachlichen Unterricht. In: *Zeitschrift für E-Learning, Lernkultur und Bildungstechnologie* 7.2, 34–46.

Heckmann, Verena & Manuela Baus (2014). What's Your Favorite Film? Mit Edu-Glogster Filme empfehlen und Poster präsentieren. *Der fremdsprachliche Unterricht Englisch* 48.128, 26–30.

Hill, David A. & Brian Tomlinson (2013). Coursebook Listening Activities. In: Brian Tomlinson, ed. *Developing Materials for Language Teaching*. London et al.: Bloomsbury, 429–42.

Howard, Jocelyn & Joe Major (2005). *Guidelines for Designing Effective English Language Teaching Materials*. http://www.paaljapan.org/resources/proceedings/PAAL9/pdf/Howard.pdf (12 February 2015).

Hyland, Ken (2013). Materials for Developing Writing Skills. In: Brian Tomlinson, ed. *Developing Materials for Language Teaching*. London et al.: Bloomsbury, 391–405.

Jolly, David & Rod Bolitho (2011). A Framework for Materials Writing. In: Brian Tomlinson, ed. *Materials Development in Language Teaching*. 2nd ed. Cambridge et al.: Cambridge University Press, 107–34.

Kervin, Lisa & Beverly Derewianka (2011). New Technologies to Support Language Learning. In: Brian Tomlinson, ed. *Materials Development in Language Teaching*. 2nd ed. Cambridge et al.: Cambridge University Press, 328–51.

Kiddle, Thom (2013). Developing Digital Language Learning Materials. In: Brian Tomlinson, ed. *Developing Materials for Language Teaching*. London et al.: Bloomsbury, 189–205.

Kultusministerkonferenz (2012). *Operatoren für das Fach Englisch*. http://www.kmk.org/ fileadmin/pdf/Bildung/Auslandsschulwesen/Kerncurriculum/Operatoren_fuer_das_ Fach_Englisch_Stand_Oktober_2012_ueberarbeitet.pdf (12 February 2015).

Masuhara, Hitomi (2011). What Do Teachers Really Want from Coursebooks? In: Brian Tomlinson, ed. *Materials Development in Language Teaching*. 2nd ed. Cambridge et al.: Cambridge University Press, 236–66.

Masuhara, Hitomi (2013). Materials for Developing Reading Skills. In: Brian Tomlinson, ed. *Developing Materials for Language Teaching*. London et al.: Bloomsbury, 365–89.

Mishan, Freda (2005). *Designing Authenticity into Language Learning Materials*. Bristol: Intellect, 2005.

Motteram, Gary (2011). Developing Language-Learning Materials with Technology. In: Brian Tomlinson, ed. *Materials Development in Language Teaching*. 2nd ed. Cambridge et al.: Cambridge University Press, 303–27.

Nation, Paul (2013). Materials for Teaching Vocabulary. In: Brian Tomlinson, ed. *Developing Materials for Language Teaching*. London et al.: Bloomsbury, 351–64.

Neumann, Günther (2012). *Gestaltung von Arbeitsblättern für den Einsatz im Unterricht*. https://www.isb.bayern.de/download/11079/kurzhandreichung_gestaltung_von_ arbeitsblaettern.pdf (12 February 2015).

Nold, Günter (2007). Die Arbeit mit dem Lehrwerk. In: Johannes-P. Timm, ed. *Englisch lernen und lehren: Didaktik des Englischunterrichts*. Berlin: Cornelsen, 127–36.

Nunan, David (2000). *Designing Tasks for the Communicative Classroom*. Cambridge et al.: Cambridge University Press.

Pachler, Norbert; Michael Evans; Ana Redondo & Linda Fisher (2014). *Learning to Teach Foreign Languages in the Secondary School: A Companion to School Experience*. 4th ed. London et al.: Routledge.

Pulverness, Alan & Brian Tomlinson (2013). Materials for Cultural Awareness. In: Brian Tomlinson, ed. *Developing Materials for Language Teaching*. London et al.: Bloomsbury, 443–59.

Richards, Jack C. (2007). *Curriculum Development in Language Teaching*. Cambridge et al.: Cambridge University Press.

Richards, Jack C. (2013). Curriculum Approaches in Language Teaching: Forward, Central, and Backward Design. In: *RELC Journal* 44.1, 5–33.

Robinson, Peter (2007). Criteria for Classifying and Sequencing Pedagogic Tasks. In: María del Pilar García Mayo, ed. *Tasks in Formal Language Learning*. Clevedon: Multilingual Matters, 7–27.

Robinson, Peter (2011). Syllabus Design. In: Michael H. Long & Catherine J. Doughty, eds. *The Handbook of Language Teaching*. Malden, MA et al.: Wiley-Blackwell, 294–310.

Saraceni, Claudia (2013). Adapting Courses: A Personal View. In: Brian Tomlinson, ed. *Developing Materials for Language Teaching*. London et al.: Bloomsbury, 49–62.

Schnitter, Thomas (2014). A Day on the Oregon Trail: Tagebucheinträge mit TitanPad verfassen. *Der fremdsprachliche Unterricht Englisch* 48.128, 18–25.

Sercu, Lies (2000). Textbooks. In: Michael Byram, ed. *Routledge Encyclopedia of Teaching and Learning*. London et al.: Routledge, 626–28.

Stranks, Jeff (2013). Materials for the Teaching of Grammar. In: Brian Tomlinson, ed. *Developing Materials for Language Teaching*. London et al.: Bloomsbury, 337–50.

Strasser, Thomas (2012). *Mind the App! Inspiring Internet Tools and Activities to Engage Your Students*. Innsbruck: Helbling.

Strasser, Thomas (2014). Them and Us: In einem mit Go!Animate produzierten Cartoon Stereotype reflektieren. *Der fremdsprachliche Unterricht Englisch* 48.128, 32–37.

Tomlinson, Brian (2011). Introduction: Principles and Procedures of Materials Development. In: Brian Tomlinson, ed. *Materials Development in Language Teaching*. 2nd ed. Cambridge et al.: Cambridge University Press, 1–31.

Tomlinson, Brian (2013a). Introduction: Are Materials Developing? In: Brian Tomlinson, ed. *Developing Materials for Language Teaching*. London et al.: Bloomsbury, 1–17.

Tomlinson, Brian (2013b). Materials Evaluation. In: Brian Tomlinson, ed. *Developing Materials for Language Teaching*. London et al.: Bloomsbury, 21–48.

Tomlinson, Brian (2013c). Humanizing the Coursebook. In: Brian Tomlinson, ed. *Developing Materials for Language Teaching*. London et al.: Bloomsbury, 139–55.

Tomlinson, Brian (2013d). Materials Development Courses. In: Brian Tomlinson, ed. *Developing Materials for Language Teaching*. London et al.: Bloomsbury, 481–500.

Tomlinson, Brian & Hitomi Masuhara (2013). Simulations in Materials Development. In: Brian Tomlinson, ed. *Developing Materials for Language Teaching*. London et al.: Bloomsbury, 501–19.

Volkmann Laurenz (2010). *Fachdidaktik Englisch: Kultur und Sprache*. Tuebingen: Narr.

Waters, Alan (2011). Advances in Materials Design. In: Michael H. Long & Catherine J. Doughty, eds. *The Handbook of Language Teaching*. Malden, MA et al.: Wiley-Blackwell, 311–26.

References unit 12

Angelo, Thomas A. & Kathryn P. Cross (1993). *Classroom Assessment Techniques: A Handbook for College Teachers*. San Francisco, CA: Jossey-Bass.

Arendt, Manfred (2006). Beurteilung mündlicher Leistungen. Eine Untersuchung. In: *Praxis Fremdsprachenunterricht*; Part 1: 3.3, 3–10; Part 2: 3.4, 3–8.

Bebermeier, Hans (1999). Neue Formen der Leistungsfeststellung (Sekundarstufe I und II). In: *Der Fremdsprachliche Unterricht Englisch* 37, 46–51.

Bohl, Thorsten (2009). *Prüfen und Bewerten im offenen Unterricht.* 4th ed. Weinheim et al.: Beltz.

Byram, Michael (1997). *Teaching and Assessing Intercultural Communicative Competence.* Clevedon et al.: Multilingual Matters.

Council of Europe (2001). *Common European Framework of Reference for Languages: Learning, Teaching, Assessment.* Cambridge: Cambridge University Press.

Eisenmann, Maria (2008). Formen mündlicher Leistungsmessung im Fach Englisch. In: *Praxis Fremdsprachenunterricht* 5.4, 26–30.

Eisenmann, Maria & Theresa Summer (2012). Oral Exams: Preparing and Testing Students. In: Maria Eisenmann & Theresa Summer, eds. *Basic Issues in EFL Teaching and Learning.* Heidelberg: Winter, 415–28.

Finkbeiner, Claudia (2012). Introduction: Assessment and Testing and the Issue of Equity. In: Maria Eisenmann & Theresa Summer, eds. *Basic Issues in EFL Teaching and Learning.* Heidelberg: Winter, 385–401.

Haß, Frank; Werner Kieweg; Margitta Kutty; Andreas Müller-Hartmann & Harald Weisshaar, eds. (2008). *Fachdidaktik Englisch: Tradition, Innovation, Praxis.* Stuttgart: Klett.

Hattie, John (2009). *Visible Learning: A Synthesis of over 800 Meta-Analyses Relating to Achievement.* London et al.: Routledge.

Huerta-Macías, Ana (2002). Alternative Assessment: Responses to Commonly Asked Questions. In: Jack C. Richards & Willy A. Renandya, eds. *Methodology in Language Teaching: An Anthology of Current Practice.* Cambridge et al.: Cambridge University Press, 338–43.

Jürgens, Eiko (2000). Brauchen wir ein pädagogisches Leistungsverständnis? In: Silvia-Iris Beutel & Witlof Vollstädt, eds. *Leistung ermitteln und bewerten.* Hamburg: Bergmann und Helbig, 15–25.

Jürgens, Eiko (2005). Lern- und Leistungsjournal und Portfoliokonzept: Verfahren pädagogisch sinnvoller Leistungsbeurteilung. In: *Schulmagazin 5 bis 10* 73.10, 9–12.

Jürgens, Eiko (2010). *Leistung und Beurteilung in der Schule: Eine Einführung in Leistungs- und Bewertungsfragen aus pädagogischer Sicht.* 7th ed. Sankt Augustin: Academia.

Jürgens, Eiko & Werner Sacher (2008). *Leistungserziehung und pädagogische Diagnostik in der Schule: Grundlagen und Anregungen für die Praxis.* Stuttgart: Kohlhammer.

Kieweg, Werner (1999a). Allgemeine Gütekriterien für Lernzielkontrollen. In: *Der Fremdsprachliche Unterricht Englisch* 33.37, 4–11.

Kieweg, Werner (1999b). Klassenarbeiten: Überprüfung der grammatikalischen Kompetenz und Performanz. In: *Der Fremdsprachliche Unterricht Englisch* 33.37, 18–25.

Kieweg, Werner (2007). Fehler erkennen – Fehler vermeiden. In: *Der fremdsprachliche Unterricht Englisch* 41.88, 2–11.

Kieweg, Werner (2010). Kompetenzen diagnostizieren. In: *Der Fremdsprachliche Unterricht Englisch* 44.105, 16–22.

Kleppin, Karin (2009). 'Fehler' und 'Fehlerkorrektur.' In: *Praxis Fremdsprachenunterricht* 6.1, 60–61.

Macht, Konrad (2007). Aufgaben als Bewertungsinstrumente. In Johannes-P. Timm, ed. *Englisch lernen und lehren: Didaktik des Englischunterrichts.* Berlin: Cornelsen, 366–77.

Müller-Hartmann, Andreas & Marita Schocker-von Ditfurth (2009). *Introduction to English Language Teaching*. 5th ed. Stuttgart et al.: Klett.

Peñaflorida, Andrea H. (2002). Nontraditional Forms of Assessment and Response to Student Writing: A Step toward Learner Autonomy. In: Jack C. Richards & Willy A. Renandya, eds. *Methodology in Language Teaching: An Anthology of Current Practice*. Cambridge et al.: Cambridge University Press, 344–53.

Rampillon, Ute (1999). Englisch lernen neu denken – und neu bewerten. In: *Der fremdsprachliche Unterricht Englisch* 33.37, 26, 35–39.

Schneider, Franz J. (2010). *Interne Evaluation im Englischunterricht: Unterrichtsbegleitende Diagnoseverfahren zur schulischen Qualitätsentwicklung*. Berlin et al.: LIT.

Thaler, Engelbert (2008). Klassenarbeiten – eine Prozessperspektive. In: *Praxis Fremdsprachenunterricht* 5.4, 6–10.

Thaler, Engelbert (2012). *Englisch unterrichten: Grundlagen – Kompetenzen – Methoden*. Berlin: Cornelsen.

Thüringer Ministerium für Bildung, Wissenschaft und Kultur (2010). *Abiturprüfung 2010: Leistungsfach Englisch (Haupttermin) – Teil B*. Erfurt: TMBWK, 1–9.

Tillmann, Klaus-Jürgen & Witlof Vollstädt (2000). *Funktionen der Leistungsbewertung: Eine Bestandsaufnahme*. In: Silvia-Iris Beutel & Witlof Vollstädt, eds. *Leistung ermitteln und bewerten*. Hamburg: Bergmann und Helbig, 27–37.

Weinert, Franz E. (2002). Vergleichende Leistungsmessung in Schulen – eine umstrittene Selbstverständlichkeit. In: Franz E. Weinert, ed. *Leistungsmessungen in Schulen*. 2nd ed. Weinheim et al.: Beltz, 17–31.

Weskamp, Ralf (2001). *Fachdidaktik: Grundlagen & Konzepte*. Berlin: Cornelsen.

Weskamp, Ralf (2003). *Fremdsprachenunterricht entwickeln. Grundschule – Sekundarstufe I – Gymnasiale Oberstufe*. Hanover: Schroedel-Diesterweg-Klinkhardt.

Winter, Felix (2010). *Leistungsbewertung: Eine neue Lernkultur braucht einen anderen Umgang mit den Schülerleistungen*. 4th ed. Baltmannsweiler: Schneider Hohengehren.

Zydatiß, Wolfgang (2006). Mündliche Prüfungen in Englisch Klasse 10: Sachgerecht gestalten und 'gerecht' bewerten (Teil 1). *Praxis Fremdsprachenunterricht* 3.4, 9–13.

Index

Acknowledgments

The cartoons at the beginning of each unit were designed by Frollein Motte, 2014. If not otherwise indicated, the copyright of the figures lies with the authors. The complete titles of the sources can be found in the references to the units unless given below. All of the websites were checked on 10 September 2014.

Fig. 1.1, William Hogarth: *Scholars at a Lecture* (1736/37), http://en.wikipedia.org/wiki/File:Hogarth_lecture_1736.jpg

Fig. 1.2, Johan-Amos Comenius, https://de.wikipedia.org/wiki/Johann_Amos_Comenius

Fig. 1.4, Wilhelm Viëtor, http://de.wikipedia.org/wiki/Wilhelm_Vi%C3%ABtor#mediaviewer/File:Wilhelm_Vietor.jpg

Fig. 1.5, CEF common reference levels – global scale, Council of Europe (2001). *Common European Framework of Reference for Languages: Learning, Teaching, Assessment*, http://www.coe.int/t/dg4/linguistic/source/framework_en.pdf

Fig. 1.6, KMK competences framework, Kultusministerkonferenz (2003)

Fig. 2.1, The reflective practice model of professional development, Wallace, Michael J. 1991: 94

Fig. 2.4, Principles of good teaching practice, adapted from Meyer, Hilbert (2006)

Fig. 2.5, The TPACK framework and its knowledge components, Koehler, Matthew J., & Mishra, Punya (2009). "What Is Technological Pedagogical Content Knowledge?" *Contemporary Issues in Technology and Teacher Education* 9.1, S. 63. Available online http://tpack.org; Reproduced by permission of the publisher, © 2012 by tpack.org

Fig. 2.6, Paradigm shift, incl. picture on the left from Onderwijsgek@nl.wikipedia, http://commons.wikimedia.org/wiki/Category:Empty_classrooms?uselang=de#mediaviewer/File:Empty_classroom.jpg, CC BY-SA 3.0 nl, on the right from Metropolitan School, https://commons.wikimedia.org/wiki/File:Unterricht.jpg?uselang=de#/media/File:Unterricht.jpg, CC BY-SA 3.0

Fig. 3.2, Second language acquisition: natural vs. instructional setting, adapted from Lightbown & Spada 2006: 110–12

Fig. 3.12, Bettina Winkler, *Teaching and learning as mountaineering*

Fig. 4.1, *The New Language Laboratory, 1970*, Library of the London School of Economics and Political Science, https://commons.wikimedia.org/wiki/File:The_New_Language_Laboratory,_1970.jpg

Fig. 4.2, Model of communicative competence, based on Canale & Swain 1980, Canale 2013

Fig. 4.3, Methodology and principles of the task as work plan, adapted from Ellis 2003: 244, 257–58, 276–78; Ellis 2012: 200–2; Keller 2013: 77

Fig. 4.5, Individual learner differences, adapted from Dörnyei & Skehan 2003: 619; Dörnyei 2010: 249; Schlak 2010: 258; Ellis 2012: 308–16

Fig. 4.6, Dynamic system of motivation, adapted from Dörnyei & Skehan 2003: 619; Dörnyei 2004: 429–30; Riemer 2010: 171

Fig. 4.7, Table of basic methods, adapted from Larson-Freeman & Anderson 2011: 222–23

Fig. 5.1, Psycholinguistic model of speech production, Levelt, Willem J. M. 1994: 91

Fig. 5.2, Processability hierarchy for English as L2 from advanced (6) to beginners (1), based on Pienemann in Keßler & Plesser 2011: 86–87

Fig. 5.3, Example of overgeneralization, Lightbown & Spada 2006: 16. Reproduced by permission of Oxford University Press. From *Oxford Handbooks for Language Teachers: How Languages Are Learned 3rd Edition* © Oxford University Press 2006

Fig. 5.4, Input enhancement techniques, based on Keßler & Plesser 2011: 153

Fig. 5.5, Proactive FonF focusing on past -ed, based on Keßler & Plesser 2011: 150
Fig. 5.6, Example of TBLT, based on Rodríguez-Bonces & Rodríguez-Bonces 2010: 172–74
Fig. 5.7, Example of ABM, based on Ziegésar & Ziegésar 2007: 292–98
Fig. 5.8, Lexical competence, based on Nation 1990: 31
Fig. 5.9, Explanation techniques, based on Quetz 2007: 277
Fig. 5.10, Word fork, based on Hutz 2012: 115
Fig. 5.11, Word ladder, based on Hutz 2012: 112
Fig. 5.12, Tonks, Robert (2012). Denglisch in Pool Position: English makes German Werbung funny! 2. Borsdorf: Winterwork, S. 2, www.robert-tonks.de
Fig. 6.3, Pre-activity phase strategies, based on O'Malley & Chamot 1996: 44–46
Fig. 6.6, Improving reading skills, based on Weskamp 2001: 133–34; Grabe 2011: 455–56
Fig. 6.7, Improving listening skills, based on Weskamp 2001: 124; Field 2002: 242–45; Vandergrift & Groh 2011: 402–05
Fig. 6.12, Exclusion, segregation, integration, inclusion; Robert Aehnelt, Historische Schritte auf dem Weg zur Inklusion auf gesellschaftlicher Ebene; http://de.wikipedia.org/wiki/Inklusive_P%C3%A4dagogik; CC BY-SA 3.0
Fig. 6.13, Differences between integration and inclusion, based on Damm & Legenhausen 2013
Fig. 7.2, The iceberg model of culture, based on http://opengecko.com/interculturalism/visualising-the-iceberg-model-of-culture/
Fig. 7.3, *Outsourced* – movie poster; http://www.impawards.com/2007/outsourced_ver4_xlg.html
Fig. 7.4, Intercultural communicative competence; adapted from Byram 1997: 49–55, Coperías-Aguilar 2007: 64
Fig. 8.2, Individual use of literature, designed by Frollein Motte, 2014
Fig. 8.3, Dynamic model of reading as experience and interactive information processing in combination with the social negotiation of meaning in an institutional framework, based on Reichl 2009: 214
Fig. 9.1, Focal areas of media pedagogy, based on Hug 2002, 8–9
Fig. 9.2, Multiliteracies model, Cazden et al. 1996: 83
Fig. 9.3, Media literacy, based on Wermke 1997: 145
Fig. 9.4, Extract from Comenius' *Orbis sensualium pictus*, https://commons.wikimedia.org/wiki/Category:Orbis_pictus?uselang=de#/media/File:Orbis-pictus-024.jpg
Fig. 9.5, Blended learning: media, methods, and theories, adapted from Wiepcke et al. 2008: 30
Fig. 9.6, Writing and illustrating a picture book, adapted from Stafford 2011: 48–49
Fig. 9.7, Weather reports with fun, adapted from Grimm & Riecken 2014
Fig. 9.9, Platform-based literature project, adapted from Klemm & Grimm 2013
Fig. 10.1, Metaphors for a lesson , based on Ur 1996: 213
Fig. 10.2, Factors forming and shaping lessons
Fig. 10.5, The reflection process, based on Richards& Rodgers 1986: 159
Fig. 10.7, The IRE pattern, adapted from Lindner 2011: 40
Fig. 11.1, Characteristics of forward, central, and backward design, based on Richards 2013: 30
Fig. 11.3, Materials design checklist, based on Howard & Major 2005: 104–07
Fig. 11.4, Language performance requirements, based on Kultusministerkonferenz 2012: 1–2
Fig 11.6, Sample popplet; pictures: Wikipedia/Wikimedia
▶ Dallas Mavericks logo: http://en.wikipedia.org/wiki/Dallas_Mavericks#mediaviewer/File:Dallas_Mavericks_logo.svg
▶ American Airlines Center: http://en.wikipedia.org/wiki/Dallas_Mavericks#mediaviewer/File:Victory_Plaza_1.jpg
▶ Head coach: http://en.wikipedia.org/wiki/Dallas_Mavericks#mediaviewer/File:Rick_Carlisle.jpg
▶ Jason Terry: http://en.wikipedia.org/wiki/Dallas_Mavericks#mediaviewer/File:Jason_Terry.jpg
▶ Jason Kidd: http://en.wikipedia.org/wiki/Dallas_Mavericks#mediaviewer/File:Jason_Kidd_drives_Feb_24_2008.jpg

► Dirk Nowitzki: http://commons.wikimedia.org/wiki/Category:Dirk_Nowitzki#mediaviewer/
File:NowitzkiWizards3.jpg

Fig. 11.8, Sample glog; http://graceigr8.edu.glogster.com/into-the-wildimagery-themes-and-symbols/

Fig. 11.9, Activity formats on LearningApps; http://learningapps.org/index.php?sorting=relevance

Fig. 12.1, The bell curve (example); http://compforce.typepad.com/.a/6a00d83451df4569e201a3f-ce9ba57970b-pi

narr | VERLAG   francke | VERLAG   attempto | VERLAG

Michael Meyer

English and
American Literatures

UTB 2526
4., überarbeitete und erweiterte Auflage 2011,
VIII, 264 Seiten
€[D] 16,90/Sfr 24,90
ISBN 978-3-8252-3550-5

English and American Literatures ist <u>das</u> Arbeitsbuch zum Selbststudium, zur Examensvorbereitung und als Grundlage für Einführungskurse in die englische und amerikanische Literaturwissenschaft. Es bietet kompaktes Basiswissen über die Analyse lyrischer, narrativer und dramatischer Texte, literaturwissenschaftliche Methoden und Theorien und die Vorbereitung auf Referate, Hausarbeiten oder Prüfungen. Zahlreiche Beispiele, Leitfragen, Checklisten und Übungen bieten hilfreiche Werkzeuge für die systematische Lektüre und wissenschaftliche Erschließung von Literatur vom ersten Semester an.

Narr Francke Attempto Verlag GmbH+Co. KG · Dischingerweg 5 · D-72070 Tübingen
Tel. +49 (07071) 9797-0 · Fax +49 (07071) 97 97-11 · info@francke.de · **www.francke.de**

narr VERLAG **francke** VERLAG **attempto** VERLAG

JETZT BESTELLEN!

Gerhard Bach / Johannes-Peter Timm (Hrsg.)

Englischunterricht

UTB M
5., aktualisierte Auflage 2013, X, 390 Seiten
€[D] 22,99/SFr 31,90
ISBN 978-3-8252-4037-0

Der „Bach / Timm" mit seinem Konzept der Handlungsorientierung hat sich seit mehr als zwei Jahrzehnten als Standardwerk der Lehreraus- und -fortbildung bewährt.

Die 5. Auflage stellt sich den pädagogischen, fachlichen und strukturellen Herausforderungen, die den fremdsprachlichen Unterricht gegenwärtig prägen: Anfangsunterricht in der Grundschule, Bilingualer Sachfachunterricht, Diskussion um Bildungsstandards und Kompetenzprofile, bildungstheoretische Konzepte, Prozess- und Lernorientierung, Lernerautonomie, Strategien effizienten Lernens, interkulturelles und projektbezogenes Lernen. Die bewährten Grundlagenkapitel wurden ebenso auf den neuesten Forschungsstand gebracht wie die Kapitel zu den gegenwärtigen Brennpunkten des Englischunterrichts, darunter „Neue Medien" oder „Bildungsstandards".

Narr Francke Attempto Verlag GmbH+Co. KG • Dischingerweg 5 • D-72070 Tübingen
Tel. +49 (07071) 9797-0 • Fax +49 (07071) 97 97-11 • info@francke.de • **www.francke.de**

narr
VERLAG

francke
VERLAG

attempto
VERLAG

narr STUDIENBÜCHER

Daniela Elsner / Jörg-U. Keßler (eds.)

Bilingual Education in Primary School

Aspects of Immersion, CLIL, and Bilingual Modules

narr studienbücher
2013, 176 Seiten
€[D] 19,99/SFr 27,50
ISBN 978-3-8233-6782-6

Bilingual education has become a major trend throughout multilingual Europe both at primary and secondary school level. This book offers a concise and reader-friendly introduction to bilingual teaching and learning at primary school level. It provides a state of the art overview of current approaches, issues, research results, and teaching practices of bilingual education at primary schools. The book is written by renowned experts in the field of bilingual education and addresses university students, teacher trainees as well as in-service-teachers. It can be used for self study purposes as well as for university seminars. The authors focus on goals, chances and challenges of the integration of bilingual teaching and learning programmes such as CLIL, Immersion, or Bilingual Modules as well as valid and practice-oriented assessment of bilingual classrooms and learners. Each chapter includes a short introduction, pre- and post-reading activities, suggestions for review, reflection, and research on each of the topics and is accompanied by further reading suggestions. The book is completed by a glossary, a bilingual sample module, a detailed bibliography, and a subject index.

JETZT BESTELLEN!

Narr Francke Attempto Verlag GmbH+Co. KG • Dischingerweg 5 • D-72070 Tübingen
Tel. +49 (07071) 9797-0 • Fax +49 (07071) 97 97-11 • info@narr.de • **www.narr.de**